**Living with Oil**

Number Seven
*Peter T. Flawn Series in Natural Resources*

# Living with Oil

Promises, Peaks, and Declines on Mexico's Gulf Coast

BY LISA BREGLIA

University of Texas Press ◆ *Austin*

The Peter T. Flawn Series in Natural Resource Management and Conservation is supported by a grant from the National Endowment for the Humanities and by gifts from various individual donors.

Requests for permission to reproduce material from this work should be sent to:
  Permissions
  University of Texas Press
  P.O. Box 7819
  Austin, TX 78713-7819
  http://utpress.utexas.edu/about/book-permissions

⊗ The paper used in this book meets the minimum requirements of ANSI/ NISO Z39.48-1992 (R1997) (Permanence of Paper).

**Library of Congress Cataloging-in-Publication Data**
Breglia, Lisa, 1972–
   Living with oil : promises, peaks, and declines on Mexico's gulf coast / by Lisa Catherine Breglia. — 1st ed.
      p.   cm. — (Peter T. Flawn series in natural resources ; no. 7)
   Includes bibliographical references and index.
   ISBN 978-0-292-74461-5 (alk. paper)
   1. Petroleum industry and trade—Mexico.   I. Title.
   HD9574.M62B74   2013
   333.8′2309726—dc23                                      2012025775

doi:10.7560/744615

# Contents

Abbreviations **vii**

Acknowledgments **ix**

Introduction **1**

PART 1. **Peaks and Declines** **23**

1. The Mexican Oil Crisis **29**

2. Natural Resources in the Laguna de Términos: Piracy and Profit **65**

PART 2. **The Pesquera and the Petrolera** **103**

3. The Peak and Decline of Fishing in the Laguna de Términos **107**

4. Capturing Compensation: Resource Wealth in the Era of Decline **146**

PART 3. **Post-Peak Politics: Energy Reform and the Race to Claim the Gulf of Mexico** **191**

5. "No to Privatization": A Battle for Energy Independence **197**

6. Energy Security on the U.S.-Mexican Maritime Border: Transboundary Oil in the Deepwater Gulf **233**

Conclusion: Post-Peak Futures **259**

Notes **265**

References **279**

Index **307**

# Abbreviations

| | |
|---|---|
| APFFLT | Laguna de Términos Flora and Fauna Protected Area |
| bcf | billion cubic feet |
| bpd | barrels per day |
| Btu | British thermal units |
| Canainpesca | Cámara Nacional de Indústria Pesquera y Acuícola |
| Conapesca | National Fisheries and Aquaculture Commission |
| EEZ | Exclusive Economic Zone |
| EIA | Energy Information Agency |
| FAO | United Nations Food and Agriculture Organization |
| FAP | Frente Amplio Progresista |
| Fexhi | Fondo de Extracción de Hidrocarburos |
| Frecoperic | Frente Común Organizado de Pescadores Ribereños del Estado de Campeche |
| IEA | International Energy Agency |
| INEGI | Instituto Nacional Estadística Geográfica |
| kWh | kilowatt-hours |
| mbpd | million barrels per day |
| NOC | national oil company |
| OPEC | Organization of Petroleum Exporting Countries |
| Pemex | Petróleos Mexicanos |
| PAN | Partido Acción Nacional |
| PEP | Pemex Exploration and Production |
| PRD | Partido de la Revolución Democrática |
| PRI | Partido Revolucionario Institucional |
| Profepa | Procuraduría Federal de Protección al Ambiente |
| PVEM | Partido Verde Ecologista de México |
| Sagarpa | Mexican Ministry of Agriculture, Livestock, Rural Development, Fisheries, and Food |

| | |
|---|---|
| Semarnat | Secretaría de Medio Ambiente y Recursos Naturales |
| Sener | Secretaría de Energia |
| Sepesca | Secretaría de Pesca y Acuacultura |
| STPRM | Sindicato de Trabajadores Petroleros de la República Mexicana |
| UNCLOS | United Nations Convention Law of the Sea |
| UNESCO | United Nations Educational, Scientific, and Cultural Organization |
| URR | ultimately recoverable reserves |

# Acknowledgments

Most of my thanks are owed to the community of Isla Aguada, Campeche, Mexico, where I began carrying out research in 2007. Despite all of the challenges thrown its way, this resilient Gulf coast fishing town is filled with vibrancy and vitality. I am especially indebted to "las hermanas cabañas"—Marina Perez Dorantes and Alma Perez Dorantes de Hinojosa and her husband, Carlos Hinojosa Shields—for their incredible warmth, hospitality, and friendship. Bertha Acosta Reyes, Nidia Hernandez Fuentes, Luisa Morales Baños, Rocio Jimenez Lopez, and Jesús Espinosa Mendoza were truly kind and accommodating. Community leaders and activists in Isla Aguada and neighboring Ciudad del Carmen were especially important in supporting this research. In Isla Aguada, I thank the *comisario* Martín Ramirez Barrera as well as Javier Aguillón Osorio. In Carmen, Lourdes Rodríguez Badillo as well as Mario Antonio Rodríguez Badillo provided valuable insight.

Both the scope and depth of research necessary for this study required the participation and patience of many friends and colleagues, especially at George Mason University. First, I owe Mason's Center for Global Studies, under the directorship of Terrence Lyons and Peter Mandaville, a huge debt of gratitude for launching this project with a grant that funded my initial research. In the Global Affairs program, which I have made my home for the entire length of this project, I would like to thank T. Mills Kelly for his support. I was able to turn my attention to this project only because I could count on Erin McSherry, Emily Jones, and Stephanie Burton holding down the fort—with uncommon competence and attention.

Countless colleagues across the disciplines and indeed across the world provided excellent and incisive feedback on this work at various stages. Ludy Grandas helped in more ways than I can say. Michael Klare, Terry Lynn Karl, Jane Collins, Chelsea Chapman, Imre Szeman, Gisa Weszkalnys, Jeanne Simonelli, Stephanie Paladino, Roger Lancaster, John Foster, Tim Kaposy, Jeff Mantz, and Andy Bickford all played roles in helping me think through the issues at different stages of this project. I was fortunate to become involved about halfway through this project with a group of like-minded "anthropology of energy" researchers, spearheaded by Tom Love, Sarah Strauss, and Stephanie Rupp. I hope this work is a valuable contribution to the ongoing efforts to establish this important field of research.

Two anonymous reviewers at the University of Texas Press were generous in their time and attention to this book in an earlier manuscript form. I am forever in their debt, as well as that of my editor, Theresa May, and the staff at the University of Texas Press. Theresa is the kind of editor who makes an author consider writing another book. My second time working with her was even more pleasurable than the first.

Drawn to the sea since my childhood spent surrounded by beautiful Floridian coastlines, I knew that my research would eventually bring me back to the ocean. Above all, the support of my family has made this possible. My parents first brought me to dip my toes in the Gulf of Mexico and gave me the sense of both the strength and vulnerability of oceans. My childhood beach companion—my sister, Deanna Breglia—generously prepared the maps for this book.

Also deserving special mention are Leslie Tingle and Tana Silva. Without Tana's heroic efforts, especially, this book—and I—would have suffered.

**Living with Oil**

# Introduction

## On Mexico's Frontlines

Cantarell, the world's largest offshore oilfield, lies underneath the warm, shallow waters of the Gulf of Mexico. From the very first drops of crude drawn from Cantarell in 1979, it was clear that the field would exceed not only the expectations of the state-owned oil company Petróleos Mexicanos (Pemex) but the wildest dreams of the Mexican state. The offshore supergiant would turn Mexico from a net importer into a robust exporter and, as in other resource-rich developing nations, enable the Mexican state to launch an ambitious national development program.

While the country celebrated its oil as both a symbol of national pride and a key economic asset, Mexico's neighbors, too, were thrilled by Cantarell. With its own economy still reeling from the pain of the 1973 oil shock caused by the OPEC embargo and in the midst of a fresh energy crisis brought on by political instability in the Middle East, the United States watched and waited for the cheap, abundant, non-OPEC crude flow from the nearby offshore Gulf into the marketplace. Production rates for the Cantarell crude oil met and exceeded expectations. In three decades of bonanza, dependence on the shallow-water oilfield in the Campeche Sound only expanded and deepened. While Mexico anchored its own national economic security in Cantarell, the United States increasingly tied its energy security to Cantarell crude. But when the oilfield demonstrated a marked decline beginning in 2005, it became clear that Cantarell was a once-in-a-lifetime discovery. Mexico's easily extracted oil was dwindling fast. The country was left on the brink of an energy crisis.

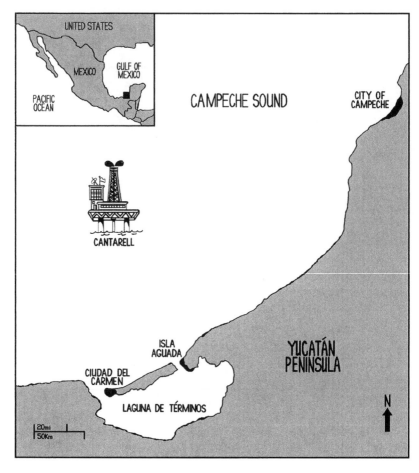

The Campeche Sound and the Laguna de Términos. Map by Deanna Breglia.

Nowhere are the visceral effects of the contemporary conundrum of declining production and increasing global energy demand more apparent than in the communities on Mexico's Gulf coast. In six coastal states, from Mexico's border with Texas to the Yucatán Peninsula, natural resources, especially those based on a delicately balanced marine ecosystem, form the basis of the regional economy (Sánchez-Gil et al. 2004). In the lightly populated state of Campeche, residents are drawn to the coastal region of the Laguna de Términos—a body of water roughly thirty miles long and fifteen miles wide situated where the Yucatán Peninsula meets mainland Mexico. Marine resources are central to everyday livelihood in Campeche through commercial and recreational fishing, tourism, and the petroleum industry. From among the industrial activities in the southeastern Gulf of Mexico, the most dramatic impacts on the social lives of residents and the stability of coastal ecosystems come from the petroleum industry—including the exploration, exploitation, transport, and refining of petroleum as well as the development of petrochemical industries (Sánchez Gil et al. 2004: 592). The intensity of the exploitation of coastal resources combined with insufficient maintenance of the petroleum-extracting and -transporting infrastructure have led to recurrent accidental oil spills and pipeline leaks, which pollute the soils and coastal lagoon systems along the Gulf coast (Vásquez Botello et al. 1992; Vásquez Botello, Ponce Vélez, and Macko 1996; Day et al. 2003; Fiedler et al. 2008). Oil development has come at a high price for communities dependent on marine resources. Campeche's claim to the highest levels of oil and gas production match its highest regional levels of coastal pollution in the air, soil, and water (Yáñez-Arancibia et al. 2009: 94).

Since oil began flowing from the country's premier oilfield, coastal communities have served as the onshore support network for an intensive exploitation effort to produce billions of barrels of heavy Maya crude. Over the past three decades, fishing communities on Mexico's Gulf coast have faced mounting pressures—social, political, economic, and, perhaps most of all, environmental—of living on the "frontlines" of the production of the world's most valuable commodity. While waiting for the promises of plenty in the midst of the boom of oil wealth, communities in the Laguna de Términos region of Campeche on Mexico's Yucatán Peninsula have slowly been brought to the brink of collapse.

Meanwhile, the offshore complex of Cantarell is Pemex's "city on the sea," a busy network of oil-production platforms approximately fifty miles north of Ciudad del Carmen in the Campeche Sound. The marine area has platforms for drilling, transportation, and telecommunications as well as for eating, sleeping ("flotels"), and recreation. More than 20,000 workers conduct the everyday operations at Cantarell, employed by both Pemex and private multinational oil-services providers including the global powerhouses Halliburton, Bechtel, and Schlumberger. Ciudad del Carmen, a thriving shrimp port from the 1940s through the 1980s, is now better known, perhaps, for oil-industry infrastructure. The sprawling city is dotted with industrial parks, dozens of one-star motels and worker-housing tracts, and a busy heliport. The city of 150,000 permanent residents and thousands of transient workers has been transformed over the past decades from a sleepy—if over-grown—fishing village into a convenient staging ground for offshore oil operations. Amid the workaday buzz of the island city the noise of helicopters overhead shuttling crews of workers in their brightly colored coveralls to platforms for twenty-eight-day shifts or back to land for two-week breaks is a constant reminder of the proximity of the offshore world that dictates the pace of onshore daily life.

The changes wrought across the municipality of Carmen, affecting a broad coastal region of dozens of mostly fishing communities, are part of a historical narrative much longer than the three decades of oil exploitation in the Campeche Sound. Nearly five centuries ago, the Laguna de Términos emerged as a strategic location in the transnational marketplace of natural resource extraction. Fought over, raided, negotiated, and occupied by competing colonial empires, merchants, and pirates, the region's history through the close of the eighteenth century was one marked by the dramatic pursuit of plunder for profit. After Mexico gained independence from Spain in 1825, the nineteenth and twentieth centuries saw renewed efforts by foreigners to once again benefit from the natural riches of the Laguna de Términos. Well before the discovery of oil, four key resources were exported through the port of Carmen: a colorfast dye made from the wood of the campeche tree, a natural chewing gum from tree sap known as *chicle*, coconut from plantation-cultivated palms, and Gulf shrimp. All had strong economic impacts on the region much earlier than oil did.

These seemingly disparate resources share several remarkable characteristics based on their strategic political and economic value. As I detail in chapter 2, because of the unique qualities of each commodity, it found high demand in the global marketplace, although each in its own geographical and historical niche. The exploitation of each resource went hand in hand with an assertion of territorial control of land and sea but also with the regulation of settlement patterns in the region. Each resource required a significant amount of capital investment, which often came from the private sector. The region's resources became increasingly vulnerable to private capital controlled mostly by foreign interests—many of which exercised land and labor management practices that had detrimental effects on Campeche's natural environment and population. Each cycle of resource exploitation repeated the pattern of failing to benefit the social or economic development of the Laguna de Términos.

Like other communities in the Global South that find oil to be both a blessing and a curse, residents of Campeche, too, have found that multiple natural resources have brought promise and despair. As a frontline community for the strategic exploitation of resources, coastal Campeche accustomed itself to a repetitive rhythm of boom-and-bust cycles as each resource peaked and declined. Given this historical experience, the hopes and expectations following the discovery of the uber-natural resource, oil, were mixed. Would oil be the commodity to finally bring social and economic benefits to Campeche? Or would the age-old cycle of boom and bust be destined to repeat itself, just another chapter in the story of natural resource exploitation in the Laguna de Términos?

In Mexico, oil holds a very special place not only in the popular imagination but also in the national budget. Mexican oil is a foundation for the economy and a cornerstone of nationalism. Lifeblood for the national economy, crude oil is strategically important for the domestic economy. Its revenues fund up to 40 percent of the national budget. In addition to supporting the energy needs of its neighbor the United States through exports, oil also serves Mexico's own ever-rising domestic energy demand. These twin pressures on Mexico's most valuable asset place the issue of resource sovereignty—the nation's ability to maintain control over the exploitation and rights to benefit from energy resources—at the forefront of contentious debates. From the steps of the famous Angel of Independence monument in Mexico City to the gates of refineries in the far-flung regions from Oaxaca to Tamaulipas, the issue of ownership of and the right to benefit from Mexican oil is one that dates back more than a century. According to Article 27 of Mexico's postrevolutionary 1917 constitution, the principle of resource sovereignty explicitly rejects foreign intervention in the exploitation of the nation's "strategic" natural resources. Resource sovereignty is a cornerstone of Mexican nationalism. But the ability of the Mexican state to maintain a de facto monopoly over oil production is a highly contested issue—within and among political parties, between state administrations and labor unions, between the state and the citizenry, and between the public and private sectors. The ability to retain resource sovereignty was exacerbated with the discovery of Cantarell. Now more than ever, when nearly every last state asset has been emptied from the nation's coffers under the pressures of neoliberal globalization, the ownership of Mexican oil is an increasingly volatile issue in Mexican public life. Vociferous nationalist protests greet even the subtlest hint of privatizing Mexico's most prized and valuable national patrimony.

In this charged atmosphere, high demands and even higher expectations have been placed on the billion-barrel Cantarell oilfield, revealing the deep dependence of the nation's hydrocarbon industry on the offshore complex. Since its discovery, Cantarell has contributed up to 80 percent of the nation's production. Of this, between 60 and 80 percent is directed to exports. Nearly all of the oil exported from Cantarell is Maya crude—a heavy, sour crude that is sent unrefined to the United States.[1] For nearly three decades, Cantarell was able to produce enough oil to meet the seemingly unrealistic demands: to fund national development programs, fuel everyday needs of a national budget, pay off Mexico's enormous foreign debts accumulated upon the supergiant oilfield's discovery, and produce enough oil to remain among the top three sources of U.S. imports. But while the oil flowed abundantly from Cantarell's shallow Gulf wells, Pemex failed to invest in new exploration. Politicians and bureaucrats of several presidential administrations holding the parastatal (state-owned company) purse strings relied on the generosity of Cantarell to outlast their own *sexenios* (six-year terms), and Mexico robustly entered the twenty-first century with record-high rates of extraction. But these could not last. Now, scientific experts, government officials, and laypeople alike agree that Cantarell, Mexico's most significant Gulf oilfield, reached its point of maximum extraction, or peak, in December 2003, only to fall into a precipitous and alarming decline.

On the frontlines, the problem of living with oil is, ironically, exacerbated by the prospect of Cantarell's collapse. Now, residents as well as state and municipal governments of Mexico's Gulf coast are facing the complex realities of dealing with a natural environment affected by thirty years of the presence of the oil industry and an uncertain future in the shadow of the oilfield's peak. Those who live and work in the fishing communities along the Gulf coast in the state-designated "oil-affected" regions of Veracruz, Tamaulipas, Tabasco, Chiapas, and Campeche are understanding resource sovereignty and making their own claims to oil and other natural heritage resources by reaching into generations of local experience with the impact of oil exploitation on their everyday lives and livelihoods. Local residents are wrestling with the legacy wrought by Pemex and private oil-services providers upon the natural environment, including the region's once-plentiful fisheries. In the face of the oil crisis, residents as well as municipal and state officials are faced with the problem of how to build a sustainable future in an oil-damaged and oil-dependent region that is confronting an imminent shortfall of oil revenues. As experience from the frontlines in Campeche demonstrates, the problem of living with oil certainly cannot be easily resolved by living without oil.

## Understanding the Local in the Global Energy Crisis

Mexico's Gulf coast is an ideal setting for confronting the meaning of "energy crisis" from the perspective of the Global South. While the Global North, historically home to the largest consumers of energy, worries about securing a steady supply of crude from geopolitically stable sources, the South is beginning to emerge with a greater appetite for energy consumption in its own right. The North, enabled by the formidable reach of multinational corporations, has long wielded economic and political power to purchase cheap crude from productive regions with little to no heed for local consequences on their populations or environments. Now a greater percentage of oil reserves are held in the hands of nation-states, allowing for the assertion of resource sovereignty over increasingly valuable—not to mention scarce—cheap, easily exploitable crude. Meanwhile, peak oil appears to everyone—save falsely optimistic oil companies—like an impending reality. These conditions are the stuff of a serious energy crisis.

But what does a twenty-first-century energy crisis look like for the South? This study provides a close look at the local experience of resource peak in the oil-affected communities on the Gulf coast in order to highlight Mexico's confrontation of the complex issues of sovereignty, security, and stability in what we might call the "post-peak" era. As in other frontline sites around the world, a tension exists for Mexico's Gulf-coast frontline communities over the presence of the oil industry and the needs and desires of local communities as they come to terms with the political, social, economic, and environmental factors that are brought to bear on local life. To illustrate the local nature of the global phenomenon of energy production and energy security, I draw on the work of an interdisciplinary body of scholarship as well as popular media. This perspective is enhanced by my on-the-ground experience of interacting with residents of coastal communities. To capture the rich texture of how people live with oil, I turn to a part of the world I already know well, Mexico's Yucatán Peninsula.

I began conducting research in the northern and western regions of the peninsula, in the state of Yucatán, in the late 1990s as a graduate student in cultural anthropology at Rice University. My concerns were heavily focused on how local indigenous Maya people living in and around archaeological monuments claim, give meaning to, and benefit from Mexico's sites of national heritage (Breglia 2006). Over the course of my studies of archaeological heritage I developed a deep interest in the rich, vivid, complicated, and contradictory lives of resources—especially as the resources are brought into social contexts, economic markets, and political frays by engaged and often contentious social actors. I learned that in Mexico the most symbolically charged national resources—no matter if they are cultural or natural—are often the most economically valuable and politically vulnerable. Neoliberal pressures to downsize government and state-owned industries throw the future of national patrimony into peril. Frontline communities stood on the brink of benefiting from the patrimony in their midst on the one hand or, on the other hand, losing access to their most valuable sources of income and identity.

Given that archaeological heritage and oil were the two most valuable national patrimonies that remained under de jure constitutional protection in Mexico, I decided to pursue an inquiry into "oil heritage" akin to my previous study on the politics of heritage. How, I wondered, do local communities work with, alongside, and perhaps even against state claims on heritage to assert their rights to maintain a livelihood from natural and cultural resources in their midst? What is more, how do citizens, state agencies, and private-sector actors respond to pressures of resource depletion, now and in the past, as they vie for territorial access to valuable heritage resources?

Communities affected by oil were less than 200 miles away on the Yucatán Peninsula's southwest coast, in the state of Campeche, and I extended my research interests to Mexico's Gulf coast, to the frontlines of oil production. In 2007 I began spending time in a coastal fishing community that was dealing with thirty years of intensive oil production off its attractive coastline. Here I put my skills as an anthropologist to work conducting ethnographic research with fishers and their families on the Gulf coast of Campeche.[2] I focus my attention particularly on Isla Aguada, a peninsula with sandy beaches fronting both the Gulf of Mexico and the Laguna de Términos and a small-craft port operating on the lagoon. Across the Puente de la Unidad (bridge) from the island of Carmen, the community's proximity to the city of Carmen and its location on the main highway draw many to its convenience. With a population barely reaching 3,000 just a decade earlier, the 2010 census

Welcome to Isla Aguada. Wall painted as part of town beautification campaign, 2011. Photograph by author.

shows that Isla Aguada swelled to nearly 7,000 residents in a short time. Longtime self-described "natives" of Isla Aguada identify the town with its small, traditional fishing-village roots and now perceive the community as overrun with immigrants from the interior of Campeche and other Mexican states as well as workers from Ciudad del Carmen. Though some twenty-five miles distant, Carmen's oil-industry-backed growth has driven up the cost of living, making housing scarce and expensive. A half-dozen informal settlements of newcomers to Isla Aguada have sprung up in recent years, putting a strain on space and infrastructural services. The sprawl to Isla Aguada's outer limits encroaches on delicate mangrove stands on the edges of town, threatening the region's environmental heritage within the federally designated Laguna de Términos Flora and Fauna Protection Area (APFFLT or ANP), which covers not only Isla Aguada but the whole island of Carmen as well.

A goal of my analysis is to highlight frontlines as peculiar spaces at once highly localized, especially as defined by their physical proximity to specific resources, and part of wider, denser, transnational networks. Living as they do near the center of intensive oil production and situated as they are within a wider landscape of the national and transnational energy marketplace, residents of Isla Aguada and across the municipality of Carmen have a unique stake in the effects of resource exploitation and resource depletion, especially in the Gulf of Mexico. To call attention to the specificity of the energy crisis faced by these communities, I examine the production of social inequalities as part of the production of the Laguna de Términos as a space of resource exploitation. Thus, I pay close attention to the spatializing tendencies and spatialized effects of resource exploitation and resource depletion not only for developing nations or regions—such as Mexico and the Laguna de Términos—but also for the maintenance of resource supplies in the name of energy security for developed nations, in this case the United States. Isla Aguada sits on the frontlines, which are often the crosshairs of these geopolitical concerns.

Spatial analysis helps us to understand representation, practice, and power on the frontlines of extractive industries across the globe. Frontlines exist where everyday life bumps up against the presence of oil. From the Ecuadorian Amazon with its cesspools of toxic waste to the conflict-ridden Niger Delta to U.S. coasts from Florida to Alaska, communities living in the midst of oil production bear the brunt and the burden of providing energy to the world. Communities on energy's frontlines host upstream activities such as oil or natural gas drilling. They also serve within the distributed network of "downstream" industries such as tanker ports, refineries, and chemical plants. Hooked into national and global economies and cutting across sovereign and deterritorialized spaces, frontlines are both real and virtual. They are drawn wherever the effects of energy are felt, anticipated, remembered, or imagined.

On the frontlines, diverse social actors are drawn and bound together to form energy communities. These social actors work in, through, alongside—and perhaps against—public- and private-sector agencies and institutions as groups and individuals pose challenges or offer acquiescence to multinational corporations, parastatal companies, or murkier joint ventures. For communities facing the challenges posed by extractive industries, a spatial analysis can highlight many of the contradictions inherent within the logic of resource exploitation—whether the relationship between natural resource wealth and underdevelopment or the collusion between resource-sovereign states and foreign capital. Though they have long existed, these contradictions are exacerbated since the 1980s as a consequence of neoliberalism, characterized by an ideological framework and a host of policies supporting deregulation, liberalization, and notably privatization.

Across more than four centuries of resource exploitation in the Laguna de Términos region, spatial and social relations have been created and re-created by these contradictions. The relatively recent introduction of an offshore extractive industry—set geographically apart from coastal communities—would appear at first glance removed from the everyday lives and experiences of residents. Today, oil is not extracted on shore in Isla Aguada or even in the immediate offshore vicinity. There are no platforms operating inside the protected waters of the Laguna de Términos or in Gulf waters within view of the shore. Yet the community lives the legacy of oil extraction and development. Tales of suspected or anticipated encroachment of oil drills constantly circulate in Isla Aguada. Residents especially worry that Cantarell's depletion will necessitate the search for oil on land and within the lagoon—locations many believe to be rich with oil deposits.

The effects of oil are, however, ever present in Isla Aguada and neighboring coastal communities. Years of social and economic development problems in Isla Aguada mirror challenges facing the municipality and the region as a whole: poor roads, lack of access to secondary education, and inadequate power and water service. Social problems among young and unemployed people plague the community, particularly the high levels of drug and alcohol consumption. The effects of oil are visceral in the natural environment as well—in the oil slicks that appear on the shoreline, the tar balls that wash up on the beaches, and the corpses of animals including dolphins and endangered species of sea turtles that appear with unnerving frequency. The everyday activity of the oil industry in the Campeche Sound produces a host of emissions through gas flaring, contaminated water discharge, drill cuttings (ground rock covered in a layer of drilling fluid), and crude-oil spills (Villaseñor et al. 2003: 3714).

Even though Pemex continually shrugs off responsibility for environmental damage in the region, residents of Isla Aguada express skepticism toward the parastatal's operations in the Campeche Sound. One resident said to me, "Look at what they *have* admitted to. Imagine what they don't tell us." According to a local environmental activist from the Carmen-based organization Marea Azul, spills ranging from major to minor occur all the time, on average once every ten days.

Though more human lives were lost in other accidents, Pemex's worst accident in terms of the volume of oil spilled was the 1979–1980 Ixtoc I blowout. For decades the Ixtoc blowout held the dubious honor of being the world's largest accidental oil spill, leaking a quantity of crude surpassed only by the deliberate spillage of oil by Iraqi forces into the Persian Gulf in 1991. In April 2010 both spills were overtaken by the Deepwater Horizon accident in U.S. Gulf waters. Multiple reports, including an official blow-by-blow account by the Bureau of Ocean and Energy Management (BOEM), familiarize us with the Macondo well under the Deepwater Horizon rig. The Ixtoc blowout three decades earlier was eerily similar. A rapid loss of pressure during the drilling process caused the well, more than two miles deep, to blow out and begin an uncontrolled release of oil and gas into the Gulf. The volatile mixture caught fire, igniting the drilling platform itself. The platform was destroyed and collapsed over the wellhead on the ocean floor. At the peak of the Ixtoc I spill, oil poured out at a rate of up to 30,000 barrels and possibly as much as 50,000 a day. For 290 days the uncapped well leaked oil into the Gulf. In total, the Ixtoc spill released more than 3 million barrels of crude into the Gulf of Mexico.[3]

Three decades later, the cumulative effects of the workaday activity of extraction match the dangers posed by single spills. Thousands of miles of intricate, aging pipes carry oil, gas, and chemicals such as nitrogen (injected into offshore wells to stimulate recovery) not only under the sea but across wetlands, marshes, and coastal residential communities, too. Leaks and spills within the dense network of pipelines accumulate over time to a heavy toll on the marine and coastal environments in Veracruz, Tabasco, and Campeche's Laguna de Términos (Bach et al. 2005: 17). Yet the public's attention is more easily drawn away from the long-term effects of oil extraction on shore to accidents involving rigs and platforms on the high seas. Disasters from Ixtoc to the Deepwater Horizon are constructed as extraordinary, once-in-a-lifetime events. As exceptional rather than business-as-usual occurrences, public perception is deflected away from the onshore daily grind of living with oil.

With its particularly high toll on human lives, Pemex's Usumacinta rig accident in 2007 brought the anomaly of offshore tragedy closer to shore. On October 23, under heavy weather, the privately contracted floating Usumacinta drilling rig struck Pemex's Kab-101 platform. A rescue operation complicated by faulty lifeboats saved almost seventy people but left twenty-two dead. Some of the survivors spent the night riding out fifty-mile-per-hour winds afloat in Gulf waters. At the accident site, a spill commenced and an oil and gas fire raged for days before Pemex claimed control over the situation (Leis et al. 2008).

After a yearlong investigation, Pemex blamed the incident on unforeseen, extraordinary weather conditions. But coastal residents sensed the injustice of impunity. After all, they were the ones who witnessed the bodies of dead workers airlifted to Ciudad del Carmen. In the wake of the accident, it was local fishers who found the empty, broken-apart rescue boats on their beaches, forewarning an ominous black tide of spilled crude soon to follow.

Framing oil crises and emergencies—ranging from rig disasters and well blowouts to the declaration of peak oil—as extraordinary events or exceptions produces a heightened sense that offshore operations at Cantarell are displaced from the quotidian experience of living with oil. Offshore represents what we could call a place of exception where, as Agamben (2005) has notably described, de jure law is suspended in favor of indistinction. Offshoring creates territories where boundaries between legal and illegal, public and private, transparency and corruption, and access and dispossession are dangerously messy and continuously renegotiated. A local environmental activist in the region described to me precisely this regime of offshore exceptionalism by detailing how offshore operations of Pemex are, to paraphrase, beyond the laws, regulations, and oversight of the de jure strictures of governance, especially when it comes to the environment. For the activist, who has decades of experience fighting for the protection of wetlands, mangroves, and native species largely in the Laguna de Términos, the Gulf of Mexico is a territory where "federal authority doesn't exist."

The offshoring of oil production can be understood alongside the broader offshoring trend in economic globalization—the deterritorialization, particularly of finance and production, through the creation of enclaves of deregulation, low-wage labor, and various financial incentives (Cameron and Palan 2004, Palan 2003). In a certain sense, the environmentalist critique of Pemex's operations at Cantarell is correct: through offshore spaces, states take advantage of distance and deregulation to suspend the expected practices of governance over labor and rights. This is the case as the Gulf of Mexico falls further under the sway of private-sector multinationals. However, offshore spaces are "fundamentally and paradoxically coincident with . . . the continued salience of the 'sovereign' state" (Cameron and Palan 2004: 108). As the authors describe, the notion of offshore undermines a particular idea of what a state should do, including how it should express claims to "national" natural resources in relationship to territory. "Offshore . . . rewrites, retroactively and proscriptively," the role of the state (ibid.). Under conditions of neoliberal globalization, Mexico can use the offshore as a space to practice a seemingly contradictory deterritorialization of resource sovereignty by giving up territorial control over the nation's most valuable resource through the extensive involvement of the private sector in the everyday activities of the oil industry.

For frontline communities, offshore oil exploitation might appear to displace the visceral experience of living with oil to the no-man's-land of the high seas. Yet the offshoring of natural resource exploitation hardly means that all of the effects of oil production are absent from local landscapes and livelihoods. As Anna Zalik points out, based on her comparative study of frontline communities in the Mexican Gulf and the Niger Delta (2009: 557), "The petroleum offshore . . . is historically embedded within socially defined space, among populations whose livelihoods form part of fluvial and marine ecosystems." Coastal communities, as the frontlines for production, are at once inextricably linked to as much as they are distanced from offshore production spaces, and intensive offshore oil production activity has profound implications for populations dependent on marine resources.

The offshore realm of Mexico's Gulf oil industry may often seem a distant world apart from the everyday challenges of making a living over the past thirty years. After all, few residents of Isla Aguada are going to find employment opportunities on the offshore platforms. But Gulf oil structures their landscape nonetheless. The oil wealth that trickles into Isla Aguada is not through secure employment with the parastatal but instead through social-development aid programs aimed at fishers in the community. The small aid packages offer little in the way of stimulative financial capital for growth or development. Oil wealth also finds its way to Isla Aguada through in-kind "mutual benefit" infrastructural development projects paid for by Pemex. These public works projects entail the construction and paving of roads and bridges, the rehabilitation of school buildings, and the extension of sewer and potable water systems.

For Campeche's coastal residents, offshore spaces are close rather than distant, intimate rather than alienated, because the Gulf of Mexico is their patrimonial sea. The abundant fisheries of the Gulf have served the local communities for generations as a patrimony inherited from one generation to the next. But Mexican sovereignty over fisheries and more recently oil should mean that as national patrimony the resources benefit all. The patrimonial sea is a highly contested space where the state struggles with foreign entities as well as the private sector for sovereignty over valuable natural resources. In the patrimonial sea, the state also struggles against its own citizenry to maintain control of the ideological charge over the ambivalent meanings of patrimonial assets (Breglia 2006). In the offshore space of neoliberalism, a fissure erupts between resource sovereignty and territorial sovereignty that nationalist rhetoric cannot abide. As we will see, residents of frontline communities must negotiate not only nationalist words but parastatal deeds within the Gulf of Mexico and the Laguna de Términos.

## Time, Space, and the Post-Peak Condition

Trying to come to grips with the complex situation of oil, politics, violence, and everyday life in the Niger Delta, Michael Watts (2009) proposes a mode of "thinking about oil" that he calls the "oil assemblage." With particular inspiration from the work of Andrew Barry (2006) and Timothy Mitchell (2007), Watts crafts a model for understanding the social, political, and economic as well as cultural and ideological dimensions of oil. Oil assemblages are multiple spaces of visibility and invisibility, with moving boundaries "ideologically draped in the discourses of nationalism, security, scarcity" (n.p.). Within the oil assemblage, whether the Niger Delta or Mexico's Gulf region, we might find a "coordinated but dispersed set of regulations, calculative arrangements, infrastructural and technical procedures that render certain objects or flows governable" (ibid.). Thinking about peak oil as an assemblage—part of a spatial and temporal matrix—rather than an empirical given helps shed light on the complicated politics of living with oil.

Standard notions of peak oil derive from a mathematical model created by Shell Oil geologist M. King Hubbert in the 1950s. Hubbert created a bell-shaped curve of the life cycle of extraction in a given field. The top of the curve, sometimes called Hubbert's Peak, represents peak oil, the point of maximum extraction after which a terminal production decline begins. While Hubbert had trouble convincing oil-industry colleagues of the limitations of oil supply, the warning bells of peak oil and its dire consequences are now reaching more ears. Experts from petroleum geologists to energy analysts and political scientists are taking up the case of the global emergency of the social, economic, and geopolitical implications of oil depletion.

Peak oil highlights what Watts identifies as the "peculiar temporality" of the oil assemblage in simultaneous orientation toward the future and its movement toward exhaustion. By calling attention to the role that peak oil plays in the oil assemblage, we may heighten our awareness of the limits of fossil fuels while also shedding greater light on the contemporary condition of living with oil on the frontlines. Empirical analyses of actual cases of resource depletion, particularly from the frontlines of the Global South, show that the end of oil is still the continuation of everyday life. Peak oil debates, abstracted from the quotidian realities of the social, political, and economic effects of the decline of supergiants such as Cantarell, are thus put aside. Instead, in the chapters that follow, I examine the post-peak condition and its wider sphere of implications for affecting people's lives not only in frontline communities but in the broader contexts of governance, policy making, social programs, and the political economy of resources.

As much as Hubbert's curves and peak oil theories have raised an awareness of the impending end of the fossil fuel age, they fail to tell us how local communities like those on the frontlines of energy production in the Global South will deal with the everyday effects of peaks and declines of oil at the micro level. The current shape of peak oil debates north of the Mexican-U.S. border continually left me frustrated in my search for a framework to understand the way the struggling Cantarell oilfield loomed over my fieldwork in Campeche's Gulf coast communities. Thinking through the circumstance of peak oil at Cantarell while working with residents in Isla Aguada and learning about their challenges, I found that peak oil per se did not seem wholly pertinent to the issues facing the frontline communities or oil nations of the South. Understandings of peak oil in the context of the dynamics of globalization are particularly lacking in their failure to address the differential nature of peak oil's effects on the Global North versus the Global South. Furthermore, peak oil has primarily been viewed through the lens of the (mostly Northern) consumer or the highly capitalized transnational oil company. A failure to understand the complexity of peak oil from the perspectives of producing and exporting communities and nations is shortsighted and dangerous. These nodes in the global energy-production chain prop up the consumption patterns of the North. Meanwhile, many producers are rapidly turning into bigger energy consumers themselves. The global landscape of energy production is not only uneven—it is a constantly shifting terrain.

By spatializing peak oil we can see that Cantarell's peak is only one element within a much broader complex of social, political, and economic problems facing Mexico, the sum of which appears not unlike a recipe for a doomsday scenario.[4] Given the forward momentum toward global peak oil, the Mexican experience surely is instructive for other nations and communities around the world living with oil at the end of the petroleum age. The case of living with oil along the Mexican Gulf offers an opportunity to gain a new perspective on peak oil, lay the groundwork for comparative study, and broaden our understanding of post-peak life and livelihood.

A true sense of post-peak life will not be based on how much or how little oil is at hand for a specific nation or for the planet, whatever the truth of the available reserve numbers. Post-peak life is not simply about the gathering fear that oil is running out. Rather, as the title of this book suggests, it is about how different people are choosing to live or being forced to live with oil now and up to this point. In Isla Aguada, Campeche, post-peak life is the everyday reality of the effects of the decline of Cantarell. For residents there are no debates over the finer points of peak-oil theory, nor do they get caught up in the heady hypotheticals of post-peak apocalyptic scenarios. There are no "doomers"—peak oil apocalyptic thinkers—in Isla Aguada. Instead, post-peak life is more about the grinding realities of living in a community on the frontlines of oil production, where spills, air pollution, and environmental degradation are commonplace. Life today in Isla Aguada, like all frontline communities, is the quotidian experience of living on the downslope, so to speak, of Hubbert's bell curve so deeply ingrained in our understanding of the rise, peak, and decline of oil production.

While popular interpretations of the Hubbert curve understand the peak to signify the end of oil and thus living *without* oil, the frontline experience of living *with* oil is quite different. On the downslope, frontline communities face the insecurity of life and livelihood conditioned by resource depletion. In post-peak life, the end of oil often means more rather than less production. The downward slope entails ramped-up secondary and tertiary recovery in existing fields using invasive chemical techniques to stimulate wells. It means living with consequences as oil industries turn to nonconventional energy resources—extra-heavy crude, tar sands, oil shale, and deepwater oil—which are technically difficult and costly to obtain. Energy exploitation on the downward slope is dirty, expensive, and dangerous.

I bring my discussion of peak oil to the frontlines of coastal Campeche in order to reassert a politics of space into the overwhelmingly temporal signification of the Hubbert curve. Simply put, while mention of peak oil typically provokes the question of "when," often asked with a sense of urgency and even alarm, I wish to shift the emphasis of our peak oil concerns to one of "where." As my familiarity with the implications of peak oil for specific communities affected by the rise and fall in crude production grew over the course of this study, I became more convinced of the need to unpack the spatialized logics of resource peaks and declines, highlighting how resource exploitation territorializes the landscape—whether by the state or the private sector, off shore or on land—and structures social relations, especially concerning labor.

My goal in this study is to map the experience of resource extraction onto the phenomenon of peak oil by detailing the sociospatial character of the post-peak condition. The condition has three major characteristics, clearly illustrated in this case study, that demonstrate the widespread, generalizable nature of the phenomenon—beyond Campeche or Mexico, beyond oil, and perhaps even beyond other natural resources. First, the post-peak condition, as a general scenario of resource depletion, encourages the interests, actions, and interventions of private-sector capital into national territories. In peak resource contexts, multinational oil companies find circumstances ripe for managing and profiting from the exploitation of natural resources, especially those ceded by the state. This is generally concurrent with neoliberal trends in privatization. The second characteristic is the reconfiguration of resource sovereignty in response to challenges mounted by a variety of social actors and institutions vying for control of resources. The third feature is the territorialization of heritage resources—in this case, the making of the Gulf of Mexico into a patrimonial sea, a space of social relations where multiple forms of heritage resources are created, claimed, and contested. As it emphasizes these three characteristics, the post-peak condition exacerbates Mexico's struggle to maintain resource sovereignty in a global age.

## Chapter Summaries

Part 1 traces the contours of peak and decline, both conceptually in the debates over peak oil and as lived through resource exploitation in the Laguna de Términos. In chapter 1 I outline the historical origins of peak oil theory—the idea that resource extraction and depletion follow a bell-shaped curve—and trace how a scientific model moved into the popular imagination through the Hubbert's Peak graph. I demonstrate that peak oil is a scientific model and an ideological representation through which the view from the North shapes an image of post-peak life that decidedly excludes communities that long served as the source communities for energy commodities. I suggest an alternative perspective, what I call a view from the downward slope, as a form of critical analysis for understanding the lived experience of frontline communities.

Chapter 2 shows how a contemporary "oil crisis" is shaped by historical cycles of resource peaks and declines in the Laguna de Términos. *Living with Oil* is not your typical tale of how the traditional lifestyle of a sleepy fishing village is suddenly disrupted by the imposition of the oil industry. Instead, the story I tell here is meant to rid the imagination of all fantasy of global modernity having such an impact on local tradition. For at least a half-millennium in the Americas and elsewhere, largely in places tied to the marketplace through colonialism and neocolonialism, globalization has repeatedly and continuously made commodities out of resources, especially those of the natural environment. In and along the shores of the Gulf of Mexico, these resources include wild and cultivated products of the sea, coastal wetlands, and tropical forests. Over the course of several centuries the Laguna de Términos region was known for a variety of unusual resources. During the colonial period the region was inhabited by pirates turned loggers exploiting a tree known as *palo de tinte*. Colorfast black and purple dye was extracted from heartwood of the tree for use in European textile manufacturing. In the nineteenth and early twentieth centuries, an enormously valuable sap known as *chicle*, bled from a different tree, the *chicozapote* or sapodilla tree, was gathered to the enormous profit of mostly U.S. plantation owners in the region. Destined for chewing-gum factories in Canada and the United States, chicle, like palo de tinte before it, was—however niche—wildly profitable though detrimental to the land and laboring populations. The exploitation of these resources over nearly 500 years can be charted as a series of boom-and-bust cycles, the ultimate of which is peak oil.

In part 2 I go directly to the frontlines to more closely examine the lived experience of the contemporary effects of resource depletion on local communities. In this central, ethnographic part of my study we see the emergence of the next resource in the cycle of commodities of the Laguna de Términos region: commercial shrimp. The goal of my ethnographic research is to show how oil directly and indirectly affects the lives of fishers in the Laguna de Términos. Chapter 3 focuses on fishing: the heritage of subsistence artisanal fishing in Gulf coastal communities, establishment of the commercial shrimping industry in the 1940s at the port of Carmen, the crisis in regional fisheries with the decline in capture coincident with the establishment of oil-drilling operations in the Campeche Sound, and local responses to these circumstances. Oil abundance has not always signified wealth for its producers or the state of Campeche. To the contrary, during the initial boom of Cantarell, the funding mechanisms were not in place to directly support the state or municipality. By the time Campeche was able to advocate for managing Cantarell's oil wealth, the field was already hitting its peak.

Chapter 4 focuses on how Campeche has attempted to avoid the classic symptoms of resource curse by managing oil wealth on the local level. For fishers, oil proceeds present themselves as Pemex-funded compensation programs. I look closely at the relationship between Pemex and the fishing sector in terms of the various aid and compensation programs but also more broadly at a model of post-peak development as the region faces growing insecurity for local economies still dependent on oil incomes.

Part 3 presents two case studies highlighting two defining features of the post-peak condition: neoliberalization of strategic resources and intensification of exploration and production activities. Chapter 5 presents an analysis of President Felipe Calderón's 2008 energy-reform proposal, known to opponents as the "privatization proposal." I discuss how the conservative political administration attempted to mobilize a variety of rhetorical strategies against a vocal Mexican Left to appease the private, multinational oil-services companies long involved with Pemex and wishing to obtain more benefits through its lucrative contracting schemes. The debates surrounding the proposal illustrate that in the face of the dramatic decline of the nation's most prolific oilfield, the state, the citizenry, and the private sector were willing to battle to the last drop of oil to benefit from Mexico's most treasured patrimony. Meanwhile, as the frontline communities faced increasing resource insecurity with the decline of Cantarell, the administration demonstrated that it was willing to leverage the de jure national patrimony into a de facto privatization.

In chapter 6 we find that the peak of Cantarell has motivated Pemex to explore new frontiers for oil, including the deep waters of the Gulf of Mexico. Mexico's challenges in the deepwater Gulf are not only the expected financial and technological hurdles but geopolitical challenges, too. At the same time, as more and more valuable hydrocarbon resources are discovered in the Gulf of Mexico, the territory is transformed into a juridically contested space as well as an ideological battleground. While the United States and Mexico sort out maritime boundaries and rights to exploit the Gulf's deepwater reservoirs, the territory is symbolically transformed into a patrimonial sea, a natural and cultural heritage resource. In the patrimonial sea, the nation's stake in maintaining resource sovereignty, most of all on the maritime border, is crucial to Mexican nationalism and the energy security of both the United States and Mexico.

I conclude by examining alternatives for constructing post-peak futures in the Laguna de Términos. While fishers displaced from the artisanal sector are becoming ecotourism entrepreneurs, Pemex is devising elaborate plans to intensify production in the Gulf. The Laguna de Términos is now at a critical crossroads between a past based on natural resource extraction and a future requiring a concerted effort toward conservation. Will the post-peak condition allow the region to pursue the sustainable option? Or will the energy-security needs of Mexico and its northern neighbor tip the scales toward a future not unlike its past?

## PART I

# PEAKS AND DECLINES

In July 2009 Ciudad del Carmen, Campeche, marked the thirtieth anniversary of Mexico's success in offshore oil drilling. Officials used the anniversary to launch more than a week of memorial activities including an orchestral concert, food festival, and artisanry fair. The celebration culminated in speeches by Pemex Director General Jesús Reyes Heroles and Campeche Governor Jorge Hurtado Valdez. But the happy façade of the events hid profound contradictions. All on hand at the celebrations—Pemex, Campeche state and municipal officials, and residents of Carmen and the surrounding area of the Laguna de Términos—had good reason for mixed feelings about celebrating three decades of extracting oil in the Campeche Sound. Between 1979 and 2009, Cantarell rose and fell as one of the world's most prolific oilfields. In those thirty years, the Pemex chief emphasized in his speech, Cantarell produced an average of 1.9 million barrels per day (mbpd) of crude oil equivalent, representing 72 percent of the national effort and 2.7 percent of global production.[1] During the three decades of prolific production, nearly 1.5 mbpd was sent to the export market, generating income for the country of $430 billion (Reyes Heroles 2009).

The thirtieth-anniversary commemoration provided workaday residents and authorities the occasion to look back and consider the region's role in natural resource exploitation, not only since the discovery of oil in the Bay of Campeche in the 1970s but long before. As Governor Hurtado pointed out in his speech, across time the ecologically rich and diverse region has generated multiple "cycles of bonanza," but time and time again the resource boom has ended in a bust. Hurtado did not have to remind his audience of the local effects of the boom-and-bust cycles of natural resource exploitation in Campeche or of the difficulties that come hard and fast following a bonanza. Indeed, peaks and declines are part of a lived reality in the Laguna de Términos. Long-time residents, despite their lack of formal education, know the stories of the parents and grandparents and great-grandparents who worked in Campeche's landscape gathering chicle and logging palo de tinte. Most everyone listening to Hurtado speak about the vicious cycle of Campeche's booms and busts knew from their own life experiences the bonanza and bust of the shrimp industry. As they stood within sight of Carmen's desperately sad and depleted industrial port, the reminder of a once-thriving shrimp industry now decimated served as a daily lesson in resource economics. More than just a quotidian experience, living this cycle became, over the course of several generations and at least four commodities, ingrained into the public consciousness. Carried from the colonial era through to the present day, this cyclical culture developed in the Laguna de Términos region as a daunting heritage of underdevelopment.

How could frontline communities in the municipality of Carmen break out of the cycle, given the weight of their terrible inheritance? What was the path to the future after the peak of Cantarell? In his speech Hurtado was caught in a position of having to be respectful and somewhat deferential as a state governor, yet he also stood absolutely firm about the strategic importance of Campeche to Pemex. Hurtado asserted that the discovery of oil in the 1970s "breathed new life into our expectations for development." Thirty years on, the governor stressed that Campeche had built a relationship of "alliance" and "growing harmony" with Pemex, revealing a less than harmonious past that needed a post-peak future with local sustainable development at its center. For state and municipal politicians, the celebration left the state poised on the edge of an abyss. On one side was the salvation offered by the proceeds of petroleum to the state. Over the dark edge was the seemingly undeniable situation that Cantarell was in a serious decline. For Campeche state officials and even more immediately for those governing the municipality of Carmen, the funding scenario was dire.

For Pemex, the thirtieth anniversary should have marked a moment of sober reflection on both successes and serious setbacks. True enough, Cantarell marked the parastatal's first offshore venture. In 1974–1975 the first exploratory well, Chac-1, named for the Maya god of rain, was drilled to a depth of 11,600 feet below the seabed forty-three miles north of Ciudad del Carmen in the Bay of Campeche. Others soon followed. By 1979 oil was flowing. By 1981 the Cantarell complex was producing almost 1.2 mbpd. Given that Pemex only had onshore experience, the project was ambitious. When it was built, Cantarell was the largest offshore development in the world. But Pemex neither developed nor drilled Cantarell without considerable help from foreign oil-services companies including Brown and Root, Bechtel, and Schlumberger that have continued to ally closely with Pemex throughout the years of offshore success to the tune of millions upon millions of dollars in contracts.

Over the course of three decades, Pemex developed an overreliance on the Bay of Campeche for upward of three-quarters of the total national oil production. At the moment of the thirtieth-anniversary celebration, however, Gulf production was in freefall. The parastatal's public propaganda machine betrayed no anxiety, showing only pride in Pemex's success at its first offshore undertaking. A fifteen-minute Pemex video, "30 aniversario de la Sonda de Campeche," released in July 2009 for the commemoration, stresses Cantarell's crucial role in modernizing Mexico. But the robustness of Pemex's claim on unmitigated success belies the harsh reality of Mexico's very real oil crisis indicated by the parastatal's own numbers. In December 2003 Cantarell reached its highest level of daily production with 2.2 mbpd. The oilfield's peak year is considered 2004, when output averaged 2.1 mbpd. Then production fell a staggering 31 percent, to below 1.5 mbpd by 2008 (Pemex 2008a). In 2009 Cantarell, once the prolific, Maya-god supergiant, contributed less than 0.7 mbpd to the national production, hitting a decline rate of just over 34 percent from 2008. Cantarell's drop in production hurt Mexico's total Gulf oil production by 14.5 percent in the same period (Pemex 2009a: 19).

Those keeping tabs on Cantarell from north of the border are painfully aware that Mexico's energy crisis is far from exclusively a domestic concern. It is also on the radar in official U.S. energy reports (and only occasionally reported by media outlets) because Mexico's energy security is U.S. energy security and therefore a matter of national security. The United States is highly dependent on Mexican oil. For three decades, Mexico has been a key supplier of crude to the United States. In 2006 Mexico was the second-largest supplier to the United States, with 1.7 mbpd, an all-time high (EIA n.d.). In late 2007 Mexico slipped from second to third top supplier of oil to the United States, a telling sign of what was to come. In 2008, when Cantarell's production fell by 30 percent from its peak in 2004, Mexico's crude exports to the United States dropped to less than 1.2 mbpd, the lowest volume since

1994 (EIA n.d.). The United States closely monitored Cantarell's decline with concern about a further drop in Mexico's domestic production. The two countries had become closely linked by the traffic in Gulf crude. As Mexico's production fell, so did the energy security of the rest of North America—with consequences that would echo across the globe.

"Carmelitas" countered the insecurity and doubt about the region's oil future in the celebratory atmosphere of the thirtieth-anniversary commemoration with a show of pride in their role in supporting offshore oil. Local residents were proud that they hosted Mexico's greatest feat of technical and industrial prowess and that "their" oil contributed substantially to the national budget. Along with transforming the country through a national development program, offshore oil production had indeed changed the course of everyday life in the coastal communities of Campeche. Certain aspects were definitely for the better. Ciudad del Carmen had more to offer as an urban space, including hospitals, schools, and a university. But residents also worried about the uncontrolled growth on the island with inadequate infrastructure. A true division between rich and poor was visible.

One of the worst facets was the palpable damage to the natural environment. The port city, burdened with hosting oil services for the world's largest offshore field, was also within the watershed of one of the ecologically richest areas of Mesoamerica. The mangroves around the Laguna de Términos provide habitat to thousands of species of water and land plants, birds, and animals. Several endangered species are trying to survive in the area. As the human population grows and industry intensifies, ecological damage has the potential of multiplying. This has occurred, it seems, even under the federal protection the entire region now has. The anniversary speakers failed to mention environmental effects over the decades of production at Cantarell.

The unwanted effects of living with oil would not be mitigated by the peak of Cantarell. Carmelitas worried about the precipitous decline of the oilfield and what this meant for local development. While the Mexican state and foreign interests had long benefited from Gulf resources in the form of oil wealth and oil energy, the municipality of Carmen had only recently negotiated with Pemex significant direct local income from oil revenues. For less than a decade, more substantial cash and in-kind revenues were directed to support an agenda for local development of sanitation, health, communication, and education. Roads were under repair, electricity was finally reaching rural homes, and potable water systems were installed. Far-flung communities were slated to receive ambulances so a person with chest pains or a woman in labor had a chance of reaching a hospital in time. Classrooms were coming online so local children had the potential to become competitive in the emerging high-tech industries. Various programs funded by Pemex as well as regular budgetary support from oil incomes were making this possible. Was it all going to end as it was just beginning?

Standing before his constituents on the shores of the Bay of Campeche, Governor Hurtado Valdez asserted, "Pemex has been here thirty years and will be here at least another thirty years more." But did the governor have the assurance of Pemex that the parastatal would commit to its end of the relationship? Given the effects of the first thirty years, was a long-term relationship with Pemex one that Campeche's frontline communities wished to have as part of their destiny? Campeche's long experience as a region of natural resource extraction left little hope for a post-peak future of economic and social development. The long-suffering, underdeveloped Carmen and hinterland communities were still without basic needs such as water and electricity and had limited access to health care and education. After all, Carmen, as the very frontline for servicing the offshore oil production, had only a few years earlier won the right to benefit from becoming an "oil-affected" municipality. The riches of Cantarell were just beginning to provide for coastal Campeche. Now that the area had come so close to these opportunities, would they all disappear?

## CHAPTER I

# The Mexican Oil Crisis

In an oft-quoted and very memorable line of his 2006 State of the Union speech, George W. Bush proclaimed, "America is addicted to oil . . . which is often imported from unstable parts of world." Bush's comment struck a chord for an energy-dependent America at the height of the Iraq war. As a nation, the United States was consuming more than 20 million barrels of oil per day. Less than 5 percent of the world's population consumed nearly a quarter of total global supply. To fuel its high energy consumption, the United States imports a large volume of hydrocarbons including crude oil. For more than fifty years the United States has cultivated dependence on energy imports and along with it, a highly politicized rhetoric on the nation's foreign oil dependence. For most of his audience that evening, still deeply mired in the aftermath of 9/11, the war in Iraq, the uncertainty of Afghanistan, and the spatial politics of the war on terror, Bush's use of "unstable parts of the world" was a very specific allusion. Without a doubt, Bush meant to evoke discomfort in listeners about the ongoing insecurity of the Middle East.

Would the 2006 State of the Union address have been received differently if the famous "addicted to oil" line were accompanied by a graphic demonstrating the actual foreign suppliers of oil, a pie chart, perhaps, clearly showing North American neighbors Canada and Mexico as top oil suppliers to the United States? When politicians, pundits, and others pontificate about the real, invented, and hyperbolized dangers of America's reliance on foreign oil, Mexico is not the first "foreign source" that comes to the average citizen's mind.[1] Whatever Mexico has been guilty of or blamed for in the past few years—illegal immigrants, drug-cartel violence, swine flu—it certainly has nothing to do with either maintaining or endangering America's energy security. Certainly no one thinks

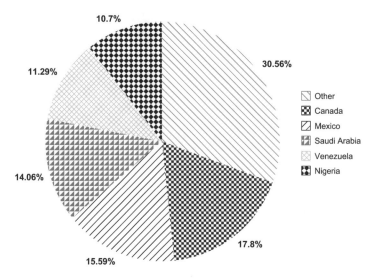

10.7%

11.29%

30.56%

☒ Other
☒ Canada
☒ Mexico
☒ Saudi Arabia
☒ Venezuela
☒ Nigeria

14.06%

17.8%

15.59%

Sources of U.S. crude oil imports, 2006. Source: EIA n.d.

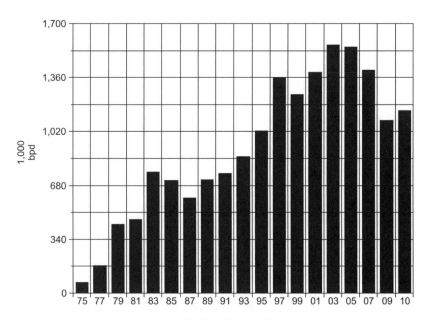

U.S. crude imports from Mexico, 1975–2010. Source: EIA n.d.

of Canada as a big bully on the global scene of energy geopolitics. The fact is that America's closest and usually most compliant neighbors, not far-flung and menacing threats, have long been supplying the foreign oil to the United States' helplessly fossil-fuel-dependent lifestyles.[2]

But at the very moment George W. Bush made his famous pronouncement promising to reduce America's dependence on foreign oil, Mexico—the number two supplier of U.S. oil imports—was indeed becoming an unstable part of the world. Adding to mounting concerns over the country's compromised security at the hands of narcoviolence, especially on the U.S.-Mexican border, Mexico was falling into an energy crisis. At the outset of 2006, news was breaking that Cantarell—Mexico's key producer—had declined by 13 percent in the previous two years. Even worse was the overall state of Mexico's petroleum sector. Along with the drop in production was a plummeting replacement rate, which fell by more than 17 percent over the same period. Pemex's replacement rate into its reserves had dropped to 49 percent—less than half a barrel for every barrel extracted (Cardoso 2006).

For the United States, the world's largest oil consumer, the quest for secure sources of foreign oil is a decades-long preoccupation. The United States, in conjunction with multinational companies, has looked to Mexico twice over the past century as a source for easy-to-access oil. The first time was during the golden age of the Mexican oil industry (roughly 1911-1922), when U.S. and other foreign companies were heavily invested in discovering and extracting millions of barrels of crude from inside Mexico's national territory, mostly on the Gulf coast of Veracruz. This period culminated in the expropriation and nationalization of the oilfields and industry on Mexican territory by President Lázaro Cárdenas in 1938. The second time the United States secured Mexican oil was in the early 1980s. Following the loss of confidence in Middle Eastern and OPEC suppliers after the oil shocks of the 1970s, the discovery of Cantarell provided the United States with the opportunity for a major, non-OPEC, Western Hemisphere supplier.[3] Cantarell's crude put Mexican oil resources at the center of U.S. energy needs and North American regional energy security.

Through two oil booms in Mexico's history, the United States and Mexico deeply intertwined through mutual oil dependence. For the United States, the public sector grew to depend on oil to fuel everything from transportation innovations to industry to world wars. For the U.S. private sector, oil development in Mexico was a profitable foreign investment opportunity. When Mexican oil is flowing most freely, political elites have aided the ventures of the foreign private sector in benefiting from the exploitation of natural resources in Mexican national territory. During the golden age, this was by design. Laws governing state ownership of subsoil resources were suspended to allow foreign exploitation of oil and other valuable mineral resources under the banner of national development. However, with the 1917 constitution's reinstatement of national ownership of the subsoil and the 1938 expropriation of the foreign-owned oilfields, Mexico instituted the most restrictive and longest-lasting holds over its hydrocarbon resources to be found anywhere on the globe. For Mexico, national ownership of oil—and oil itself—became an increasingly powerful symbol of Mexican nationalism. The peak of Cantarell brought the issues of resource sovereignty and energy security—as not only domestic and but transnational issues—into sharp tension with one another.

At the root of Mexico's domestic problem is another strain of oil addiction. Two years after George W. Bush, Mexican Finance Minister Agustín Carstens, speaking on the television news program *Primeros Noticias*, pointed out that Mexicans, too, are addicted to oil. However, for Mexico, oil addiction is not a problem of foreign-oil dependence or excessive energy consumption. Instead, for the exporting country, it manifests as a compromise to the nation's financial health. When Carstens accused Mexico of oil addiction, he admitted that Mexico's government finances were *petrolizadas*, "petrolized" or "oiled" (*El Universal* 2008). Since Mexico reconverted itself into a major exporter in the late 1970s, helped along by offshore discoveries in the Gulf of Mexico, between 35 and 40 percent of the national budget has been directly dependent on oil incomes, or rents. Though the petroleum dependence in Mexico's national economy is far lower than in true petrostates like Nigeria and Venezuela, rents have played a vital role in Mexico's development over the past few decades. Income from oil has allowed the state to use its sovereign resources to finance national development. However, dependence on a finite natural resource is dangerous for Mexico, a large and diverse country with its own social and economic challenges and facing powerful neighbors.

Oil dependence shapes the workaday activities of Pemex and the parastatal's relationship to civil society. The use of oil rents in lieu of a robust and reliable taxation system to fund the nation's ongoing budgetary needs consistently diverts funds away from Pemex that could be used for oil exploration, exploitation, and processing. This form of oil dependence also creates expectations among the citizenry about maintenance of national territorial sovereignty over valuable natural resources, especially one proven so valuable as oil. Given that Gulf oil is a key asset for local development, Mexico's national security, and regional energy security, what can be done to mitigate the decline?

## Peaks and Declines in Mexican Oil Production

Along Mexico's Gulf coast, petroleum and its derivatives have been part of the natural landscape, known for centuries to indigenous inhabitants, the Maya, their neighbors, and their trading partners throughout Mesoamerica. Reports of oil in the Laguna de Términos region were frequent over the centuries, dating back to pre-Columbian culture and the early European colonists. Called *chapopote* in the Nahuat language, oil from naturally occurring asphalt was used to make murals and decorate ceramics and was applied to bodies for ritual and medicinal purposes. In the colonial period, chapopote was used as a varnish for finishing wood, and Spanish and English sailors used tar washed ashore from natural seepages to repair leaky ships during the course of their long voyages (Moreno Gullón 2004).

While an onshore oil industry boomed in Mexico in the early twentieth century, the offshore riches beneath Mexico's Gulf waters were not discovered until much more recently. The origin of the billion-barrel oilfield, Cantarell, is part of the heritage of the Gulf-coast fishing community of Isla Aguada. Here, fishers guard the origin story of Cantarell as a cultural legacy. When fishers of Isla Aguada roll out the yarn, they themselves, of course, tend to play a central role in the story.

The origins of Cantarell are as humble as the fisher whose name the field carries. Rudesindo Cantarell Jiménez, known as Chito, first encountered the signs of offshore oil in the Bay of Campeche about forty-five miles offshore from Ciudad del Carmen in 1961. At the time, he was working on a shrimp boat, the *Centenario del Carmen*. According to local lore in Isla Aguada (a village from which many Cantarells hail), the oil slick, called a *mancha*, that Chito discovered was in fact well known. Local fishers used the nearly 300-foot-long oil slick as a regular point of reference to navigate to some of their favorite fishing grounds. Far from naïve, Cantarell and his colleagues knew that the slick was indeed some sort of oil or kerosene, as they referred to it as *el chapopotero*. A noxious odor of fuel emanated from the bubbling surface of the water. Fishers knew that it was not the remnants of a fuel spill because the strange mancha constantly replenished itself.

Although Rudesindo Cantarell could not possibly have guessed the magnitude of what lay beneath the ocean floor, he took it upon himself to report the mancha to officials. It was not easy to get Pemex to pay attention to a simple fisherman. In 1968 he twice tried to bring the oil slick to the attention of marine authorities, once in the municipal seat of Ciudad del Carmen and again in Frontera in the neighboring state of Veracruz. Then, on a trip to Coatzacoalcos bringing fish to market, he met an engineer who, upon hearing his story, relayed the information to Pemex officials. Within days experts arrived in Ciudad del Carmen to locate and collect samples from the mancha, thus setting the wheels in motion to initiate the exploration that began in 1971. While many might consider that Don Chito's compensation for finding the oil slick was the fact that the supergiant would go on to carry his name, he requested work at Pemex for himself and his two sons. One son was eventually granted a position—unusual and coveted job security for a fisher from a village in Campeche. But Cantarell himself lived the rest of his life in obscurity—and, according to some accounts, in misery—in Isla Aguada. He had a heart attack and died in 1997 at age eighty-three.

The find inspired hopes that oil could be converted into a platform for national development by bringing Mexico back into the invternational market as an oil-exporting country (Ortiz, Romero, and Díaz 1979). Considering that the Mexican energy company had not undertaken offshore drilling before, the operation went relatively quickly. The complex Pemex constructed was huge, covering more than sixty-two square miles. But the task was simplified because the water was shallow and the seabed allowed straightforward access to the oil. In 1974 drilling commenced in the Campeche Sound, and in 1975 Pemex sank Chac-1, then wells in adjacent fields in the Cantarell complex—Bacab, Abkantún, Akal, Nohoch, and Cantarell-1 (Bolívar Aguilar 2001: 79). The field's first commercial production began modestly with 4,290 barrels per day (bpd) in June 1979. At the time, Mexican officials expected that Cantarell would contribute up to 37 percent of the nation's crude production (Ortiz, Romero, and Díaz 1979). The whole operation consisted of twenty rigs, none in more than 300 feet of water, with wells drilled down to depths of no more than 3,500 meters, about 10,500 feet (Campeche 2004). Through three decades of drilling, Cantarell grew to nearly 200 wells.[4] Though in the infancy of Mexico's offshore production the Bay of Campeche contributed only a small fraction of Mexico's national output, Cantarell soon proved to be the biggest oilfield ever discovered in Mexico, producing prodigious quantities of Maya crude—a heavy (meaning high-density), sour (indicating sulfurous) oil. According to Pemex statistics, in the 1980s Cantarell contributed about

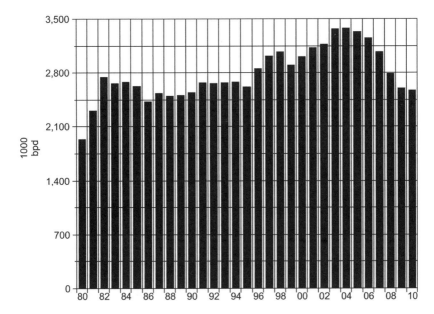

Pemex annual average crude production, 1979–2010. Source: Pemex 2008a.

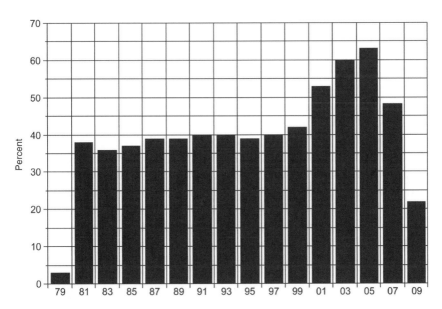

Cantarell contributions to national crude production, 1979–2009. Sources: Pemex 1990, 2001, 2010b.

37 percent to total national production. In the 1990s the supergiant contributed nearly 41 percent, and its contributions rose again to average almost 57 percent of national production from 2000 through 2007 (Pemex 2008a). During its year of peak production, Cantarell contributed more than 60 percent to national production. The oilfield's decline is marked by a plunge to 22 percent just four years later.

Cantarell, dubbed by Mexicans "el salvador del país," the country's savior (Ortiz, Romero, and Díaz 1979), also inspired great hopes and expectations across the border. When commercial production commenced, the U.S. reaction showed the transnational importance of Mexican Gulf oil: "No aspect of the Mexican petroleum situation has so fired the popular imagination as the possibility that Mexico will become a major oil producer" (Ronfeldt 1980: 34). This statement from a 1980 report to the U.S. secretary of energy prepared by the Rand Corporation demonstrates the expectations regarding Cantarell for shaping a U.S.-Mexican energy policy. When the extent of Mexico's Gulf reserves became known (in 1980 estimated between 10 and 20 billion barrels), Mexico's oil became an issue of public policy discussion and debate in the United States. The estimated size of the find promised the only supergiant outside of the Middle East, northern Siberia, the North Sea, and the Permian Basin of Texas and New Mexico and the only one discovered in 1970–1980, a decade marked by U.S. energy insecurity (17, 34–35).

The report points out that these debates and discussions were shaped by three assumptions: the strategic importance of Mexico's oil for meeting U.S. energy needs; the salience of oil in serving as the foundation for U.S.-Mexican relations; and the high degree of pressure the United States would be able to exert on Mexico to produce and export as much oil as possible (viii). Despite the hubris of these assumptions, several conclusions regarding U.S. interests in Mexican oil remained in evidence. First, U.S. domestic oil production inarguably peaked in the mid-1970s, and other major producers were beginning to reach their peaks as well. Second, as the oil shocks made clear, the geopolitical stakes of import partners were high. The United States was under increasing pressure to find non-OPEC alternatives to Middle Eastern energy sources. Third, given these conditions and Mexico's proximity as a stable, developing country, Cantarell indeed looked like an exciting prospect for abundant and potentially quite cheap crude. Cantarell crude is heavy oil and difficult to refine; thus it fetches a lower price than the more desirable lighter, "sweeter" crudes.

Three decades and 11 billion barrels later, the persistence of Ru-

desindo Cantarell and of Pemex in building an offshore oil industry obviously paid off. Mexican national development, U.S.-Mexican relations,
and local livelihood strategies would be brokered over Cantarell oil.

## Foreign Ownership in Mexico's Oilfields

The issue of Mexico's security as a source of foreign oil—and as a territory for foreign investment—harkens back to the country's earliest oil
boom, in the first quarter of the twentieth century. During that golden
age of oil production, foreign oil companies, mostly from the United
States and Britain, experienced a bonanza of production made possible by Mexico's relinquishment of territorial sovereignty over its oil resources. The golden age coincided with the three-decade dictatorial regime of Porfirio Díaz (1876–1911), known as the Porfiriato, during
which the Secretaría de Fomento (Ministry of Development) launched
an elaborate and aggressive campaign to make Mexico's resources known
to the world, advertising the country as an abundant frontier ripe for
foreign investment. In his drive to open Mexico to foreign investment
and spur national development, Díaz had to create an environment un-
encumbered by state intervention, particularly in the strategic and profitable areas of natural resources. Though the Porfiriato represents a period of rupture in a centuries-long genealogy that gave legitimacy and
stability to the state's claims of direct dominion over subsoil resources,
it was a critical period in the modernization of Mexico. Heavy foreign
investment and vigorous national infrastructural development left a legacy of railroads, highways, and oilfields.[5]

The success of the foreign companies working in Mexico depended
on the free flow of oil, a highly contingent process. In order for Mexico's oil to flow without trouble, companies backed by foreign interests such as El Huasteca, Mexican Eagle, and the Mexican Petroleum
Company had to have luck with nature, unrestrained and unambiguous
mineral rights, and a compliant labor force. Laws enacted during the
Porfiriato—changing legal precedent to allow oil companies the outright purchase of lands and permitting exclusive private access to mineral rights—ensured the domination of the oil companies formed by
Edward Doheny, Weetman Pearson (later known as Lord Cowdray),
and others. The Porfiriato conditioned the possibility for wild success
on all counts. Porfirio Díaz's scheme for the foreign capitalization of
Mexico's resources worked—in a sense. From 1911 to 1922, production approached and then exceeded tens of millions of barrels a year.

Nearly 2 billion barrels were drawn from Mexican wells before the subsoil was renationalized and the foreign-owned oilfields were expropriated in 1938 (Meyer 1977: 35).

By the time oil resources were brought back into the national fold, Mexico's oil boom was over. When President Lázaro Cárdenas nationalized oil in 1938, Mexico was experiencing faltering production as foreign companies were losing the confidence to make investments in exploration and infrastructure. Mexico became less attractive to foreign companies. The oil companies were ready to move on, growing more interested in other fabulous finds such as Lake Maracaibo, Venezuela. Beginning in the late 1920s, foreigners flocked to Venezuela, where more abundant oil came with the more favorable legal conditions provided by the ready-to-deal dictator Juan Vicente Gómez. Other oil-production regions around the world also became attractive, predominantly among them the Middle East. Meanwhile, Mexico's production plummeted. In what would become its last decade of foreign-operated oil production, Mexico moved from being the world's second-largest producer to sixth place—from producing almost 200 million barrels annually in 1921 to less than 50 million in 1937 (Koppes 1982: 64). Through the 1950s and 1960s, Mexico was a net importer of oil, producing only a quarter of a million barrels a day in 1960. (When Cantarell came online in 1979, the field would initially produce that entire amount by itself.) As oil tumbled from its peak in 1921, the country would not see significant production levels on the global stage again until the 1970s.

However, during this final decade before expropriation, even in the midst of decline Mexico began to get the flavor of oil rents. Although production had fallen and foreign firms were mostly repatriating the profits they earned from Mexico's natural resources, because of the real taxation imposed on the foreign oil companies Mexico finally began to benefit from the oil industry.[6] The first substantial revenue was drawn from oil in 1920, and revenues from Mexican oil became critical to the federal budget. Oil revenues amounted to 25 percent of the national budget in 1921 and up to 31 percent in 1922 (Gordon 1976: 54). Mexicans began to get a sense of what oil might mean as national patrimony, as the wealth of the nation.[7]

## Mexico's Offshore Boom

The energy relationship between the United States and Mexico has an eerie serendipity. Just as U.S. production was reaching its peak in the early 1970s, Mexico was on its way to becoming an oil exporter. At the time, Mexico was a very attractive alternative for the United States, whose demand was growing and whose own domestic surplus had diminished. As its neighbor and a non-OPEC major producer, Mexico was geopolitically ideal for assuring American energy security well into the contemporary oil age. After years of hearing critics decry U.S. dependence on Middle Eastern oil, policy makers now seemingly could afford to take a harder line against Persian Gulf states. As a silent but steady top supplier, Mexico appeared as the answer to American energy-security anxieties.

Mexico had long been suspicious of U.S. designs on its national patrimony and took steps to set export policies. Officials wanted to make good financial sense and good political sense at the same time. Even though the López Portillo administration (1976–1982) found, in 1980, high prices, an abundant flow coming from Cantarell, and a needy neighbor to the north, it wanted to be sure to exercise prudence and maintain sovereignty in the face of resource riches, particularly in regard to export policies. Mexican leaders were loath to subject their great plans for using the new oil incomes for national development "to US political pressures and economic vicissitudes" (G. Székely 1989: 1780). But as soon as Mexico started revving up its oil production, bilateral business opportunities opened across the border, leading to "a greater direct penetration of U.S. firms in Mexico" (Corredor 1983: 139). Accelerated transnational ties led to growth in sectors from automotive to *maquiladora*.

In this second Mexican boom, oil was safely secured under Article 27 of the constitution as the nation's patrimony. Oil was protected because Article 27 defined "crude oil, hydrocarbons, and basic petrochemicals" as strategic resources under the aegis of the state. As such, their control was an extension of state sovereignty and their management a feature of the state's security apparatus.[8] During Mexico's second boom (1978–1981), proven oil reserves jumped from 6.3 billion barrels at the end of 1976 to 16 billion barrels a year later and soared to 40 billion barrels in 1978 (G. Székely 1983).

Even before Cantarell started flowing, Mexican oil was finding its way to the United States. From 1977 through 1979, 86 percent of Mexican crude exports were heading north of the border. For the United States, by 1980 Mexican oil accounted for 10 percent of all imports (Corredor 1983: 139). Thus the first national energy plan, developed during the administration of José López Portillo, protectively stated than no more than 50 percent of oil exports could go to one single country. Furthermore, the plan dictated that Mexican oil should not account for more than 20 percent of any foreign nation's total imports (G. Székely 1989: 1780).

López Portillo insisted on the autonomy of oil resource sovereignty in terms of maintaining the Pemex monopoly, yet the oil riches provided Mexico with virtually unlimited access to capital from private companies and international lending agencies such as the World Bank. Most of what Mexico borrowed was from private foreign banks. During the López Portillo administration, the borrowed money bought an expansion of the public sector, including nationalization of the shrimping industry. The stated goal was for state-led development backed by guaranteed oil revenues to lead to growth. The expectations of the oil prices against which Mexico was borrowing very large sums of money proved not to be the reality that emerged in the global marketplace during the oil glut of the early 1980s. During the oil boom, the increasing crude oil, oil derivatives, natural gas, and petrochemical exports profoundly raised Pemex's contribution to the national totals, jumping from 15 percent in 1975 to 75 percent in 1983. Pemex oil provided almost $65 billion that led to the financial boom in the late 1970s.

The petroleum bonanza set the stage for a new development model for Mexico that offered compensation for the internal inequalities across the country brought about by a reliance on the import-substitution model (Millor 1982: 125). As Negrete explains (1984: 7), the import-substitution model brought growth (from 1940 to 1970 at an annual rate of about 6 percent) "at a high cost to both Mexican citizens and the state." Inequalities abounded within and among sectors of the economy, regions, and income groups. Unemployment and underemployment rose as exports were neglected in favor of imports (ibid.).

A greater than 19 percent annual growth in oil exports during the boom with a 54 percent annual growth in exports led economic expansion to the tune of a 9 percent GDP increase from 1977 through 1981. In those years, oil-export incomes were twice what the government expected (Moreno-Brid and Ros 2009: 131, 135). An early spurt of economic growth did not indicate that Mexico's oil was fueling long-term national development, however. High international oil prices during the boom guaranteed favorable short-term effects for the country's economy. But Mexico showed signs of "Dutch disease" common among developing countries rich in natural resources. The country failed to diversify across sectors. While public investments showed a strong bias in favor of oil, agriculture and manufacturing were neglected (ibid.: 133).

Mexico began to rely solely on exporting oil instead of adding other exports, continuing the damaging legacy of the import-substitution industrialization model.[9] Meanwhile, Mexico's newfound oil wealth drew international lenders to its doorstep. As Mexico already was indebted following currency crises of the 1970s, new loans from foreign banks would eventually place it in an untenable financial position, compromising not only its development plans but its fiscal health overall.

Over the course of the boom, Mexico's economy became petrolized, particularly in foreign trade, making it vulnerable to fluctuations in international oil prices. When these dramatically tumbled from $33.20 per barrel in 1981 to $11.85 just five years later, a profound economic crisis set in (Suárez and Palacios 2001: 39). The bottom fell out of world oil prices in 1981, and Mexico's heavy borrowing, ballooning foreign debt, and inability to sustain the peso's value at artificially high levels any longer led to its 1982 debt crisis. Price controls at home on everything from gas to tortillas that had been kept artificially low could no longer be maintained. To keep the situation in check and especially to keep inflation down and maintain some real value to the peso in relation to the U.S. dollar, prices on commodities were repeatedly and dramatically increased. Gasoline, utilities, and staple foods that already had risen to high prices were increased overnight by 100 percent, inciting panic. Devaluation would bring the peso from 26 to 1 against the dollar in 1982 to 2,300 to 1 in 1987 (Joseph and Henderson 2002: 462).

In 1982 the cost of debt servicing reached more than 62 percent of export revenues (Lustig 1998: 31). By August the country announced defeat. Mexico could no longer pay the $90 billion or so owed to foreign banks. The reaction among those who held any money at all in pesos was to convert them to dollars. Gentleman notes (1984: 224), "The crisis brought massive layoffs and the devaluations meant an erosion of purchasing power that affected citizens equally across all income levels." What is more, the crisis drove Mexicans across the U.S. border, doubling the estimated number of undocumented migrants.

Chained now to the global economy through its debt, Mexico was far from alone in experiencing the fallout. Home to many of the creditor banks, the United States had a vested interest in finding a solution to Mexico's crisis. In August 1982, Mexican Finance Minister Jesús Silva Herzog along with Pemex officials went to Washington over what was called the "Mexican weekend" to meet with U.S. Department of Energy and Treasury officials to negotiate an assistance package that would feature among its measures an oil deal. Pemex and the

U.S. Department of Energy were already under contract to sell the U.S. government 110 million barrels of Mexican oil to stock the strategic petroleum reserve at a price slightly below market value.[10] In this additional contract, the United States would give Mexico a $1 billion advance payment for oil exports to stock the U.S. strategic reserves. Under the terms of what was called an "aid contract," Mexico would supply the United States with its lighter-grade Isthmus oil at "wellhead" price, with the United States taking a bet that world oil prices would not go up substantially in 1983 and thus significantly lower the volume of delivery to the strategic petroleum reserve. The U.S. negotiators gambled conservatively. For its $1 billion the United States received 36–37 million barrels of oil for about $29–$30 a barrel, just below market price (Beaubouef 2007: 129).

The International Monetary Fund (IMF) then stepped in with a more permanent solution to reschedule Mexico's overall debt. The economy was forced into rapid liberalization. Mexico tried to stimulate the domestic manufacturing sector. However, if any correction to the trade deficit was made or if any surplus was garnered, this went to debt repayment, not development programs in the budget (E. Ortiz 1994: 161). Thus, despite the government's national development ambitions, the oil boom ended with fewer safeguards in place to fight Mexico's problems of social inequality. With the country subject to "shock treatments" of structural adjustment programs following the debt crisis, economic sovereignty had effectively been ceded. Health care, education, and antipoverty programs promised on the flow of oil rents were slashed as the state stepped back from national development promises. Oil thus opened the door and paved the way for Mexico's neoliberal turn.

### Oil Apocalypse?

From its discovery until 2004, Cantarell rose to join the world's exclusive rank of supergiants: producers of at least 5 billion barrels of oil. Right in America's backyard, Cantarell—the world's largest oilfield no one had heard of—produced millions of barrels a day to make Mexico a leading global exporter and a top-three supplier to the United States and made Pemex one of the largest companies in the world. But the production bonanza could not last forever. From a peak of almost 3.4 mbpd in 2004, oil production fell at a rate of 13 to 15 percent in the following years. By 2008 Mexico's total production decreased by

20 percent, to 2.8 mbpd. Within another year, production had slipped to 2.2 mbpd. The supergiant indeed reached peak oil, its maximum rate of output, and subsequently production slipped downward.

When George W. Bush alluded in 2006 to the dangers of depending on oil from "unstable" parts of the world, he was not referring to the real crisis of energy stability that the world is now facing: peak oil. For Mexico the critical issue was whether the peak of Cantarell per se indicated a more generalized peak oil condition for the nation's reserves. Given the overwhelming importance of this single field's contributions to Mexico's overall production, it seems that Cantarell's peak indicates a general peak. Empirical evidence gathered and reported by international agencies, private sources, and the Mexican government all agree that national oil production is in decline.

The monumental significance of Cantarell is only magnified by the loss of its contributions. Those who believe in the notion of peak oil do not have to look far to find evidence of an oil apocalypse in Mexico: long-term production prospects certainly do look grim. Peak-oil blogger and oil and gas industry insider Martin Payne calls Cantarell "a 'poster child' for Peak Oil concerns" (2008). As a prototypical representation of peak oil, Cantarell embodies issues on the agenda of a growing community of petroleum geologists, engineers, environmentalists, academics, policy makers, and ordinary citizens. The issues vary from economic instability, transportation gridlock, food shortages, climate change, and geopolitical realignment to a host of national security threats.

While peak oilers view the decline of Cantarell as emblematic of peak oil's imminence, they scarcely look beyond the boundaries of the oilfield to the onshore social or political context of Mexico's oil production for the domestic effects of Cantarell's decline. The failure to understand this broader context of Cantarell's peak is shortsighted. The Gulf of Mexico is more than simply a workaday space of oil production. Instead it is a space where citizens, the state, and the private sector vie to assert control over the world's most valuable commodity. It is also a space of the contestation of the meaning of oil as a natural and national resource not only for generations of Mexicans but for those who watch the peak and decline of Mexican oil from across the border.

The famous Hubbert's Peak bell curve emerged in an atmosphere bullish on oil production and potential. When Hubbert began to speak of peak oil in the 1950s he intervened into a cornucopian atmosphere when the United States was the world's largest global oil producer and most oilmen and scientists alike held very optimistic positions on an extreme abundance of the oil supply. In his model of resource production and depletion rates, Hubbert calculated that U.S. production would reach a maximum between 1966 and 1972 (Hubbert 1956). Hubbert's prediction proved right on target when it became apparent in 1971 that U.S. production did indeed peak the previous year. Even though Hubbert's curve was originally set to model individual fields, in 1969 Hubbert shifted his sights to the global oil supply. Hubbert predicted a peak in the year 1995 (Grove 1974). While contemporary research may differ on the precise year, there is growing evidence, and some could argue consensus, that global peak oil is imminently upon us.[11]

Production decline at Cantarell is indicative of global peak oil, according to recent comprehensive, comparative studies of oilfields across the world. The peak and decline of giants and supergiants apart from Mexico's Cantarell, including Saudi Arabia's Ghawar and Kuwait's Burgan, are significantly contributing to the effect of global peak oil (Simmons 2005: 15). The peak of these megaproducing fields is key to global oil supply, given that no supergiants have been found since the 1970s. While there are tens of thousands of producing oilfields around the world, only a relative minority produce a vast majority of the global production. Of the world's approximately 70,000 oilfields, just 25 of the 507 giant fields account for one-quarter of the global production of crude oil, 100 fields account for half of production, and up to 500 fields account for two-thirds of all discoveries (Robelius 2007; Sorrell et al. 2009: ix). Even though the giants (fields with at least 500 million barrels of recoverable oil) of the world are only a small fraction of the total number of fields, their importance is huge. More than 60 percent of world oil production came from giants by 2005, and more than half of the world's reserves are found in giants (Höök, Hirsch, and Alekett 2009). The maturation of the giants, most of which were discovered in the 1950s, is of serious concern in terms of regional and global peak oil. Of the 507 giant oilfields, 430 are in production, and of them, 261 are in decline (ibid.). In 2007, production from 16 of the top 20 producing fields was also in terminal decline (IEA 2008). Cantarell fits the global trend of recently peaked supergiants now in terminal, irreversible decline. The preponderance of the evidence drawn from the performance of the major global producer led the International Energy Agency to suggest in the 2010 *World Energy Outlook* that global oil production would never again reach production levels achieved in 2006 (IEA 2010). From the IEA data, one analyst concluded, "peak oil is not just here—it's behind us already" (Rudolf 2010).

## From Doomsday Scenarios to Failed States

This whole scenario, what Michael Klare (2009a) calls the "era of xtreme energy," is, in line with the poles established by debates on peak oil, welcomed by some and dreaded by others. According to Klare, the current era of decline is an interim between the petroleum age and a new era of renewable energy that is yet to emerge. The current post-peak period is a painful and ugly time of transition "characterized by excessive reliance on oil's final, least attractive reserves." Attractiveness, of course, is in the eye of the beholder. Indeed, private energy companies and multinational oil-services providers (Halliburton, Brown and Root, and so forth) are in fact very attracted to the profitable opportunities in going after "tough oil" (Klare's term) and unconventional fuels. Doing this could range from drilling into the ultradeep waters of the Arctic and Gulf of Mexico to using hydraulic fracturing to extract natural gas from rock formations. Given the dangerous equipment, chemicals, and infrastructure required for such operations, most often in delicate and otherwise pristine ecosystems, it is no wonder some dread the extreme scenario.

Klare's projections show us what is here and now rather than off in the distant and unknowable future. It is not a Mad Max world portrayed in end-of-oil accounts in movies and on the Discovery Channel, per se, but one in which we have to account for a broader geopolitics of resource depletion. The case of Mexico and the peak of Cantarell has geopolitical ramifications of the highest degree. But to date, Mexico's peak-oil status has been tangentially brought into the fray overshadowed by typical sticky subjects of U.S.-Mexican relations, border politics, migration, and trade. In the September 2010 document "Mexico-U.S. Relations: Issues for Congress" prepared by the Congressional Research Service, the only mentions of oil are the failure of the Calderón administration to pass a comprehensive energy-reform package that would have allowed the opening of Pemex to the private sector, Calderón's efforts to ally Pemex with Petrobras (the Brazilian national oil company), and the small-scale bilateral promotion of wind-energy programs in Mexico (Seelke 2010). Considering the role oil plays economically, not to mention socially and politically, the more strident supporters of the position that peak oil portends the collapse of civilization would eagerly await the contribution of Mexico's oil crisis to the host of other familiar (and severe) problems, namely drug cartels and the general toll of the global economic recession.

While a lot of peak-oil hype conjures hypothetical doomsday scenarios, the reality of peak oil began to wash over Mexico quite soon after Cantarell's 2004 peak as a political and economic apocalypse of sorts. Just four short years after record production rates from the world's largest offshore field, not only was the shallow-water Gulf complex dramatically giving out, but global economic recession was setting in, showing that Mexico's post-peak condition would be far more complex than that for which Hubbert's metric could account. In 2008 Mexico's top three sources of hard currency—oil, remittances, and tourism—were dealt a reverberating series of simultaneous blows. Remittances, revenue sent back home to Mexico by family members working mostly in the United States, are second only to oil as a major legal source of national income. Mexico is the largest remittance-receiving country in Latin America, owing to approximately 12 million Mexican nationals living in the United States. Remittances are an unstable form of income, as their value is highly sensitive to economic downturns and currency fluctuations at home and abroad. Following the onset of the global recession, according to Banco de Mexico figures, remittances showed a 15 percent drop from 2006 to 2009, from just over $26 billion to just over $21 billion (in Alba 2010). This significantly affects daily life for families at home, given their dependence on funds from abroad. According to the Inter-American Development Bank (IDB 2009), 57 percent of remittances to Mexico go toward such basic necessities as food, medicine, and housing. The remainder is often invested in small businesses or education.

While the economy was in the throes of the recession-induced drop in remittances, tourism (the third-largest source of national income) took a double hit. The first blow was when drug-cartel violence splashed across TV screens and newspapers. This was redoubled when the H1N1 swine flu turned would-be visitors away from Mexican vacations. The tourism industry accounts for 8 percent of Mexico's GDP, employing some 2 million people across the country. As if a global economic recession was not enough to hurt the tourism industry, Mexico was contending with the impact at home and abroad of the drug-cartel violence that killed more than 5,000 people in 2008 and by spring of 2009 was on track for an even higher figure. U.S. State Department travel alerts warned travelers that "recent Mexican army and police confrontations with drug cartels have resembled small-unit combat, with cartels employing automatic weapons and grenades" and that during some "large firefights" across the country but mostly in the border towns, "U.S.

citizens have been trapped and temporarily prevented from leaving the area" (Booth 2009). Federal troops, Mexico's newest weapon in combating drug-cartel violence, even moved onto the streets of Mexico's most popular tourist destination, Cancún. This followed the February 2009 torture and assassination of a retired Mexican brigadier general who was on his first day of the job as Cancún's new top antidrug official, along with an aide and his driver, the mayor's nephew. The assassination of General Mauro Enrique Tello Quiñonez launched Operation Quintana Roo, a militarized offensive against drugs and corruption in and around the popular tourism destination. In this beach resort far from the known violence of Mexico's border towns, one might have felt a world away from the possibility of getting tangled up in cartel violence. Yet images of black-masked, machine-gun-wielding anticartel special forces cruising past Carlos 'n' Charlie's and Señor Frog's—as played out on American television—would certainly give pause to spring breakers just about to book their trips.

When the swine flu hit that April, the tourism industry was already extensively damaged. Early estimates of the cost were enormous, in the neighborhood of $2.3 billion, or between 0.3 and 0.5 percent of Mexico's GDP (according to Finance Minister Carstens) to as much as 1 percent (according to Foreign Minister Patricia Espinosa) (Ness 2009). The federal government countered U.S.-style, with a tourism stimulus package. It pumped money into credit packages, loan restructuring, and a marketing campaign called Vive México: Experience Mexico. Nevertheless, months after the flu outbreak, a decline of 40 percent was felt across the tourism sector. Resurgent cases of flu, notably along the Maya Riviera of the Yucatán Peninsula, continued to fuel visitors' fears and keep their much-needed cash away. Hotel occupancy in Cancún, for example, dropped to 20 percent in summer 2009, forcing up to two dozen hotels to close their doors. Meanwhile, occupancy in other tourist destinations such as Acapulco and Puerto Vallarta dipped as low as 9 to 12 percent (SourceMex 2009).

Rounding out the triumvirate of top income sources is oil, a major contributor to Mexico's national budget since it became a net exporter with production from Cantarell beginning in the 1970s. Since the peak of Cantarell in 2004, Mexico has tried to balance declining production with rising oil prices. During its highest moment of oil production, December 2003, Pemex recorded nearly 3.4 mbpd. At the end of 2007 Mexico was producing 2.9 mbpd. In 2008 production dropped to a fourteen-year low of 2.8 mbpd. Exports were also down substantially in

2008, to 1.4 mbpd on average, a drop of 16.8 percent from 2007 (Gentile 2009).

Oil sales numbers from the close of 2008 demonstrate how Mexico's top source of revenue stood to fare in a global economic crisis. In the fourth trimester of 2008, income from exports of Mexican crude mix earned just under $6 billion, 48 percent less than in the comparable period the previous year. Production in 2009 began the same way: not quite 2.7 mbpd in the first four months, down 7 percent from 2008. Exports for this period averaged just under 1.3 mbpd at a value of $6.14 billion, down 60 percent from the same period in 2008 (Pemex n.d.b.). In 2008, oil and gas extraction made up 8 percent of the nation's gross domestic product (PEP 2009).

The trend of serious earnings decline can be attributed to the deadly confluence of two factors: the fall in oil prices combined with a fall in output. The price per barrel of Mexican mix dropped from $77.31 to $45.31, more than a 41 percent fall between the end of 2007 and the close of 2008. Exacerbating this price fall was a drop in production for the all-important export market. Mexico simply had less oil to sell. After reaching a 2007 export level of almost 1.7 mbpd, Pemex failed to meet its 2008 export production goal of slightly less than that and in fact closed 2008 with a 1.4 mbpd average. Exports of Mexican mix generated a total of more than $43 billion in 2008 (CEFP 2009: 8). In Pemex's report of export market projections for 2008-2017, slight but steady gains would be made through 2013, with a significant drop-off in overall export production, ending the period with 875,000 bpd in 2017 (Sener 2008: 57). One interesting transformation in the oil export profile is in the balance of quality. An increase is expected in the share of light and superlight crude (significant in the former and modest in the latter), both of which are more valuable than the bulk of Mexico's heavy Maya export crude drawn from the dying Cantarell field. Also factored in is Mexico's growing refining capability, with its first new refineries in three decades expected to come on line by the middle of the projection period. Once the country can refine more of its own heavier crude, then it can focus exports on the less abundant but more valuable lighter and sweeter product.

Over the course of 2008, Mexico's worsening energy economy was somewhat masked by sky-high oil prices in the global marketplace. At the same time, the Mexican public's attention was captured by Felipe Calderón's explosive energy-reform bill before Mexico's federal legislature, the Congreso Nacional. The declining production volume was mitigated by high prices, and the federal budget contributions were cushioned. Meanwhile, the federal government used the high prices at the pump to double its political advantage. Endless government-sponsored commercials on the Televisa network showed middle-class Mexicans hit hard by high gas prices. The ads, sponsored by Calderón's right-wing Partido Acción Nacional (PAN), stressed the importance of supporting private-sector participation within Pemex in order to reduce reliance on imported refined petroleum products. Economic pressures were converted into political opportunity as the conservative Calderón administration looked to use declining production, rising domestic consumption, and the popularization of energy independence to capitalize on a long-sought neoliberal reform: the privatization of Pemex.

Given the triple hit on oil, tourism, and remittances, the general atmosphere of global recession, and the unabating violence on the border, certainly Mexico was facing major problems. Outside perceptions of Mexico—very much unappreciated domestically—characterized the country as chaotic with the state losing its grip. One source voicing this particular opinion was the U.S. military. In a report produced by the U.S. Joint Forces Command, Mexico was considered, compared to Pakistan, the less likely of the two "large and important states" to pose the potential for "rapid and sudden collapse." To its south this presented a "worst-case scenario" for the United States due to pressures from criminal gangs and drug cartels on Mexico's government, politicians, police, and judicial system (US JFCOM 2008: 36).[12]

Even though official accusations emanating from north of the border regarding Mexico's potential or achieved "failed state" gave little heed to the country's energy crisis, the peak-oiler community did not fail to connect Cantarell's peak to collapse scenarios. In fact, peak oilers have been closely watching Mexico for several years now, long before murmurings of generalized implosion. Jeff Vail, a contributor to the peak-oiler website *The Oil Drum*, has been watching for and expecting Mexico's collapse since 2006. According to Vail, the decline of Cantarell will be the root cause of the imminent collapse of the economy and governance in Mexico. Discussion boards and forums have picked up on a similar sentiment. For example, a forum launched in 2008 on the user discussion boards to peakoil.com called the Mexico Collapse Watch Thread served as a news and commentary source on current events in Mexico and the fallout effects of the declining trend of oil production.

Discussion topics in 2008-2010 did not stray very far from questions of drug-cartel-related violence and the interconnection of border security with energy security.

The discussions on peakoil.net are among many in which interlocutors draw connections in Cantarell's declining production, Pemex's inability thus far to find alternative resources, and the implications for an imminent apocalypse scenario. This leads some peak oilers to perceive a direct security threat on the U.S.-Mexican border as the declining oil and deteriorating situation create a new kind of border crosser: the peak-oil migrant.[13] Even though outmigration from the United States to Mexico fell by more than half between 2006 and 2009 (OECD 2011), Jude Clemente (2008) argues that an "extensive socioeconomic crunch" spurred by declining oil revenues could rapidly reverse this trend.

The linkage between Mexican oil and migration across the U.S.-Mexican border has historical precedence in the popular imaginary and in legislative circles as well. The 1973 oil shocks found the United States looking toward Mexico for oil resources. The U.S. government proposed a guest-worker program (after ignoring Mexico's repeated requests for such a policy following the demise of the Bracero program of the 1940s–1960s) as a concession to Mexico in exchange for privileged access to its reserves. Backed by nationalist bravado and the promise of oil-backed domestic development in 1974, President Echeverria refused the American offer (Fitzgerald 2006, Rico 1992). According to Alexandra Délano (2011), Echeverria's confidence that oil would bring prosperity to Mexico supplanted the need to engage in immigration negotiations. The discovery of offshore oil and initiation of production at Cantarell only strengthened the position "that oil reserves would give [Mexico] an economic boost and therefore cooperation with the U.S. on various issues, including migration, was no longer a priority" (84).

But U.S.-Mexican relations only strengthened over the traffic in Gulf oil and the two countries' mutual—however distinct—problems of oil dependence. The issue of migration, as Délano points out, morphed into a "policy of no policy" on migration from Mexico to the United States. As the ebbs and flows of ideological discourse brought the sensitivity of migration issues to the fore, Mexican oil was once again brought to the table as a bargaining chip for politicians. In 2003 the U.S. House of Representatives Foreign Relations Committee passed an amnesty resolution for undocumented Mexican migrants living in the United States. The resolution, which was only a recommendation and not legally binding, offered immigration amnesty in exchange for access to Mexico's oil market. The resolution accused Pemex of corruption and inefficiency and said that only by opening to outside investment would an adequate supply of oil products to Mexico and the United States be ensured. Mexico responded negatively, including President Fox's definitive statement that Pemex "is not and will not be up for sale" since it belongs to all Mexicans (in Ballve 2003).

Though it is unlikely such a bold statement formally linking oil to migrants will be made again, the intimate connection between them remains alive in political discourse. In May 2010, in the atmosphere of heightened emotion of the Deepwater Horizon accident, Republican Senator Jim DeMint compared the influx of undocumented immigrants to the uncontrolled oil spill in the Gulf of Mexico in an attempt to secure more funding for the border fence, saying, "We need to seal that leak as quickly as possible to minimize the cleanup later" (in Nill 2010). The Republican turnaround on oil-for-migrants in a few short years surely comes as a recognition of the precipitous decline of Cantarell and the country's precarious post-peak condition.

Under multiple social, political, and economic pressures at home, the Calderón administration struggled to contain an energy-security crisis that increasingly overlaps with the nation's ongoing threats from *narcotraficante* (drug-trafficking) cartels whose activities plague the nation and compromise the security primarily of border states. In some cases, drug-trafficking violence has directly coincided with Pemex's ability to secure the production and transport of oil and gas.

Oil theft from Pemex pipelines, money laundering by way of service stations, and worst of all, provocative kidnappings of the company's executives and those of service companies working with the state firm are all on the rise (Martin and Longmire 2011). The increasing overlap of activities of drug-trafficking organizations and Mexico's oil industry—*after* the initiation of Calderón's stepped-up antinarco campaign—causes disruption in production and threatens the security of workers and residents on the frontlines. Just a few months' worth of incidents shows the frightening and expensive toll taken by cartel violence at Pemex installations. In December 2010 a gas pipeline explosion rocked the town of San Martin Texmelucan (fifty-five miles east of Mexico City), leaving twenty-eight dead and dozens injured; it was the result of oil thieves "hot-tapping" the pipeline. The line tapping, widely attributed to Los Zetas drug cartel, was only one of 60 illegal taps in that very pipeline and one of 550 illegal taps in pipelines nationwide (Hernandez 2010).

Cartels also use their more familiar tactics of kidnapping and extortion—along with seizure and occupation of installations—to threaten and intimidate as well as gain access to oil and gas. In May 2010 armed groups affiliated with Los Zetas seized one of the largest gas plants, Gigante Uno in the Burgos Basin, a hydrocarbon field that stretches across the northern Gulf state of Tamaulipas. For a full month the group held five Pemex workers hostage while siphoning fuel from the well. The Mexican army finally regained control of the well. The seizure happened at the same time that Los Zetas kidnapped a group of contractors. Oil installations are increasingly prime targets for narco groups. Three dozen Pemex workers and contractors (for companies including Halliburton, Schlumberger, and Weatherford) have been kidnapped, disappeared, or held for ransom from the Burgos Basin region alone (Wilkinson 2010). The cartels are able to profit from the illegally obtained oil and gas mainly by selling the product across the border in the United States. The loss of oil and income is compounded by the loss of security. Unofficial figures place thefts from the Pemex network at roughly $2 billion annually (Martin and Longmire 2011), yet a true value cannot be placed upon the encroachment of cartel activities into the bastion of Mexico's economic and symbolic lifeline.

**Facing the Precipice or Falling Off?**

Though peaks are more and more often predicted and can most accurately be described with the clarity of hindsight vision, the 2004 peak of Cantarell was so quick in coming that it eluded prediction and seemed to require no historical perspective. The decline of Cantarell was definite and precipitous. By 2007 crude oil production was just under 1.5 mbpd, and it was predicted to drop to about 1 mbpd by the end of 2008 and less than 0.3 mbpd by 2017 (Sener 2008: 48). By August 2009 the decline of Cantarell was elevated to a state of emergency. A leaked memo from the legal affairs office of Sener, the Secretaría de Energía (Mexico's Ministry of Energy), warned that by December 2009 Cantarell would be producing just 550,000 barrels. That was down 75 percent from its peak output just five years prior. The warning turned out to be pretty much on target. After averaging production of 647,000 bpd in 2009, in May 2010 Cantarell production fell below an alarming threshold: less than 500,000 bpd. Numbers dropped again to a new low of 497,000 bpd in July 2010 (Rodríguez 2010a).

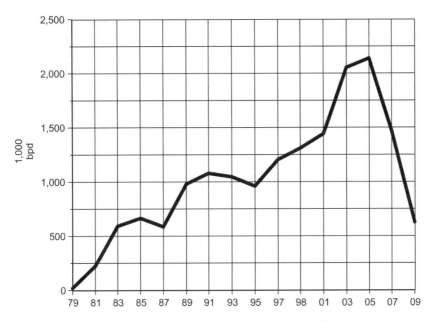

Cantarell crude production, 1979–2009. Sources: Pemex 1990, 2001, 2010b.

This decline at Cantarell is affecting Mexico's overall production and exports and is starting to sting the federal budget, of which 40 percent normally comes from oil revenues. The revenues pay for roads, hospitals, schools, and welfare programs. Social programs ranging from Oportunidades (formerly known as Progresa), the federal government's main antipoverty program consisting of grants to poor families to promote health education and nutrition, to the social development fund directly administered by Pemex Exploration and Production (PEP) in oil-affected municipalities. The stability of these programs is directly dependent on oil revenues. The ongoing drop in production, combined with less than robust oil prices, forced Mexico to move away from its ideal plan of using oil for discrete national development projects and now rely on oil to fund everyday budget items. The quick decrease not only hit the federal budget for social spending but reduced the overall GDP by half a percentage point (Serrano Cruz 2009a).

Following the lines of controversy regarding peak oil more generally, debate continues over the issue of Mexico's management of petroleum resources. Those concerned over the true status of energy resources want to know whether the problems are political or geological.

Those falling on the side of a political critique have plenty of ammunition, and it is hard to find anyone who is not critical of some aspect of Pemex. Politicians, economic analysts, the media, and even the public often blame Mexico's declining production on Pemex. Time and time again, even Pemex itself has complained that Mexico has incredibly rich reserves, but because of multiple problems, from chronic lack of research and development to an archaic political code that prevents risk sharing, the parastatal cannot access valuable crude. One of the largest national oil companies (indeed, one of the largest companies of any sort) in the world, Pemex appears bloated, cumbersome, old-fashioned, and corrupt. As a national oil company (NOC), Pemex is surpassed in size only by Brazil's Petrobras, which is, much to the contrary, a model of corporate and technological success. Petrobras's recent achievements are in deepwater and ultra-deepwater exploration and in partnership with other NOCs and Big Oil private companies for major exploration and production projects across the globe.

Pemex is not solely to blame for its problems, which lie far within the administrative and financial relationships of this parastatal corporation to the federal government. Pemex certainly generates huge incomes, but as a state-owned company it also carries an enormous tax burden and can find itself operating in the red even in years of high production. With $103.8 billion in net sales, Pemex topped the *Latin Business Chronicle*'s Top 500 Companies list in 2008.[14] Taxed at up to 62 percent, Pemex is the largest single contributor to Mexico's federal budget, paying on average about 40 percent of revenues. Pemex is thus at the base of a dependence that extends through Mexico's federal structure to states and municipalities that all rely in turn on oil money to cover their own budgets. The creation just since 2000 of extrabudgetary funds such as the oil stabilization emergency fund to adjust for price fluctuation and the hydrocarbon extraction fund for directly oil-affected regions (both discussed in chapter 4) has only complicated the parastatal's task of meeting ever-growing demands. Also, despite high production, Pemex continually operates with an enormous debt—upward of $1.5 billion—and has operated in the red every year but one since 1998.

Some of the situation can be glimpsed if we look at the year 2004, under the presidential administration of Vicente Fox Quesada (2000–2006), a very good year in terms of both production and exports. During this apex of production, Mexico became the sixth-largest producer in the world and the top offshore oil producer. But even during this year of record production when income hit $69 billion, a tax rate of 61 percent meant that Pemex recorded a shocking but typical net loss. This was part of a general pattern: between 1998 and 2005 debt quadrupled, with liabilities reaching 115 percent of sales. It seems that in effect the Pemex model has been—increasingly over time—to build a business that generates losses.

Former Pemex director Antonio Bermúdez (1946–1958) suggests a series of reasons for Pemex's difficulties: its history of poor prioritization, putting other activities before looking for new reserves; the use of time and money in other activities outside of the oil industry; and excessive political interference in the management of the oil industry (in Pazos 2008: 45–46). Bermúdez also finds fundamental fault in "the deterioration of oil mysticism" (46). At one point, "they even thought of placing gains for Petróleos Mexicanos before the ideal of service to the nation" (47). The original charge of the parastatal—to operate in the nation's interest, to use the nation's oil patrimony to fund national development—raises the question of whether the Pemex model is justifiable. As long as Mexico's oil industry is not a business-as-usual, rationalized, capitalist enterprise but instead operates as a catch-as-catch-can cash machine for the federal government, then Pemex's is far from the ideal business model. But are the voices of reform reasonable, either, when many of them call for an increased role for the private sector, whether through privatizing certain aspects of the industry such as refining or by modifying the complicated contracting process to allow for oil-services companies to share risks and rewards?

Despite the terms of the economic debate over Pemex's business model, different social actors within Pemex itself hold opposed and divergent interests. Holding the center of gravity in defense of Pemex as a traditional Mexican institution per se are the unionized workers. From the point of view of labor, Pemex was formed out of workers' strength and determination, and they are not ready to see the parastatal dissolved and oil disappear as the nation's patrimony into the hands of right-wing elites complicit with the interests of the multinational private sector. The political elites in positions of power within the parastatal—non-union, appointed positions *de confianza*—tend to side with the presidential administrations that support (and usually appoint) them. Those Pemex officials are most likely to diverge from political positions taken by the union and will support reform efforts proposed by the executive branch of government.

## Replacing Losses at Cantarell

The beginning of the decline of Cantarell showed that heavy indebtedness without reinvestment in exploration and new technology was not the right model for a competitive oil company in the twenty-first century. The heavy taxes leave the parastatal without the capital it needs to upgrade its infrastructure and to search for new oil reserves. Simply put, Pemex does not make large investments in safe and sure production efforts, especially possible alternatives to Cantarell. Demonstrating a continued overreliance on that aging and declining field, in 2008 the greatest proportion of the PEP budget still went to Cantarell for "administration of the decline" (Cardoso 2008). It is hardly surprising that critics scoff at the hand-wringing of Pemex officials and politicians about the decline of the supergiant field since the decline at Cantarell threatens exports from the United States' third-largest supplier and promises to turn this major exporter into a net importer by 2020 or sooner.

It is completely disingenuous to say that Cantarell's—and thus Mexico's—peak came either suddenly or shockingly. Most analysts look at that peak as part of an overall curve and through raw production numbers. But what the bigger picture, which includes extraction methods, tells us is that the race against the decline of Cantarell began long before its highest production years. Already by the 1990s it was clear that Cantarell was faltering, given that by mid–decade secondary recovery techniques had to be put in place—namely the nitrogen-injection process that began in earnest in 2000. Nitrogen injection is a stimulation technique used along with a host of other secondary and tertiary recovery methods including water pressure and reinjection of natural gas, carbon dioxide, steam, and surfactants. The purpose is to lower the viscosity of heavy, dense oil while increasing pressure in the reservoir. Output that had naturally slowed during the primary recovery phase should pick back up, causing oil to flow once again.

Huge amounts of nitrogen are not naturally occurring out in the Gulf of Mexico, so a source had to be created. Pemex was able to mobilize the nitrogen-injection method thanks to a gas supply provided by the world's largest nitrogen gas plant, a privately contracted facility constructed onshore to provide more than a billion cubic feet of nitrogen needed daily to keep fields in the Campeche Sound pressurized. (Later I examine the effects of the nitrogen-plant construction on the Peninsula of Atasta within the Laguna de Términos wildlife protection area and the community reaction to its presence.) Nitrogen injection at Cantarell was successful, boosting production from about 1 mbpd to 1.6 mbpd, then to 1.9 mbpd in 2002, and to a peak of 2.1 mbpd in 2004. At the time this made Cantarell the second-fastest-producing oilfield in the world, behind Ghawar Field in Saudi Arabia (*OffshoreTechnology.com* n.d.). In terms of production numbers, the injection method was exactly what Pemex ordered: it staved off the decline of Cantarell for a few more years by squeezing out extraordinary numbers that were especially noticeable at a period when barrel price was high.

Production efforts over the past few years across Mexico are all geared toward making up for losses in the face of declining production at Cantarell. Critics view Pemex's plans here as far from viable realities. Nonetheless, Pemex presses on with a two-pronged strategy for future production. To mitigate the losses at Cantarell, sights are set on two other production efforts: Ku Maloob Zaap (KMZ), an offshore complex sixty-five miles northeast of Ciudad del Carmen, adjacent to Cantarell; and the Chicontepec Basin, an onshore development east of Mexico City in the Gulf state of Veracruz. KMZ is similar to Cantarell in that it produces a heavy crude that is difficult and expensive to refine. Ku began initial production in 1981, Maloob in 1984, and Zaap in 1991. These three fields, together with Bacan and Lum, form the KMZ complex, touted since its discovery as being able to make up for Cantarell's losses. Though KMZ yielded just over 700,000 bpd in 2008, Pemex predicted the field would supplant Cantarell as the nation's top producer in 2009 (Gentile 2009). But the decline at Cantarell far exceeds the increase in output from new, less promising oilfields. KMZ now accounts for 63 percent of the total increase in production from other oilfields, and in January 2009 it surpassed Cantarell as Mexico's primary contributor with 825,000 bpd, not a terribly difficult feat. The field reached its highest production level in February 2010 at 856,000 bpd but was unable to sustain the output, and it slipped to maintain a 2010 average of less than 850,000. But the reality of production at KMZ is clearly not meeting Pemex's hopes or the country's needs in terms either of increased domestic availability or of the export revenues needed to finance nearly half the federal budget.

Meanwhile, Pemex continues to invest, to the tune of $4 billion, in the Gulf of Mexico as the nation's primary oil source. Together, the declining Cantarell and the underperforming KMZ account for 59 percent of Mexico's total daily crude output. Although there were anxieties in mid-2009 about the newer field's imminent decline, Pemex continued to coax KMZ into higher outputs through enhanced recovery techniques. Part of the state oil company's strategy was to drill more technically advanced horizontal wells at KMZ. Using these higher-yielding methods in combination with opening more wells, Pemex hoped to sustain KMZ's production at around 830,000 bpd for seven more years (Millard 2009b). In autumn 2010, however, PEP director Carlos Morales Gil finally confirmed that the field would peak in 2014 (Rodríguez 2010c).

## Reviving Chicontepec

Pemex's second major decline-mitigation effort is onshore in the Chicontepec Basin, the site of 54 percent of Mexico's proven, non-Cantarell reserves (Clemente 2008). Chicontepec is a mature field discovered some ninety years ago during Mexico's first age of oil exploration. Spanning 2,400 square miles in four Mexican states along the Gulf coast, it was initially exploited in 1926 by the Anglo-Dutch partnership El Águila, otherwise known as Mexican Eagle. The fields were later abandoned in favor of more easily accessible oil, but Pemex turned to this field again in the 1990s and recently made a major discovery there. Such an effort is a clear example of the historical strategy of "high-grading" oil exploitation—in other words, extracting the oil first that has the highest quality and is easiest to obtain.

With a combination of drilling new wells and utilizing secondary recovery techniques, Pemex officials are hoping to access eventually an 18-billion-barrel reserve at Chicontepec. In recent years, hundreds of wells have been drilled there, but the oil is not exactly flowing as planned. The field is "unconventional," meaning that the geological formations are extremely difficult and expensive for oil extraction. With $4.5 billion already invested in Chicontepec, expectations for tangible results at the field were high. But once again, the predictions were a bit overblown. Although Pemex originally estimated it could retrieve 70,000 bpd, by early 2009 actual production was only at 33,000. Pemex's goals for 2009–2017 were to reach an average of 443,000 bpd in crude production and another 546 billion cubic feet of gas, with an expected peak in production around 2016 (Rodríguez 2010b). Though PEP was prompt in lowering its expectations to 50,000 bpd, Chicontepec's advance has been modest at best. By 2009 the field was only producing 29,500 bpd, representing 1.1 percent of national crude contributions (ibid.). At the outset of 2012 Chicontepec was producing 63,313 bpd through the combined efforts of a coalition of private-sector contractors (Rodríguez 2012).

Chicontepec exploitation has caught the attention of critics for its hefty budget, much of which goes to lucrative private contracts with oil-services providers including Weatherford International, Schlumberger, and a division of Mexican billionaire Carlos Slim's industrial and retail conglomerate, Grupo Carso SAB. Pemex has long used oil-services companies to shoulder a lot of the work in oilfields. While constitutional prohibitions have limited the benefits the private sector could derive from participating in oil-exploitation activities, the breadth and depth of private-sector contracting grows exponentially, spurred by the introduction of the "multiple-service contract" during the Fox administration and helped by further reforms in late 2008 that introduced "integrated service contracts." The constitutionality of contracting arrangements is highly contested by the Left and by some moderates as well, as will be discussed in more detail in chapter 5.

Contract liberalization efforts use the rationale of "necessity" to bring private-sector tangibles and intangibles to the exploitation of national patrimony at fields such as Chicontepec. According to the logic, falling production requires the technology and expertise that outside companies can bring to challenging situations such as those at Chicontepec. Yet the help of millions of dollars in private contracts has not boosted production. When in 2007 and 2008 these companies fell behind schedule, they blamed Pemex for lagging in its provision of infrastructural support at drilling sites, even for the most necessary things such as building access roads. While the public began to notice the combination of heavy foreign presence and lack of production at Chicontepec, Pemex announced more rather than drawn-down investment, with a $2.3 billion investment plan for 2009. This time, Halliburton was awarded a $169 million contract to drill 170 wells (Millard 2009a).

Recent further explorations of the Chicontepec Basin in the states of Veracruz and Puebla suggest that the reserve is well above the previously estimated 18 billion barrels. In February 2009 Morales Gil, the head of PEP, announced an unprecedented reserve of 139 billion barrels at Chicontepec, making the field nearly four times the volume of Cantarell and more than big enough to revive Mexico's faltering production. However, he admitted, there was a catch: "Right now the technology does not exist that would permit us to exploit those hydrocarbons," not in Mexico or anywhere in the world (in Serrano Cruz 2009b).[15] It would be at least another generation, maybe two, before anyone would draw upon this megareserve at Chicontepec.

Soon after efforts to revive the mature field were initiated, Chicontepec began to look like a boondoggle. Pemex had spent approximately $11.1 billion dollars and earmarked another $2 billion in 2009 alone for Chicontepec (Martin 2009). Mexico's own regulatory agency, the National Hydrocarbons Commission (CNH), issued a report criticizing the production strategy and questioning expectations at Chicontepec; the head of the CNH called for a halt to the project until a more effective development plan could be devised (ibid.). Although it is only an advisory body, the CNH drew the attention of President Calderón and Secretary of Energy Georgina Kessel. Even though the project is failing to produce as promised and is very expensive, PEP director Morales Gil stressed in response to the CNH that Pemex could not abandon the project that played an important role in future production plans (Iliff 2010).

### Deepwater Potential?

Beyond KMZ and Chicontepec, Mexico's greatest hopes for the future of the nation's oil supply are off shore in the deep waters of the Gulf of Mexico. Pemex estimates that Mexico has more than 50 billion barrels of reserves lying in deep water. Exploiting this crude through deep and ultradeep drilling is the biggest technical challenge the parastatal has yet faced, one that successive years of paltry research and development budgets have left the company unfit to confront. Pemex has a disadvantage in comparison to American and Cuban competitors in the Gulf of Mexico, as the deepwater projects require enormous capital investment that the private sector is willing to gamble for the rewards of deepwater crude. However, Mexico's constitution prohibits the private sector to have its own leases or to enter into production contracts (and share some of the oil) or "risk contracts," the types of arrangements that allow companies to see profitable returns on their investments. Further complicating the challenge is the location of these new deepwater reserves, on the fringes of international maritime limits that are already the targets of multinationals operating under U.S. leases and by various state-owned oil companies working for Cuba. (In chapter 6 I will discuss at length the issues of negotiation and disputes over the Gulf of Mexico's transboundary reservoirs.)

What is more, deepwater oil has been a political hot potato under the Calderón administration, which has repeatedly mobilized the issue of deepwater reserves to justify a call for energy reform, including privatization. But the sometimes vague and often quite explicit promise that deepwater oil will mitigate Mexico's peak is more rhetoric that reality. By 2010 only eight wells had been drilled in water deeper than 1,640 feet (the average well depth at Cantarell is just under 200 feet of water). Pemex's 2009-2017 outlook projects sixty exploratory wells in the Gulf's deepwater but nowhere indicates when or how much oil will flow from the supposedly abundant reservoirs of this new frontier. Deep water would remain, throughout the Calderón administration, promise and potential rather than actual crude.

**The Politics of Reserves**

In the dwindling euphoria of Mexico's oil boom, it became clear that the nation's supplies were not infinite. What was the actual state of Mexico's reserves? The question was crucial not only domestically but also as part of the strategic energy calculations of the United States, which very quickly had become dependent on large quantities of Mexican imports. The actual status of Mexico's reserves is not a wholly transparent matter. The details of proven reserves and daily production capacity may seem like technical jargon, behind-the-scenes language exclusive to the realm of specialists and technocrats. However, since Mexico's federal budget depends on oil profits, or rents, for funding everything from education to health care to vital infrastructure projects across the nation, such numbers very much concern the average Mexican citizen. When these numbers appear constantly in the newspaper and on television, their decline causes even greater concern.

In 1984, during the era of abundance, Mexico had proven reserves of 72.5 billion barrels of oil. Over the next years, the reserves declined annually (Shields 2007). Part of the problem was wells simply running dry. Exacerbating the conundrum was Pemex's failure to explore for new sources of oil to replace what it pumped. But another key factor has been the methodology employed in quantifying the reserves; the total fluctuated because the methods used in calculating reserves changed. In other words, at different times, Pemex and the Mexican government have presented reserves in different ways for different purposes.[16]

At the beginning of 2010 Mexico's proven hydrocarbon reserves were

14 billion barrels of crude oil equivalent, of which 74 percent was crude oil and the remainder gas and liquids. In the 1990s Pemex expanded the scope of its reserves by changing the definition of "total reserves" to include the "three P's": proven, probable, and possible. Proven reserves are those commercially recoverable hydrocarbons that can be extracted with reasonable certainty in the foreseeable future; they can be broken down into the categories of developed and undeveloped. Probable reserves are, according to geological and engineering data, those with a greater than 50 percent likelihood of recovery. Possible reserves only have a 10 percent chance of commercial recoverability. Total proven, probable, and possible reserves at the outset of 2010 were 43.1 billion barrels of oil equivalent (boe). This broad definition of reserves inflated numbers enormously. Reserves plummeted when Pemex adopted a new set of international definitions and the nation's reported reserves necessarily became "proven reserves" only. From 1998 to 1999, the reserves plummeted from more than 60 billion barrels to less than 25 billion (Shields 2007).

Reserves are highly politicized numbers and can be presented to great rhetorical public effect. An example of this occurred in 2007 during the first blush of the Calderón administration, when Mexico's reserve numbers were translated to the public into an oil-apocalypse scenario. The front page of nearly every newspaper of the country sounded a frightening alarm—Mexico would run out of oil in less than seven years! "Seven years" came as a worst-case scenario based exclusively on the figure of the proven developed reserves, almost 9 billion barrels of economically recoverable oil. Pemex would have to keep pumping at the same production rate to exploit the whole reserve in less than seven years. The apocalyptic scenario looks slightly further into the future, adding that investment in the proven undeveloped reserves of nearly 4 billion barrels could stretch production almost another three years (Serrano Cruz 2007a,b).

Such a pronouncement as the 2007 alarm bell was not without its political motivations. The alarming numbers were boasted about rather than hidden by the administration of President Felipe Calderón. Hopes were that the shock of the announcement would strengthen Calderón's case for an administrative and operational overhaul of Pemex in the form of the 2008 energy-reform initiative rolled out by his National Action Party (PAN). Calderón hoped that creating an oil-apocalypse scenario would serve as impetus to drive a wedge into the nationalist sentiment that kept oil the property of the Mexican state and finally enable him to open the industry to private investment.

Meanwhile, numbers continued to make the administration's case. In 2009 Pemex reported a decrease of just over 2 percent in reserves from the year before. Fresh numbers produced in 2009 by Sener again focused on the three P's to encourage the public about the viability of the industry. By focusing less on proven reserves and more on total reserves, Pemex and the administration have been able to accomplish a sleight of hand that helps to distract from the decline in the proven category. Total reserves of a more comfortable 43.6 billion barrels are calculated by adding together reserves: possible (14.7 billion barrels), probable (14.5 billion), and proven (14.3 billion) (Pemex n.d.b). To play up the positive aspect of the probable reserves, PEP followed up its 2009 announcement with a strategic plan for a 100 percent replacement rate of reserves by 2012, staking its hopes on exploratory activities in the deepwater Gulf of Mexico and other fields such as onshore Chicontepec.

According to Pemex data, between 1979 and 2007 the parastatal produced 29 billion barrels of oil, 13 billion drawn from Cantarell alone (Pemex 2008a). With 45 percent of the national production coming from a single field, its decline causes serious implications for Mexico's domestic and international stability if its contributions cannot be replaced. Given the weakness of the alternatives of other offshore and onshore projects including KMZ, Chicontepec, and the deepwater Gulf, the EIA's *International Energy Outlook 2010* forecasts that Mexico will become a net oil importer by 2020, with net oil imports of more than 1 mbpd by 2035 (EIA 2011a).

### Peak Concerns

Michael Watts notes that in a post-9/11 world, "alternative non–Persian Gulf sources are central to American geostrategic interest" (2008: 27). While Watts along with countless social scientists and energy policy specialists have looked especially to Africa and South America and even Southeast Asia to understand today's geopolitical landscape of energy security, there is far less consciousness that the closest neighbors of the United States are its most critical energy partners. Since the early 1980s North American energy security has come to depend on Gulf of Mexico oil. Rhetoric around foreign-oil dependence invokes a specific cartography of energy security that denies America's key energy ally in its current, very real energy crisis.

A report prepared more than thirty years ago for the U.S. Department of Energy (Ronfeldt 1980) makes several key points regarding the future of Mexico's oil production. Prepared while Cantarell's output was beginning to reveal its stunning capacity, the report emphasized that while Mexico would "never reach rates of production as high as ten million barrels per day or more," the country was "destined to become one of the world's leading oil producers." However, Ronfeldt predicted, "if Mexico decides to become a major producer and thus a major exporter, it will be choosing a role that its resource base can sustain for only a few decades" (vi). That time has now come.

The peak of Cantarell, similar to those of many of the world's maturing supergiants, appears to be a clear-cut case of simple geophysics. The oil is running dry (Höök 2009; Höök, Hirsch, and Alekett 2009). However, like Mexico's first boom and bust, Cantarell's peak involves the deep interplay of the political dimensions of sovereignty and territory. Here, political administrations play an active role in exposing the vulnerability of Mexico's patrimonial energy assets, especially in the Gulf of Mexico. Cantarell's peak was helped along by the forces of international economic institutions in leveraging oil against insurmountable debt. As in other resource-depletion scenarios, peak oil opens the door for tension between the internal forces supporting moves toward liberalization of energy resources and the entrance of the private sector on the one hand and, on the other, the subsequent dismantling of constitutionally protected resource sovereignty.

## CHAPTER 2

# Natural Resources in the Laguna de Términos: Piracy and Profit

Peaks and declines are a part of everyday life on the shores of Mexico's Gulf coast, shaped by centuries of natural resource exploitation. The oil industry represents only the most recent in a nearly half-millennium of endlessly repeating cycles of natural resource extraction in the Laguna de Términos. Local residents are all too familiar with the production cycles of a series of peculiar tropical commodities—a wood-based dye, hardwood timber, and natural chewing-gum fiber—known for rising to the highest peaks and declining into utter obscurity. Campeche's well-known and lamentable booms and busts all share the same features: foreign territorialization, occupation, and ownership; labor exploitation; and serious pressure on the natural environment. The exploitation of various natural resources in the Laguna de Términos over the past 500 years has contributed to the same local net effect—the failure to generate sustainable social and economic development at the local level.

Political and economic policy from the export-led mercantilism of Spanish colonialism through Mexican state-led national development projects of the twentieth century demonstrate that the primary factor in shaping Campeche's development agenda has been the protection of the interests of foreign and private capital over resident populations. Not only did the exploitation of Campeche's resources fail to build the regional economy, but because the practice was so invested in foreign capital and resource extraction, ecological destruction, and the accrual of debt for recruited workers, it produced a physical and social landscape indelibly marked by the export-oriented strategies used in the region. This chapter traces the cumulative effects of a series of cycles of natural resource exploitation in the Laguna de Términos culminating in the region's current post-peak condition. I demonstrate how the historical legacy of natural resource exploitation continues to affect the social dynamics of contemporary Campeche.

## Cycles of Exploitation

*From the dawning of global trade initiated with the conquest of the Americas to the globalization of the market hastened by advanced technologies of production and communication, the worldwide commodification of natural resources has tended to proceed . . . as if they were inexhaustible.*

CORONIL 1997: 23

At the time of the Spanish arrival, indigenous residents of settlements around the Laguna de Términos made use of resources of the wetlands, lagoons, and rivers of the watershed (Jiménez Valdez 1989: 103–104). Coastal inhabitants used *cayucos* (canoes) to access marine resources. Salted fish, shark meat, and shells were important regional commodities brought from the Laguna de Términos to markets as far as the Mexican mainland and Central America (ibid.). Soon after the Conquest began, Campeche's port of Carmen became a key node of the incipient global marketplace of the seventeenth-century Atlantic world. But the trade in Campeche's resources neither began nor ended as a project of colonial empire building. Spain's first endeavors in the region were either half-hearted or thwarted by other means. The first profit-generating European settlers in the Laguna de Términos region were not *conquistadores* but English, Scottish, and French pirates who cut and shipped the valuable dyewood palo de tinte (also known as *palo de campeche*) to Europe and New England. Although Spain regained control of the territory in the eighteenth century, palo de tinte did not see a golden age of profitable resource exploitation until after Mexican independence, during the Porfiriato (1876–1910). The fall of the palo de tinte market, coinciding with the deforestation surrounding the Laguna de Términos, occurred with the rise of another highly profitable tropical export commodity: chicle, raw chewing-gum sap. Mexican national policies at the turn of twentieth century enabled foreign capital to buy extensive land tracts from the Mexican Gulf coast across Campeche to Guatemala to enable the export of natural resources to mostly U.S. markets. It was not until the cultivation of the Gulf and lagoon fisheries in the 1940s (after the collapse of the transnational chicle market) that the local population began to use local resources for local markets. Although the region had long supported artisanal and subsistence fishing among the coastal population, in the 1940s a new commercial fishing boom occurred with the shrimping trade based in Ciudad del Carmen.

## Palo de Tinte

The first journeys to the Yucatán Peninsula were made by Francisco Hernández de Córdoba in 1517 and Juan de Grijalva in 1518. Each sailed from Cuba, and, according to the appraisal of colonial chronicler Diego de Landa, a prime motivation was to gather slaves to replenish Cuba's dwindling labor force (1978: 4). The expedition of Córdoba navigated from the northeast Caribbean tip of the peninsula, where they explored Isla Mujeres before landing on Cape Catoche. They continued around the peninsula to the Gulf coast without violent incident until their approach at Champotón. Here, the Spanish engaged in battle with armed indigenous Maya warriors, resulting in casualties and many wounded on both sides (de Landa 1978: 5; Díaz del Castillo 1844: 23).

Inspired by otherwise favorable reports, notably one of gold obtained by the Córdoba crew at Isla Mujeres, the governor of Cuba sent his own nephew, Juan de Grijalva, to continue the expedition. Grijalva and his crew landed at the mouth of the Laguna de Términos, where they found refuge in the place they called Puerto Deseado, a desirable place for its good harbor and abundant supplies including fresh water. The head pilot for the Grijalva expedition, Antón de Alaminos, dubbed the place Términos, or endpoint (del Castillo 1866: 19, 151), believing they had arrived at the end of the island land mass of Yucatán (Díaz del Castillo 1844: 24).[1] Grijalva's crew spent more than a week resting and replenishing water, wood, and food around the Laguna de Términos without making contact with local inhabitants before eventually going on to the coast of mainland Mexico, founding New Spain, and inspiring the next major Spanish expedition, that of Hernán Cortés (ibid.).

Even though the Yucatán Peninsula itself was vital to the Spanish colonial endeavor, the Island of Carmen was not a mainstay of Spanish colonial settlement following the Conquest. Unlike the rest of New Spain, which had amazing mineral riches or verdant agricultural potential, the Yucatán Peninsula inspired little in the eyes or imaginations of the conquistadores. Carmen was an especially neglected part of the Spanish

Main. Well into the Conquest, the Yucatán inland remained unsettled by Spanish colonists; the city of Mérida in the peninsula's northwest was established at the location of an indigenous city; and on the Gulf coast the City of Campeche, established in 1540, became an important port on the Spanish Main and a vital center of trade, including the Atlantic slave trade (Restall 2009). But Campeche's lively commerce and convenient location on the Gulf shore left it open to pirate attacks, often by some of the most notorious pirates operating in the Caribbean. Pirates turned to the shelter offered by the Laguna de Términos as early as 1558 as a convenient respite from local marauding.

Far from the watchful eyes of Spanish settlements, in an area of sparse indigenous population, the Laguna de Términos was an ideal location for organizing invasions of nearby ports and for launching attacks on Spanish vessels on Gulf and Caribbean waters (Pinet Plascencia 1998: 135–136). Situated less than 125 miles from the city of Campeche, a favorite target for raids, and other haunts such as the port of Veracruz, here pirates could find safe harbor, no threatening indigenous population, and fresh water. For centuries the area would prove to be an ideal liminal space between authorized and unauthorized activity, between legitimacy and illegitimacy. When their usual privateering trade slackened, the buccaneers settled on Campeche's coast and took up a legitimate trade, becoming palo de tinte cutters. Logwood cutting was not an end in itself. Rather, it was a way for the buccaneers to bide time. And thus the Laguna de Términos became a shelter for piracy's reserve labor pool with up to 200 Dutch, English, and French pirates living in the wetlands and forests of the Laguna de Términos and participating in the highly profitable palo de tinte trade.[2]

Palo de tinte (*Haematoxylon campechianum*), popularly known as logwood, was Campeche's primary natural resource commodity, recognized by the Spanish, who otherwise were quite disappointed with the spoils found in the Yucatán Peninsula. Friar Diego de Landa, perhaps the best-known chronicler of the history of the region, commented that Yucatán was the land with the least amount of soil he had ever seen, leaving little doubt as to the low opinion of the region's natural potential. But the palo de tinte tree thrived. Growing to twenty-five feet in height, it is not a tall tree. It has a gnarled trunk that splits not far up from the ground, and it grows in almost impenetrable stands called *tintales* along the edges of lakes and in low-lying wet areas. The tree thrives in salty soil, such as where the mangrove meets the forest. Never such an ideal ecology for it can be found as around the Laguna de Términos, with its extensive watershed, vast network of rivers and tributaries, and marshlands.

The rasped, boiled, and mashed heart wood of the campeche tree produced a high-quality, colorfast dye that textile makers in European markets desperately sought. The precious dye creates blue, violet, bluish gray, or blacks, depending on the "mordant" or chemical additive used.[3] The rich and stable palo de tinte dye also served as an intensifier and toner to make a range of other colors such as bottle green, dark brown, lavender, and claret (McJunkin 1991: 12–14). The importance of the Campeche dyewood for the industrializing European textile manufacturers linked the Laguna de Términos to the global marketplace.

Upon discovering and surveying New Spain, the royal authorities decided which colonial commodities they wished to monopolize and those to which they would permit access to the commercial sector. Dyewoods and minerals were among those monopolized. Of these dyewoods, found from Mexico to Venezuela, "during the colonial period, logwood was by far the most valued and politically significant of all" (Offen 2000: 117–118). But despite the monopoly laws, the colonists had little actual control over the export enterprise. Spain never captured resource sovereignty over palo de tinte for three reasons. First, Spain's own domestic textile market was not the most developed in Europe; that advantage in the early eighteenth century went to the Netherlands, and so Spain lost profits to be gained through vertical integration and instead had to reach the wider marketplace in Europe through middlemen (McJunkin 1991: 277). The second major problem the Spanish crown faced was the loss of product due to privateering and piracy. From the sixteenth through the eighteenth centuries, Spanish ships were regularly attacked and sacked by French, British, and Dutch buccaneers or privateers for the sake of what was at the time a precious cargo. And lastly, during the colonial period, Spain did not establish a stable population in the coastal regions where palo de tinte grew, notably the Laguna de Términos, with a reserve labor pool capable of exploiting the logwood. Despite the best efforts of the crown to maintain sovereignty over its economic interests, it could not control certain colonial territories or the high seas. After pirates actually settled around the Laguna de Términos and began shipping directly, resource sovereignty was fully lost.

An incomplete historical record makes it difficult to discern the effects of palo de tinte extraction on local populations and the environment. However, one pirate-turned-logger, William Dampier, left a substantial and colorfully written account of his time in the Laguna de Términos circa 1675–1676. His account indicates that the region seemed to be a kind of no-man's-land in the cartography of the Spanish colonial regime. The accessible and resource-rich Laguna de Términos was unsettled by the Spanish and free for the taking—whether by indigenous Maya, African slaves brought to work in the trade, or European pirate and privateer loggers.

During his brief stint as a logger, Dampier encountered both Africans and Maya in the mangroves and tropical forests of Campeche's coast. His encounters with Africans were limited but key to his survival. When his leg and ankle became infected with worms, African slaves offered a cure (1699: 89-90). Dampier was cognizant of the plight of the region's indigenous population. He tells of whole towns of refugee Indians recently settled in the "unfrequented woods" of the Laguna de Términos "to enjoy the freedom; if they are accidental discovered they will remove again, which they can easily do; their household goods being little else but cotton hammocks and their calabasa [gourds]" (94).

However, the Laguna de Términos was not an entirely safe place for the Maya, given the threat posed by the loggers, who engaged in raiding indigenous settlements. These raids were slave-hunting expeditions. Captured indigenous women were brought to live with the loggers in their palm-thatched huts, and men were sold into slavery in Jamaica. Indigenous communities remained lightly and furtively settled around the loggers' camps throughout the years of privateering, perhaps, as Dampier suggests, "so they might see their friends and acquaintances that had been taken some time before" by the Europeans (95).

Palo de tinte loggers covered the whole of the Laguna de Términos watershed in their exploitation efforts. Dampier's firsthand account is an unlikely source of rich description of the flora and fauna of the region. New to his eyes and ears were monkeys that flung their feces at him, wild pigeons and turkeys good for eating, and the vulture.[4] Dampier could not imagine a place in the universe so well stocked with alligators as the creeks, rivers, and lagoons of the Bay of Campeche. The loggers' dogs were perhaps more terrified of the alligators than were the men. Snakes, iguanas, and hawksbill turtles made better reptilian meals, as Dampier describes the quality of alligator meat as "musky." Manatees, on the other hand, were "sweet." Luckily for the Europeans a source of beef was close at hand on none other than Beef Island, the present-day Peninsula of Atasta, or Xicalango, the pre-Conquest crossroads of culture and commerce; hunters regularly made excursions there to shoot the animals, whose flesh was eaten and hides were tanned by the loggers.[5]

English loggers dominated the Campeche coastline and began to penetrate the forests in the latter part of the seventeenth century and into the eighteenth. Not just pirates but privateers worked the logging trade. The question of the legitimacy of the endeavor certainly hung over the activity, and the consternation of the Spanish was evident in their increasingly violent confrontations with the loggers beginning in the 1660s. Dampier claims, "It is not my business to determine how far we might have a right to cutting wood there, but this I can say, that the Spaniards never receive less damage from the persons who generally follow from that trade than when they are employed upon that work" (131). While it might have been true that Spain was spared a great deal of privateering and outright piracy on the high seas because the men were otherwise occupied in their onshore activities, Spain hardly would have been content with the trade-off. The crown could not continue to turn a blind eye toward logging in the Laguna de Términos, even if it meant disturbing a pirate's den.

## Spanish (Re)Assertion of Territorial Sovereignty

By the second decade of the eighteenth century, the nonsanctioned cutting of logwood was about to meet its demise but not before rising to a boom period in illegal exports. While the trade had declined at the turn of the century due to Queen Anne's War, during which the Spanish repeatedly attacked logging camps in Campeche, the end of the war brought a renewed vigor to English activity. The signing of the Treaty of Utrecht in 1713 inspired imports to Britain to triple over the next four years (Jarvis 2010: 224). Although the Spanish had long been attacking the Campeche coast with periodic violent raids on the logging camps around the Laguna de Términos, they made no serious or sustained effort to occupy the territory, station a garrison, or build an outpost there themselves. But finally, in an all-out 1716–1717 maritime campaign Spanish forces dislodged the loggers from the Laguna de Términos. The loggers were pushed into present-day Belize (Justo Sierra 1998: 60–64).[6]

Despite the crown's inability to maintain a foothold in the Laguna de Términos region from the Conquest through the seventeenth century, the Spanish eventually regained a physical presence through a decisive naval military victory and killing, kidnapping, and deporting the pirate and privateer loggers. Retaking the Laguna de Términos and establishing the settlement at the fort called Presidio del Carmen at the western tip of the island asserted Spanish occupation of the territory (ibid.). Life for those at the presidio and the newly founded town of Carmen was bleak and can hardly be considered a rush for colonization. A half-century after the town's establishment, a 1774 reconnaissance report filed by Spanish naval officer Matías de Armona notes only 600 to 700 people living in the two settlements—the military post and the town (Weddle 1995: 131). Nevertheless, the humble origins of Carmen are its definitive origins as a Spanish town.

Over the eighteenth century, the Spanish faced three problems that made the transfer of logwood cutting into a colonial enterprise a difficult task: ongoing insecurity, a labor shortage, and resource depletion. Even if they were successful at getting the pirate loggers out, they were not nearly as successful at getting the area settled themselves. Nor were they successful in recapturing a profitable monopoly over the palo de tinte trade. Even though the colonial administration awarded free licenses for extracting palo de tinte (not to own land but only a right to cut and sell the wood), the development of Campeche's logwood export into a commercial success was hard fought.

The most substantial problem of the Spanish endeavors in the Laguna de Términos was securing territorial sovereignty to ensure resource sovereignty. As the Spanish were trying to secure control of the palo de tinte trade, the British were still a thorn in their side as they continued fighting for the right to exploit logwood. A battle of international law fought with diplomacy ensued between Britain and Spain over sovereignty, territory, and resource rights in Mesoamerica. As the Spanish tried to push the pirate loggers out of Campeche, the English tried to take a stand for resource rights to palo de tinte and other tropical hardwoods. Though the British and other Europeans were cleared out of the Laguna de Términos (some were killed, others returned to a life at sea, and some were sold into slavery by Spanish captors), the English continued to make claims to that territory as well as other parts of Yucatán and well-forested areas of the Bay of Honduras.

The Spanish countered British territorial claims using the retaking of the Laguna de Términos and the founding of Carmen to reestablish their presence in the hinterlands across the region, particularly those with rich resources. Stepping up their game, the Spanish sent official word to the British crown that it would have to vacate all areas of the

Spanish empire that the British had occupied without royal consent. These included the strategic resource-exploitation locations around the Yucatán Peninsula—the loggers' huts at Cape Catoche, Isla Mujeres (off the coast of present-day Cancún), and the Laguna de Términos (Headlam and Newton 1939: 20). The British resisted, believing they had a right to the natural resources of the New World in the areas where they themselves had established territorial occupation, as outlined in the 1670 Treaty of Madrid (also known as the American or Godolphin Treaty). While this treaty established the Spanish crown's official dominion over territories of the Americas, it contained a proviso (Article 7) that "the King of Great Britain shall have, hold and always possess in full sovereignty and propriety all lands, regions, islands, and places be that what they will lying and situate in the West Indies or in any other part of America which the said King of Great Britain or his subjects now possess" (Anderson 1787: 77).

Given that the 1670 Treaty of Madrid laid out the principle of occupation for territorial claims, the tactic the British employed was to demonstrate their own de facto presence in regions such as the Laguna de Términos in the face of the Spanish crown's absence. According to an investigation conducted by the British Council on Trade and Plantations, logwood cutting was of "great importance to our Navigation and the American Colonies [and] is in danger of being lost" by the threats of the Spanish to expel the settlers on the Yucatán Peninsula (ibid.). The British gave evidence to assert their own territorial claims over the coastal wetlands and forests where palo de tinte grew in great and profitable quantities.

Physical presence was the key to claiming territorial sovereignty—and by extension, resource sovereignty. In a missive sent from the council to the king of England in September 1717, the case was argued: if the privateer loggers were in fact able to settle in an area "wholly desolate and uninhabited" and live for many years around the Bay of Campeche (before, during, and after the signing of the Treaty of Madrid), how could the Spanish claim that they "possessed" this region? (Council of Trade and Plantations to Mr. Secretary Addison Whitehall, September 25, 1717, in Headlam 1930). The Spanish demanded proof of British habitation prior to the enactment of the 1670 treaty, and the British complied. Using depositions gathered from former loggers under the supervision of the governor of Jamaica, Thomas Lynch, the proof was assembled. The English argued that apart from the three cities the Spanish held, "all of this great peninsula was a veritable desert in which the Spanish had not forts, fortifications, or magazines," characteristic indications of possession in the Americas (ibid.). The loggers, on the other hand, made the marks of settlement by sustaining a long-term trade, moving inland in search of resources, building houses, and even planting:

> That they have us'd this trade for three years past, at first finding it by the seaside, but afterwards being forc'd to go four or five miles up into the country for their refreshment, they had planted Indian provisions, and built houses there, to keep themselves and their provisions from the sun and rain, that, altho' they had gone 6 or 7 miles further into the country, to kill deer etc. This possession, in the West Indies, is held the strongest that can be, falling of wood, building of houses and clearing and planting the ground. (Ibid.)

The testimony collected from the loggers demonstrated their claims never "to have seen any Spaniard or other person in all the time of their working" (ibid.). In other testimony witnesses verified that there were "300 persons living winter and summer in Yucatan not within 45 leagues of any Spanish plantation" for the eight years preceding the 1673 investigation of the matter (Council of Trade and Plantations to the Duke of Newcastle, March 21, 1733, in Headlam and Newton 1939).

In this case, the acts of piracy and privateering in the Laguna de Términos were used as a basis for legitimating the British territorial claims to portions of the Yucatán Peninsula and the strategic resource exploitation of a valuable commodity. Given that by 1669 numbers of settled loggers were significant and large quantities of wood were being shipped to New England and Jamaica, the British case seems strong. In the face of sovereignty challenges, Spain responded with physical attacks on the logging settlements. The attacks succeeded in pushing the English farther along the western Caribbean coast into modern-day Belize and Honduras. The new settlements turned into very productive British colonial possessions (Jarvis 2010: 228).

Adding to its sovereignty troubles, Spain had two other problems in establishing its own palo de tinte trade in the Laguna de Términos. First, the sparse population along Campeche's Gulf coast following the pirates' logging venture left little hope for a willing labor pool. Spanish settlers' logging enterprises would have to look down other avenues for labor sources. The sparse population spurred an increase in the slave labor previously known in the logging trade of Maya of the Yucatán, other indigenous peoples from across Mexico, Africans, and even Native Americans from U.S. territories. Among the predominantly English privateer loggers, some enslaved labor was used. Decades earlier, one New Englander attempted to force two dozen Native Americans captured in New England into cutting logwood. They killed their ship captain and escaped overland (Dampier 1699: 131). More commonly, however, pools of enslaved labor were Maya and Africans.

Africans were brought to New Spain in the earliest days of the Conquest. Owing to its very position as a port city on the Spanish Main, Campeche had a surprisingly large concentration of Africans. In the colonial period, most of the blacks in Yucatán lived in and around Campeche and worked in all areas of Spanish economic activity. The Spanish used a two-tiered system of Maya and Africans in labor, as summarized in Restall and Lutz 2005 (194): "Wherever Spaniards sought to exploit natural resources, they invariably brought Africans in small numbers to carry out the most skilled tasks or to supervise skilled or unskilled Maya workers." This was no different in cutting palo de tinte in the Laguna de Términos, where black slaves acted as overseers to the indigenous workers. The Spanish turned to the option of slave labor for reviving the logging as a colonial enterprise after the expulsion of the pirate loggers from the Laguna de Términos.

Correspondence in an archival document from the South Sea Company gives us a clue as to the kind of commercial reliance between the Spanish and English after the expulsion. The British joint stock company was allowed to send one ship per year to New Spain with slaves under the *asiento*, a contract arranged between Britain and Spain in the Treaty of Utrecht by which Britain agreed to supply the Spanish colonies with slaves. Ledward (1930: 195) describes the document: "South Sea Company had agreed to take logwood of the Spaniards in return for their negroes; had settled a factory at Campeachy [*sic*] for that purpose, and carry negroes thither for sale, which had encouraged the Spaniards to drive out the English logwood cutters settled there before." Shortly following this correspondence was another short notice indicating that the factory plans went bust.

While certainly Africans were on the Yucatán Peninsula since the Conquest, a lack of intensive development prevented their wholesale participation in exploitive labor regimes.[7] In the Laguna de Términos region, labor recruitment was especially a problem for the Spanish settlers at the fort of Carmen who struggled to revive the logging trade. Businesses like the South Sea Company demonstrated that labor provisioning for the smaller-scale logging enterprise could solve the settlers' problem by privatizing the provision of slaves to the Campeche logging industry. Spain attempted to launch the agricultural industrialization of this otherwise dangerously underoccupied and underdeveloped territory with palo de tinte as the platform. The plan was to replace the privateers with slaves supplied by English businessmen in Jamaica and pay them in precious dyewood.

Another major problem the new incarnation of the palo de tinte trade had to reckon with was the ecological impact of the privateer logging era. After decades of willy-nilly exploitation, this natural resource was considerably depleted. As time progressed, the unexploited tintales, or tree stands, were farther and farther from any navigable waterways of the watershed that could be used to transport the wood to the port of Carmen. This made exploitation difficult and costly. To make logging profitable whatsoever, substantial taxes were levied on transportation through the Laguna de Términos watershed (Hernández Montejo 2007: 29–30). It was not until the last quarter of the eighteenth century that the colonial exportation of palo de tinte finally brought a relative prosperity to the 2,000 Spanish military families settled in the presidio of Carmen (Leriche Guzmán 1995: 49), as the dye finally reached ports across Europe.

Three hundred years after the initiation of the Spanish Conquest on the Yucatán Peninsula, resource sovereignty was finally achieved. Spain regained an industrious palo de tinte trade out of the port of Carmen. However, Spanish control over the palo de tinte trade lasted only a short while, as the Spanish crown ceded political sovereignty to an independent Mexican state in 1821. The colonial experience of palo de tinte exploitation presents an intriguing case of resource insecurity in the history of the Laguna de Términos region. Under such an ideal colonial extractive economy, palo de tinte should not have been insecure. But the Laguna de Términos was not part of the Spanish strategic settlement plan, and its resources were not immediately required as part of the wealth of New Spain.

Spanish colonialism in southern Mexico represented a dilemma of sovereignty. Palo de tinte, more than other colonial commodities, exposed a deep fissure between the crown's desire for economic sovereignty and a distinct inability to establish territorial sovereignty over the Yucatán Peninsula. Palo de tinte thus represented the first in a troublesome legacy of efforts to extract natural resources in Campeche. Palo de tinte is emblematic of the ongoing problem of resource security, territorial sovereignty, and development that unfolds over several centuries in the Laguna de Términos, beginning in the colonial period and passing through the contemporary oil age. The to-and-fro tension between state and private interests and the concomitant cycles of resource peaks and declines are twin dynamics that will return time and again to haunt resource extraction in the Laguna de Términos.

## Privatization and Resource Extraction across Campeche

Half a tumultuous century after independence, Porfirio Díaz presided over a nation that was vast, poor, and underdeveloped but rich in natural resources. One of the primary goals of the Díaz administration at the turn of the twentieth century was to fund the modernization of Mexico with foreign capital by means such as attracting oil companies from the United States and Britain. A necessary step in Díaz's playbook for attracting foreign investment and modernizing Mexico was the liberalization of the nation's resources. His legislative acts allowed for the suspension of tight controls over the government ownership of subsoil resources that the Mexican nation had carried over into independence from Spain after the colonial period. Porfirio Díaz intervened in a deep legal and cultural tradition of subsoil resource ownership that was much older than the still-young Mexican nation. He also profoundly altered the nation's agricultural landscape by privatizing an enormous proportion of the Mexican countryside. The concentration of forest and agricultural land into private hands had profound, lasting effects for Campeche.

The long history of underdevelopment of the region intensified while Campeche was still in the height of palo de tinte extraction. Campeche had neither a substantial urban nor a significant rural population. Rather than living in cities, the population—only a labor force subordinated to the exploitation of palo de tinte—was dispersed throughout the riversides and tintales. Because its economy had long been based in gathering rather than cultivating, Campeche did not even have the rural peasant population base typical of the rest of the Mexican countryside. This condition continued after independence and into the nineteenth century. The policies of the Porfiriato exacerbated the circumstances of underdevelopment, since they emphasized the power of private and especially foreign capital over the landless laborers.

Now the real distortion of Campeche's development began to show itself. As Campeche historian Carlos Justo Sierra puts it (1998), the profitable export of palo de tinte along with other precious tropical timbers such as mahogany and cedar underwent a resurgence. These profitable export commodities ensured that land would not be used for another stream of development in Campeche. The new golden age of palo de tinte in the Porfiriato "stimulated ambitions that blocked the production of coffee, cacao, and rice, because rural residents were lured to the tintales with the promise of high sums of money" (33). Cattle raising and crop growing, activities that would have provided an economic subsistence base for a rural peasant population, were pushed aside in favor of the more lucrative logging effort to benefit an extractive economy. The labor supporting the extractive economy was in theory wage labor but in practice more commonly debt peonage. Labor contractors widely used the practice known as the *enganche* (literally "hook") whereby a worker would be roped into a contract through an advance offer that seemed too good to refuse. The same method was used for the chicle industry, as we will see.

Campeche did indeed have other resources besides extractive commodities. Fertile soils across the Laguna de Términos watershed made possible the cultivation of various crops. In coastal areas, coconut palms—containing valuable *copra* (dried meat pressed for oil)—flourished. But these resources were subordinated to palo de tinte and confined to privately owned tracts of land. As the state was beginning to take shape, people in the different regions were making decisions about the role that palo de tinte extraction would play in their economies. Rather than a platform for growing and diversifying Campeche's economy, palo de tinte served, at least while it flourished, as a crutch for development.

By the turn of the twentieth century, the apex of the palo de tinte trade came to an end. Tied as it was to the international market, the local economy would suffer from the bottom falling out of prices as the European market turned to chemical dyes. Sufficient support to convert southeastern Mexico's economy to another commodity could come only from an injection of foreign capital, and a plan to make this happen was already in place. Not only did this plan propose to rescue Campeche from the demise of palo de tinte, but in keeping with the Porfirian ideology, it promised foreign capital to fund a vision of progressive modernization for Mexico. By 1900, one-half of all American foreign investment was in Mexico (Schell 1990: 222). As we have already learned, oil did not become a factor in Mexico until after 1901, so investments through 1900 were based mostly in the tropical products of southeastern Mexico.

Why had these changes taken place, and how did they set the stage for more changes in the Laguna de Términos? The rise in exports is helped along by the rise of a very specific set of commodities. While strong mineral exports from central Mexico accounted for half of the monetary value of exports, commodities from southeastern Mexico began to assert their presence in the export market. Though these are all agricultural exports, they are regionally specific and differently produced. On the one hand we have an explosion in production of henequen fiber, mostly in Yucatán and northern Campeche rather than the Laguna de Términos. Henequen (*agave fourcroydes*) plants produce a hemplike fiber that was exported mainly to the United States for commercial use as binding twine in mechanical harvesting machines. Henequen plantations, occupied by local Maya and imported debt peons, dominated the state of Yucatán. In the 1890s it was estimated that approximately seven-eighths of the state's population was involved in some aspect of cultivating, processing, or marketing henequen. It was by far the most profitable resource commodity to come out of the Yucatán Peninsula during the Porfiriato. Although some henequen haciendas crossed over the border into Campeche, the production of a different export commodity, chicle, dominated the rest of the Yucatán Peninsula. Insignificant as an export in 1875, in just fifteen years chicle rose to become a half-million-dollar export product.

The tropical resources of the Yucatán Peninsula played a large role in the "Americanization" of Mexico through millions of dollars of investments in multiple enterprises and, as we will see later, through an extensive privatization of Mexican territory. During the Porfiriato, Mayer and Ober wrote at the time, "the financial invasion from the United States [was] in full swing . . . sweeping over the country in a tidal wave of seemingly irresistible power" (1906: 420).

### Chicle, Another Boom-and-Bust Commodity

In the nineteenth and early twentieth centuries in the forest and coastal zones of southern and southeastern Campeche where land and climate did not favor henequen production, an alternative product was abundant: chicle, the raw sap of the chicozapote, or sapodilla tree, from which natural chewing gum is made. In the year of the highest exports of palo de tinte in Campeche, 1895, the surge of chicle production began. The era of chicle extraction would last from 1903 to 1945 (Vadillo López 2001: 95). Like palo de tinte, chicle was gathered rather than cultivated, and chicle gathering required hard work and specialized knowledge of how to bleed trees for their latex without cutting them too much and risking killing them. Workers came from across southeastern Mexico on the enganche, just as in the palo de tinte trade, on the lure of a promise of good pay and working conditions. Men even brought their families to live in new settlements in the Laguna de Términos and the southeastern forest to work the nine-month annual chicle-gathering season (Knight 1990: 88).

Archaeologist Jennifer Mathews (2009) points out that pre-Columbian indigenous populations in the region used chicozapote gum, fruit, and timber for a variety of practical and ritual purposes. They chewed chicle gum, mixed it with rubber to burn incense, and carved its timber for use in monumental construction such as the intricately detailed lintels at the archaeological sites of Chichén Itzá in Yucatán and Tikal in Guatemala. The pre-Hispanic Maya may also have cultivated the tree; at least, they did not destroy it when clearing the forests for their cities and ceremonial centers (11–13).

At the turn of the twentieth century, however, chicle had just one use. The sap of the chicozapote tree was the raw material to make chewing gum. U.S. companies turned to the natural resource's abundance in Campeche for their supply. The political and economic climate in Mexico was more than hospitable to foreign companies in need of raw commodities or the land to grow or, in the case of chicle, gather them. As we saw with foreign companies during Mexico's first oil boom, liberal capitalist national development in Mexico during the Porfiriato was built upon the principle of foreign investment and commercial agricultural export crops. Thus, the concentration of land into the hands of American companies such as Wrigley, Adams, and the American Chicle Company was spurred by Mexican national policy during the Porfiriato as part of the early stages of a dangerously collaborative effort between U.S. companies and Porfirian development ideology.

The Porfirian drive to modernize and rationalize the landscape created a system of land tenure that would be commercially productive by taking advantage of foreign capital. The Díaz administration enacted a host of laws designed to aid the privatizing drive of liberal capitalism. The 1883 Ley de Colonización y Terrenos Baldíos allowed state or private surveying companies to delimit *terrenos baldíos*, lands that were considered vacant, unclaimed, unused, otherwise without title, or public. Under the legal mechanism, approximately fifty private companies surveyed a third of the Mexican territory—more than 60 million hectares. In accordance with the law, they received a tenth of the national territory in compensation for their efforts. The remainder was to be auctioned off at a public sale (Holden 1994).

The 1883 law was designed to overhaul Mexico's landholding system, aiding in the general efforts of Porfirian state modernization. The effect of the liberalization of landholding was to privatize the Mexican countryside. This was accomplished through making large plots of untitled, "public" land available to private owners. Federal water laws worked in conjunction with the law of terrenos baldíos, declaring that all land not explicitly claimed under a legally recognized title should be considered public, even if it was occupied. These public lands, including the resource-rich forests of Campeche, became subject to "denunciation," or the staking of claims by interested parties (Knight 1990: 95; Vázquez Castillo 2004: 24-25). The 1883 law originally limited landholdings to 2,500 hectares per colonist; this provision was dropped only a year after implementation. The net result was the conversion and concentration of public lands into private estates. Knight has found that "throughout the Díaz regime, nearly 39 million hectares of untitled land were converted into private property, an area equal to California, comprising one-fifth of the surface area of the country" (1990: 95).

Ironically, by taking the land into the public patrimony, Díaz was paving the way for privatization. Díaz used land surveying as an instrumental arm of land rationalization under capitalism and made the practice mandatory after he came to power in 1876. Díaz's cronies formed surveying companies to take advantage of the opportunity allowed by the privatization law. The surveying companies, which were often American-owned, "served as a crucial link in attracting foreign investments for the growth of individual landholding, capitalizing commercial agriculture, and infrastructure and industrial development" (Hart 2002: 167). The Porfirian land surveys resulted in an extensively privatized and commercialized Campeche state. The surveyor who undertook the job, engineer Manuel Avila, ended up with 6,200 acres. By 1890 word spread to world capitals that cheap land was available in Carmen (Vadillo López 2001: 106).

Campeche, from coast to deep forest, was now prime for foreign investment. A 1903 news brief by Edward C. Butler in the *Los Angeles Times*, "Americans in Mexico: Astonishing Natives with Their Energy," reports on the inroads of American businesses into Mexico:

> In Southern Mexico, the mahogany has been depleted from the forests along most of the streams deep enough to float the logs, but back from the deeper waterways the forests remain untouched. American companies in Illinois, Pennsylvania, and Iowa are contemplating taking up tracts of the virgin forests and making roads there too. Something like 600,000 acres have thus been recently taken up in the State of Campeche.

This foreign mahogany-logging boom particularly affected the municipality of Carmen, a focus of intense chicle exploitation. Not only did the naturally occurring chicozapote trees grow there, but landowners found the proximity to the already developed port of Carmen another boon.

By the turn of the twentieth century, foreign ownership across the region surged. Likewise, the period 1901–1911 saw a tremendous rise in foreign exports, up to three-quarters of which went to the United States. And the conversion from extraction of palo de tinte to chicle could not have happened without, according to the Porfirian plan, foreign capital to fund the vision of progressive modernization for Mexico. However, like palo de tinte before it, chicle would have a quick rise and an even quicker fall, with a single extractive commodity proving too unstable for either the market or Campeche's environment.

Just as would be the case with Mexico's discovery of oil reserves in the 1970s, "tropical investment contributed substantially to Mexico's international reputation as an excellent credit risk" during the 1910s and 1920s (Schell 1990: 238), when Campeche became the primary producer of chicle in Mexico. At this time, the industry relied heavily upon the participation of residents of the area for a product that was nearly exclusively shipped to the United States. But due to the nature of the industry and chicle's place as part of a transnational commodity chain, the ground-level workers saw little of the rewards of this heyday. Between 1901 and 1910, the chicleros extracted and exported 10 million kilograms (22 million pounds) of chicle from the state of Campeche. In 1910 chicle exports were valued at 2 million pesos (Pan American Union 1911: 189), and chicle was Mexico's fifth-largest agricultural commodity export, below henequen, rubber, guayule (a shrub that produces a natural latex), and coffee. A large percentage of all of these top-five commodities went to the United States. The greatest value of exports passed through Gulf ports, nearly twice as much as for the next-biggest point of export, Mexico's northern land border (Pan American Union 1911). Nearly all of the chicle went to the United States, some by way of Canada or British Honduras (Belize).

The innocence of America's chewing-gum addiction, beginning in the fin de siècle, was based on turning a blind eye to chicle's transnational commodity chain, to the origins of raw chicle, and to the labor force and land-tenure system that produced it, not to mention the state-sponsored political climate that nurtured the whole system. The primary beneficiaries of chicle production were foreign companies that owned large tracts of land in the state, some upward of a quarter of a million acres. The tracts included lands for chicle gathering as well as established plantations for the cultivation of tropical agricultural products. Beginning around 1880 the companies became involved in logging hardwoods (cedar, ebony, and mahogany) and cultivating fruits and other crops. The plantations necessarily relied upon the forced labor of thousands of debt peons, as was the custom on the henequen haciendas in northern Campeche and in Yucatán.

Although many companies were involved in chicle exploitation and processing, the biggest and most powerful was Wrigley and Company of Chicago. As was the typical practice of the foreign companies operating in Mexico, Wrigley worked by way of a development corporation on the ground in southeastern Mexico, the Laguna Corporation. This development company proved to have remarkable staying power, remaining in Campeche, particularly in Carmen, through times of political upheaval that spanned the Mexican Revolution and its reforms. Wrigley used 9 percent of the land of Campeche and 45 percent of the territory corresponding to the municipality of Carmen (de la Peña 1942: 72; Leriche Guzmán 1995: 60). Wrigley also controlled land in Guatemala.

John Mason Hart provides a well-researched, detailed account (2002) of the activities of American business interests in Mexico during the Porfiriato. In the first decade of the twentieth century, Americans including members of the Hearst and Du Pont families owned half of Campeche's land area extending from the Gulf of Mexico to Guatemala. The holdings were vast, the largest among them 604,000 acres (228). Porfirio Díaz enabled such extensive foreign ownership. He bent laws and adjusted national policies (and constitutional prohibitions) to extend foreign ownership to the $n$th degree.

The Porfirian impulse to privatize land and resources was a practical outgrowth of the regime's liberal ideologies of national development and economic growth. "The Porfirian land enclosure process was a necessary step in the country's capitalist economic transformation" (Hart 1987: 158). The scale was staggering and effected profound changes in the magnitude, if not nature, of resource exploitation all across Mexico. But the southeast was hit especially hard. From the oilfields of Veracruz to the tropical plantations and forests of Campeche, local ecologies were scarred for life. Not only did land suffer, but so did labor, as it became just another natural resource to exploit under the logic of Porfirian capitalism.

The Mexican Revolution broke out in response to this exploitation of the peasantry during the Porfiriato. Some agrarian reformers sought to improve the conditions of the most exploited of all Mexican workers, the *enganchados*, or contract laborers, who voiced a host of complaints. For example, a group of laborers left their homes in Veracruz in 1897 to work in Campeche after being promised a wage of 1.5 pesos a day. The owner actually paid them 25 centavos a day, provided no health care, and refused to let any of the enganchados leave (Henderson 2000: 187). Indeed, the state's borders were patrolled by militias making sure workers did not leave the plantations (Wells and Joseph 1996: 154).

Although discontent had to be high among the residents across Campeche, the early years of the revolution were relatively smooth for the operators of the plantations. However, further into the revolution, insurgency started to cross Mexico. The 1912 resignation of Porfirio Díaz did not bring about the real reforms needed to satisfy the growing sense of peasant empowerment—*zapatismo*—across the Mexican countryside. Attacks on the landed estates of foreigners began in earnest. By the third year of the revolution, a wave of violence had begun to move south across Campeche directed at the extensive private landholdings that covered most of the state's territory, as groups calling themselves *villistas*, after the revolutionary leader Francisco "Pancho" Villa, moved into the Chiapas, Oaxaca, and Campeche countryside (Hart 1987: 14). In 1913 a Hearst property near Ciudad del Carmen and a property of the American-owned Mexican Exploitation Company were "occupied by insurrection forces under the leadership of Manuel Castilla Pascual," and federal troops were dispatched (*Washington Post* 1913).

In the spring of 1914 it became apparent that Americans in Carmen were not faring well. The *New York Times* reported in 1914 that Americans on their Campeche plantations were left without means of communication and were starving as violence intensified. A party of six Americans went missing as they attempted to cross the jungle and reach British Honduras. But the entrepreneurial spirit could not be daunted, and a year later the *Tribune Investors' Guide* advertised the Campeche-Laguna Corporation (controlled by the Laguna Corporation) as a "good investment" on the basis that "this territory has not been ravaged by the revolution so much as the northern part of Mexico and the company is understood to be in good condition and to be paying interest on its $1,682,000 of bonds" (*Chicago Daily Tribune* 1915: 15). It is true that through 1919, the Laguna Corporation persevered to profit, while nearly all of its foreign neighbors became defunct.

It seemed that no war, no reforms, no new constitution, and no administration in Mexico City could stop the American interests in the Campeche chicle trade. In 1919 chicle officially surpassed timber as Campeche's most valuable export. In the 1919–1920 season, the region produced just under 4.5 million pounds, nearly 60 percent of Mexico's national production. Most of this came from Carmen, Candelaria, Escarcega, and Xpujil (Hernández Montejo 2007: 54), making Campeche the biggest producer of chicle. The private landholding domination of Campeche is marked at the end of the first decade of the twentieth century by statements by representatives of American companies, owners of the southern two-thirds of the state, claiming that they had successfully "cleared the jungle" from the Bay of Campeche to the Guatemalan border (Hart 2002: 230).

In 1930–1947 chicle peaked. The period was productive but rife with problems. During the 1930s Campeche, along with Yucatán and Quintana Roo, accounted for 75 percent of the global production of raw chicle for the U.S. market. When faced with overproduction of the product and a fall in prices, the companies began to stop buying chicle from the producers on the ground. However, a chicle boycott would not be tolerated by the Mexican state, which stepped in and nullified the exploitation licenses held by any foreign development corporations that would not guarantee the purchase of a full harvest (Hernández Montejo 2007: 55).

The state's strategy under the guidance of President Lázaro Cárdenas was to wrest control from the private companies and gain control of the production process through expropriation of land and establishment of worker cooperatives. The Yucatán Peninsula territory was divided into concessions, and starting in 1936 cooperatives were established across the chicle-gathering area.[8] For American companies 1940 was a watershed year for land loss. Cárdenas nullified the land titles for 1.5 million acres held by three major chicle producers: the Laguna Corporation, the Mexican Gulf Land and Lumber Company, and the Pennsylvania Campeche Land and Lumber Company. All were parcels originally part of the Manuel Avila land survey conducted in the Porfirian land rationalization project. The Cárdenas administration claimed that the companies had never been the legal owners of the land. Furthermore, the administration charged that the holdings were contrary to the Mexican constitution's prohibition on monopoly. The Laguna Corporation attempted to save a single large tract by converting it into a Mexican company, the Compañia de Terrenos de Laguna, carving out a 300,000-acre parcel of the Laguna Corporation holdings in Carmen and Champotón, up the coast from Isla Aguada. The Cárdenas administration identified this maneuver as sleight of hand and successfully initiated an expropriation of the property (Cortesi 1940).

Some 20,000 chicle workers were cooperatized (Mathews 2009: 58), mostly in Quintana Roo and some in the interior forests of Campeche. Nonetheless, chicle was already on the downward curve of its peak production. After reaching its maximum volume and value during World War II, when chicle was declared essential to the U.S. strategic war effort (for gum-chewing soldiers in European trenches), the demand for chewing gum fell. Synthetic chicle derived from petroleum at a fraction of the cost quickly replaced the natural latex. Finally, in 1947 the collapse of the powerful Laguna Corporation marked a significant milestone for the industry in Campeche. Camps—population centers that served only as outposts for chicle gathering and timber cutting—were completely depopulated and ceased to exist. Others were reinvented as ejidos, communal agricultural landholding villages, through the agrarian reform provisions under Mexico's 1917 constitution that had not been forcefully enacted in the heavily privatized hacienda districts until the Cárdenas administration.

Hart (2002) connects the commodity of chicle to a much more immediate issue, suggesting that the extensive holdings were a cover for the real interests of the U.S. businessmen: oil. By 1910 there were early indications of oil deposits on the Gulf coastal plain from southern Tamaulipas to Campeche. Although more than thirty American and British companies were operating in the region, just a few majors dominated. The Mexican Eagle Oil Company (El Águila) and Mexican Petroleum Company with its affiliate Huasteca already were producing in northern Veracruz and controlled the drilling and refining at Minatitlán. When a large gusher was found in December 1910, output more than tripled overnight, and 1911 saw 11.5 million barrels produced, making Mexico the world's third-largest producer, below the United States and Russia (Secretaría de Hacienda y Crédito Público 1912: 154).

The discovery of oil on the Gulf coast instigated a rush for foreign oilmen to occupy oil-rich territory. In order to secure their resource rights under Porfirian legislation, as Brown notes (1993b: 74), "the oilmen who came seeking leases desired precise legal titles," causing strife around ownership and exploitation rights as a newly fraught extension of the resource politics occasioned by the chicle industry. In Campeche, the rising potential of oil finds and their value triggered political tensions, although, as Hart points out (2002: 334), the struggle between American and Mexican interests was often hidden: "The likelihood of large oil and gas deposits under the Campeche shoreline brought the powerful American interests that were incorporated as the Laguna Corporation into the fray against . . . Mexican administrations."

While the corporations could not yet get at the most valuable resource, oil, they mined the region for other natural resources: hardwoods, cultivated crops, and, as we have seen in this section, chicle. None of this commercial presence could have been sustained without the Porfirian land and labor policies that made Campeche so attractive to foreigners.

It was clear that the reformers had won when Lázaro Cárdenas finally enforced Article 27 of the 1917 constitution, ending the large-scale land privatization in Campeche. The cooperatization of chicle was not terribly successful because the market fell, but Cárdenas had other plans to incorporate working-class and *campesino* Mexicans into production activity. We will see how one plan played out for Gulf coast residents: the cooperatization of commercial fishing crews. When the next boom industry, commercial shrimping, came to the Laguna de Términos as chicle declined, cooperatization, at least in theory, leveled the playing field to allow workers without capital to benefit from a lucrative industry based at the port of Carmen.

Palo de tinte and chicle exploitation in the Laguna de Términos demonstrate the long and deep history of boom-and-bust cycles in the region. These two historical cases clearly show that privatization and foreign control are central themes that characterize Campeche's experience of development. Porfirian land policies in the name of Mexico's national development plan allowed for the territorialization of the region by foreign, private capital from the Gulf coast to Mexico's border with Guatemala. Only after the Mexican Revolution was land secured back into the national patrimony. The tension between privatization and public patrimony is a theme that would repeatedly reemerge out of the past and into the future in Campeche's hopes for development in cycles of resource exploitation including the fishing and oil industries.

## The Resource Landscape of Contemporary Campeche

The long history of intensive natural resource exploitation in the Laguna de Términos as well as in Campeche's interior forests leaves an indelible mark on the social and physical landscape. Centuries of resource exploitation shape the region's distinctive identity and lend it a sense of being apart from the rest of Mexico. This distinctiveness hinges, for the most part, on the region's multiple cycles of extractive economies, foreign capital investment, and the associated patterns of land tenure and labor organization that supported resource extraction. The orientation of the industries in Campeche toward global markets instead of Mexico itself was a factor in the extractive economies of palo de tinte and chicle. During the colonial period, products were shipped to Europe, and trading with the United States and Caribbean nations began during the colonial period and continued into the twentieth century. The pattern of infrastructural development during the growth of the main industries and even following their demise only added to the area's long-standing sense of apartness. The separation increased in the nineteenth century with the privatization of large parts of the peninsula including southwestern Campeche. A federal highway running directly along the Gulf coast connecting the Yucatán Peninsula to the Mexican mainland was not completed until 1967. Furthermore, the island of Carmen was not incorporated into the highway system until the 1980s. Two bridges—Puente de la Unidad, connecting Carmen's Puerto Real to Isla Aguada, and the Zacatal, at the Peninsula of Atasta—were not completed until 1982 and 1994, respectively. Before the bridges were built, ferries (*transbordadores*) had to be used to reach Ciudad del Carmen from either the Yucatán Peninsula (northeast) or mainland Mexico (west-southwest).

The history of natural resource exploitation shaped modern Campeche demographically, making it into a state with a very low population density. Because population centers were only inhabited for short-term, seasonal resource exploitation and for gathered rather than cultivated commodities, few areas were permanently settled. During the chicle-production era, for example, even though the state was producing a major export commodity, the population remained quite low. In the years 1900–1940, the population for the whole of the state varied between only 87,000 and 90,000 inhabitants; it had the third-lowest population density in Mexico in 1940 (Ponce Jiménez 1990: 35). The pattern of resource exploitation that discouraged and even actively prevented long-term settlement had the lasting effect of low population density that can still be seen in Campeche today: about a quarter of the national average at thirteen inhabitants per square kilometer in 2005, rising to fourteen in 2010 (INEGI 2011b: 13). Campeche ranks thirtieth in population, above only two other Mexican states, Colima and Baja California in northern Mexico.

Campeche's approximately 822,000 inhabitants in 2010 (up from 755,000 in 2005) are regionally and ethnically varied; the population encompasses indigenous groups that speak Yucatec Maya, Ch'ol, and Tzeltal, making the state more linguistically diverse than its neighbors on the rest of the Yucatán Peninsula (INEGI 2011b). The diversity is owed to the number of regional and transnational migrants drawn to Campeche. Some residents and their descendants came to the region as refugees from violence, whether during the 1840s–1850s Caste War or the more recent civil war in Guatemala (1960–1996). The latter refugees, thousands of Maya of various linguistic groups who managed to flee Guatemala, were relocated to camps in Campeche and Quintana Roo.[9] Others are part of a centuries-long historical chain of resource migration. The regional economy of resource exploitation beginning in the colonial period and intensifying through the nineteenth century drew migrant workers to the Laguna de Términos region. Mayas, Yaquis from northern Mexico, other mestizo Mexicans, and even African slaves were put to work exploiting the region's resources, hooking the Laguna de Términos into the global marketplace. In the nineteenth century and first part of the twentieth century migrants came, and many left after the commerce in resources such as timber and chicle declined. Others stayed.

In recent years Campeche has been receiving migrants from other parts of Mexico and from Central America. In 2010 a considerable proportion, 22.7 percent, of Campeche's population was not born in the state (INEGI 2011b: 17). As a general trend, more people now move to Campeche than leave the state. For 2005, statistics show that 26,845 immigrants came to Campeche and 20,818 persons over the age of five emigrated from Campeche (INEGI 2006a: 363). Even though Campeche may have its own development challenges, its urban centers do offer an alternative for rural populations from other parts of the state and from neighboring states such as Chiapas. This is demonstrated in that Campeche is not one of the major states sending migrants to the United States. Rather, Campeche's urban centers continue to grow. The highest population density is gathered in two urban centers, both situated on the Gulf of Mexico: the capital city of Campeche in the north and Ciudad del Carmen in the south. This is not to say that rural and peripheral areas of Campeche are the only migration poles. In the 1960s and 1970s, government incentives opened the forests of the interior of the state, notably Calakmul, to settlement from migrants from all across Mexico (Haenn 1999a). In Isla Aguada as in other communities around the Laguna de Términos, migrants from Chiapas began to arrive in the late 1990s to participate in the coastal fishing industry.

Campeche's attractiveness to a growing population is not owed to a diversifying economy. The economy of Campeche is, as it has been for centuries, highly dependent on natural resources. Since the discovery of oil in the 1970s the dependence is reaching a point of even greater distortion. Gross income in Campeche increased dramatically between 2003 and 2008, helped by strong performance in the petroleum sector, in which the extraction of more than 689 million barrels of oil—the highest by far among Mexico's seven oil-producing states—represented 73.3 percent of the national production. The income from oil extraction increased over this five-year period from less than $230 million to more than $540 million (INEGI 2010).

The profile of the state's economy from 2003 to 2008 gives a good indication of the current state of affairs, showing that Campeche is dangerously tipped toward a dependence on the oil industry as the primary sector of economic activity, with oil contributing 80 to 87 percent of the state's GDP in those years (INEGI 2010: 174, figure 137). This is a major jump from the previous five-year period; from 1997 to 2002, oil incomes represented about 40 to 54 percent of the contribution to state earnings (INEGI 2004: 44, figure 9). Significantly, the second-largest productive sector in 2003–2008 was construction, unsurprising given the phenomenal growth of Ciudad del Carmen. Commercial construction and public works projects (many in support of oil infrastructural development) have been undertaken in the region with funds to the state and municipality from Pemex. Mid-range contributors to Campeche's economic activity—transportation, storage, communication—likewise demonstrate a deep connection to oil-related growth. In the context of a larger region where tourism dominates the cultural and economic landscape, Campeche's own service sector is a paltry contributor to the economic activity. In the period 2003–2008, hotel and restaurant incomes accounted for less than 1 percent of state GDP (ibid.).

From the mid-1940s through the 1980s, Campeche had a strong commercial fishing sector. This now plays a significantly decreased role in the state's economic activity. In the late 1990s the sector that includes fishing contributed up to 4 percent of the state's economic activity. By 2003 fishing fell below 0.6 percent, and in 2008 it contributed less than 0.4 percent of the state's economic activity, a total of just about 3 billion pesos annually (ibid.), paling in comparison to the enormous oil incomes. Nonetheless, fishing continues to contribute more than emerging innovation activities such as mass media, financial services, and health services. Even though the economic activity generated by the fishing sector is dwarfed by the oil activity in Campeche, it has remained an area of economic concern for residents and policy makers at the municipal, state, and federal levels over the past three decades. This is precisely because the enormous oil incomes registered on the state's accounts were not staying in the state, while fishing was truly a local economic activity. Concern abounded for keeping fisheries afloat by whatever means necessary, and fishing continues to be vital, especially in smaller coastal communities in the Laguna de Términos where it is culturally as well as economically significant.

Oil production at Cantarell began to affect coastal fishing communities almost immediately after the discovery of offshore crude in the early 1970s. After 1980 the oil industry really began to make its mark in the municipality of Carmen. Even though the actual oil production is offshore, the island of Carmen serves as host for headquarter offices for Pemex and oil-services providers, housing for oil workers, and other activities including some heavy industry. Crude oil from the Cantarell complex is not brought to Carmen but instead is loaded onto tankers in the Campeche Sound or is taken by pipeline to tankers farther out to sea at Cayo de Arcas or to storage tanks on shore at Dos Bocas, near Paraiso, Tabasco. From Dos Bocas, the largest part of the production is exported, and the balance is transported inland by pipeline to other facilities.

While most of the oil is diverted elsewhere, Campeche does directly receive natural gas. Almost half of the nation's natural gas production comes from the Campeche Sound, and it arrives on shore at the Peninsula of Atasta on the far eastern end of the Laguna de Términos. Amid cattle-grazing and other small-scale agricultural and fishing activities is the Gas de Atasta recompression plant. The Campeche plant gathers and processes gas for transport along a pipeline that will pass through several industrial facilities along the Gulf Coast: Cactus in Chiapas, Nuevo Pemex and Ciudad Pemex (both in Tabasco), and onward to Cempoala, Veracruz. (Eight of the country's ten gas-processing plants are in southeastern states.) In Cempoala the gas is diverted into a nationwide pipeline forty-eight inches in diameter and 780 miles long from which it will move out into an even broader network of Mexico's nearly 6,000 miles of natural gas pipelines, feeding mostly central and northern Mexico.

The capital city of Campeche is known for its beauty and undeniable colonial charm, while Ciudad del Carmen is decidedly unattractive and instead offers the modern, Western comforts found in any global city today such as the Holiday Inn, Sam's Club, and KFC in an urban landscape that feels haphazard, uncoordinated, and disjointed. Carmen is two places at the same time. It is at once an incredibly large but surprisingly provincial fishing village and an unpleasant industrial processing zone. City leaders have attempted to reconcile its identity crisis with a bronze statue of a giant shrimp at the center of a *glorieta*, or traffic circle, to memorialize the community's heritage based in commercial shrimping. The giant shrimp was recently refurbished along with the downtown waterfront, or *malecón*, refocusing attention away from the shabby and increasingly violent suburbs and semi-slums to a pleasant seaside vista where a history of resource exploitation is sanitized as a heritage of the arts of *pesca*, or artisanal fishing.

But new streetlamps, sidewalks, and ice cream carts on the malecón cannot counter Carmen's darker industrial personality. Heavy traffic, poor sanitation, and frequent, severe flooding plague a city that has grown too fast for local government to keep up. The ever-widening industrial outskirts spread daily as multinationals buy up properties on the small island for business and pleasure. Meanwhile, housing shortages plague residents, many of whom are drawn to the city from Campeche's rural countryside as well as from neighboring states where opportunities are limited. Carmen may be two places at once, but today's Carmelitas and new migrants must find a way to live in both.

High oil earnings and a low population combine to produce a distorted per capita income in Campeche. In 2008 Campeche had the third-highest per capita income in the nation, after Mexico's Distrito

Federal and Nuevo León (INEGI 2010). On the ground it might be hard to see evidence of that, especially in frontline communities. Given the problems that I have only begun to hint at, it is obvious that the wealth brought by the oil and gas boom of the past three decades has not stayed within the municipality of Carmen. Like other state oil companies in extractive regions across the world, Pemex initially undertook very little local reinvestment in the municipality of Carmen. Though this would change after more than twenty years of intensive oil exploitation in the region, the first few years created a great deal of noticeable social and economic inequality. Roberto Rodríguez C.'s 1984 study of Ciudad del Carmen in the early 1980s suggests that oil was to follow the same model of resource extraction as palo de tinte and chicle, leaving no local basis for development. When Pemex started work in the Campeche Sound, little of the work was offered to locals. In the words of a local Carmelita interviewed in the 1980s, "They don't give any work on the platforms to the people of Carmen. Only to outsiders" (18).

Pemex had no need to hire locally since the parastatal already had an available workforce of tens of thousands, many from the neighboring Gulf-coast states of Tabasco and Veracruz. Besides that, the unionization of Pemex workers made it notoriously difficult for new workers to enter. Traditionally, Pemex jobs are a birthright, and the elite blue-collar jobs are kept in closed circles. Jobs with foreign oil-services companies were initially filled mostly by foreign workers. Thus, direct employment levels have been quite low. In 1990, some 13,500 people were employed in the oil industry's operations in Campeche Sound, Carmen, and Atasta. Of these, 3,288 were local, less than 2.2 percent of the actively employed population of 149,983 in the whole state of Campeche at the time. Rather than improving, the situation of local employment is worsening. In 2005, when the number of offshore oil workers dropped to 11,890, local workers were hit hard: 2,166 were local, not quite 0.9 percent of the actively employed population, a decrease of 65.8 percent (Hernández Montejo 2007: 92).

The arrival of oil operations did not give back locally and even created new hardships for the resident population in Carmen by distorting the local economy. The presence of an essentially new class of people in Carmen, earning Pemex wages and benefits or working for the foreign multinational oil-services providers, caused an abrupt price inflation in Carmen. The prices of everything from food to property to transportation were driven up as soon as the industry moved in. Meanwhile, Carmen's middle- and working-class families experienced no trickle-down effect from the oil workers' high wages: "Those who work on the platforms, after they get paid, they go back home, leaving nothing here. The only thing left is a high cost of living" (in Rodríguez C. 1984: 19). An editorial in the local newspaper *Tribuna Campeche* in the early 1980s sums up the problem perfectly: "Oil may be good for the nation, but it definitely represents a serious issue for the great majority of people who inhabit the areas where it is produced" (ibid.). In the early years in Carmen, the notion of the nationalist rallying cry "El petróleo es nuestro" (The oil is ours), borrowed from the moment of the 1938 expropriation, began to sound more like "The oil is our problem," especially for frontline communities.

Due to the oil boom, the whole municipality of Carmen experienced a population explosion across the following decades, putting a strain on the island's limited economic and environmental resources. The 2005 population of 199,988 represented an annual growth rate of almost 2.7 percent between 2000 and 2005 (INEGI 2006a: 23).[10] Carmen's growth is mirrored by a similar rate of population increase in the small *villa* of Isla Aguada, twenty-five miles to the east-northeast across from Carmen Island at Puerto Real. Isla Aguada, bursting at the seams with nearly 7,000 inhabitants, had many new residents who migrated from neighboring states as well as workers from Carmen seeking affordable housing. Insecurity there over public safety, the economy, and the future has become one complex issue with oil at its center.

Though Isla Aguada and neighboring communities along Campeche's Gulf coast are indeed on the frontlines of Mexico's intensive hydrocarbon-extraction industry, they are only tangentially involved in the actual labor of offshore oil drilling. Almost no one in Isla Aguada works for Pemex. A few people work directly in the industry for oil-services companies, and some others work indirectly in service-sector jobs that support the industry and its operations. When a real need arises and the funds can be gathered, Mérida rather than Ciudad del Carmen is the preferred destination for a medical consultation—not to mention emergency—or a major purchase. Residents on the frontlines feel isolated by a lack of transportation, paved roads, and communication infrastructure (especially the Internet) but also because of the education gap. Statistics from 2010 show that nearly 12,000 adults in the municipality of Carmen had not finished primary school, leaving more than 7,000 unable to read or write (INEGI 2011b). I observed communities across the municipality of Carmen lacking not only modern technologies such as Internet access and computers but also the most basic necessities of proper furniture, bathrooms, and schoolbooks. On the frontlines of the oil industry, communities on the margins of development express the urgent need for municipal and state authorities to step up access to a variety of resources—an appeal that grows louder and harder to meet in the post-peak energy crisis.

### The Laguna de Términos Protected Area

The municipality of Carmen has 120 miles of coastline, well more than one-third of the state's total. Three-quarters of the Campeche state population lives in coastal zones (Campeche 2004). The resources provided by the coastal and marine environments are potentially limitless. Whether for those dedicated to fishing or to jobs related to the oil industry, the two most productive sectors of the state's economy, the sea is an invaluable resource. The lagoon itself, the largest in Mexico, is a body of water so vast that on first sight the Spanish were convinced it was a strait and that the Yucatán Peninsula was an island. The Island of Carmen acts as a barrier protecting the lagoon from the Gulf of Mexico, save for two inlets—the Puerto Real inlet on the east and the Carmen inlet on the western side of Isla del Carmen. Although most of the lagoon is shallow, with an average depth of thirteen feet and maximum depth of fifteen and a half feet, the inlets have deeper channels (forty to fifty-five feet) spanned by the two longest bridges in Mexico.

The Laguna de Términos is an exceptionally rich hydrological ecosystem with an incredible diversity of plants. It is a winter haven for migratory birds. Dense but delicate mangrove swamps and coastal forests support a variety of land and sea animals. Aquatic reptiles including the American, Morelet ("Mexican"), and brown caiman crocodiles and hawkbill, Kemp's Ridley, and green sea turtles breed along beaches and marshes in these coastal zones. Scores of bobbing bottlenose dolphins can be regularly seen in the lagoon from the shores of Isla Aguada. In a colorful passage, Friar Diego de Landa records the fauna of the Laguna de Términos on his historic visit at the time of the Conquest, and through his evidence we can note that the rich diversity of the Laguna de Términos has a long history:

> There are many kinds of large and small herons, some white and others brown, in the Laguna de Términos. Many are of a very bright red, like powdered cochineal; and so many sorts of small birds, as well as large, that their numbers and variety are causes for wonderment; and still

more is the seeing them so busy hunting their food on the shore, some entering the incoming breakers only to break away from them, others hunting food on the beaches or hurrying away; but most of it all is seeing how God has provided for it all. (1978: 109)

In 1994 the region was declared a protected area and officially designated the Área de Protección de Flora y Fauna Laguna de Términos.[11] Ten years later it was recognized by the Ramsar Convention, an intergovernmental treaty for the protection of wetlands. It is, according to the International Union for the Conservation of Nature, a category 6 site, a protected area managed mainly for sustainable use of natural resources, a designation that explicitly acknowledges that the area and its resources are open to human use. The protected zone includes more than 1.7 million acres, or more than 2,700 square miles, of associated shoreline, Isla del Carmen, the Peninsula of Atasta, and the coastal zone of water up to thirty feet deep. In October 2008 the Laguna de Términos and the adjacent Pantanos de Centla in Tabasco were nominated by Mexico into the first stages of consideration for World Heritage status with the United Nations Educational, Scientific, and Cultural Organization (UNESCO). Voting within the organization for inclusion on the prestigious list of natural and cultural heritage sites across the globe usually takes place within five to ten years of nomination.

Wetlands and coastal zones like the Laguna de Términos are among the most productive environments in the world, containing complex ecological processes with the potential of providing vast socioeconomic benefits. Furthermore, they are a rich source of biodiversity and are vital in sustaining global fisheries. Coastal zones and wetlands provide critical habitat for vulnerable species. The Laguna de Términos has historically served the national industrial fisheries as a breeding ground and "nursery," as local fishers say, for fish and shellfish. However, in the Laguna de Términos (as well as similar situations in the Caribbean), "the importance of mangroves and wetland resources to rural communities has been overshadowed by the dedication of these vulnerable coastal areas to the energy sector" (Baptiste and Nordenstam 2009: 15).

The Laguna de Términos is Campeche's "other" protected area, second to Calakmul, which was established by presidential decree in 1989. Calakmul is about equal in size (at almost 1.8 million acres) and the focus of more intense attention not only by state development agencies and nongovernmental organizations (NGOs) but by scholars as well. The Calakmul biosphere reserve in the state's inland tropical forest extending to Mexico's border with Guatemala covers 13 percent of the state's surface area. It is the largest block of protected tropical forest in Mexico and was accepted into UNESCO's international system of biosphere reserves in 1993 (Nations 2006: 164).

Nora Haenn, a leading scholar of the Calakmul area, points out that Calakmul was created as an "ecological municipio" (2002). The designation of the area marking it a zone slated for protection and conservation programs was a bureaucratic act not welcomed by Calakmul's residents. To the contrary, the label did not reflect the local understanding of the space. Farmers resisted environmental management they saw as working against their subsistence use of forest resources. This did not mean, however, that they opposed conservation of the protected area. The long-term research of Haenn and others demonstrates that farmers used their identity as campesinos to create a movement to press the state for aid.

The cases of Calakmul in the state's interior and Campeche on the Gulf coast represent an important study in contrasts that highlight the distinctiveness of how local ecologies shape destinies in terms of both resource exploitation and conservation programs. In Carmen, ordinary citizens, environmentalists, and multiple state agencies worked together to make the Laguna de Términos into a federally protected area. On the Gulf coast, though, another designation overlies and perhaps even competes with that of the protected natural area. The Island of Carmen and its surrounding communities carry the special political designation *municipio petrolero*, oil municipality. Local officials and citizens welcomed and embraced this designation, which signifies that they will share in the proceeds of oil wealth on the local level. While the interior forests of the state were destined to be targeted for environmental sustainability, the Gulf coastal watershed would be targeted for energy recovery—two projects that have different objectives but share a common history of land and labor exploitation. The designation as an oil municipality signifies for Carmen the recognition that it is, despite any other hopes or aspirations, a center of oil production. It also means Carmen will receive funds from the proceeds of oil recovery in the Campeche Sound under a variety of agreements and arrangements by Pemex, the federal government, and the state of Campeche.

Fishers and campesinos, keenly aware of the wealth of petroleum resources in their midst, know that the 1994 designation of the Laguna de Términos as a protected area was a thin mantle of cover for the region's delicate ecology. While oil is indeed Mexico's national patrimony and oil revenues comprise some 40 percent of the national budget, the marine environment holds another valuable patrimony that sustains tens of thousand of residents along the Mexican Gulf coast encompassing six states: Tamaulipas, Veracruz, Tabasco, and (on the Yucatán Peninsula) Campeche, Yucatán, and Quintana Roo. Besides oil and gas production and petrochemical industries, the main economic activities of the region are fisheries, agriculture, cattle ranching, and tourism. More than 80 percent of the economic activity of each of the six Mexican states is in or associated with the coastal zone. Some believe that fishing and oil go hand in hand, but the fishers of the Laguna de Términos view the *pesquera* (fishing sector) and the *petrolera* (oil sector) as necessarily at odds with one another, especially as both resources have peaked in the Campeche Sound.

The tensions between oil development and the everyday lives of fishers and farmers in the towns and villages around the Laguna de Términos formed the basis for a grassroots mobilization beginning in the early 1990s. The movement brought together social actors—local residents, NGOs, academics, and politicians affiliated with the Partido de la Revolución Democrática (PRD)—calling for Pemex to be made accountable for the pollution of fields and water. The core of the social movement is based in the Peninsula of Atasta, one of the most marginalized areas of the municipality of Carmen. Atasta hosts heavy onshore infrastructure such as the Gas de Atasta recompression plant and the world's largest nitrogen plant. Before the declaration of the APFFLT, citizens held demonstrations and protests against Pemex. For example, in 1992 groups blocked the arterial highway to mainland Mexico, protesting twenty years of damage to their land and asking for investment in social development. The citizens group Movimiento de Campesinos y Pescadores de la Península de Atasta was soon established. Working with a local environmental NGO, Marea Azul, it negotiated with Pemex, state, federal, and municipal officials toward an accord guaranteeing Pemex's adherence to established environmental regulations, particularly in the Atasta region, and three consecutive years (beginning in 1995) of Pemex investment in local social development through the establishment of an annual fund of 4 million pesos (Hernández Montejo 2007: 124). This was the beginning of what would become a long and extremely complicated arrangement of social and economic development vis-à-vis Pemex payouts to communities throughout the Laguna de Términos, largely in the municipality of Carmen.

The APFFLT's roots in political mobilization have not necessarily

translated into subsequent years of building a community-interest conservation corridor. Nor has it ended the cycle of resource curse—far
from it. Since the declaration, the APFFLT has continually revealed itself as a source of contradictions in regard to the zone's plants, animals,
and people. The wide biological diversity of the zone encompasses commercial species (several kinds of shrimp and crab as well as fish including
the robalo and the corvina) and endangered species (the jabirú stork,
peregrine falcon, crocodile, ocelot, jaguar, and manatee, among others). The protected area encompasses the most delicate of natural ecological habitats, most of all in the coastal mangroves, but equally houses
the worst kind of urban sprawl and blight in the ever-expanding Ciudad
del Carmen. Even though these factors form the deep contradictions
of everyday existence of the APFFLT, what remains the most shocking
and striking is that within those very same waters oil is being drilled.

## Conserving a Critically Threatened Landscape

On a dark night the sparkling lights of offshore platforms are sometimes apparent from the shores of Isla Aguada. But one day a hulking
platform was clearly visible to my own naked eye on the horizon during
broad daylight; certainly the installation had moved very close to the
protected area. I visited the APFFLT site manager, Humberto Reyes, at
his office in Ciudad del Carmen and asked why a platform had appeared
just off shore near Puerto Real, across the inlet from Isla Aguada, seemingly inside the protected area. He registered a subtle recognition at
the mention but went on to produce for me a heroic feat of bureaucratic runaround. *The platform is not actually there,* he told me. At first
I thought the previous long days in the sweltering heat had indeed produced mental short-circuiting on my part. But no, I saw it! (I wanted
to insist.) Several times, in fact. I even took pictures of it. I talked to
many people in Isla Aguada about the platform, and that in turn produced a series of heated discussions among the fishers about the rumors
of more platforms (three, according to most reports) set to encroach
upon the lagoon itself. *Not there? Yeah, right!* With my head spinning
but without protest, I allowed Reyes to continue his explanation. His
office had no knowledge of any proposals or plans for the establishment
of platforms near Isla Aguada or anywhere in the APFFLT. Any project,
whether Pemex's or any other kind of development inside the APFFLT,
had to be fully vetted and assessed by its parent organization, the Min-

istry of Environment and Natural Resources (Semarnat), for environmental impact. Semarnat then gives a technical opinion. Given that he received no proposals and Semarnat thus did not approve any projects, logically the installation could not be where I said it was. I thanked him for the clarification.

My experience at the protected area office illustrates the thick bureaucracy, relative lack of power, and huge burden of managing the Laguna de Términos protected area. Access to the APFFLT is not restricted. Highways run through it, and one of the major cities of southern Mexico, Ciudad del Carmen, sits within the protected wildlife area's borders. A growing population, unchecked urban sprawl, unabated pollution, and insufficient infrastructure for drainage and sewage, for instance, present a constant threat to the delicate ecosystem of the estuary and mangroves. Great socioeconomic disparity exists in different parts of the APFFLT, corresponding to those who live in the urbanized area of Ciudad del Carmen and those who live in the highly marginalized hinterlands of the protected area. The APFFLT has incipient slums in the urban areas. In the rural zones, cattle ranchers, beekeepers, and farmers try to eke out a living off the land, but state-sponsored aquaculture programs are replacing their efforts.

Parks Watch, a monitoring organization based at Duke University that works in-country with NGOs (in this case, Naturalia) to protect the biodiversity of tropical protected areas, completed an assessment of the APFFLT and came up with a list of the most significant threats to conservation in the protected area (2003: 11):

- Petroleum exploration and production (Pemex)
- Contamination of the lagoon system by bacteria and agrochemicals
- Population growth and land-use change
- Wetland destruction to establish shrimp farms
- Deforestation and habitat destruction
- Wildlife poaching and illegal fishing
- Exotic species introduction
- Hurricanes

Based on this assessment Parks Watch determined that the APFFLT's status was "critically threatened." Despite awareness of the dangers that all these risks pose to conservation of the delicate ecosystem in the APFFLT, every single one of them is only getting more serious as time passes.

The establishment of the protected area gives local residents a political voice by helping them feel justified that their surroundings should not be ignored, but in nearly two decades since its establishment, no revision to the zone's founding plan has been presented to the public. Meanwhile, in 2010 Pemex began new incursions into the Laguna de Términos—this time clearly inside the APFFLT. Pemex intended to drill five wells to extract crude and natural gas (Ribereño wells 11, 33, 31, 13, and 35), with the expectation that each would produce a modest 1,000 barrels of condensate and 11 million feet of natural gas per day. Without waiting for the environmental agency to issue the results of its environmental impact study, Pemex went ahead in clear violation of the law and initiated work in the area where the exploratory well Ribereño-1 is located, easily within the protected area, near the small town of Nuevo Campechito. Later, after much public outrage, Pemex clarified in a press release that the wells were only exploratory and not for exploitation and would be capped except for Ribereño-11, which would be exploited. The press release added that the project was key to helping strengthen the nation's proven reserves.

The Ribereño well project implies that when done in the nation's strategic interests, oil development will win out over the mandate to protect the Laguna de Términos. Certainly, incursion into the protected area will only mount in the post-peak period as traditional sources of oil and gas decline and new ones are sought. In recent years Pemex's activity inside the protected area, rather than being limited to infrastructure and support services, is now veering toward actual exploration and production. In other words, it seems at least to residents to be on the increase. The director of Marea Azul, Lourdes Rodríguez Badillo, has responded that "due to the economic crisis, all the barriers that protect the environment are being broken through, in order to drill and extract every last drop of oil in the area" (in Chim 2010). Was the economic crisis the root cause or just a superficial excuse, however, for the intensification of Pemex activity in the Laguna de Términos? Was it really the much broader post-peak condition under which environmental policies, citizens' voices, and the political process no longer applied?

## PART 2

# THE PESQUERA AND THE PETROLERA

From the smallest towns to the largest cities across Mexico, the annual celebration of a community's patron saint's feast day is a greatly anticipated and much-lauded event. In Ciudad del Carmen, the veneration of Nuestra Señora del Carmen, the Virgen del Carmen, is no exception. The patron saint's feast stretches across several days each summer in the blazing heat and occasional deluges of late July. The height of the fiesta is the procession of the Virgen del Carmen, a delicate, bridelike statue in a brown brocade dress, draped in a white lace mantle with her head surrounded by a huge gold coronet. The city takes to the streets to watch the eighteen-inch-tall brunette virgin atop a flower-strewn platform carried in procession through Ciudad del Carmen, passing under colorful flags and swirling foil confetti.

Known as a patroness and protector of sailors and fishers, Our Lady of Carmen is similarly celebrated in port cities throughout the Catholicized world, from the tourist mecca of Ibiza, Spain, to the small fishing village of Ocumare de la Costa, Venezuela. Fishers and other Carmelitas alike turn out in droves each year to watch the Virgen proceed through the streets and on a maritime peregrination. Each year the port of Carmen officially closes to all other traffic for three hours in the middle of the afternoon of the procession, and hundreds of small, decoratively festooned fishing boats accompany the figure on its *recorrido* through the Laguna de Términos.

The Virgen del Carmen was named patron saint to the island on July 16, 1717, the day the Spanish finally recaptured the island of Tris from the English palo de tinte plunderers reluctant to give up their settlement. As patroness of the sea, the Virgen del Carmen offered hope, solace, and courage to many a sailor on the Spanish Main. The centrality of the Virgen's dominion over the port of Carmen and coastal

Campeche through the centuries would see her relevance as patroness of the sea only strengthen. The Virgencita, or Little Virgin, witnessed the transition of the port of Carmen to commercial fishing, offering her blessings over shrimp trawlers.

The Virgen's annual procession through the streets and the more participatory phase through the Laguna de Términos carries a deep symbolism that resonates with the region's political economy. Rather than an ancient tradition rooted in the community's distant past, the practice of carrying the Virgen is instead quite modern. The figure's first *paseo* through the Laguna de Términos began in 1956 by fishers under the guidance and inspiration of a much-revered priest who rose through the ranks to become a bishop, Monsignor Faustino Robelledo Blanco. The modern tradition of carrying the Virgen aboard the shrimp boats anchored itself within the coastal community's cultural heritage. Thus, the maritime procession is explicitly linked to the success of the commercialization of the shrimp industry in the port of Carmen and the veneration and propitiation of the Virgen as the patron saint of fishers.

For fifty-two years the Virgen figure was carried by a commercial shrimp boat in a stately marine procession through the Laguna de Términos to the delight of Carmelitas and visitors from near and far. For decades while shrimping carried the economy of Carmen, a shrimping boat, or *cameronero*, carried the Virgen. However, after the decline of commercial shrimping—and indeed all fishing activity, including the region's long-vibrant artisanal, or *ribereño*, sector—a thriving competitor stepped up to carry the figure instead: the petroleum industry. Thus, it should not have come as a surprise when in 2009 Cotemar, just one of the dozens of private offshore oil-services providers contracted by Pemex, stepped up to assume the mantle. Surely the aging and decrepit shrimp trawler was unfit and unsafe to carry out the important public ritual. The shrimp trawler, one of only a couple of dozen remaining of Carmen's fleet of hundreds, was a sign of a once-robust industry now in decline. Now, a new era would be ushered in, distinguished by new traditions shaped by the ever-changing cycle of commodity exploitation in the Laguna de Términos. Even though the age of oil arrived in Ciudad del Carmen three decades earlier, the thought of passing the Virgen figure from cameronero to *petrolero*—from shrimp boat to commercial oil boat—was a shocking indecency. At the same time, the commercial shrimp industry in the port of Carmen peaked and since has died a slow and quite public death in the city that grew famous and dependent on the profitable crustacean known as *oro con patas*—gold with feet.

Meanwhile, the petroleum industry loomed on the same horizon. In the year oil production began in the Bay of Campeche, Carmen was registering significant volumes of catch in its shrimp fishery: half of the state's total and, together with Isla Aguada, three-quarters of the state's shrimp catch (Rodríguez C. 1984: 22). But as offshore oil production took off, the fishing industry withered and waned. Their intertwined lives in the Gulf waters were, for many years, inverse destinies. Thus, by the time of the preparation of the July 2009 annual fiesta, the honor of carrying the Virgen del Carmen became a battle over much more than religious devotion. It was instead a fight for staking a territorial claim to the celebrated tradition and, as came to pass, a last gasp in a symbolic battle over resource sovereignty in the waters of the Bay of Campeche.

In the annual pilgrimage in Campeche's waters, the Virgen was entering a contested space of two competing local and national resources: oil and fisheries. The Virgen's passage highlighted the contested nature of the sea's two patrimonies, the *pesquera* and the *petrolera*. A fierce debate ensued in the run-up to the fiesta over not just the privilege but the right to carry the figure on its procession through the glassy green waters of the Laguna de Términos. Fishers were indignant at the announcement that the honor of carrying the Virgen atop the cabin of a shrimping boat would pass to an oil-services boat, from the realm of the *cameronera* to the petrolera. How could a half-century precedent be overturned? Moreover, how could the deep cultural significance of fishing be eschewed for the crass economic importance of private oil contractors? Hundreds appeared in demonstration in front of the city's nineteenth-century church, wrote letters, and held audiences with priests and port authorities alike. The fishers demanded and beseeched that the long tradition not be broken.

At the eleventh hour, officials finally conceded to allow a cameronero to carry the Virgen figure for the fiesta. The *Michelle M.*, built in 1995, was selected for the task. The newest of Carmen's aging fleet, the boat could carry fifty to sixty passengers to accompany the figure through the Laguna de Términos. At 6 a.m. on July 19, 2009, the day's activities began with a ninety-minute procession through the downtown streets, from the church to a baseball stadium where thousands heard a mass celebrated by the bishop of Campeche. Only then did the Virgen travel to the port to board the *Michelle M.* The shrimping boat carried the dark-haired figure flanked by scores of *lanchas*—the outboard motorboats of the artisanal fishermen—and a couple of dozen big shrimp boats. Some of the small, narrow fiberglass boats, lots decorated with balloons and outfitted with canopies, carried up to ten people and sat dangerously low in the water. The crowds gathered downtown along the malecón to see the Virgen take her place atop the *Michelle M.*'s cabin at the Puerto Pesquero.

I went out that day to line up along the malecón with the crowds of Nuestra Señora's devotees. The freshly painted *Michelle M.* put on a bright façade atop the sparkling water as the *patrona* bobbed along to a catchy *cumbia* beat. But the impatient buzz of the Halliburton helicopter overhead served as the ever-present reminder that even tradition in Carmen has to make room for oil. This was a small victory for Carmen's fishing tradition—perhaps a final concession to the Gulf shrimpers in the waters of their patrimonial sea.

## CHAPTER 3

# The Peak and Decline of Fishing in the Laguna de Términos

The rich and varied resources of the warm waters of the Gulf of Mexico and the vast, shallow Laguna de Términos have served the residents of Isla Aguada through thick and thin for generations. "Aquí, todos viven de la pesca" (Here, everyone lives off fishing), one native Aguadeño explained to me; even those residents who appeared to earn their income by other means live by fishing. "If there isn't fish, there isn't bread. Fishing is the source of income for everyone." Others have insisted that "Isla Aguada es cien por ciento pescador," 100 percent fisher, a fishing community through and through. Most households in Isla Aguada have at least some members, usually one or two generations of men, who self-identify as fishers. "Soy pescador" (I am a fisher) is a primordial marker of identity that overrides any other sense of being or belonging.

That is why I grew more and more curious when early each morning I set out for a walk along the villa's malecón and found every fiberglass lancha neatly lined up on the narrow beach, exactly the same as the day before. Among the few stalls at the central market, none sells fish. After a couple of nights of a delicious *empanizado* (lightly breaded and fried) fish filet at the *posada* where I was staying in town, the host announced to the guests: no more fish. As an alternative, I was offered frozen burger patties brought in from the Bodega Aurrera, a big-box discount store owned by Wal-Mart that sells everything from tequila to tires, twenty-five miles away on the highway to Ciudad del Carmen. In Isla Aguada everyone is a fisher, but no one goes fishing.

It has not always been this way in Isla Aguada and the other fishing communities along the Laguna de Términos and the Gulf coast. And the reason is a matter of some controversy, at the heart of which is how much the presence of Pemex in the Campeche Sound has de-

*Lanchas* lined up on the Laguna de Términos shore. Photograph by author.

stroyed fishing in this self-proclaimed 100 percent fishing community. Isla Aguada's fishers are of two minds on the decline of fishing: either Pemex is to blame for the low capture, or the absence of a decent catch in these waters is unrelated to Pemex. An overwhelming majority unabashedly and bitterly attribute the community's misfortune to the former, while many fewer will try to convince me of the latter. Two fishers of relatively the same cohort illustrate this difference. Seventy-year-old fisher Don Enrique has lived in Isla Aguada for forty-five years and considers himself a "naturalized" resident, though he was born in another fishing town up the coast. He was drawn away from the busier fishing port of Champotón to the smaller village decades ago because of the "riqueza sobre el mar," the richness of marine life, to be found at Isla Aguada. El Cangrejo, as he is known among his fishing buddies, has witnessed a dramatic decline in the abundance of fish available to Isla Aguada's fishers. When queried as to why, he cites the coming of the oil industry in the Campeche Sound that he believes has contaminated the waters. One of his cohorts, known as El Gato, prefers to take a broader perspective on Isla Aguada's fishing problem. Over the past decades, he explains, he has witnessed not only the rise of the oil industry's activities but also an increase in the number of lanchas in local waters. Fishers from "outside" have increased the pressure on local fisheries. What is more, El Gato says, the nonnative fishers catch very small, immature fish. This breaks the life cycle of the fisheries, preventing replenishment. Even though El Gato only completed a fifth-grade education, he prides himself on his intellectual, "scientific," and even-handed approach to the problems plaguing Isla Aguada's fisheries. Regardless of the exact cause of the decline of fishing at Isla Aguada, all walks of life in the community are affected by it, whether state-owned Pemex is blamed directly as the culprit or not.

Even if residents find it increasingly difficult to make a living from fishing, Isla Aguada remains 100 percent pescador because fishing is a deep part of the cultural heritage of Mexico's Gulf coastal communities. As long as the Yucatán Peninsula has been inhabited, in the warm waters of the Bay of Campeche as well as the Laguna de Términos the arts of fishing have brought an abundant yield. As far back as we can trace the historical record, intrepid coastal fishers appear carrying out their arts of pesca with nets and harpoons from canoes in the sea, lagoon, and rivers. One chronicler of the Spanish Conquest, Friar Diego de Landa, described the sixteenth-century Laguna de Términos as "a great lake abounding in fish of all kinds" (1978: 3). De Landa observed that the indigenous residents captured fish in the lagoon in the shallow waters with arrows, although they preferred the coastal waters of the Gulf if they had nets. The abundant fisheries provided subsistence as well as enough catch to take to market "throughout the country" (97), a distance he then noted as twenty to thirty leagues. The Indians preserved their catch of skate (*liza*, "very fat and good"), bream, sardines, tilapia, and flounder, not to mention oysters, each by its own proper treatment of salting, cooking, or drying in the sun (97).

In the seventeenth century the privateer William Dampier observed fishers in the Laguna de Términos region fishing for snook, tarpon, and dogfish. Dampier saw "the great tarpon caught not with lines but with harpoons." He noted a curious practice of the "very shy" fishers when their canoes were sighted by a European ship. They would allow their canoes to fill with water to sink the vessel just enough to make the canoe level with the surface of the water, remaining with just their heads above water until the ship passed by (1699: 12).

Though de Landa recorded the regional marketing activities of Laguna de Términos fisheries in the sixteenth century, like most indigenous commercial activity, this would have been rapidly curbed by the increasing presence of the Spanish as the Conquest intensified. The thriving marketplace on the Campeche-Tabasco border, Xicalango, ceased to function as an indigenous commercial and cultural hub of exchange after the Conquest. Xicalango was in the area of southwestern Campeche controlled by the Chontal Maya, called by some the Phoenicians of the New World (a reference to their great drive toward trading, even across remarkably long distances around the region). Xicalango, on the Gulf coast, was a strategic location for moving goods between the Yucatán Peninsula and the highlands of Mexico and into Central America (Farriss 1984: 15). Even before the conquistadores subdued the Maya of Yucatán, enough damage was done to other nodes of the long trade routes to disrupt the indigenous trade networks (ibid.).

With compromised trade routes and a population decimated by fighting and disease during the Conquest, fishing returned to a subsistence level. Fishing remained outside the realm of the marketplace for centuries as the exploitation of other natural resources took precedence. For the Laguna de Términos, external forces ranging from colonial power struggles to the Industrial Revolution to Western habits of taste and style dictated which natural resources would be most competitive in the global marketplace. From 1650 to the 1940s, palo de tinte, tropical hardwoods, and chicle supplanted fisheries as the leading exports.

In a now familiar boom-and-bust cycle, the decline of one resource led to the rise of another. As chicle met its ultimate demise, shrimping was poised to become the principal economic activity of the region for the 1940s–1980s. Even though the riches of the region's waters would come to be just another exploitable commodity, fisheries are not wholly commensurable to other resources in the Laguna de Términos. Unlike palo de tinte or chicle, fishing is part of the cultural heritage or patrimony of coastal communities. The centuries-long pattern of artisanal subsistence fishing for the coastal residents of the Laguna de Términos region anchors cultural life and came to define livelihood for families in communities such as Isla Aguada. Thus, distinctive from other extractive economies, fishing is deeply connected with local identity and personhood for the *hombres del mar* of the Laguna de Términos, shaping patterns of everyday life as much as it sustains livelihoods. As inherited cultural patrimony, the arts of fishing—including knowledge of the sea and fish, traditional fishing grounds, weather patterns, and capture techniques—were passed from one generation to the next.

In the 1940s the discovery of a lucrative shrimp fishery off the shores of Carmen prompted the development of a parallel industrial fishery in the region. Like its artisanal counterpart, industrial fishing too became a kind of patrimony as the Mexican state realized the significance of marine resources for both regional and national economic development. From the time of their discovery to the peak of Mexico's fisheries in 1981 (Hernández and Kempton 2003: 509), until the decline of Carmen's shrimp fisheries in the 1990s, the Mexican state struggled to assert sovereignty over fisheries as well as marine territories. Well before the discovery of offshore oil, shrimp exploitation in the Gulf of Mexico and Laguna de Términos demonstrated the historic and ongoing tensions among local, national, and foreign interests in Campeche's resource-rich waters. The battle for sovereignty over fisheries set the legal as well as sociocultural precedents for claiming the Gulf and its multiple resources as a patrimonial sea—the assets of which belong to the state and the citizenry.

## Shrimping in the National Interest

Feverish interest in exploiting oro con patas—gold with feet, as the crustacean came to be known—hit Ciudad del Carmen after the chance discovery of "giant shrimp" in 1946 on the banks of the Campeche Sound. Prior to the discovery, fishing was an artisanal practice in the Laguna de Términos region. Using small craft and no navigational aids, fishers utilized hand-cast nets and lines to catch a variety of finfish including snappers, snook, and sardines. In Isla Aguada, fishers also specialized in the capture of *cazón* (small sharks) and sea turtles. Fishing was a subsistence practice as well as a commercial activity, but local markets were few, and transportation, refrigeration, processing, and cold storage problems hampered distant marketing. Thus, through the mid-1940s fishing contributed little to the regional economy. Technology, ready markets especially in the United States, and foreign investment for production infrastructure coincided to rapidly develop a booming commercial industry of national significance based in Ciudad del Carmen. Waves of migrants came to Carmen, workers and businesspeople alike. Given that industrial fishing in the scorching hot Gulf did not use salting, curing, or canning, shrimping required the massive manufacture of ice.[1]

In a very short time, a matter of months, the waters of the Laguna de Términos went from producing only a supplemental foodstuff for the tables of the region's humblest households to being a source of wealth, causing Campeche Governor Lavelle Urbina to wax eloquent in his 1948 Informe de Gobierno that "the discovery of the giant shrimp has arrived providentially in order to resolve the terrible situation that the people of the Isla have been suffering" (in Leriche Guzmán 1995: 70). By the time Cantarell was discovered in the 1970s, the transformation of Carmen from a fishing village to an industrial shrimping port was complete. The addition of infrastructure in support of offshore oil operations only supplemented the industrial feel of the port city.

Since the beginnings of commercial shrimping out of the port of Carmen, a tension has existed between public and private interests in controlling and benefiting from marine resources. For most of this history, shrimping has appeared, at least on paper, as a national enterprise. Shrimp initially became a patrimonial resource when the Cárdenas administration (1934–1940) passed reforms ensuring fishers' access to a marine commons in the Gulf of Mexico. In the same spirit as the legislation that tightened up territorial sovereignty over Campeche's forests and cooperatized chicle operations, a fishing law passed in July 1940 reserved the exploitation of shrimp in all national waters specifically for cooperative societies formed by Mexican fishers (Soberanes Fernández 1994: 9). National cooperatives maintained exclusive access to shrimp through the 1950s. In the 1960s, laws changed to allow private investors to rent boats and equipment to the cooperatives and to own and lease processing facilities. In this manner a greater degree of privatization has crept into Mexico's fishing sector. By 1992, under the wave of privatization initiated by the Salinas administration, harvesting rights and control over all facets of production and distribution were liberalized.

The presence of strategic living or mineral resources readily spurs conflict, arbitration, and negotiation. When fisheries and oil—among the most contentious issues in contemporary resource geopolitics—coexist, stakes are high for developing nations seeking to benefit from resource wealth. Conflict takes the form of maritime boundary disputes and the setting of new maritime borders. Mexico's attempt to maintain sovereign control over Gulf fisheries set into motion a series of international disputes that reverberated across the latter half of the twentieth century and echo loudly today in ongoing disputes and negotiations over offshore hydrocarbon deposits.

Maritime disputes date back to the days of the Spanish Main and the destructive presence of the palo de tinte exploiters, the privateers-turned-pirates, along Mexico's Gulf coast. The colonial cases concerned the Spanish crown's assertion of its exclusive right to navigate the waters of the claimed empire. The Spanish wished to control the trade routes as an extension of the vertical integration of the monopoly they claimed over the colonies and their resources. In the recognized international law of the sea in contemporary times, such assertions would not be tolerated. While coastal nations have a right to territorial waters (a strip of sea), the high seas are commons. Such rules are established in the United Nations Convention on the Law of the Sea (UNCLOS).

From the time of the discovery of the shrimp in Campeche's waters almost through the peak catches of shrimp in the 1970s, the Bay of Campeche was plagued by the presence of "foreign boats," known as *barcas piratas*, from the United States and even Japan. This is because of differing international interpretations of the precise measure that constitutes a nation's territorial sea, definitions of which have changed over time and varied among nations. Differences in consensus over the delimitation of Mexico's territorial sea in the Gulf provoked international dispute. Through the nineteenth century, Mexico's customary claim to its territorial waters was "three leagues from land," and the claim can be found explicitly stated for the Gulf of Mexico in the Treaty of Guadalupe Hidalgo (1848) and the Gadsden Treaty (1853), both of which discern maritime borders between the United States and Mexico as an extension of the delimitation of land borders. The three-maritime-mile rule was reiterated in the 1902 Ley General de Bienes Nacionales that was, over time, revised to become in 1935 a nine-mile and in 1969 a twelve-mile territorial sea (Schmitt 1982: 139).

Significantly, in the Mexican constitution of 1917 the actual delimitation itself was left ambiguous, as Article 27 states that the nation's territorial waters were only the same as those established by international law. However, Article 27 does specify and assert Mexico's national sovereignty over resources within that territorial sea. The same provisions that guarantee the nation's dominion over strategic natural and cultural heritage resources ranging from oil to archaeological monuments also allow for the protection of fisheries as national resources. This protection converts the territorial sea into a *patrimonial* sea in the sense that Mexico's territorial waters, especially those in the Gulf of Mexico, contain strategic national patrimonial assets such as fisheries and hydrocarbons. Within the patrimonial sea, sovereignty over resources should be guaranteed.

As Mexico tightened its jurisdiction over territorial waters in the Gulf, illegal shrimping became the cause of some political friction between the United States and Mexico. The fishing law of 1940 declared the exploitation of shrimp in national waters to be the exclusive right of

Mexican fishers, but American and some Japanese crews nevertheless attempted to fish in the Gulf waters for the profitable catch. The American fleet's efforts redoubled following World War II after enormous amounts of shrimp had already been hauled out of U.S. Gulf waters. Huge penalties threatened the foreign vessels that ventured to shrimp in the Bay of Campeche. But indeed they did, and the Mexican coast guard intercepted, sanctioned, and detained these barcas piratas, their catches being decommissioned at the port of Carmen.

The 1941 revision of the Ley General de Bienes Nacionales set the limits of national waters at nine nautical miles, but U.S. ships were respecting Mexico's territory at only three. Leriche Guzmán (1995: 85–86) recounts an episode of the shrimp boat of one Felice Golino of Louisiana, caught on September 9, 1946, along with five other boats by the Mexican coast guard in the disputed territory between three nautical miles recognized by the United States and nine nautical miles established by the Mexican government. Captain Golino sought the help of the U.S. ambassador to avoid penalties and continue fishing in Mexican waters, but after spending ten days detained in the port of Carmen he paid $800 in fines and was advised to seek a proper license to fish in Mexican waters or else stay outside the nine-mile zone.

His was just one story among many. Violations of the boundary and the subsequent seizure of U.S. ships became so frequent that in 1954 the U.S. Congress passed the Fisherman's Protective Act to guarantee reimbursement to boat owners for ships caught in the disputed area between three and nine nautical miles off Mexico's coast (Schmitt 1982: 142). In 1969 a set of short-term agreements was negotiated with the United States and Cuba that would be phased out by the end of the 1970s. Under these agreements, foreign vessels would still be allowed in Gulf waters, but Mexico would benefit from the unequal power of the limited incursion allowed to the U.S. fleet over the ever-growing Mexican fleet. In the period 1970–1974, 10 percent of the U.S. Gulf states' catch came from Mexican waters, using a fleet of upward of 600 boats (Griffin and Beattie 1977: 1, 12). The Texas fleet was particularly dependent on Mexican shrimp, drawing 17 percent of its catch, amounting to almost 20 percent of its revenue, from Mexican waters (12).

Just over the horizon, the debate over three, nine, or even twelve nautical miles of territorial waters would become redundant as nations including the United States and Mexico began to adopt the much more expansive delimitation of 200 nautical miles. By constitutional amendment in 1976, Mexico established an "exclusive economic zone" (EEZ) of 200 nautical miles "in which it would control all resources living and non-living, free-floating and attached to the sea-bed, and under the ocean floor" (Schmitt 1982: 144). The United States and Mexico negotiated a treaty to phase out U.S. shrimping in Mexico's waters, and Mexico agreed that licenses would be sold to foreign fishing boats—but only for the catches that the Mexican fleet could not itself harvest (ibid.). However, the most controversial issue was shrimp, a species Mexico definitely reserved for Mexican boats only. By 1979 U.S. shrimping had been phased out of Mexican waters (Aguilar and Grande-Vidal 2008: 235).[2]

The foreign threat to the Mexican national fisheries was not the only problem in the boom period of Carmen's commercial shrimp industry. The local fishers were little prepared for large-scale, industrial work on the high seas. After all, they were ribereños, artisanal fisherfolk, accustomed to different tools, techniques, and catches. This added to the problem of quickly growing an authentically national Mexican fleet. As legal shrimping was limited to Mexican cooperatives, sometimes they had to hire foreign shrimp boats to work on their behalf. Such foreign boats registered themselves in the names of Mexican nationals (using *prestanombres*, or aliases). In other cases, some shrimp boats were privateers (*armadores*) masquerading as cooperative boats. The Gulf was reverting to the eighteenth-century outlaw regime of resource exploitation.

The cooperative system designed by the Mexican state was, in theory, an egalitarian way to share the patrimonial waters and resources among those who, by dint of their class position and lack of access to capital, would not otherwise benefit from national fisheries. The state created cooperatives to control the exploitation of the nation's most valuable fisheries: shrimp, abalone, octopus, and squid. The cooperatization, one of many such nationalistic acts under the Cárdenas administration, turned out to be key to the shrimping operation out of the port of Carmen and for the economy of the Laguna de Términos region. As the emergence of commercial fishing on Campeche's Gulf coast coincided with the final collapse of the chicle industry, it came at a moment of regional collapse too and helped provide new social and economic opportunities for the average resident. The chicle industry that had attracted many migrants and their families to the region left many jobless in its wake. Unlike other parts of Mexico or its close neighbors in the Yucatán Peninsula, the municipality of Carmen suffered from stunted agricultural development, the legacy of decades of the privatized plantations and an extreme extractive economy. The fishing industry thus became an important source of employment and income for residents of the municipality of Carmen, in the newly urbanizing city of Carmen itself, and in the smaller fishing villages from Isla Aguada to the Peninsula of Atasta.

The assertion of territorial sovereignty and cooperatization failed, however, to regularize shrimping activity in Gulf waters. The rush to exploit the lucrative oro con patas stirred up conflict and competition among cooperatives, businesses, fishers themselves, fuel distributors, and peelers and packers in factories. Even though the system was cooperatized, the shrimping cooperatives out of the port of Carmen did not quite work in practice as they were designed in theory. According to the law, in Mexican territorial waters shrimp was national patrimony. This meant that the catch was closed to foreigners. In practice that meant in some cases that foreigners invested capital behind the names of local Mexicans. The cooperatives were circumvented by the de facto system of capitalization in which boats were owned by armadores who held a great amount of power over the cooperative members (*socios*). In effect, the socios of the cooperatives were workers for the armador. The system was not really any different (beyond its technical legal arrangement) than a system of wage labor. The early cooperatives functioned less as an egalitarian system of laborers sharing resources and more as a patron-client system dominated by business owners. Because the cooperative would lack capital to finance the boats, they would be subject to the more powerful business interests.

Foreigners from the United States were not the only outsiders to compete with the Laguñeros, residents of the area, for the shrimp catch. As soon as word of the presence of the valuable oro con patas spread, boats from fishing ports across Mexico arrived at Carmen. Some of the boats were actually foreign boats illegally rented through Mexican businesses involved in clandestine shrimping for export to the United States. The local cooperatives wished to claim exclusive rights to exploit the resources of the Bay of Campeche or at least to charge outsiders for fishing in Campeche's waters. But they knew such exclusive territoriality was futile (Leriche Guzmán 1995: 109). Despite the de jure intentions of the nationalized, cooperatized system, the de facto practice of shrimping was distorted so that it became driven by private and often foreign capital.

The early phase of the boom, beginning in 1947 and lasting through the mid-1950s, was one of chaos and disorder for Ciudad del Carmen.

Many jobs were generated, but the pattern of rapid, unchecked growth also had its downside for the local population: inflation, a decline in public services, and a housing shortage (ibid.: 89). The rapid commercialization of the shrimping industry turned Carmen from a fishing village into an industrial port overnight. The old docks and piers that served the palo de tinte and chicle industries were razed in order to modernize Carmen's port, much to the dismay of many of the citizens. It was a process of modernization that would, however, anaesthetize Carmen to its reindustrialization decades later with the coming of the oil industry.

The shrimping industry took full advantage of modern trawling technology and a twenty-four-hour work cycle to exploit three main species of shrimp: the pink shrimp (*Farfantepenaeus duorarum*), the brown shrimp (*Farfantepenaeus aztecus*), and the white shrimp (*Litopenaeus setiferus*). Through the mid-1950s the shrimp catches reached a peak that resembled the initial boom of 1947, which lasted three years, and the fleet size reached a record number of 401 boats (taking in 7,260 tons) in 1957, with 75 more under construction in the state of Campeche (Leriche Guzmán 1995: 131). Prices for shrimp destined for the U.S. market increased 50 percent from 1954 to 1957, and the supply seemed inexhaustible.

Toward the end of that decade, though, overexploitation caused the catch to decline severely, and the Carmen market crashed. By 1960 only 3,000 tons of shrimp were landed. All signs pointed to the now-familiar cycle of peak and decline, "as if it were a repetition of the events that fatally repeat themselves ever since the 18th century in El Carmen that maintain its place in history as an export center" (ibid.). Local overexploitation, the resulting decrease in capture, a decrease in the price of shrimp, and production in other areas brought competition to Carmen. Part of the fleet dispersed to other waters.

Yet the industry worked its way back from the slump. Between 1966 and 1976 in the port of Carmen alone, the industrial shrimping, or *altura*, fleet increased from 268 to 405 boats (Melville 1984: 91), and the industry supported an extensive local infrastructure of twenty-two freezing and packing plants, four shipyards, a fishing school, and two biology stations (Justo Sierra 1998: 88). However, alarm bells should have been sounding as the catch did not grow commensurate with the size of the fleet: 6,700 tons in 1966; 8,800 tons in 1972; and 7,100 tons in 1976. At this time, no regulation such as an annual *veda* (closed season) was yet in effect, no limits were placed on the catch, and foreign fleets still encroached into the area. A decade earlier, boats would spend four to five days out at sea; now they had to spend twenty days out to make their catch. The fleet was getting bigger, and the capture was simply not registering proportional increases. The seeming abundance of the valuable oro con patas did not look limitless any longer, and it was becoming clear that the shrimp population was stressed.

In the 1970s, when the rest of Mexico and indeed the rest of the world was experiencing economic crisis, shrimping was one of the few activities that maintained not just its stability but also its prosperity during the most severe years of the crisis (Melville 1984: 89). Shrimping may have persevered, but it also was about to see its peak. Still, the peak of shrimp was far from the end of shrimping, although the industry did undergo some serious changes. The administrative structure of the industry was a façade: private investors who operated their vessels disguised as cooperatives ran the shrimp industry. Meanwhile, the government was heavily subsidizing the industry as one of Mexico's last productive export sectors.

Catches were strong, though few were prepared for the effects of the emergence of the oil industry in the Bay of Campeche. Initial exploration offshore produced the Ixtoc I disaster, which halted shrimp capture in the Bay of Campeche (Leriche Guzmán 1995: 143). The oil spill from June 1979 to March 1980—the result of a blowout due to the loss of pressure during the drilling of an exploratory well—closed Gulf coast fisheries for months and affected captures for at least two years. Fishers in the industrial and artisanal sectors along the Gulf from Yucatán to Tamaulipas and extending along the U.S. coast were affected despite the official stance of minimizing the effects of the spill.

One effect of the otherwise harmful oil spill was the revelation of the extent of Mexico's oil riches. Banking on this and other oil on shore in Tabasco and Veracruz, the administration of José López Portillo (1976–1982) chose the path of expansion rather than austerity. A result for Campeche's fisheries was the 1981 initiation of "deprivatization" of the shrimping fleet. The goal was to regain productivity and profitability in the fishing sector through cooperatization, or the "transfer of the fleet" back to the legitimate hands of the socios. To support this nationalization process, a state-run fisheries bank, Banpesca, was founded with a directive to provide loans to the socios. Other conditions for nationalizing the fleet remained less than ideal. The nation's economic situation was precarious, and the local situation of the newly nationalized shrimp fleet was equally so.

Although Mexico had finally gained control over shrimp as a national patrimonial resource, it did so perhaps too late. López Portillo nationalized the fishing fleet while carrying out a massive fiscal expansion that involved the purchase of private-sector firms across the industrial and manufacturing sectors and their conversion into enterprises. The administration, in theory, was attempting to expand the state's role in the economy, particularly in terms of production and employment. However, in practice, the strategy was unsustainable largely because it was based on deficit spending tied to the nation's number one asset: oil. Mexico's principal source of foreign exchange and income, oil, was in a serious slump. López Portillo's fiscal expansion and the associated national development project were contingent on the success of Mexico's oil in the global market. Prosperity would require high oil prices that simply were not forthcoming. The newly nationalized shrimp industry was thus born into Mexico's 1982 debt crisis.

Meanwhile, several other factors complicated nationalization of the shrimp fleet. First, socios of the cooperatives were ill-prepared to handle the administrative and bureaucratic burdens of managing the fleet. As Hernández Montejo points out, there was insufficient aid to support nationalization, and corrupt administrators acted with impunity (2007: 65). Second, the loans taken out by the cooperatized fleet from Banpesca seriously indebted the new ventures—ironically, to private capital investors. The goal of López Portillo's nationalization plan was to reassert the true cooperatization of the fleets that had been de facto privateers operating under the guise of cooperatives. Now they were truly cooperatives but caught once again in the clutches of the private sector. Third, the volume of shrimp production was headed in the wrong direction. Just a decade later, by 1992, the fleet was reprivatized subsequent to constitutional amendments to Article 27, and the catch has significantly declined since that moment.

Perhaps the key to the equitable exploitation of the Gulf's shrimp fishery was to maintain it within the commons. But a major reversal of years of shrimp fisheries management policy came with the withdrawal of the cooperatives' historic rights in the 1992 fisheries law and their replacement with a system of permits and concessions. Since 1992, private-sector entrepreneurs have been officially permitted to purchase and use the boats and equipment belonging to the debt-ridden cooperatives. Banpesca, the public-sector fisheries support bank, was shut down. Additionally, a system of standards was put in place by the state—the Mexican official standards (NOMs)—to define and regulate the permits and concessions for different fisheries, gear specifications, seasonal closures and prohibitions, quotas, and so forth. The 1992 reform "provided a clear signal to private investors" that the national patrimony was no longer the commons (Thorpe, Aguilar Ibarra, and Reid 2000: 1693). As a privatized commodity, fisheries including shrimp were threatened with being converted into just another extractable and alienable resource like palo de tinte or chicle. Campechanos, who once worked as hired laborers in extracting the patrimonial resources of their land, would now work the sea in just the same way.

The period of reprivatization marks a decline and even collapse in the shrimping industry. Between 1988 and 1998, the shrimp catch decreased by 60 percent, from 4,388 to 1,708 tons. That decrease represented a 59 percent loss in income for Campeche's fishing sector (Campeche 2004). After reprivatization, the robust fleet began to shrink and with it the whole industrial fishing sector, as Vásquez León and McGuire describe: "Active trawler fleet size was reduced to some 40 percent of its level during the 1980s. Cooperatives have closed, their boats repossessed by private banks and sold, frequently well below value, to private investors" (1993: 59). The drop in production and reconfiguration of the industry led to a demise in employment and output of fisheries-related industries—boatyards, processing plants, and outfitters (ibid.).

Neoliberal economic reform in Mexico in the 1990s clearly privileged private interests over cooperatives in the fishing sector. But the strategy was not successful in terms of maintaining a robust commercial shrimping industry. Several factors combined to create an insurmountable pressure on Gulf shrimping—overcapitalization, an increasing deregulation of offshore fishing regulations, and the introduction of new harvesting technologies that increased captures—leading to overexploitation (ibid.). Once again, the state had to intervene. Since the early 2000s, state and federal programs have oscillated between subsidizing the weakened industry and trying to buy out shrimpers, decommissioning older vessels, and thereby reducing the fleet.[3]

Shrimp trawlers continue to bring in pink and white shrimp from the Gulf, and other fishing boats catch finfish such as grouper, sea bass, red snapper, mullet, and mackerel in the Bay of Campeche. The fleet is much diminished, however, and the season is very short. Now, only 17 boats make up the port of Carmen's resident commercial shrimp fleet. For the whole of the state of Campeche, the commercial fleet stood at around

350 boats but shrank rapidly to only 107 shrimping boats in the 2010 season. Due to the Deepwater Horizon oil spill, this shrunken fleet was expected at the start of the season to gain strong sales to the United States, the state's primary market. But in spring 2010 the trade relationship was severely jeopardized because Mexico lost its certification to export wild-harvested shrimp to the United States because of its failure to comply with the use of turtle-excluder devices on shrimp trawlers. Mexico was recertified by inspectors by the end of the 2010 *veda*. For the 2010 season the state of Campeche sent 1,500 tons of shrimp to the United States valued at about 350 million pesos (García Mendez 2010). In 2009, half of the 2,800 tons was sent to the United States.

The peak of shrimp came just in time to usher the age of petroleum into the Campeche Sound. The severe decline not only in the shrimp fishery but across all catches, however, has been linked to a multiplicity of factors, the activities of Pemex only one among them. Even with the growing clash of the pesquera and the petrolera, Campeche and especially the Laguna de Términos continue trying to maintain what is still the most important Gulf fishery and indeed one of Mexico's important national catches. Today, shrimp remains the most valuable fishery in the Bay of Campeche. Alongside Campeche's industrial fishing force, workaday artisanal fishers pull in their own hauls of robalo, pámpano, guachinango, jurel, and shrimp, too, trying to make a living in the post-peak environment.

### Pescadores Ribereños, Artisanal Fishing

Commercial shrimping is far from the whole story of fishing in the Laguna de Términos region. The realization of a commercially viable shrimp fishery in Campeche's waters in the 1940s precipitated a new distinction among fishers in the region: *pescadores de altura*, who work on the commercial shrimping boats, and *pescadores ribereños*, the small-scale fishers who use artisanal tools and techniques for subsistence and commercial fishing. The Puente de la Unidad, the bridge connecting Isla Aguada to the island of Carmen at Puerto Real, is a structure approximately 1,000 feet long completed in 1984 that joins two pieces of land and divides two bodies of water. To the north of the bridge is the Bay of Campeche (part of the Gulf of Mexico), and to the south is the Laguna de Términos. Largely since the commercialization of the fishing industry with the discovery of shrimp, these two bodies of water

Fishers prepare nets to catch fish for bait at the foot of the Puente de la Unidad.
Photograph by author.

have evolved into distinct territories. Each has its own master. Due to the arts and techniques of fishing, the ribereños held more sway over the lagoon. The ribereño fishers travel short distances using small fiberglass lanchas that were equipped with outboard motors in the 1970s. Even after motorizing the lanchas, the ribereños cannot comfortably travel very far into Gulf waters. Thus the Gulf waters are the realm of pescadores de altura, leaving the lagoon to their artisanal colleagues.

The Puente de la Unidad divides the territories of the Gulf and the lagoon, which historically defined the areas of the two categories of fishers. Given the severely declining captures, however, the lagoon was declared a reserve for shrimp in 1974 and closed to fishing. The total fishing prohibition in the lagoon, designed to protect the adult shrimp fishery in the Gulf, had a disproportionate impact on the ribereño fishers, as they once made their livelihoods from lagoon and coastal fishing. In the early decades of shrimping, artisanal fishers could catch reasonable quantities along with their usual variety catch including abalone, oyster, squid, octopus, conch, sea urchin, crab, and various finfish.[4] The complete closure of the lagoon significantly restricted their fishing grounds. The ribereños' small boats could not make the long trips and handle the nets and large hauls of the industrial shrimping operators.[5]

Today, the small-scale and artisanal pescadores ribereños number around 200,000 nationally. Ribereños contribute 35 percent of national fishing production and 46 percent of its value (Sagarpa 2005). They constitute the backbone of local and regional economies in fishing zones across Mexico. While the altura fleet in Campeche has seriously declined after the shrimping peak in the 1980s, the ribereño fleet has undergone a concomitant increase. The industrial fleet declined from 605 ships in 1982 to 334 in 1998 (of which only 269 were active). The artisanal fleet increased considerably in the same period, from 1,144 boats in 1982 to 4,402 in 1998 (Ramos-Miranda, Flores-Hernández, and Do Chi 2009: 4). The Mexican state encouraged the growth of the fleet through loans and subsidies in various forms: subsidies for fuel, credits for equipment, and aid to fishers' unions and cooperatives. One contributor to the benefits programs is Pemex. The dependence of fishers on these programs in the era of declining captures is a major symptom of Campeche's post-peak condition.

In Campeche the official number of state-registered and credentialed ribereño fishers is just under 12,000, with approximately one-third of the state's credentialed fishers operating in the municipality of Carmen. The size of the ribereño fleet currently is not easy to estimate. This is in part because it is difficult to know how many of the boats are actually fishing. But there are many more fishers than boats because it is becoming more financially difficult for fishers to own, operate, and maintain their own boats. Although the fishers themselves might move between fleets, the equipment, techniques, and markets utilized in the two fleets are quite different. The ribereños use artisanal rather than industrial methods of capture with tools such as hand-cast nets, short harpoons, and traps, and they bring in much smaller catches than industrial fleets. The ribereño fishers first began participating in commercial fish markets alongside their industrial counterparts through the exploitation of shrimp in the Laguna de Términos and along the coast. Now the ribereño fleet exploits the limited coastal shrimp and a range of other species of finfish (collectively known as *escama*) for commercial purposes. It is important to remember that the "ribereño" distinction does not exclude these fishers from market aspects of the fishing industry: most are small-scale commercial fishers. However, ribereños do also continue to exploit local fisheries on a small-scale basis for subsistence catches.

When shrimp fisheries began to experience exploitation pressures in the late 1960s to early 1970s, artisanal fishers were blamed. While the altura fleet out of the port of Carmen found success with the oro con patas in deeper Gulf waters, a newly transformed, more competitive artisanal fleet was developing to take advantage of the lucrative catch. Modern technology transformed wooden lanchas to fiberglass, and the boats were equipped with outboard motors in the 1970s. The more efficient artisanal shrimpers became known as the *chaquiste* (mosquito) fleet, as they operated their smaller-scale competitive shrimping work inside the Laguna de Términos and along the Gulf shorelines. It was not long before the ecological strain of overexploitation on the balance of the fishery became apparent.

The shrimp fishery in the Laguna de Términos region is especially vulnerable to overexploitation as a "sequential fishery," meaning that juvenile shrimp are likely to be caught by artisanal fishers in the lagoon itself while mature shrimp at breeding age are caught by the pescadores de altura out in Gulf waters. Catches made by the artisanal sector affect those of the industrial sector and vice versa. Sequential exploitation leads to overexploitation of stock itself (Díaz de León et al. 2004: 458). Because the ribereño fishers concentrated their efforts on the lagoon and coastal waters, they were assigned the blame for overexploitation of the fishery.

In 1974 a fishing ban was placed on the waters of the Laguna de Términos. The exploitation of immature shrimp by the artisanal fleet was prohibited through the federal powers vested in the Ley Federal para el Fomento de la Pesca. An accord was struck that declared shrimp a public resource of the nation and that it was necessary to conserve and protect the resource in the interest of the national economy. Recognizing that too many fish were being caught below commercially viable size (in fine-meshed nets, some with holes less than one inch), the 1973 accord established a regulatory scheme for net sizes to establish the lagoon as a reproductive area, a nursery where fish are born and can grow. The new regulations called for the use of nets with minimum openings of three inches so only mature shrimp would be caught and the reproductive waters would be protected (*Diario Oficial* 1974a,b).

After the Laguna de Términos shrimping prohibition went into effect, some artisanal fishers were cooperatized into commercial fishing on the trawler fleet based in Carmen. The fleet continued to grow through the 1970s. Despite the prohibitions in the lagoon, fishers did continue to shrimp in its waters. Sometimes the shrimp capture appeared unintentional. Roberto Rodríguez C. (1984: 30) recounts the story of one Aguadeño who began fishing with nets made of nylon monofilament introduced into the market in the late 1970s. Ostensibly using nets to fish for the legal, sustainable capture of three-year-old (mature) finfish, this ribereño ended up with more than 650 pounds of shrimp in his net through "incidental capture." However, it is also well known that illegal fishing, *pesca furtiva*, has taken place for decades inside the lagoon. It is estimated that more than 20 percent of the annual national shrimp catch comes from artisanal shrimping, but much of this occurs below the radar of official activity (Aguilar and Grande-Vidal 2008).

Evidence shows that commercial exploitation is not the only stressor on the region's fisheries. The artisanal fleet has especially exploited one particular shrimp species that prefers to make its home close to shore from the Peninsula of Atasta to Ciudad del Carmen, in traditional ribereño territory: the *siete barbas* (*Xiphopenaeus kroyeri*). A ten-year evaluation (1994–2004) of the siete barbas shrimp fishery demonstrated that the levels of the catch were too high and that the resource exploitation was at its maximum capacity (Wakida Kusunoki, Amador del Angel, and Santos Valencia n.d.). The researchers attributed this to a combination of two factors: too large an artisanal fleet that was fishing over too large an area. In the winter of 2009, constant cold fronts limited the ribereños in their search for siete barbas shrimp to approximately one week of fishing for every month of the short open season. By the end of the October 1–May 1 season, the catch was much lower than in the previous year, not because of stress on the resource but due to the weather; 10 percent of normal fishing days were lost to the closure of ports in inclement weather (*Tribuna Campeche* 2009d).

Though much attention is paid to the shrimp catch because of its high value and contribution to the national catch, the region has other important fisheries. Ribereños are responsible for several fisheries, all of which are experiencing declines. *Pulpo*, or octopus, is one of Campeche's most active and important fisheries for the ribereño sector. More than 90 percent of the nation's pulpo comes from the Gulf coast of the Yucatán Peninsula, and approximately 15,000 people are employed directly or indirectly in the seasonal pulpo capture along the Campeche coast. To regulate the catch, the state awards around 1,500 licenses for two-person boats to participate in the octopus catch in the shallow Gulf waters mostly to the north of the Laguna de Términos. These fishers are mostly from Champotón, Seybaplaya, Sabancuy, and Isla Arena. The residents of Isla Aguada do not participate to a large extent in octopus fishing. A portion of the catch is reserved for local markets, where it is popular, but most of it is sent to international markets such as Spain, Italy, and Japan. In 2007, the most recent year with an above-average yield, eight and a half of the nearly twelve tons caught went to these international destinations (*Por Esto* 2010).

Many Campechanos pin a lot of their income hopes on the pulpo season that opens annually on August 1 and lasts until December 15. A single pulpo fishing expedition can cost around 700 pesos in fuel, and there are times when boats return empty. It is difficult to catch enough to make it worth the trip when pulpo is selling at only $1.55 a pound. During the course of a season, a fisher may invest an average of up to $530 in the capture of pulpo. Even with such an outlay of funds, Sagarpa insists that pulpo fishing is still profitable, and it remains one of the fisheries that keeps ribereño fishing alive in Campeche. One reason for the profitability of the pulpo trade is the far-reaching appeal of the catch. Octopus-fisher cooperatives on the peninsula's Gulf coast participate in Mexico's global trade agreements that send octopus to Europe and Asia.

With a catch of 5,439 tons in the 2008 season, the average earnings for the 7,000 families involved in octopus fishing were 22,000 pesos, about $1,672 (*Tribuna Campeche* 2008c). The following year was a different story. Before the end of the summer 2009 season, officials were already able to estimate that the catch was dangerously below average. *Pulperos* (octopus fishers) had brought in only 806,709 pounds of product, valued at $661,275, a 57 percent decrease in volume and 63 percent decrease in value compared with the 2008 season. The final figure for the 2009 season (3,840 tons) represented a 33 percent decrease and made this the worst pulpo season in eleven years (*El Universal* 2009).

Often, a low catch is blamed on a broader environmental crisis. While it is widely known that pulpo is the target of a great deal of poaching, there are more complex reasons based on the balance of the regional ecosystem. The balance of marine ecology is very delicate, and some authorities blame the overfishing of *pepino del mar*, or sea cucumber, upon which octopus feed. Sagarpa officials also have looked to blame out-of-season capture of pulpo, such as during vulnerable times of the reproductive cycle. They stepped up their vigilance and even caught sea-urchin poachers with several tons of illegal capture during the winter of 2009. Perhaps these conditions continued, or other reasons for the decline were at play. In any case, only a week into the 2010 season, Conapesca officials estimated that the catch would be only half of the paltry 2009 catch. Various aid programs for the pulperos were introduced. To mitigate the decline in volume, prices were artificially set at 70 percent above those of the previous year. To offset capital investment, fuel sub-

sidies were awarded, and more fishers were integrated into a motor upgrade program. To begin the 2010 pulpo season, the outboard motors
of eighty-four lanchas were upgraded from the inefficient and polluting two-stroke motors to four-stroke motors at no cost to the owners.
But as a large number of the state's ribereños depend on the seasonal
pulpo catch for the bulk of their yearly incomes, more measures would
be needed. As Campeche's fisheries succumb in turn to declines, disillu-
sioned fishermen predict that ribereño fishing will soon disappear.

## Post-Peak Fishing

The normally threatening and unpleasant winds of a late-autumn storm
known as a *norte* sometimes stir up a surprise in the Gulf's waters. One
November dawn, for residents of the San Nicolás and Tierra y Liber-
tad neighborhoods in Ciudad del Carmen, it was loads of siete barbas
shrimp carried to a distance of only thirty feet from shore. At dawn,
with waves and riptides providing no obstacle, the shrimp gatherers collected up to twenty pounds each using the artisanal nets known as *pa-
ños de arrastre*. Such stories of plenty are getting to be fewer and farther
between in a coastal landscape that looks as if it should be abundant but
simply is not. Indeed, the decline in catches in the Laguna de Términos
region is part of a global phenomenon. Shrimp fishing worldwide is under pressure and is also increasingly under the scrutiny of global governing bodies. According to a study prepared by the United Nations
Food and Agriculture Organization (FAO), problems for the shrimp
fisheries across the globe include overexploitation; the catching of ju-
veniles of species that are both ecologically important and economically valuable; the degradation of coastal habitat; illegal trawling; the
destruction of ocean beds; and, on the social front, conflicts between
artisanal and industrial fisheries (Gillet 2008). Mexico's Gulf coast fisheries increasingly suffer from many of these intersecting and overlapping issues. The result is that Gulf fishers are experiencing the same
generalized effects of pressure and deterioration that their counterparts
across the country and even the globe are facing in the contemporary
moment. In Mexico more than 80 percent of fisheries are already fully
exploited or are overexploited (Hernández and Kempton 2004: 524).
Ribereño fishers now find themselves in a post-peak condition. Fishers in Isla Aguada cite three major challenges of the contemporary conundrum: contamination of the waters of the Gulf and the Laguna de

Fishers haul fuel from the *bodega* to their lancha along Isla Aguada's waterfront. Photograph by author.

Términos, the ever-increasing prohibitions of seasonal closures known as vedas, and the ever-widening restrictions on fishing grounds due to Pemex offshore operations.

## Contamination

Shrimp became Mexico's most important fishery in the early 1980s. At the very same time that shrimp production peaked for fishers in the Laguna de Términos, Pemex's production activities began to intensify in the Campeche Sound. Fishers associate early shrimp declines with the Ixtoc I oil spill. Following the blowout, oil "mousse" washed up on beaches along with dead marine life, from fish to sea turtles and dolphins. The smell of the oil fire burning on the sea's surface for weeks on end reached Campeche's shores. Some residents were sure that it was the fouled air—as much as the polluted water—that irrevocably harmed the Laguna de Términos. The coincidence between the oil spill and the initiation of the decline in fisheries was too strong for many to ignore. It seemed that after the blowout and the nine-month-long spill, nothing was the same again.[6]

The extent of the effects on the multiple Gulf and lagoon fisheries of millions of barrels spilling into the Bay of Campeche for more than nine months during the Ixtoc I blowout are not well documented. Nor is the overall effect of thirty years of oil exploration and production in the Campeche Sound. Gold-Bouchot (2004) points out that the few studies done in Mexico show that oil activities can have detrimental effects on coastal organisms. For fishers, scientific studies are hardly necessary to chart the correlation between Pemex's offshore operations and their consequences on fish stocks. High hydrocarbon levels have been reported for the Laguna de Términos—higher than other regional lagoons—albeit without massive mortalities (Gold-Bouchot, Noreña-Barroso, and Zapata-Pérez 1995). Álvarez-Legorreta, Gold-Bouchot, and Zapata-Pérez (1994) reported very high hydrocarbon concentrations in clams (*Rangia cuneata* and *Polymesoda carolineana*) from the Laguna de Pom in Campeche. But the available information is not sufficient to allow the conclusion that the magnitude of the observed effects (decrease in fishery catches and other environmental degradation) often attributed to Pemex is a result of petroleum activities (Gold-Bouchot 2004: 419).

Though fishers believe it to be true and have what they consider irrefutable anecdotal evidence, contamination is nearly impossible to prove, according to Pemex's standards.[7] Because of the complexity of the watershed system, when found, contamination stems from several sources including agricultural runoff of insecticides and herbicides from farming and cattle ranching such as the historical intensive use of DDT and other pesticides in the region (Vásquez Botello et al. 2005), and parsing out the precise contribution of hydrocarbons on the decline in fisheries is a difficult task. Historically, Pemex has been negligent in either conducting or publishing environmental studies. Long-term studies that can detect changes in levels of pollutants are nonexistent, and what is more, monitoring programs are not in place to detect concentrations of contaminants along the coast (Gold-Bouchot 2004: 418). As comprehensive environmental impact studies are now emerging, they are not producing the results some have been expecting: a firm link between hydrocarbon exploitation and marine toxicity (ibid.).[8]

To the contrary, other researchers have found that oil activities can have harmful effects on coastal organisms even if their conclusions are not strong enough to scientifically prove the culpability of Pemex for the decline in fisheries due to ecological degradation. What studies do convincingly show is that hydrocarbons in the Gulf of Mexico and the Laguna de Términos exceed the safe standards set out by various regulatory agencies including the United Nations Educational, Scientific and Cultural Organization (UNESCO) standard set in 1976 and the U.S. Environmental Protection Agency (EPA) water quality standard (Ponce Vélez and Vásquez Botello 2005). The lagoon itself has undergone a process of fossil fuel contamination. The first recorded level of anthropogenically produced contamination in the lagoon was in 1982, with much higher levels recorded by researchers than acceptable by international standards—even though no hydrocarbon exploitation was going on in the lagoon itself but only in open seas at a distance of eighty kilometers, about fifty miles (279).

## Vedas, Seasonal Closures

Contamination is not the only cause of decline in capture cited by the fishers of Isla Aguada. The other causes require less scientific study and are more apparent on the surface: longer vedas (official closed seasons), more fishing days lost to closed ports, and higher operation costs due to high fuel prices and subsidy cutbacks are making it nearly impossible for fishing to be profitable. "It's just mathematics," one fisher explained the logic of fishing decline to me. He said his primary school education taught him everything he needed to know about why he can't make a livelihood from fishing under the current conditions. "The season is becoming shorter and shorter, while the daily catch is smaller and smaller," he said. Indeed, during the 2009 winter shrimping season, when the veda was lifted in February, a nightly catch might reach 150 kilos; by the time the closing date of April 30 was in sight, boats were pulling in only a fraction of that amount, between 30 and 50 kilos. It is difficult for a fisher to decide whether to risk life and limb—and boat—going out in bad weather during the high season. It is a catch-22 since the fishing season is also the season of poor weather, the season of nortes, when ports are frequently closed because of storms. But the risk is par for the course. "When you set out to fish," an Aguadeño explained to me, "you never know how long it will be. Maybe just a few hours, maybe all night. You don't wear a watch, and you never tell your wife when you'll be back."

Campeche's fisheries are managed through the mechanism of seasonal closures, which are used in fisheries management across the globe. The veda, imposed upon fisheries experiencing declining catches under provisions established in the federal Ley General de Pesca y Acuacultura Sustentables, is a method of exercising control over space through the management of time. The vedas are implemented and regulated by Sagarpa, and breaking a veda carries the penalty of fines and confiscation of catch. The imposition of vedas—suspension of fishing activities that might be for one month or might be permanent prohibitions—is the state's way of trying to regenerate depleted fisheries, protect the reproductive process, and maintain the commercial viability of the catch. The multiple vedas across the Gulf coastal region from Tamaulipas to the Yucatán Peninsula were designed to protect stocks during the most intense periods of reproduction. The goal of instituting closed seasons was to increase "recruits," the young among the exploitable stock. Tracking studies used by the federal government in establishing veda dates for the Campeche Sound demonstrate that the highest reproductive and growth activity occurs June through August. The recruits born during the first part of the veda (May) contribute 45 percent of the catch in the first half of the season. The rest of the season's catch is possible only because of the growth of the principal cohort of shrimp born in the first third of the year and protected by the veda (*Diario Oficial* 2010).

The use of closed seasons has been in effect in Mexican waters for decades for species conservation, for example, for shrimp spawning and growth. The monthlong, mandatory seasonal fishing prohibitions as we see them today went into effect for pescadores de altura only in the mid-1990s. Even though shrimp has the highest production value of all of the Gulf's fisheries, closing the season for six months of the year obviously restricts fishers' ability to make a living from it. Dates for vedas vary depending not only upon particular species' reproduction and growth cycles and region but also upon fleet. The ribereño fishers were greatly affected by the permanent veda imposed inside the Laguna de Términos in 1974, yet the coastal waters were still open to shrimping. However, beginning in 1993 the Campeche Sound had its first extensive shrimping veda.

Most closed seasons are consistent as to dates, but this can vary by as little as a day or two on either end to more than a week. Some vedas may be short. The veda for *mero* (grouper) lasts just one month in winter (February 1 to March 15); others may last more than half the year, such as those for the profitable pulpo (December 16 to July 31). Vedas and open seasons are regional. In Campeche, permission for catching some species of fish is open year-round, while it might be on prohibition elsewhere. *Robalo* (snook), for example, a popular year-round catch for fishers of Isla Aguada, is on veda at various times from May to August for Mexican states bordering the Gulf from Tamaulipas to Tabasco to Veracruz. A long veda dominates the yearly shrimping cycle for the Gulf fishery, and the Laguna de Términos is under a permanent shrimping prohibition. The normal parameters for the all-species shrimp veda are May 1 to October 31; the precise dates may fluctuate based on specific species, local region, weather or seasonal conditions, and even economic circumstances. The 2009 veda lasted from May 20 to October 31, covering the region from the mouth of the Río Coatzacoalcos in Veracruz to Mexico's Caribbean border with Belize—except for an open season for ribereño shrimping in coastal Campeche and Tabasco for one specific species: the siete barbas shrimp (closed season May 1 to September 30). Otherwise, for ribereño shrimpers around Isla Aguada, there are only the slimmest of pickings. A permanent veda exists within the Laguna de Términos and for the Gulf coastal zone from zero to fifteen miles seaward from Isla Aguada all the way to Mexico's border with Belize (*Diario Oficial* 2009).

Because the closed seasons vary by region, pescadores de altura from the ports of Carmen and Campeche seek and obtain licenses to fish other Gulf waters where the shrimping veda lifts sooner. The waters off Tamaulipas, for example, open in late summer, and in 2009 a thirty-five-day open season began there on August 15. Fishing the Tamaulipas waters would tide the shrimpers over until the end of the veda in the Campeche Sound. The altura fishers have more options; with their larger boats and crews they can leave the Bay of Campeche for other, more abundant waters. Yet even if altura fishers from Campeche manage to make good catches in Tamaulipas to supplement their local catches, the Carmen fishers have to live with knowing that the Tamaulipas fleet will also shrimp alongside them in the dwindling waters of the Campeche Sound when the open season rotates from one part of the Gulf to another. Julio Alejandro López Garcia, president of the Federación de Pescadores de Altura, Maricultura y Acuacultura, describes how the altura fishers have lost access to fishing in their patrimonial waters: "The legacy [*herencia*] that Pemex has left behind is that the fishers have to leave the Campeche Sound in search of better catches" (in *Tribuna Campeche* 2009g).

The biggest problem the Campeche fishers experience with the veda is not that their right to fish is infringed upon but rather that the institution of the veda appears arbitrary. While dates for the opening and closing of seasons are more or less regular, occasionally they will be altered by two weeks or more. The altering of dates is typically on the side of a delay in opening the capture season. State fishery officials cite studies of juvenile shrimp size (too small) as the reason for the delay. Yet the cooperatives complain that there is no scientific backing to the annual prohibitions. Shrimpers certainly understand that there is a serious decline in catches and agree that measures to protect the species and prevent overexploitation should be taken. Indeed, they feel this quite keenly. At the same time, fishers experience the veda as punitive rather than as a measure of sustainability. Fishers also perceive the 150-day annual vedas as inflexible. This is connected to the larger issue of marine resources management as a top-down enterprise in Mexico. Fishers often talk of this hierarchy in terms of its arbitrariness, insensitivity to local conditions, bureaucracy and red tape, partisan politics, and even corruption.

"Veda" has become synonymous with "hardship" as well as state intervention. And even though some argue that it may work against their own interests, there are fishers who put up some covert resistance against the vedas. It is widely known that vedas are broken and that some amount of illegal catch takes place. Illegal catch is defined as shrimping in the wrong place, at the wrong time, or by the wrong person. The history of illegal catches on the part of ribereño fishers goes back to the first prohibitions placed on shrimping within the Laguna de Términos itself. Roberto Rodríguez C. (1984) provides a detailed account of fishing in Isla Aguada and the surrounding area in the 1980s, when Laguna de Términos fisheries were still abundant yet already clearly endangered. At that time the ribereño fleet did some illegal fishing, and in some cases the poaching was quite deliberate: hauls of up to 100 kilos were trucked out, camouflaged underneath a legal catch, and shipped to market, often via the airport in Carmen. Often the Mexican practice of the *mordida* (bribe) would be employed to ensure that officials looked the other way. If a lancha was seized by authorities, fishers were usually pulling in enough money from illegal shrimping to cover the cost of another. If their contraband was ever discovered, it was always easy enough to recover the loss (29-30). Catches are not simply plentiful enough to carry out poaching on this scale today, even if fishers could get away with it.

Effective external policing systems are almost nonexistent, and the region relies on self-monitoring by its citizens. Recently, altura and ribereño fishing societies have been working in partnership with the authorities including the Mexican navy to slow the depletion of species during their closed seasons and to protect natural resources along the

Campeche coast. In 2009 the Frente Común Organizado de Pescadores Ribereños del Estado de Campeche (Frecoperic) and the Cámara Nacional de Industria Pesquera y Acuícola (Canainpesca) signed an accord with Conapesca to establish a special program of inspection and safeguarding and protection of marine resources according to the guidelines established by the fisheries law. This arrangement is unique to the state of Campeche. In another recent move, Sagarpa instituted a program aimed toward children in fishing communities to promote a culture of conservation in regard to certain marine species and to teach the children about the rules and regulations of seasonal vedas. As part of this awareness program, Sagarpa representatives visited schoolchildren in mostly rural ribereño communities and gave lectures, distributed posters, and provided a toll-free hotline number for reporting poaching (Méndez Romellón 2009).

Both alturas and ribereños experience extreme hardship due to the vedas. Because these last five months a year, the fishers have to find other work to eke out livelihoods. The difficulties are compounded by the problem of those who emerge from an unprofitable fishing season because of personal or family problems, bad weather, environmental problems such as oil spills, and high fuel prices. Villegas Sierra and Martínez Beberaje (2009) link the establishment of ribereño fishing organizations beginning in 1994 to the initiation of the veda in 1993. The collective response of the ribereños to the hardship of the vedas, especially of siete barbas shrimp, was to organize themselves into organizations known as *sociedades de solidaridad social* to fight the state-led deregulation of the fishing sector and the reforms of the *ley de pesca*. Their major organization, formed in Isla Aguada and other communities across the municipality, is the Unión de Pescadores de Ckiquixocoq. According to members of such organizations in Isla Aguada, it is thanks to the strength of their cooperative action that they were able to work on a local and regional level to gain access to state and federal aid programs. This union is made up of several hundred fishers from Isla Aguada under the leadership of Javier Aguillón Osorio. Originally from the state of Guerrero, Aguillón is a local fisher turned powerful politician who now plays the role of negotiator, spokesman, and intermediary with municipal, state, and Pemex officials on behalf of Isla Aguada.

In response to this activism the state government instituted the Programa de Veda y Baja Captura, the closed-season and low-capture aid program that makes payments to qualified and credentialed fishers during the summer months. Shrimp-factory and shrimp-boat workers have asked for similar aid, and even retirees from the trade have made their case for aid. The demands of these downstream workers and others for inclusion in the closed-season and low-capture aid program demonstrates just how many workers and families in Carmen and Campeche at large remain dependent on fishing, even as the industry moves into what looks to be its waning years.

Not all the fishers simply sit around during the veda and wait for aid money. After all, the closed season is very long, and the aid payments are hardly enough to live on or support a family. Therefore, during the veda up to 70 percent go to work in another sector, often in semiskilled or unskilled labor such as in construction. However, that kind of work is much likelier to be available in an urban area like Ciudad del Carmen than in a village more singularly dedicated to fishing, like Isla Aguada. During the shrimp veda in Isla Aguada, many pescadores continue to set out in their lanchas a few days a week during the low-catch season searching for fish such as *jurel* (jackfish), robalo, pargo, rubia, macabíl, mango, and siena. An off-season trip may last no more than three or four hours, taking a crew of two experienced fishers and a younger helper to fishing grounds seven miles or so from the Gulf shore. The typical haul is small, usually not more than about twenty pounds. A catch like this is a subsistence rather than commercial catch. Few, if any, of these fish will be sold outside of the fisher's own cohort. Traditionally, the fishers have had a system of gifting fish to each other, paying with fish for favors, and using fish for barter. With a small haul, it is more than likely that the fisher owes them all already.

## Territorial Restrictions

The prospect of more than 200 drilling platforms in the Campeche Sound did not automatically spell the end of fishing in the region's territorial waters. Instead, initially the areas surrounding the platforms were known to be particularly rich fishing grounds. Given that oil-platform structures attract fish in ocean waters, it might seem that their presence would be a boon for the fishing industry rather than a crutch. But as Pemex increased the amount of infrastructure in the northeast and southeast marine regions of the offshore development area, more and more fishing territory has been closed to fishing. Fishers claim that the territorial restriction around the platforms imposed by Pemex is the number one problem they experience in relation to the petroleum industry.

Under the guise of heightened security following the September 11, 2001, attacks in the United States, Mexico reterritorialized and militarized the Campeche Sound. The September 11, 2003, Acuerdo Intersecretarial 117 established a restricted area covering 6,100 square nautical miles around the Cantarell installations plus a smaller zone of 450 square nautical miles around the Dos Bocas terminal.[9] The restricted areas—a tight inner zone of exclusion and a wider zone of prevention—are patrolled under the military security operation known as Sonda III with missile ships, interceptor boats and aircraft, and Hawkeye helicopters. At 2,200 square nautical miles, the zone of exclusion is designed to "prevent transgressors of the law from carrying out acts of sabotage and terrorism that could cause partial or total damage to the strategic marine and terrestrial facilities involved in the extraction and refinement of hydrocarbons" (Martinez Tiburcio 2005: 5).

At the time of the establishment of Acuerdo 117, Pemex justified its terms by stating, "We must remember that we are a principal provider of hydrocarbons to the United States, a country under a terrorist threat since September 11, 2001 . . . Because we provide this type of service to the United States, we find ourselves put in a highly vulnerable position to such threats" (*Diario Oficial* 1998). Thus, Mexico's Gulf fishers were placed in the position of significant loss of catch in the name of Mexican national security—in the name of U.S. energy security. Like other laws and policies enacted in the post-9/11 climate, the zone of exclusion was enacted using heightened security concerns to justify the new territoriality in Mexico's national waters. However, measures to designate exclusive Pemex-only zones were already taken in 1998 (Arias Rodríguez and Ireta Guzmán 2009: 14). The decree prohibits non-petroleum-related boat traffic inside the designated zone within the Campeche Sound and establishes twenty-four-hour marine traffic surveillance at Cayo Arcas, the Pemex-controlled offshore shipping terminal (*Diario Oficial* 1998).

Given the presence of the exclusion zone and the militarized security regime, the fishers were put at risk of becoming poachers at best and de facto terrorists at worst on the nation's patrimonial sea. Pescadores ribereños and pescadores de altura alike perceive the restrictions as an abrogation of their resource rights to the sea as a commons. As citizens, they say they should have access to their traditional territorial waters, which are, in fact, coextensive with Mexican national territorial waters. They say they should subsequently have the right to benefit economically from resources that are defined as the patrimony of the nation. Nevertheless, should fishers enter an area restricted by Pemex, they risk being intercepted by the Mexican navy. The penalties they face include losing their catches, their licenses, and even their boats, a threat taken very seriously by Isla Aguada's fishers. Pemex has exclusive access to exploit hydrocarbons, but there is no area where fishers have exclusive and protected fishing grounds.

Meanwhile, the newly "secure" seas have become more dangerous to fishers in the Laguna de Términos region. In this area, known as a zone of passage for the narcotraficantes of the Gulf cartel, a fisher at sea in his lancha is vulnerable to threats, shake-downs, assaults, and even murder. Several fishers from Isla Aguada report having had their motors stolen off their boats while on the water inside the lagoon, leaving them stranded—and terrified. Others have been shot at while navigating their lanchas on the lagoon's far shores near the mouths of the Candelaria and Palizada Rivers. Outside of the militarized zone that guarantees the security of oil exploitation, the rest of the coastal area is freed up for trafficking as drugs are moved from South and Central America through the Yucatán Peninsula and then on to the United States.

## Social Transformations

The decline in fishing and concomitant reterritorialization of the Gulf is paralleled by a shift in social relations within fishing communities on Mexico's coast. This transformation has accelerated in pace and intensity with the rise of oil production in the Campeche Sound and is found in the organization of labor. As soon as avenues to commercial markets were opened in the mid-twentieth century, most fishers in the Laguna de Términos region ceased to work as autonomous, self-employed individuals. While the system of cooperative organization in the industrialized, or altura, sector of the shrimp fishery was legally dismantled, it technically persists in the ribereño (artisanal) sector. However, it has changed over time.

As Hernandéz and Kempton describe (2003), cooperatives have a unionlike structure in which individual small-scale fishers get together to obtain credits and governmental subsidies and to protect monetary and labor rights. Frequently fishers in cooperatives are the owners of their own gear and boats, and most of them get variable but generally low incomes from fishing. The ideal of communal operation was what fishers had in mind when they first began to pursue the cooperative model in Isla Aguada. Don Oscar was a principal organizer of one of the biggest and most important cooperatives in Isla Aguada in the early 1970s, born out of the need perceived locally by him and his cohort of fishers. At that time, the Aguadeños were being taken advantage of by *coyotes*, or buyers from out of town. The coyotes used the situation of Aguadeño fishers as small, noncapitalized, independent producers with no access to markets. This is an especially delicate situation for fresh fish and shellfish, when ice, refrigeration, and rapid, reliable transportation are of utmost importance. Through their cooperative, the fishers would have sufficient product and power to represent their own interests. Once established, the Isla Aguada–based cooperative was self-sufficient and able to represent its own product and its own interests to external, even far-flung commercial markets. One of the cooperative members himself drove the catch in a truck to market in Mexico City.

It soon happened that multiple and competing cooperatives flourished in Isla Aguada. The traditional cooperative system functioned in Isla Aguada through the 1980s. The main feature of the system was the façade of a personalistic relationship covering the transactional relations of bringing the catch to market. Membership in a cooperative has benefits for its socios. Beyond having a buyer for a socio's catch and a provider of fuel, the cooperative offers benefits known as *préstamos*, bonuses or favors. While these might be strictly work-related, such as resources for fuel and boat maintenance, they extend to helping a sick fisher or family member get transportation to the doctor and pay medical bills, put food on the table for a holiday meal, or advance cash for a needy family's special circumstances.

### Phantom Cooperatives

The old cooperative system had its drawbacks. The prices offered by cooperatives were fixed and controlled, and a high percentage of the price stayed with the cooperative and not with the individual. Some fishers, even some socios, admit to seeing the cooperatives as too powerful. The préstamos, which the socios came to expect and indeed rely upon, were often available only in high season or when the catch was good. And as fishing declined, so did the social benefits of cooperative membership. Today, fishers in Isla Aguada report that the cooperative system no longer exists and has been replaced by *bodegas*, or "minicompanies." Or rather, the cooperatives continue in a modified way, working in conjunction with bodegas. The modified system reduces the social security function of the cooperative system and maintains the business tie of the fisher to the buyer. In other words, the practice of préstamos has become abstracted from the relationship. The fishers are no longer socios but simply workers, or *bodegueros*. Technically, the bodegas are still cooperatives, but in the words of one fisher, they are, in effect, "phantom cooperatives" that only appear to be cooperatives. In other words, like the previous system in the mid-twentieth century shrimping industry, they are only smoke and mirrors. For the workaday fishers, they do not fulfill the proper social functions of a cooperative, emphasizing instead the transactional relationship between fisher and buyer. "They'd let you die of hunger," said one fisher bitterly.

The current bodega system is explicitly an economic system. At the core of the transactional tie between the bodega and the fisher are the high costs of capture and distribution. A primary economic preoccupation is fuel. Every trip a fisher takes is calculated according to fuel expenditure, and every catch is measured against how much fuel it requires, in other words, the fisher's return on investment. The bodega buys fuel for the lancha, and a fisherman thus indebted sells his catch back to the bodega at lower than market price.[10] The bodega helps the fisher maintain a lancha and fishing gear, especially nets, a costly undertaking. Once a catch is brought in, the bodega provides the physical space for freezing and storage, and it also connects to buyers. Cooperatives have a social function, too, acting as a safety net for the fishers in a community poorly served by federal, state, or municipal agencies. Furthermore, when it comes to bargaining for and receiving government aid or Pemex donations, cooperatives represent the interests of fishers on the local and municipal levels.

The bodega system is, obviously, hardly without its flaws. From the point of view of the fishers, bodega owners are getting rich off the fishers' labor. The heads of the cooperatives, supposedly fishers themselves (they do collect fishing aid checks, as we will see later), no longer bother to go out in their lanchas to fish. The head of one of the bodegas in Isla Aguada drives a new, American-import truck, has a bigger and nicer home, owns several businesses in town, and generally seems to be thriving while others are struggling to get by on the low fixed prices for declining catches. The bodega owners claim that they are in dire straits, too. They worry that business is so bad they find themselves in the past few years operating in *números rojos*, in the red.

From the perspective of a bodega owner, the fishers have no other option to sell their catches under the current system. One bodega owner reported to me that he saw his role as providing a social service to the fishers. Another explained the current bodega system in terms of its natural, historical evolution from the former cooperative system. Delfin, a bodega owner from Progreso, Yucatán, has lived in Isla Aguada for twenty years. He arrived with nothing, starting out as a fisherman and working his way up. From his point of view, he works diligently to comply with the standards the state authorities set out. Because of its historical affinity with the previous system and the categories set by the government, he said his bodega is indeed a cooperative—in the legal sense, that is. He showed me a thick, somewhat ragged folder with every last document he has carefully filled out, signed, stamped, and notarized for his business. At every place where the name of his bodega appears it is followed by "SCPP: Sociedades Cooperativas de Producción Pesquera." He turned to me and said, "Now, how can they say there are no cooperatives? It says so right here!" This is an example of what many of the fishers are calling a phantom cooperative.

While most fishers are caught in the cooperative/bodega system, Isla Aguada also has a small number of *pescadores libres*, free or independent fishers. However, these fishers regularly sell their catches to specific bodegas. There is no other market except standing on the highway hawking the fresh catch dangling on a rope. Free fishers share the following characteristics: they own lanchas, they buy their own fuel, and they negotiate their own prices for their catch. But recently one problem the free fishers of Isla Aguada have been facing (as have some of those associated with the bodegas) is that the bodega owners dominate possession of the limited number of fishing licenses for many species. Thus, Pacífico, a seemingly successful longtime pescador libre in Isla Aguada, finds himself outside the network of access to fishing licenses. This should not be allowed to happen, as one person is allowed only a certain number of *permisos*. But according to local accounts, bodega owners register permisos in the names of their friends and family members who are not even fishers. Because of his problem in accessing permisos, the free fisher could easily become an illegal fisher. By being outside this system of patronage that masquerades as a system of social solidarity, the pescador libre risks running up against the law. By the same token, if a bodeguero wanted to end his ties with the bodega, he would be in that position as well.

The problem of licensing is magnified on a larger scale throughout the region. Sagarpa estimates that among the ribereño fleet, only 30 percent of the fishers hold permisos for escama, while an overwhelming 70 percent hold only shrimping licenses (*Tribuna Campeche*

2009d). This means that during the long closed seasons, 70 percent of the pescadores ribereños are not legally permitted to take out their lanchas in search of commercial catch. The problem of the scarcity of permisos stems from the overexploitation of fisheries; Sagarpa and environmental authorities are loath to issue more permits for capture. The problem of access to the permisos, though, is rooted in the complex micropolitics within the fishing communities. Holding permisos means holding livelihoods, however tenuous, in one's hands.

Exacerbating the problem of access to licenses is the age-old problem of access to markets. Local markets are not consistently good outlets for ribereño fishers, especially in times of economic downturn such as began in 2008; local markets merely reflect consumers' pinched pocketbooks. Ciudad del Carmen's wharfside Alonso Felipe de Andrade municipal market ought to be an ideal outlet for local fishermen to sell their catch. Here dozens of sellers offer a variety of fresh seafood—camarón (shrimp), pargo (snapper), cazón (dogfish), ostión (oyster), caracol (conch), pejelagarto (freshwater gar), jaiba (crab), and huachinango (red snapper). Prices range from $1.55 per pound for the common mojarra (tilapia) to around $2.73 per pound for pámpano (pompano). But the public perceives the prices as high compared with supermarkets; the freshness of the market offerings compared to frozen fare in the supermarket does not seem to matter. With far from steady sales, it is mostly famine for the fishmongers. The only sure sales are during Lent, when the local Catholic population eats fish as part of religious custom. Things only became worse at a moment when the market should perhaps have looked up, during the swine flu crisis. Fish might then have seemed a good alternative to put on local tables, as many refused to purchase pork, erroneously believing that pig meat carried disease. But fish sales continued their slump through the ongoing economic crisis.

Occasionally fishers can bypass the market system that seems otherwise stacked against them, and "free fishing" happens on the bodega's watch. An occasional fishing trip may yield a small catch that will be divided up among friends or family members rather than sold back to the bodega. The sharing of a small catch—just enough for a family meal or a casual roadside sale—is usually ignored by the bodega owners. On a hot summer day during the shrimp veda, a lancha arrived on the beach at an odd time. The two fishermen, whom I knew to be bodegueros, just in with their catch, threw the sparkling fish up on top of the seawall lining the malecón. Yet again, they rehearsed the names with me, but I faltered. "What's the skinny one? A big sardine?" I asked. "No, a *macabil*," he corrected. I wrote it down. Passing over the unfamiliar (unattractive, piranha-like) fish, I chose a safe-looking, medium-size robalo for my dinner. A yellow plastic rope was strung through its gaping mouth for me to carry, dangling, back home. While the price was negotiated for my fish (about $4.50 for the three-pound fish), a group of five men who had been lingering across the road in the shade approached and had a few words with the incoming fishers. In a flash, two of them took off with a fish each for their families' tables, and two others left the remaining catch strung up on another yellow rope, no doubt destined for hawking on the side of the highway.

### The Aquaculture Alternative

Looking to the future, it seems that no amount of compensation or subsidy will ever make traditional fishing profitable, at least not in the foreseeable future. And what is more, it is impossible to predict for how much longer Pemex's commitment to funding aid programs will continue, given the declining nature of the oil supply in the Bay of Campeche. Rather than continuing to expend funds on nonrenewable fuel, the state has set aside resources for the purchase of land to be used in aquaculture projects through the Fideicomiso del Fondo de Reconversión Pesquera del Golfo de México (Fifopesca), established in 2004 following regionwide protests of the zone of exclusion.

Most of the Fifopesca funds are dedicated to aquaculture, which is increasingly touted as the alternative for traditional producers in the era of global fishery declines. Indeed, aquaculture is the global alternative to the worldwide decline in fisheries. According to FAO statistics, between 1996 and 2006 growth in farmed fish amounted to five times greater volume produced worth seven times more value worldwide. Farmed fish began to contribute to Mexico's national fisheries production in a modest way in the mid-1980s, but the real impact of aquaculture and mariculture began to emerge in Mexico's national marketplace after 2000. According to Sagarpa statistics (in *Informador* 2008), aquaculture grew nationally at an average annual rate of 4.1 percent from 2001 through 2008. Shrimp cultivation represented 42 percent of Mexico's aquacultural production, with an average annual production of 75,000 tons.

In the first years, it was found that the reconversion funds for aquaculture were not in fact going to those fishers most affected by the zone of exclusion, and Fifopesca failed to make a great impact in Campeche at the outset (Arias Rodríguez and Ireta Guzmán 2009: 22). This follows the general trend in Campeche, where aquaculture has been slow to develop. The state fishing agency, Sepesca, began in earnest only since about 2005 to fund fish-farming projects under a state program, the Fishing Conversion Fund, by offering grants for *proyectos productivos*, projects alternative to traditional fishing. The aquaculture alternative is not based on a substitution of farmed shrimp for wild-caught shrimp. Other parts of Mexico are already quite strong and well-established cultivators of shrimp, for example, the northern state of Sonora on the Gulf of California. Although some shrimp projects have been initiated, aquaculture in the Laguna de Términos region overwhelmingly favors the cultivation of tilapia. The tilapia production is geared toward both local and export markets. Tilapia is attractive because these robust, tolerant omnivores are flexible and compliant in a variety of conditions (Hartley-Alcocer 2007: 17). Tilapia is produced by farming throughout Mexico and represents the nation's third-largest fish product; it is the main freshwater species catch by weight. Sepesca has worked as a development agency across the country giving loans to communities for aquaculture projects, and government tilapia hatcheries supply young tilapia (fry and fingerlings) to small producers, ejidos, and cooperatives (Fitzsimmons 2000: 181).

Most of the demand for tilapia is in domestic markets. Up to forty tons of tilapia were raised for local and regional markets in 2006. Production is organized in associations through which funds for proyectos productivos are requested. One of the problems experienced acutely in the realm of aquaculture is lack of knowledge and training; the costs of start-up are high, and many small proyectos productivos fail early. A few across the region have been successful, among them members of the Asociación de Acuacultores de la Península de Atasta. In small groups the fish farmers had trouble with their tilapia production, but after affiliating seven cooperatives into an association with more than 150 people operating forty tanks, their production skyrocketed to thirty-one tons twice yearly by 2009.

The state and the private sector consider Campeche an ideal location for the development of an intensive aquaculture industry. For unemployed ribereños who seemingly have nothing to lose, aquaculture is presented as a viable alternative in the form of subsidized government programs. The position of Canainpesca, the private-sector fishing chamber of commerce, is that *acuacultura* is a "salvation" for Campeche's fishers, the only real option for the future, given that shrimp production stopped being profitable a long time ago (*Tribuna Campeche* 2009a).

Aquaculture does pose some very real risks, however, making it far from a salvation in the eyes of environmentalists, among others. It has little regulation and few established guidelines. In a delicate hydrological ecosystem, fish farming can be a destructive and even devastating undertaking. Since the fish are nonnative, environmentalists consider them an invasive species that upsets the ecological balance in the Laguna de Términos watershed. Tilapia are mostly cultivated in raised pools lined with geomembrane, nonporous polymer sheets designed to prevent seepage from the aquaculture ponds into the ground, but this is not always effective protection. Therefore, given the shape of the state's endeavors thus far, environmentalists in the Laguna de Términos region are distinctly critical of current aquaculture projects.

The fishers themselves have given it a mixed reception. Leaders of the Unión de Sociedades de Pescadores Ribereños of the municipality of Carmen are pushing Pemex, Campeche, and the federal agencies to further finance aquaculture and mariculture projects. While the fishers I talked with in Isla Aguada said aquaculture is a good idea, they did not necessarily see fish-farming projects in their own immediate futures. The Fifopesca reconversion rationale tells them, "Para lo que obtienen en el mar lo puedan obtener en tierra" (For what you can obtain in the sea you can get on land) (Arias Rodríguez and Ireta Guzmán 2009: 26). The desire to be a fish farmer does not exist strongly among the pescadores ribereños of Isla Aguada.

Municipal officials agree that Isla Aguada is not the most conducive location for aquaculture projects. The official reason is the extremely limited amount of available land in the community. The unofficial reason is that no one has the energy to get caught up in what some perceive as an underfunded, state-sponsored, Potemkin fish tank. After all, investment money is already spread thin. Countless other aquaculture projects have already been started across the region, many of which have thus far proved less than successful. The greater hope of many fishers in Isla Aguada, however aspirational, is for an alternative future in another industry built upon the villa's fishing heritage: tourism. Plans for tourism ventures in the Laguna de Términos shaped by the post-peak condition were already on the horizon. Without the support of state officials and the endurance of the delicate ecology of the protected area, the region would settle into the trough of another bust.

## Colliding Patrimonies

Two patrimonies—fisheries and oil—struggle to share the Gulf of Mexico. While the Mexican state fought to extend sovereignty over the resources of the Gulf, local residents of coastal communities found ways to integrate themselves into a transforming economy, especially during the shrimping boom. As fishing changed from a strictly subsistence to a commercial activity in the mid-twentieth century, local fishers in both the altura and ribereño sectors faced a rapidly changing set of social and economic circumstances, affecting their work as fishers and their relationships within their communities and with the natural environment.

The simultaneous decline of the Campeche Sound's most valuable resources challenges citizens and the state to address the post-peak condition. In Isla Aguada as in other frontline communities, the post-peak condition highlights the complicating and intersecting effects of resource depletion on social and economic life in coastal communities. Post-peak fishing is an economically grim, ecologically uncertain, politically contested, and socially fluid state of affairs. Along with the decline in catches, post-peak fishing coincides with the intensification of Pemex activity and an array of ecological changes in the coastal and marine environments. While economic pressures on making a living from fishing intensify, the social life, embedded in the heritage of artisanal fishing, is affected as well. Social transformations, indicated by the formation of local organizations fighting for compensation benefits, have accompanied the peak and decline of fishing in Isla Aguada.

## CHAPTER 4

# Capturing Compensation: Resource Wealth in the Era of Decline

"The only benefit that the discovery of oil brought to Isla Aguada is a few jobs for people out there on the platforms, just a couple of them in Pemex. That's all, nothing more," said Don Ysidro quite bitterly. A fisher in his seventies known in the community as El Pichón, he has seen the community struggle through peaks and declines throughout his lifetime. On Mexico's Gulf coast, like other resource-rich places in the world, frontline communities perceive oil as more a curse than a blessing. Since oil was first discovered onshore, the exploitation of this valuable natural resource has damaged the natural environment, reinforced unfair labor practices, and failed to bring sustainable development to the region. These failures are characteristic of "resource curse" cases in which nations with oil-wealth windfalls fail to convert their rents into positive development experiences. Studies show that since the 1970s, countries highly dependent on extracting and exporting natural resources, especially minerals and most notably oil, demonstrate overall poor economic performance compared with their mineral-poor counterparts. The presence of valuable mineral resources promotes an environment that compromises not only a developing nation's economic performance but also the structures of governance and income equality (Auty 1998, 2001; Eifert, Gelb, and Tallroth 2003; Sachs and Warner 1997, 2001). Terry Lynn Karl, in her 1997 study of Venezuela, aptly calls the phenomenon the "paradox of plenty."

According to Andrew Rosser (2006), existing explanations for the resource curse do not adequately account for the role of social forces or external political and economic environments in shaping development outcomes in resource-abundant countries. Rosser asks useful questions about the assumptions of the resource-curse approach in the predominant literature on the political economy of mineral resources in developing countries. He concludes that oil is neither a curse nor a blessing. It is important to understand a stance like Rosser's because Mexico's experience of resource curse—and the relationships among resource wealth, the state, and national and local development—are changing according to the flows and ebbs of production of Gulf of Mexico oil.

My approach is also critical, though I come at the issue from a different angle, more organic to the problem of oil and development I encountered in the Laguna de Términos. While most studies of resource curse are scaled to national experience, here I am interested in examining a regional experience of the effects of natural resource wealth on development. I find that rather than constituting a straightforward case of resource curse across the nation, in Mexico both development and the curse of underdevelopment have been differentially experienced across the decades, across different sectors of the economy, and across specific regions. Nationally, Mexico is not—like Venezuela or Nigeria, for example—an exemplary case of resource curse. In fact, it is a relatively weak case in light of evidence of Mexico's economic performance and governance structures, especially in comparison with its cohort of oil-exporting nations across the Global South. It is true that during the oil boom of 1979–1981 Mexico participated in no internationally competitive activity other than extractive industries (Auty 1993: 5). However, since the 1970s, Mexico's national economy has diversified in manufacturing and services. The economic diversification extends to a growing portfolio of exports, though most of these are concentrated on a single market—the United States. While resource-cursed nations are often plagued by governance problems on the order of severe corruption, authoritarianism, dictatorship, and civil war, Mexico is an electoral democracy that at times has shown great strides toward political freedoms and civil liberties.

However, regionally, dependence remains on very specific commodities, many of these natural resources. Is it possible that the national picture of Mexico masks a host of regional inequalities produced by oil wealth? Only when we examine Mexico on a regional level do we see that oil-producing regions, Mexico's frontlines, do indeed exhibit the classic features of resource curse in terms of problems of governance and economic development. The frontlines absorb the greatest impact in the nation's struggle to "sow"—or make productive use of—the benefits of the oil proceeds from Cantarell's bonanza production beginning in the 1980s. This failure is magnified in that fishers share a resource with the oil industry: the marine and coastal environment of the Gulf of Mexico and the Laguna de Términos.

As Michael Watts points out, "Oil dependent economies are, in spite of their vast resource wealth, some of the most sordid, chaotic, socially unjust and inequitable of all political economies" (2005: 384). How, then, can states with de jure resource sovereignty manage resource wealth in such a way as to ensure that they protect the welfare of citizens? With large amounts of oil wealth, a state may do two things. On the one hand, the state may enact a policy of large-scale distribution that funnels oil rents into national endeavors such as social programs to support health care, education, and social security (Basedau and Lacher 2006: 11). In this system, oil wealth is national patrimony and benefits the citizenry. In such a system, the government may rely more on oil rents than on income taxes for revenues.

On the other hand, history has shown that governments can also use oil wealth through a system of patronage. In this system, oil proceeds are selectively distributed to networks of clients. In other words, oil proceeds benefit politically important groups. Through this mechanism, oil revenues are distributed to a comparatively small part of the population, and access is granted through personal ties (ibid.). In Mexico, the de jure system according to the constitutional promotion of oil as a strategic national resource and, historically, the role of oil in national development plans is the redistributive system. However, Mexico has long employed both systems simultaneously. Alongside the formal system of large-scale distribution, politicians and high-placed union bosses have funneled oil rents through the patronage system. Revenues (known as *excedentes petroleros*) went in most cases to governors during the seventy-year political domination by the Partido Revolucionario Institucional (PRI) and began to move to municipalities as well after political party pluralism came to characterize the Mexican landscape and the PRI lost its hold on state offices. This occurred primarily after the election of Vicente Fox of the Partido Acción Nacional (PAN) in 2000. In this chapter we will see how at the state and municipal levels oil revenues are used and abused as wedges for political power over and against local development needs and interests.

Though oil had been a part of everyday life in the municipality of Carmen for many years, it was not until the mid- to late 1990s that the state made a concerted effort to vie for direct, formalized access to oil revenues. After production at Cantarell began, Campeche state and municipal officials started strategizing to win greater access to oil revenues.

Only much more recently have they undertaken these efforts to fund development programs in earnest, spurred by the necessity to mitigate the effects of regional resource curse and the mounting risks of post-peak life. Campeche became an oil state later than others, and Carmen likewise achieved the status of an "oil-affected municipality" as bureaucrats and activists alike looked back on the previous several oil-soaked decades as a blight visited upon Campeche. Looking for reparations and for present and future development funds, the state is still figuring out ways to assert its rights to benefit from the national patrimony. Campeche's citizens, by dint of living on the energy-production frontlines, wish to be acknowledged as the legitimate heirs of Mexico's national patrimony. Living on the frontlines in an oil-affected community, they have earned the right to benefit from oil's proceeds.

Pemex and the Mexican state have been forced to put something back into local, state, and municipal development. Furthermore, fishers have pushed Pemex to pay compensation for loss of catch and other indemnities such as in the case of major oil spills. But how significant are these responses? By looking at the micropolitics of Pemex aid distributions in post-peak Mexico, in this chapter I trace how the nation faces the challenge of converting oil revenue into the development of oil-affected regions along the Gulf coast and in the Laguna de Términos area of Campeche. Given the post-peak condition of Cantarell and black gold's 40 percent or more of Mexico's national budget slipping away, it would seem that Campeche's chance for long-term, comprehensive development has perhaps already been compromised. In addition, impending energy reforms to further open Pemex to the private sector (as I will discuss in the following chapter) threaten a slimmer budget for development programs.

## Aid to Fishers

It is payday and the Aguadeños begin to gather: dozens by dawn and then it seems like hundreds by the time the eight o'clock sun is roasting hot. The men of Isla Aguada assemble at the downtown *comisaría* to collect their midsummer *baja captura*, or low-capture and closed-season aid benefits. The baja captura fund is one of several that help to keep fishers afloat in Campeche's post-peak environment. The aid program is financed by the state of Campeche and administered by Sepesca, the state fisheries agency. The aid is not a very substantial amount of money, given that it has already been three or fours months since many fishers have had a profitable day's work. On this July day, already well into the low season and the shrimp veda, 674 fishers would collect their share of Isla Aguada's allotment, meaning a take-home of 1,180 pesos.[1]

The aid distribution is a tense and unpleasant scene. Because of the scores who have gathered and the apparent expectation of trouble, the street is closed to traffic by police tape and by the several armed municipal officers. The oldest fishers are the most critical of the baja captura aid program, perhaps because they once were the most successful fishers among those now living in Isla Aguada. They genuinely built their lives from fishing and had the tangible experience of providing well for their families from their own nets. There is not one among the elderly fishermen who spoke with me who did not tell me that he earned his house from the proceeds of his nets. The thousand or so pesos for the low-capture aid program are not much, and to the senior fishers it is, as one octogenarian puts it, "a joke." One went so far as to consider refusing the aid as a matter of pride. In the end, poverty won over pride for Don Eusebio, who still works well into his seventies fixing motors for lanchas and motorbikes. He collected the payment.

Wives and mothers-in-law might stand on the fringes of the aid collection, watching carefully and stoically over the proceedings. Yet, as is typical in rural or marginalized communities, women are at the very center of the post-peak household economy in Campeche's Gulf coast communities. Thus, as they bear the brunt of maintaining the home, putting food on the table, and keeping the kids in school, women are there on the aid distribution day, too. Spouses cannot appear as beneficiaries of aid on the rolls, only the fishers themselves—almost exclusively male in coastal Campeche. The indignant view held by many of the women who share households with fishers in Isla Aguada is that it is the women, not the men, who should be given the aid money directly!

By lunchtime, early morning patience transforms into grumbling restlessness in the growing crowd. As the sun reaches it merciless peak, it emerges that something is clearly wrong with the benefits rolls. Names are not matching up with the official lists and the claimants present. Winning the battle to be recognized as entitled to the compensation is only half the struggle for the ribereños. Getting the money in hand is the other half, and it is sometimes never actually achieved by some fishers. Some are frustrated at seeing their neighbors, whom they know to not be fishing-license holders, easily walking off with benefits. Unlike the other main aid program, the Fideicomiso Pesquero (fishing fund), whose beneficiaries stand at a fixed number, annual enrollment in the baja captura program is flexible. Local leaders of the Unión de Pescadores in Isla Aguada as well as Sagarpa recognize this as a problem but have thus far been unable to tighten the official ledgers of what is called the *padrón pesquero*. Due to the flexible enrollment in this particular aid program, the pool of claimants keeps growing. The laxity of the state's rules on defining just who is and who is not a "true fisher" and thus eligible for aid causes a constant struggle among leaders of different associations of ribereños, Sagarpa, municipal authorities, and Pemex fund contributors.

Knowing the problem with the official registries, leaders of fisher associations from Isla Aguada to the Peninsula of Atasta initially called for a *reordenamiento pesquero*, a revision of the fideicomiso's membership, to clarify who qualified for aid several years earlier. An association leader described to me how the trust works: "The revision of the roll books of the fishers who belong to the cooperatives in the federations within the fideicomiso is aimed at directing Pemex resources to those committed to fishing as an everyday activity instead of to those who have nothing to do with the fishing industry of the municipality." In early 2009 the process of regularizing not just those in the municipality of Carmen but also the more than 12,000 ribereños across the state of Campeche began in earnest. The identification and credentialing process entailed conducting a census, documenting fishers' membership in their local cooperatives, and issuing photo IDs. The official photo credential permits a ribereño access to the different programs offered by state and federal agencies. The authentic artisanal fishers eligible for aid would be identified, counted, and properly credentialed. Most likely, an accurate census would significantly reduce the number of claimants for aid in the baja captura program and thus increase the amount of aid to each verifiable claimant.

In the early months of 2009, Sagarpa, in conjunction with Conapesca, carried out a fishing census. By March the results (delivered through the contracted services of a private company) listed 257 legally registered ribereño fishing boats in Isla Aguada (*Tribuna Campeche* 2009g). The same process was used in fishing communities throughout the region, but it was slow, cumbersome, and, as the community-based cooperatives and associations claimed, full of corruption. By the start of the shrimp veda in May, the census process had broken down. Campeche Governor Hurtado Valdéz addressed the problem: "Three or four years ago we made another attempt at the reordenamiento pesquero, and at the start of the vedas, like magic, more fishers appear—which means that the benefit doesn't reach the authentic hombres del mar because of those who are popping up now and then to receive benefits" (in Mendoza Novelo 2009).

Coming to terms with receiving compensation benefits partially shapes what it means—both in the legal sense and in the sense of cultural identity—to be a *verdadero pescador*, a true fisher, in the changing reality of Mexico's Gulf coast. This reality is even starker when a fisher and his family must fight to receive the modest benefit. The larger number of beneficiaries reduces the already paltry amount of low-catch aid. These aid payments are so small that some recipients see their only value to be a few days of forgetting their troubles through drug or alcohol use. The morning after a payday in Isla Aguada the previous evening's revelry is palpable. I visited with Doña María, an older woman who lives in a humble, precarious dwelling of sticks, palm, and corrugated metal across the street from a popular bar on the lagoon. Our encounter was fortuitous: she seemed the only person out and about, hanging her laundry in her *solar*, or yard, at the early hour. "The noise last night!" she exclaimed to me after we made our introductions. "How they were carrying on. They were throwing bottles in the street, smashing them practically on my doorstep." Indeed, I could see the evidence. She was particularly bothered by the flagrancy of breaking returnable bottles. Quickly assessing the utter humbleness of her home, I could easily see that the few pesos in deposits would matter to Doña María.

She kindly invited me inside, out of the searing morning sun. She sat on a hammock and I on a plastic stool as I explained that I was visiting families to discuss the history of the villa. Many residents of Isla Aguada, especially those who identify themselves as natives, reflect on how the community has changed. Notably, residents worry about the rampant alcoholism, the drug use, and the escalating violence they attribute to a spill-over effect from Ciudad del Carmen. As it became increasingly challenging to make a living in Isla Aguada, more residents traveled to Carmen for work. Families split up and fractured. At the same time, Isla Aguada received new residents. The high cost of living in Carmen, driven up by the oil industry, prompted the low-paid working class to far-flung communities like Isla Aguada looking for affordable housing, even if the housing was little more than a beachside shanty without water or electricity. Now Carmen and Isla Aguada were tied together in facing contemporary urban problems.

Doña María asked if I had heard the recent news about the grisly murders in Carmen a few days before. Three police officers were shot, execution-style, and to the shock and horror of the locals, one of the suspects hailed from Isla Aguada. The community was on high alert. For the previous three days, convoys of pickup trucks carrying assault-rifle-bearing *federales* had been driving ominously up and down the wide avenues of Isla Aguada and turning down even the narrowest sea-shell-paved lanes. The constant presence of armed police and the military was felt by the older generation of the once-quiet villa as a threat rather than a comfort.

Doña María remembered a time, not too long before, when the camaraderie of the town brought everyone together in a time of crisis, and the government came to the people's aid. It was October 1995, and the crisis came in the form of Hurricane Roxanne, which left Campeche unreachable by sea, air, and land for days. The highway between Campeche and Carmen was washed away, leaving dozens of communities cut off and literally starving. More than 3,000 Pemex workers were evacuated from the Gulf's platforms, paralyzing Mexico's oil industry and costing millions of dollars a day.

Doña María remembered the events of the hurricane with a steady shaking of her head. Fishers saved their lanchas by moving them from the water and the beaches into the center of town, lashing them together, some in front of the church. When Roxanne passed over Isla Aguada, the bay and the lagoon joined. There was barely any dry land in the whole of the villa. "Here in this very house, the water was up to here," she said, reaching over her head to point to the top of a large wardrobe, to this day the only real piece of furniture in the room. Somehow it survived the storm's devastating impact. "We stayed here as long as we could, and then we went to the shelter in the primary school. My daughter was pregnant at the time. And wouldn't you know it! Her baby was born right there on the floor of the primary school during the hurricane. Everybody wanted to name the baby Roxana!" Doña María described how helicopters buzzed above the villa for days afterward dropping food and water. "They even dropped chickens!" But now, in an Isla Aguada that has changed so much, "if a hurricane came, no one would leave their house for fear of looting." Memories of crises such as Hurricane Roxanne in 1995 show how quickly the perception and reality of community security as well as the role of the state in providing for welfare and security have changed, along with the decline in the ability of residents to earn their livelihoods from fishing and the rise of the oil industry.

Fishers receive funds from several sources administered through a combination of federal, state, and municipal agencies. The original source of the vast majority of the benefits is Pemex. The parastatal's officials are not straightforward about why they give aid to the fishing community, and they certainly do not admit that fishers' aid is compensation for loss of catch due to contamination. For a number of years, in general and on the occasion of specific accidents and spills, Pemex has asserted that the decline in fishing in the sound is not due to the activities of oil exploitation. Pemex makes its position clear in a 2002 brochure, *Support to Protected and Sensitive Areas*: "Marine waters meet world environmental quality criteria and standards for the survival of aquatic organisms. Therefore the decline of fishing cannot be attributed to the oil sector's activities" (in Robadue et al. 2004: 33). Pemex has denied causality and consistently refuses to link its aid to compensation for contamination.

At one donation ceremony in March 2008 in which 6 million pesos (less than $450,000) were distributed, the director of PEP's social development office, Yolanda Valladares, chose her words carefully, saying that the funds were granted to ribereño fishers of Campeche to "mitigate the effects caused by Pemex." But everyone knew the payment was directly tied to compensation for the October 2007 Usumacinta accident. In heavy seas during a storm, a floating platform, the Usumacinta drilling rig, collided with the Kab-101 platform, causing an explosion. Many workers were plunged into the cold and rough seas and waited overnight for rescue; twenty-one workers were killed, and one was never recovered. An estimated 11,000 barrels of oil spilled into the sound. The leak went on for days, with residents gathering on beaches to watch the tide bring in the clumps of heavy crude, all sorts of debris, and dead and injured fish and wildlife, including endangered turtles that breed on Gulf shores. Even though it was public knowledge that Pemex and the municipal officials had been negotiating a settlement to compensate fishers for damages, Valladares explicitly denied that the aid was compensation for damages incurred for the spill. Instead, PEP was simply carrying out an already planned aid payout proposed by municipal president José Ignacio Seara Sierra (Cruz Idiáquez 2008).

In addition to extraordinary aid, Pemex also pays regular benefits to fishers through the Fideicomiso Pesquero. In 2001, fishers from Isla Aguada, Atasta, Sabancuy, and the city of Carmen worked with municipal authorities from the municipal Office of Social and Economic Development and state authorities from Sepesca to solicit compensatory funds from Pemex for the decline in catch. Fishers in four communities of the municipality of Carmen began to receive annual disbursements from the Fideicomiso Pesquero following years of lobbying the state and municipality. The Fideicomiso Pesquero is a bank trust funded by Pemex and set up in accord with and administered through the state of Campeche and the municipality of Carmen. Each fishing sector, altura and ribereño, would receive a fixed grant distributed in three payments per year to groups representing the fishers in the local communities. Among themselves, many fishers understand this compensation as damage payments for contamination. However, Pemex has never admitted to any contamination as a result of thirty years of offshore drilling. Technically the payments are for loss of catch due to the restricted zones Pemex has imposed around platforms in the Campeche Sound. Nevertheless, fishers from across the region agitate for compensatory aid and do indeed understand payments, or "donations," as compensation and even as an admission on the part of Pemex of culpability for damage to the fishing industry.

As discussed in chapter 3, the Unión de Pescadores de Ckiquixocoq is a political organization of fishers at the local level in Isla Aguada through which fishing aid is distributed. It was founded as a way to organize fishers and mobilize them to seek benefits in the era of declining catches. The Unión de Pescadores fights for fishers' compensation directly from Pemex and pulls in other funds to the municipality. In recent years it has become the body and mechanism through which aid funds—all originating from Pemex—are distributed to fishers of Isla Aguada. Other communities of the Laguna de Términos in the municipality of Carmen have similar associations known as unions. Isla Aguada is unusual because it has only one organization representing the 683 fishers who receive benefits through the fideicomiso. In the municipality of Carmen there are a total of 21 organizations representing 4,208 fishers who receive benefits from the fund. In the city of Carmen, 1,689 fishers are members of 121 cooperatives and 12 associations; in Atasta there are 3 associations and 44 cooperatives for 1,047 recipients of fideicomiso distributions; and in Sabancuy 5 associations and 38 cooperatives distribute aid for 789 fishers (*Tribuna Campeche* 2009b).

Since the establishment of the fideicomiso, the annual payment has been set at more than $1 million in 2009 granted to each sector, ribereño and altura. A proportion of the funds is released periodically, seemingly on no guaranteed, fixed schedule, throughout the year. In 2010, for the first time in nine years, the state of Campeche and the municipality of Carmen negotiated with Desarrollo Social de Pemex the granting of an additional $379,000, increasing the funds by 33 percent each to more than $1.5 million in 2010. The ribereño sector has long complained about the pretext of maintaining parity between the sectors: the ribereño sector has many more fishers in considerably more difficult economic circumstances. As opposed to the more than 4,000 beneficiaries of the fideicomiso Ribereño, the altura sector only has 370 beneficiaries.

The Fideicomiso Pesquero pays a fixed annual amount to fishers across the municipality of Carmen. Due to the regularized amount of the annual payment and beneficiary pool (unlike the baja captura payments), the claimants receive a fixed amount of 3,000 pesos ($228) each per year. However, in Isla Aguada's fishers' association, not all of this is in the form of a cash payment; only half is delivered to the fisher in cash, and the rest is "invested" back into the Unión de Pescadores under the umbrella "proyectos productivos" for a variety of purposes, from the replacement of worn-out nets or other fishing equipment to engine repair. For other communities, major project investment has gone to aquaculture. Not all the fishers in Isla Aguada are happy with this model, yet the points of criticism differ among the members. As could be expected, some of the union members would like to receive the full 3,000 pesos in cash. They see the investment model as paternalistic: "Why can't each person be trusted with his own money?" one asked. Another member made his point to me: "If they want it invested for the future, they'll invest it themselves." Others say no money from the fideicomiso should be distributed in cash but that larger amounts should be apportioned to proven projects that can provide real alternatives in the community.

The investment mindset perhaps worked a little bit better for fishers who already had security, and it is a common view among those who hold financial and cultural capital in the community. Most had some connection to the villa's *familias antiguas*, the dozen or so founding families who over the generations gained a financial and political foothold in the community that was hard to break. The older members of these families grew their nest eggs from fishing as they watched a market grow in the 1970s and into the 1980s. Innovators of the cooperative system in Isla Aguada, they were savvy fishers. But now in the postpeak era, with the emphasis shifted away from the market and toward a whole new politics of compensation, they know the rules are different.

The older Aguadeños, at least those who still fish, have little respect for the contemporary state of affairs.

Some fishers want to see the union act more paternalistically in terms of social responsibility toward its members. The benefits money held back for investment could be used as a social safety net. One fisher who suffered a severe cut on his leg while out on his lancha said he expected more from the union in helping him out with medical expenses, transportation to Carmen for surgery and doctor visits, and compensation for the many months he could not fish. The union failed to come through for him in a time of real need. The union, founded on principles of political mobilization against Pemex, is clearly not a social institution in any broader sense. It is an economic institution dedicated to managing and distributing resources at the local level.

As such, it cannot help but be a political institution as well. The Unión de Pescadores holding back some of the fideicomiso benefits is, in the opinion of many fishers, evidence of serious political corruption in the union's administration. The leader himself is the target of most of the criticism. Not a native-born Aguadeño but married into one of the most established families, the union leader has transformed himself from an activist for resources for fishers to more of a politician of fishers' issues. He is deeply in league with PAN politicos as well as with Pemex and at times would appear to be an emissary for Pemex in the community. It is hard not to appear that way when he drives a pickup emblazoned with the Pemex logo. And wears a Pemex hat. And uses the ice factory built by Pemex in town for his own office. True, the truck was another of the benefits provided to the fishers' association by Pemex so the leader could make his frequent trips into Ciudad del Carmen to carry out the business of the community. But still. The many resources he garnered gave him an elite status not appreciated by others in Isla Aguada. Many of those who find themselves dependent upon those scant but critical resources are particularly sharp in their criticism—far from grateful for the little they are getting. By the leader's own fascinating self-criticism he is a "mercenary," by which I understand him to mean that he fights on behalf of the fishers for benefits from Pemex and for Pemex among the fishers, all the while seeking his own personal benefits as well. The way he is perceived by many fishers in the community, as a sell-out to the parastatal, is the personal price he pays for his leadership position.

The leaders of the local associations of fishers play a key role in managing the numbers of fishers from their community for the benefactor agency. This is because compensation benefits, whether from the state or directly from Pemex and funneled through the municipality, are not given in direct transactions between the government or parastatal entity and the fisher claimants. Instead, these benefit transactions are mediated by a fishers organization at the local level. The association can be a cooperative, a federation, or a union. In 2009, when the ribereño sector was preparing to receive 5 million pesos as the first installment of an annual benefit of 15 million pesos (about $1 million total), the leaders of the various associations organized to tighten the eligibility framework in the wake of the failed fishing census; they added a new bureaucratic layer, the Comité de Validación Pesquero, which would act as a safeguard against ineligibility over and above the local associations. The state warned that of the 1,708 fishers from Ciudad del Carmen, 743 from Isla Aguada, 907 from Sabancuy, and 1,159 from Atasta, only 60 percent would maintain their eligibility under the new, stricter guidelines for receiving benefits (*Tribuna Campeche* 2009b).

The credentialing process was fraught with accusations of corruption and numbers inflation. In Isla Aguada the main discrepancy was in the number of pescadores libres that was completely out of proportion to the number of boats in the villa. Early in the process, as it was becoming clear to the Sagarpa and Conapesca census takers that only about 250 boats were registered in the villa, the number of free fishers already topped 400 even before the census was complete and before those belonging to the cooperatives were counted. The charge was that on the list of those receiving benefits of the Fideicomiso Pesquero, under the category of "pescadores libres," one might find men who worked in Isla Aguada as moto-taxi drivers or construction workers who lived in Carmen. There was even a charge that a name appeared on the benefit recipient list as a pescador libre of someone who actually lived in the United States. The inclusion of these names is justified by family members, especially women, intent on collecting benefits in the fishers' absence.

When 11,420 fishers were included in the new eligibility list, absent were the names of the women who had long been trying to find some way into the system to obtain direct access to benefits. Despite the women's political activism, largely in the municipality of Campeche, they did not succeed in securing a permanent place on the benefits rolls. Rather, the state agency, Sepesca, promised two women's cooperatives at the center of the protest, the Pulperitas and the Esposas de Pescadores, that they would look into the possibility of awarding them aid for carrying out their own fishing-related activities such as the commercialization of pulpo. Two weeks later, Sepesca announced a cash benefit of 500 pesos ($40) for each woman who had attempted to receive a benefit under the baja captura program. Additionally, the state office promised to funnel money into a women's cooperative aquaculture venture (*Tribuna Campeche* 2009e).

The normal political tensions in local fishing politics become heightened in election seasons, when state and federal representatives use benefits as a wedge issue. That was the case in Isla Aguada and the municipality of Carmen in Mexico's July 2009 midterm elections. Across Mexico the PRI was set to reassert itself over the incumbent PAN. With local fisher associations being led for several years by PAN activists, what effect would the broader political party changes have in Isla Aguada fishing politics? The complications could not have come at a worse time. Not only were the catches continuing to decline, but bad weather in the winter shrimping season was compounded by a markedly poor summer's fish catch during the shrimp veda. If any aid was forthcoming, late summer was indeed the time it was needed.

The PRI swept the local and state government elections, but as it turned out, there was no change on the ground in Isla Aguada. The same association leadership was reelected by Isla Aguada's 700-plus fishing electorate. A disgruntled group from Isla Aguada, clearly emboldened by the political tide change and suspicious of the financial management of the community's disbursements from the Fideicomiso Pesquero, took the opportunity to petition the municipal government for an audit of the fideicomiso disbursements from 2005 through 2008. Was there corruption in benefit distribution close to home?

The question of the politics of distribution of previous seasons' resources turned to panic as to whether the fishers would receive any resources at all. Toward the end the summer of 2009, two to three months late, the resources still had not been distributed. With lame-duck administrations occupying all levels of state and local government, the immediate and perhaps even long-term distribution of Isla Aguada's and other fishing communities' aid was imperiled. When the 5 million pesos in funds pertaining to the Fideicomiso Pesquero that were originally expected in June and then delayed until July due to the midterm elections had still not been received by mid-August, the ribereños held a series of demonstrations. They did not want municipal politics to get in the way of receiving money from the long-established Pemex fund, so they directed their criticism not at Pemex but at the Panista munic-

ipal government. For the fishers of Isla Aguada, it was an obvious connection. In their own town they claimed to witness a PAN vote-buying
scheme in the July 2009 election that threatened the disbursement of
fideicomiso funds. One fisher told me, "The PAN advised them that if
they didn't vote for that party they wouldn't give them money from the
Fideicomiso Pesquero" ("Los del PAN les advirtieron que si no votaban
por ese partido no les darían dinero del Fideicomiso Pesquero").

Demonstrations were held on the steps of Carmen's city hall, with
fishers from across the Laguna de Términos turning out to demand
their aid. Pemex, appearing to rise to the defense of the municipality,
negated the demands of the fishers by imposing a stringent new set of
rules on the fideicomiso disbursement. Previously the local associations
received lump sums for their proyectos productivos and used them at
their own discretion, but now Pemex would require that local proposals
be approved beforehand by Pemex's administrative board, the Consejo
de Administración. In order for the fishers to receive some aid immediately, the state government stepped in and advanced the twenty-one
representative fishers organizations across the municipality the disbursement of 5 million pesos.[2] That Pemex and the municipality backed each
other up in delaying the distribution of funds reveals only the first layer
of deep complicities between the parastatal and local politics in Mexico,
especially in oil-producing areas of the Gulf coast.

## Oil-Affected Zones

On March 18, 1996, the fifty-eighth anniversary of Expropriation Day,
President Ernesto Zedillo of the PRI made the customary presidential commemorative address from Ciudad del Carmen, during which he
delivered some customary platitudes. But he also had another piece of
business on this trip to Campeche: to reaffirm the Convenio de Desarrollo Social, a social development aid accord between the state government of Campeche and Pemex. In an era of rising oil production—and
intensifying oil impact—Zedillo would oversee an increase in state aid
from 17 million pesos ($1.3 million) to 65 million pesos ($5 million) as
well as the specific targeting of aid on the municipal level. Zedillo used
the occasion of his 1996 Expropriation Day speech to announce the
first *convenio de colaboración* between Pemex and the municipality of
Carmen, an accord specifying in great detail works, projects, and programs to take place in the state of Campeche:

What I want to tell you, friends from Campeche, friends from Carmen, is that I am absolutely convinced that today, exactly on this date which is so important to all Mexicans, begins the payback of a historical debt to the state of Campeche.

For some time, the Campechanos have felt that although their contribution to oil development of the country has been very important and instrumental, also you all have felt that there hasn't always been a fair correspondence between the Nation toward the state, for its participation in such an important process in the development of the country.

Today, with this agreement . . . I think I can return to the capital with a clear conscience. We have begun to settle up with Campeche. We have begun to fulfill our obligation to the Carmelitas, and it couldn't be any other way. This is a great state with great people that is doing its part in the construction of a better Mexico that we all want. For this, the government of the Republic will do right by Campeche.

Thus in 1996 Zedillo promised to step up the commitment of Pemex in its recognition of Campeche as an oil-affected state. Although the federal government had long acknowledged that Campeche, one on a growing list of states, deserved some monetary compensation for hosting the national oil-production effort, it had been a hard fight for Campechanos to get the compensation they thought they deserved. The promises of the 1990s turned out to be just the tip of the iceberg, opening the door to an era of extensive funding and financing for Campeche and especially the municipality of Carmen that would restructure the vision and practice of development in the region based on its status as an "oil-affected" zone.

Oil revenues have long gone back into national development, just not specifically into oil-affected zones. Since the federal government first began to levy significant taxes on oil in the 1920s, the resource has been mobilized to provide for the nation. Initially, this was to the great irritation of foreign companies. After the 1938 nationalization of the oil industry it became the legal obligation of Pemex to convert oil into income for the nation. In hindsight, it is easy to see how the Pemex model—whereby the state taxes the parastatal to a degree of extraordinary indebtedness—emerged. An otherwise low national tax effort since the post–World War II period compounds the need for the Pemex income: there is no other steady source of financing from which the federal government can maintain itself. The state has imagined Pemex as funding the dream of national development. Increasingly, however, rather than being put toward specific, targeted development projects on the federal level, Pemex funds go to the general operating budget and are subsequently distributed to other sources, including state budgets. The model of taxing Pemex to fund the federal budget is logical in theory. If you want to treat Pemex like an independent corporation producing a valuable commodity, taxation for the purposes of producing government income is perfectly appropriate. But with Pemex the model became irrational to the point of being dysfunctional, with the state "willing to sacrifice Pemex's status as an energy company and turn it into an instrument for the state's financial engineering" and causing government managers to "view Pemex as a supplier of cash needed to stabilize the Mexican economy" (Stojanovski 2008: 7). Oil revenues have continued to fuel ever-growing government spending, yet they have not left any surplus, even during times of high oil prices and high production, such as in the sexenio of Vicente Fox (2000-2006) that was comparable to the famous "administration of abundance" presided over by José López Portillo (1976-1982) in the initial gush of Cantarell's oil. During the Fox administration, the Bay of Campeche generated some $38 billion in oil revenue. High prices for large volumes of oil generated substantial revenue yet left no surpluses.

In Mexico's post-peak era, the federal government is becoming more rather than less reliant on oil in its budget. In 2008 the petroleum sector contributed the equivalent of 8.4 percent of the GDP of the public-sector budgetary gross income, approximately 1 trillion pesos ($77.5 billion). Even though the global recession hit the Mexican economy hard, in part by bringing down the price of oil, the federal government did not adjust its dependence on oil incomes. Facing a downturn that would result in a GDP shrinkage of nearly 10 percent in the first half of 2009, the Ministry of Finance (Secretaría de Hacienda y Crédito Público) clung to oil, expecting Pemex contributions to increase rather than decrease as a percentage of the federal budget—64 percent in 2009. Even though the proportion of oil contributions to the budget hovered between 30 and 34 percent from 2005 to 2010, the actual amount of the Pemex contribution was expected to continually grow. When Finance Minister Agustín Carstens commented on Pemex propping up the everyday operations of the state, he called an expected 2010 shortfall of 15 million pesos in Pemex contributions "four years' worth of police, security, and judiciary operations" (G. Smith 2009).

Perhaps this reliance on oil rents for the nation's everyday operating budget is too precarious, especially given the insecure nature of energy

supplies and markets. As it continues a high level of oil-income dependence, Mexico needs stable production and pricing. The 2008–2009
recession demonstrated that such stability is often out of reach. At the
close of 2009, Mexico experienced a 4.4 percent decline in oil incomes.
The price of oil per barrel dropped at the same time production was diminishing. The trend continued through 2009, with production falling from almost 1.5 mbpd to 1.3 mbpd. While federal policy makers
drafted a 2009 budget expecting a price of $99.60 per barrel, in reality
the price sank to the low seventies (OECD 2009).

Regardless of these strains and fluctuations, all thirty-one states still
relied for their own budgets upon funding by Pemex proceeds. The federal budget's dependence on high, short-term revenues from Pemex
trickles down to the state and municipal level across Mexico. Recently,
ten states defined as "priority states" due to the impact of the oil industry on their infrastructure, population, and environment have become
eligible for funding from Pemex over and above the ordinary federal
budget distribution. Campeche is one of the top three priority states.

Campeche was not always an oil state. Even after it started producing oil, it was difficult for the state to demonstrate that the region was
oil-impacted. The designation is based on a changing definition of what
constitutes oil impact; since production began at Cantarell in 1979, the
definition has changed frequently. It is important to track the definition of "oil impact" over time because it often determines what a state
or municipality and its population will receive in benefits from Pemex.
According to the 1979 Ley de Impuesto sobre el Petróleo y Sus Deri-
vados, only four states are petroleros: Tabasco, Tamaulipas, Veracruz,
and Chiapas. A states is defined as "petrolero," petroleum producer,
based on the contributions to national oil production emanating from
the physical infrastructure within its territory. Appendix 2 of the law
estimates the proportion of national production that each of these oil
states contributes. The 1979 oil-tax law designates that 50 percent of
the total income would be reapportioned to the states. This lessened
over time. Thirty years later, about 40 percent would be redistributed
to states (Campeche 2004: 13-14).

What excludes Campeche from the 1979 definition of "oil state"
is the lack of physical installations in the form of actively producing
oil wells on the mainland of the state. At the time, by definition, only
states and municipalities physically hosting Pemex installations in the
form of rigs and wells on their land were eligible to receive distributions. This was ironic for Campeche in the early days of Cantarell as

the region was experiencing the worst man-made oil spill in history, Ixtoc I, which began in June 1979. Even though the Laguna de Términos was yet to be declared a protected area, the flora and fauna of the region were in a delicate balance when the drilling operations commenced. By 1980 Campeche achieved the status of petrolero and began to receive a flat-rate compensation of 250,000 pesos (in 1980, the inflated exchange rate rose to more than 20 pesos per U.S. dollar). The money was not intended (as Pemex money never is) as compensation for environmental damage. Rather, it is more or less a "bonus" for oil-production states. Cantarell burst into production, and in 1981 the Campeche Sound quickly became the largest contributor to Mexico's national production, at 50 percent; it soon swelled to 75 percent, and that output held strong for many years.

Into the 1980s and 1990s, as Cantarell became synonymous with Campeche and Campeche with Cantarell, the state government began to actively seek its own cut of the nation's patrimony above and beyond the usual state share of the federal budget. Campeche was not born an oil state; it had to become an oil state, a feat all the more difficult when the petroleum is off shore. If Campeche was to become an authentic oil state, it would have to convince the federal government to part with a greater proportion of its budgetary lifeblood: oil money. If Campeche was to benefit from the oil wealth it produced, then it would fall most heavily upon the shoulder of the municipality of Carmen to demonstrate oil impact.

The best chance Campeche had for becoming an oil-affected state was to demonstrate a greater impact from onshore installations or to expand the notion of oil presence and impact to the physical proximity of drilling infrastructure in residents' cornfields. And here it had a lot of leverage. For Campeche's thousands of ribereño and altura fishers, certainly Pemex had affected their livelihoods. Ribereños in Isla Aguada were ready to demonstrate impact. Farmers, beekeepers, and small-scale cattle ranchers on the Peninsula of Atasta were likewise ready. They had uneasily negotiated an agreement for the construction of two gas plants on their ejido land in the 1990s. Now people were getting sick. Pipes were leaching contaminated water into their grazing land, and the corrugated metal roofs of their houses were becoming pitted by acid-rain showers, a result of continuous gas flaring at the plant. They, too, felt an impact. Workaday residents of Ciudad del Carmen were feeling the same pinch of price inflation, especially in housing, that had begun more than a generation earlier. The industry still saved the best jobs with benefits and security for outsiders. Meanwhile, rural residents in the tiny settlements around the Laguna de Términos suffered the curse of Campeche's long history of underdevelopment. For them the impact of oil was precisely their exclusion from its bonanza: amid the wealth of the oil industry they had no roads, no medical care, no educational opportunities.

By the early 1990s the federal government and Pemex recognized the need to respond to claims from residents in the Laguna de Términos region who demonstrated adverse effects from the presence of the oil industry in their communities. Residents formed organizations including the Movimiento de Campesinos y Pescadores de la Península de Atasta and took part in protests and public demonstrations with marches and highway blockages. Pemex responded to the claims of the residents on an ad hoc basis with cash payments. However, Currie-Alder and Day have found, "rather than basing compensation on evidence of damages, payments were often allocated in proportion to the inconvenience protests caused either through media attention or through interference with Pemex's operations" (2003: 353). This initiated a cycle of compensation in the Laguna de Términos, but it began and seems to residents as if it will continue as compensation without culpability.

Part of the acknowledgement of the oil industry's effects on local communities was the establishment of Laguna de Términos Flora and Fauna Protection Area. More significant than the federal government's 1994 decree founding the protected area was the invitation extended to the nongovernmental sector and local residents to join state and federal government agencies in developing the site management plan through a process of public consultation (Currie-Alder 2001, 2004; Currie-Alder and Day 2003). What arose from the consultation process, in hundreds of meetings and participation of dozens of organizations and citizens groups, is that while the express purpose of a protected area may be the conservation of rare and endangered species, many other social and environmental problems exist within its borders (Currie-Alder 2001: 18). It was during the early years of the establishment of the protected area and the exercise of citizens' voices about their interests in the zone that the role and impact of Pemex on the region really came to the fore.

Haenn (2002), following Escobar (1996), discusses how the establishment of protected areas incorporates undercapitalized areas into larger economic structures. In the interior of Campeche, the establishment of the Calakmul protected area turned the region from being characterized as a depopulated, "forgotten frontier" in the trough of the bust cycle of the chicle industry into Mexico's first "ecological municipality" where residents receive aid to support the sustainable exploitation of forest resources. Residents, many of whom were migrants resettling in the Calakmul tropical forest, were restricted from participating in subsistence activities as they were presented with alternative "environmentalist" projects ranging from agroforestry to reforestation to ecotourism.[3] Would protection imply the same transformation in the Laguna de Términos? Would the protected-area designation bring not only attention in the form of environmental consciousness but also the force of law and the power of the peso to protect what some have called the most important watershed in Mesoamerica?

It is true, but how it is true is not immediately apparent. While the actual establishment of the Laguna de Términos protected area in 1994 did not itself bring much in the way of resources, the declaration did stand as a proxy for laying a baseline for otherwise bringing compensation to the municipalities in the Laguna de Términos affected by the petroleum industry. By looking at the multiple funds and aid programs, we can examine in detail how the region became properly, effectively, and appropriately incorporated into a "regime of compensation" whereby the federal, state, and municipal governments diagnose an oil-affected region and issue funds to compensate for the effects.

One result of the growing awareness around oil impact was the designation of the municipality of Carmen and two neighboring municipalities in the state of Campeche as municipios petroleros. Carmen would join 121 others across ten states to officially become municipios petroleros. Campeche's affected population was very small, not exceeding 400,000 people, only 4 percent of the target population for the whole of Pemex's social development program. But the impact of becoming a priority oil state, like the impact of the oil industry itself, would shape the future development of the region. And becoming an oil municipality would turn out to be a blessing masking a curse for the 10 million people nationwide affected by oil in these zones.

## Social Development Programs and Benefits

Pemex has institutionalized and regularized its payments to oil-affected zones. In doing so, it attempts to preempt admissions of damages and the administration of actual compensation claims. Since the first recognition of oil-affected regions, the agreements to, in effect, compensate for the presence of Pemex have been regularized, payments have tripled, and extensive networks of programs have been established. The most significant of these is the sustainable community development program under which Pemex funds *donativos* and *donaciones* (cash and in-kind aid packages), while the parastatal's subsidiary PEP channels funds to the *obras de beneficio mútuo* (OBM), or mutual benefit program of public works. In 2008 the sustainable community development program awarded various states and municipalities cash and in-kind aid packages amounting to just over $150 million. In both 2008 and 2009 it gave about $26 million to the state of Campeche (compared to the 2001 figure of not quite $10 million), fulfilling an agreement known as the Convenio de Marco de Colaboración. In 2008 another payment of $58 million was channeled through PEP, the subsidiary in charge of distributing funds for and carrying out OBM projects (Pemex 2009a). Most OBM projects have focused on communities in areas of greater petroleum activity. In Campeche many of the OBM projects are in the municipality of Carmen.

## Mutual Benefit Projects

A substantial part of the parastatal's vision of social development is in infrastructure, the nuts-and-bolts public works. The most obvious kind of mutual benefit project takes place where Pemex has to build or improve a road to access its own facilities. Another example is when Pemex adds to the infrastructure of a town or city through potable water, drainage, or electricity when it moves into the community. OBM projects are requested by state or municipal governments by applying to PEP. The applications are accompanied by technical reports and assessments. In the case of the OBM, according to Marina Noreste, a Pemex spokesperson for the region,

> we continue to contribute parallel to the regional development of the communities influenced directly by our oil activity. We acknowledge that the current urban dynamism of Carmen can be attributed to the migratory processes and to the floating population that arrived alongside Pemex. The infrastructural development projects . . . are directed toward reducing the deterioration of roads, mitigating floods and the collection and conduction of residual waters, solving the problems of road mobility, water, and groundwater contamination, not to mention the works on the storm drain system. At the same time, we continue to

promote the social development of the ribereño fishers and productive projects of the communities around Carmen. (In *Tribuna Campeche* 2009c)

In 2008 PEP completed 189 OBM projects on the national level at a total investment of almost $58 million in fifty-six municipalities in the states of Campeche, Chiapas, Nuevo León, Puebla, San Luís Potosí, Tabasco, Tamaulipas, and Veracruz (Pemex 2009b: 91). The following year, 243 OBM projects were undertaken in fifty-two municipalities across the same states, with a total of $91 million invested (67). Across eight states over three years, Pemex maintained or constructed about 1,000 miles of paved and dirt roads and dedicated $18 million toward rehabilitating and building bridges, just over $11 million toward paving and resurfacing streets, and $1.4 million toward constructing sewer and drainage systems.

OBM projects are typically large public works projects. One example of an OBM project commonly undertaken in the municipality of Carmen is street paving and repair. Since 2000, Pemex has been working on a variety of projects to solve the severe drainage problem on the streets of Ciudad del Carmen during the extensive rainy season (June–October). On some of the busy city's main thoroughfares, an afternoon soaker could make getting around nearly impossible. One of the most notoriously flood-prone routes is Calle 31, a main street running parallel to the Gulf shoreline from downtown Carmen to Playa Norte. Neighborhood streets like those in the Francisco Madero and Pedro Sainz Baranda *colonias* (neighborhoods) are just as prone to flooding. Through OBM projects, Pemex is conducting public works projects to pave streets in the city with hydraulic cement (the most common kind of cement used in construction, particularly in wet conditions) to reinforce them against flooding.

Although Pemex does not use the word "compensation" when awarding fishing benefits, in the case of OBM awards, compensation is made explicit. A document I obtained outlining an OBM award for street paving, storm sewers, and drainage systems in Ciudad del Carmen states the typical purpose of the OBM: to "compensate for the accelerated effect of urbanization and population growth"; the work is directed to the benefit of the community and the *familias petroleras* that are part of it. PEP suggests that among the benefits of such a project, a drainage system would increase productivity by allowing workers to arrive on time at their worksites in a safe and comfortable manner without delays caused by flooding, integrate and link Pemex into the local communities where Pemex carries out operations and activities, and improve Pemex's relationships with communities and government (Pemex 2007a). All OBM projects follow similar lines of justification.

Because of the arbitrary nature of defining these projects and the considerable resources directed toward them, OBM projects are highly politicized. Some guidelines have been put in place to control OBM awards. While Pemex may use its own crews and resources to carry out the OBM projects, it also contracts private-sector companies to complete public works projects. Regulations prohibit funding projects that are political or religious in nature, and state and local governments are responsible for following federal and local laws regarding receiving funds during election times.

The latter became an issue during the 2009 midterm elections in Campeche when in May Pemex suspended resources to the state under this particular rule. The purpose of the suspension of resources is to allow Pemex to avoid funding vote buying by incumbents and thus avoid the politicization of what are essentially federal and national resources—federal in the sense that they come out of the federal budget and national in the sense that petroleum, as a subsoil resource, is part of the wealth of the nation. The suspension of resource allocations that year coincided with the annual summer suspension of the fishing season when hundreds of heads of households are out of work. Other kinds of resources were frozen, as well. Ex-fishers, taking the option of moving out of fishing into aquaculture, mariculture, and hydroponics, found their Pemex funding suspended in the "apolitical" stance of the highly politicized atmosphere.

## Donativos and Donaciones

The second category of funding under the social development benefits is donativos and donaciones, the cash and in-kind grants administered by the Pemex Office of Social Development. The social development program has expanded rapidly since the late 1990s, and over time the funding pattern has remained consistent, overwhelmingly favoring infrastructural endeavors in a few priority states, with the aid going directly to state governments. In the period 1995–2005, cash and in-kind aid from Pemex granted to states, municipalities, and civil-society associations across the nation amounted to an average annual sum of $57 million. In those ten years, Pemex donated just over $685 million principally to nine states (out of thirty-one states and the federal district).

Pemex guidelines stipulate that cash and in-kind funds must be applied to projects and programs for the social benefit of communities affected by the oil industry. Pemex does not distribute aid to "oil-affected areas" proportionally based on oil production. If this were the case, Campeche would receive a higher distribution of aid than it has since the late 1990s, given that Mexico's crude production was disproportionately based on the state's marine platform (Sales Heredia 2007: 8). Instead, Campeche shares approximately one-third of the donativos and donaciones with Chiapas, Tabasco, and Veracruz—all states heavily affected by oil production. The amount awarded to a specific zone depends on a range of indicators of oil impact. Over the first decade of the twenty-first century, the definition of "oil impact" has become more expansive than the 1980 "no drilling, no impact" notion. According to the guidelines that went into effect in 2008, oil impact should be determined using a methodology based on seven indicators. The first indicator is oil production in the area (onshore or offshore crude or natural gas, refined products, basic or secondary petrochemicals). The second indicator is the presence of an actual installation, namely, wells in production or in the drilling process. Also included are any number of installations under the category of "strategic installations." This category encompasses zones affected by seismic studies (an exploration method that detects subsurface geological features using sound waves). The third indicator considers how local residents are affected in the activities of their livelihoods (fishing, agriculture, commerce, service industry).

Another indicator considers how many Pemex workers are in the municipality. The next consideration is how much Pemex has invested in the community in terms of the works and maintenance already undertaken. According to official guidelines, oil impact is also measured by environmental impact: "It will take into account the environmental impact that Pemex as well as the subsidiary branches (PEP, etc.) have had on the air, water, and soil. It will also consider environmental protection measures put into place when carrying out new projects" (Pemex 2007b: 20-21). Seventh and last, the methodology of determining oil impact includes measuring where the community ranks on the marginalization index as indicated by Mexico's National Population Council. These indicators are to be used by the PEP administrative council when it decides on the distribution of a benefit as well as in the annual review of benefits received by the oil municipalities.

**Table 4.1. 2008 cash (*donativos*) and in-kind (*donaciones*) distributions for high-, medium-, and low-impact states (in pesos)**

|  | High | Medium | Low |
|---|---|---|---|
| Cash | 808,631,100 | 151,053,900 | 23,284,100 |
| In-kind | 639,900,800 | 145,270,200 | 104,060,400 |
| Total | 1,448,534,900 | 296,324,100 | 127,344,500 |
|  |  | High-impact total: 1,477,560,000 |  |
|  |  | National total (in billions): 2.667 |  |

Sources: Pemex 2009b,c; 2011

For the purpose of rationalizing its social and financial responsibilities toward communities, Pemex divides the nation into a three zones: those affected to a high degree by oil extraction, those affected to a medium degree, and those that only host Pemex installations. Campeche is one of five states in the high-degree category, along with Chiapas, Tabasco, Tamaulipas, and Veracruz. The medium-degree states are Coahuila, Guanajuato, Hidalgo, Nuevo León, and Oaxaca (the states where Mexico's major refineries are located). The states of Aguascalientes, Baja California, Chihuahua, Colima, Durango, Jalisco, Mexico, Michoacán, Morelos, Puebla, Querétero, Quintana Roo, San Luís Potosí, Sinaloa, Sonora, and Tlaxcala have Pemex installations, but not of significant influence or impact. Together, the high- and medium-impact states are known as the priority states, and those ten priority states receive 90 percent of Pemex social development funding through the donativos and donaciones program.

Donations in cash or in kind are distributed quarterly either to states or directly to municipalities. Approximately three-quarters of the benefits go to state governments, and the remainder is directed toward municipalities. Not all municipalities in a state, however, get access to the funds. In Campeche the state government receives funds, as does the municipality of Carmen; on rare occasions the municipality of Palizada, a rural municipality adjacent to Carmen in the Laguna de Términos region, also has received funds. Of the funds that are initially distributed to the state level, approximately 80 percent reach the municipality of Carmen.

Cash and in-kind funds are primarily directed toward serving the basic needs of the public. Typically, one-third of the aid is given in cash

**Table 4.2. Social development funds (*donativos* and *donaciones*) in priority states with high and medium impact, 2005–2009 (in millions of pesos)**

|           | 2005   | 2006 | 2007 | 2008   | 2009   |
|-----------|--------|------|------|--------|--------|
| Campeche  | 173.46 | 192  | 320  | 350.00 | 175.00 |
| Chiapas   | 132.23 | 93   | 121  | 101.58 | 94.00  |
| Tamaulipas| 87.71  | 197  | 302  | 290.82 | 267.65 |
| Veracruz  | 221.30 | 267  | 314  | 361.93 | 247.02 |
| Tabasco   | 282.43 | 78   | 318  | 411.46 | 272.83 |
| Coahuila  | 21.13  | 33   | 25   | 31.11  | 28.55  |
| Guanajuato| 12.20  | 19   | 33   | 56.53  | 79.91  |
| Hidalgo   | 29.85  | 56   | 77   | 60.32  | 46.03  |
| Nuevo Leon| 36.81  | 32   | 95   | 97.74  | 53.16  |
| Oaxaca    | 38.84  | 43   | 29   | 50.61  | 121.05 |

Sources: Pemex 2008c; 2009a,c; 2010a,b

donativos, while the greater proportion is given through in-kind dona-ciones. While the in-kind aid may consist of consumer goods such as construction materials, Pemex prefers to donate its own industrial prod-ucts. Asphalt and fuel (gasoline or diesel) are the top items in donation contracts between Pemex and a state. Millions of gallons of gas are des-tined for use in official vehicles such as ambulances, in machinery, and for powering public works systems and generators.[4]

Cash donations do not go directly to government agencies. Instead, recipients of the lesser-funded cash donativos are nonprofit organiza-tions of an educational or cultural nature or in health, science, or tech-nology sectors. They may also go to any federal agency or fund known as a fideicomiso created by either a governmental or nongovernmental agency. NGOs along with agricultural associations or ejidos, states, and municipalities are also eligible to receive in-kind aid, which may include real estate and commodities. Foreign institutions with purposes other than humanitarian or scientific research are prohibited from receiving donaciones.[5]

States with greater oil influence receive the most commodities (*bienes muebles*), approaching 5 million pesos in value in 2008. This stands in sharp contrast with states of mid-level oil influence, which receive just over $75,000 in commodities, typically items like computers for librar-ies or classrooms, an ambulance for a town's Centro de Salud (health center), or even oil barrels that a village can convert into trash cans for a community sanitation project. Across Mexico, funds distributed to the state governments go toward road and highway construction, paving, and widening projects, potable water installation, electrification, bridge construction and repair, and even the construction of a museum. In Campeche, state-level distributions form the backbone of annual budgets for other projects that will elevate the quality of life for residents of the municipality of Carmen and surrounding communities as well as provide assistance for altura and ribereño fishers (Pemex 2008d). Municipal distributions, on the other hand, may partially or wholly fund the construction of a local police station, refurbish the public marketplace, construct recreation facilities, effect school improvements, or make housing improvements such as floors, roofs, and plumbing. In Isla Aguada, one project was to build an ice factory to help the ribereño fishers by providing an essential step in getting their products from sea to market. Without their own access to ice, the fishers remained dependent on the powerful bodega owners who controlled the whole chain of production.

In addition to funding projects and bestowing goods, Pemex's social development program aims to change the nature of Pemex's relationships with oil-affected communities. Pemex asserts that an effective way to do this is to further integrate local people into the work of the oil industry. This is not done by hiring local workers into the unionized ranks of the parastatal itself, but rather Pemex purports to cultivate and support local service providers through the social development program so it can strengthen its ties with oil-affected communities, specifically by offering workshops and training programs to prepare local people to work in the oil industry (Pemex 2008d). However, as Pemex subcontracts more and more of its work, from the everyday exploration and production in the Campeche Sound to the provision of the social development public works to the private sector, it will no doubt be more difficult to keep the promises of this community-oriented mission.

## The Pemex Benefits Chain

Despite the large amounts of money, the multiplicity of funds, and the comprehensiveness of their scope, the benefits awarded by Pemex to the state of Campeche and the municipality of Carmen have not created viable options for diversified development or social change. Pemex's mission of social development is compromised—not only by the institutional notion of what constitutes how communities are affected by oil but also how these effects are mitigated. The problem may go deeper than this, however. Studies of the parastatal's Office of Social Development carried out by Fundar, a well-known transparency and accountability watchdog group, as well as thorough investigative reporting by the magazine *Contralínea* indicate corruption and cronyism at multiple levels of the Pemex benefits chain (Pérez 2007, 2009a; Pirker, Arias Rodríguez, and Ireta Guzmán 2007). Specific problems include those with transparency in awarding funds, accountability in both the distribution and reconciling of funds and the results of projects, and circumventing local concerns in favor of state needs.

For residents the infrastructural projects, most of which are carried out in the urban center of Ciudad del Carmen, are top-down rather than bottom-up. Decisions about what neighborhoods and communities need are not generated at the local level but instead often driven by what goods and services Pemex has to supply at any given time. This often leads to conflict at the very local colonia level, especially when the OBMs appear to serve Pemex interests rather than those of the residents.

Pemex exercises control over the types of works offered and the works themselves. The OBM projects do not require a transfer of resources to the state or municipal government but are carried out directly by the parastatal. However, in many cases, Pemex contracts private companies to perform the public works jobs. For workers and business owners, part of the putative benefit of public works is Pemex giving them a part in the project as another dimension of giving back to the community. Yet, in the contracting process Pemex tends to award very large contracts (or consolidates contracts for small jobs) to national or national multinational companies that exclude the participation of smaller, local businesses.

The NGO Fundar examined Pemex's social development program of donativos and donaciones for 1995-2006. Fundar found fault both with Pemex's reporting and with its corporate accountability in the social development program. According to Fundar, even though it is possible to consult the lists of distributions by state and of beneficiaries on the Pemex website, information concerning the actual application of the resources in the oil-affected zones is scarce. There is no way, that is, to verify that the resources are applied in accordance with the established norms. In addition, information is missing about the impact of the aid on the conditions of life of the population or the development of the beneficiary communities.

The study showed that the distribution of cash funds was heavily concentrated in three priority states: Tabasco, Veracruz, and Campeche together received more than 50 percent of the aid, with Campeche receiving a total of 21 percent of the donativos and about 11 percent of the donaciones. Fundar found that the distribution was skewed in favor of benefits awarded directly to state governments rather than to municipalities: in 2006, of the approximately $70 million in cash benefits, 91.6 percent went directly to state governments, with $36 million of the total going to the state of Tabasco.

The Fundar report points out that Pemex's social development distribution lacks indicators to measure the problems of social and economic development in the priority municipalities. In other words, despite the seven ways that Pemex established to measure oil impact, there are no follow-up measures for evaluating the effectiveness of Pemex's contributions in mitigating the impacts. Likewise, there is no tool for measuring the viability of solutions offered to solve the problems created by oil impact. However, the biggest weakness is not in Pemex's system of reporting but in the parastatal's actual legal framework. Fundar's criticism of the legislation in effect through 2006 was based on the baroque and opaque procedures routinely employed by Pemex in distributing development assistance. Fundar found that cash donativo funds lost their public character as soon as they moved into the hands of a third party, whether a state, a municipality, or a private person. As soon as cash donativo funds were received, for example, the third party was accountable only for assuring that the funds were indeed received. A greater problem exists in providing a paper trail documenting the name of the recipient, the amount awarded, and the purpose of the award (Fundar 2007: 26). The social development program did not have a mechanism in place for tracking or following up on the applications of beneficiaries or for compliance in the use of funds. The documents Fundar received through Mexico's freedom of information act demonstrated that the administrative system in place at Pemex required no genuine accountability as to the use of funds. Nor did it provide a way of measuring the mitigation of "oil impact" in priority states.

When a state company like Pemex manages a substantial share of the national wealth, such as spending 9 billion pesos on social development through PEP, demands for accountability and transparency as well as measurable results arise to ensure that the nation's patrimony is indeed being used for the good of the nation. Establishing expectations of transparency and accountability along with measurable outcomes for success is part of only a very recent adoption by Pemex of private-sector norms and standards. The truth of the matter is that Pemex was forced to change. By the end of the Fox administration, accountability was low. Writing for *Contralínea*, Ana Lilia Pérez (2009a) reports that state employees were using the Pemex social development funds as a *caja chica*, a petty-cash box for staff to use freely without any accountability. Similar corruption was found in state agencies including the Consejo Nacional para la Cultura y las Artes (Conaculta), Instituto Mexicano del Seguro Social (IMSS), and Instituto de Seguridad y Servicios Sociales de los Trabajadores del Estado (ISSTE) (ibid.).

A lack of public confidence in state agencies due to a widespread perception of corruption and lack of transparency led the Calderón government to address the issue from the outset of the administration in the 2007–2012 national development plan. Calderón called for a national corruption and good governance survey to obtain the public's opinion on the performance of the nation's public sector (Mexico, Office of the President 2007).

Previous scandals inside Pemex revealed a highly personalized misuse of funds, as when Director-General Raúl Muñoz Leos was accused of paying for his wife's plastic surgery with state funds. This time the investigations of Fundar found that the manipulation of funds in and out of the social development account followed a particular pattern that revealed a consistent partisan politicization of Pemex funds. A comparison of Pemex's reported authorized and executed budgets between 1998 and 2006 reveals increases of more than 60 percent for each of the years 2000, 2003, and 2006, all federal election years (Pirker, Arias Rodríguez, and Ireta Guzmán 2007: 28). According to an investigation by *Contralinea*, in 2006–2007 multiple cases of influence peddling were uncovered in which the right-of-center PAN stood to benefit from suspect donations to Panista candidates from the Pemex social development fund. Multiple in-kind grants of asphalt and fuel, valued at more than a million pesos in each instance, were made to municipalities that had no Pemex installations or other oil-related activity (Pérez 2009a).

Meanwhile, another blatant case of partisanship was revealed. Municipalities in the state of Oaxaca, many with supposedly extremely marginal Pemex installations, did not receive any Pemex social development funds. These were municipalities governed by the left-of-center Partido de la Revolución Democrática (PRD). In 2007–2008, among all the oil-affected municipalities in the state of Oaxaca, only two under PRD leadership received any funds, for a total of 400,000 pesos, while the municipalities under PAN leadership received 42 million pesos (ibid.).

In 2007 a host of new rules and regulations were put in place to end the discretionary allotment of resources by instituting the fixed category of *estados petroleros prioritarios* for priority distribution. Beginning in 2008 the financial scheme of the program also was regularized to prevent discretionary allotments, especially in municipalities that could not demonstrate oil impact. The new scheme guaranteed that 90 percent of the resources in each year's budget would go to states and municipalities identified as priority zones (Campeche, Chiapas, Coahuila, Guanajuato, Hidalgo, Nuevo León, Oaxaca, Tabasco, Tamaulipas, and Veracruz). The remaining 10 percent was to be made available, in this order, to the priority states, the rest of the states, and the civil-society sector in the priority states and municipalities including NGOs and citizens groups such as cooperatives.

For Pemex's social development program, this involved many concrete changes. One of the major transformations was to create a new atmosphere of transparency in the area of donativos and donaciones. At the top of PEP's social development agenda was transparency in reporting. Before the restructuring all information regarding recipients, amounts, and descriptions of projects was restricted to Pemex, donors, and recipients. Now PEP's social development division has a webpage to publish details of the most "relevant" aid grants.

Another transformation was in the application process for the solicitation of funds. Previously irregular and personalistic, the application process was broadened and clarified. Rather than the previous system in which a group applied by letter to the director general's office, a new standard application form was drawn up requiring data such as the technical specifications of the project, the benefit to the community the project would offer, and exactly what type of aid would be required and in precisely what quantities. The use of a standardized form signed by the applicant's legal representative allows for a more equitable basis of comparison among projects competing for funds.

The division employed technology to a greater extent. Pemex proposed the creation of the Sistema Integral de Donativos y Donaciones (SIDD), a web-based system for tracking and reporting disbursements. Through the new system, the old manual system of archiving requests and filing reports on completed projects would be changed to an online system. Another effort toward transparency was the integration of the

SIDD system and the website to make project verification results publicly available (listed by state and broken down by project), going back to the year 2007. The implementation of this online system would be crucial for Pemex's stated goal of following up on the expenditure of public funds. It is also important for the assessment process itself. For example, one of the indicators for determining oil impact is the amount of Pemex investment already in a municipality, and the online archives would help to track projects in a given municipality across time.

The proposed changes were a breath of fresh air for the social development office. But the SIDD system was slow to get up and running. For nearly three years following the reforms' effective date of January 1, 2008, the system was not in place and the hodge-podge of information previously available regarding donativos and donaciones by state was replaced by short summaries of total amounts distributed (by year). Less information was available than before the reform. In 2011 the Office of Social Development created an accessible website that fulfills the promises of the reform, listing (by state) allocations, project descriptions, and indicators as to the project's completion (2007–2010).[6]

## Politicization of Benefits from Top to Bottom

These "technical" issues of reporting are highly politicized matters. Pemex's Office of Social Development, sitting high above Mexico City in Pemex Tower, was a nest of political cronyism with the deepest and most problematic ties being those of its director, Campeche political functionary Yolanda Valladares Valle, who was named to the post in January 2007 (Pérez 2007). Her appointment demonstrated the partisan mission of the Calderón administration to internally restructure Pemex. Valladares Valle wasted no time in carrying out a so-called Panification of the office, quickly revamping the personnel of the parastatal's social development arm in Mexico City and the southeastern regional offices. Notably, the Campeche office was stacked with PAN cronies (Pérez 2007).

With both PRI and PAN connections (she was a Priista until converting to the PAN in 1994), Valladares was a family friend and no doubt the personal choice of President Calderón's right-hand man, Juan Camilo Mouriño, who was undersecretary to the president while Calderón was secretary of energy in the Fox administration. Mouriño later headed Calderón's presidential campaign team and his transition team after the election. When Calderón took office, Mouriño became his chief of staff and later Mexico's interior minister, the highest nonelected post in the country, at age thirty-six.

The status of Mouriño at the center of political power placed Campeche's oil politics at center stage. At the rocky outset of Felipe Calderón's disputed term, Mouriño was perhaps even more despised by the Left than the president himself. The Left's ammunition consisted of the most heated stuff that a nationalist can dream up in politics on either side of the U.S.-Mexican border. At the center of the controversy was Mouriño's citizenship (he was naturalized at the age of eighteen) and a scandal over suspect oil deals with private multinationals. The two scandals came together in an explosive confluence of oil nationalism.

The interior minister's family emigrated to Campeche from Spain when Mouriño (known by the nickname Ivan) was a child. In Campeche the family amassed considerable wealth through business contracts with Pemex in the Gulf of Mexico. According to accusations that brought Mouriño before a congressional inquiry in March 2008, between 2000 and 2004 the interior minister signed several contracts with the subsidiary Pemex Refinación, for a total value of $4 million, as the representative of his family's Transportes Especializados Ivancar, a fuel carrier company (Méndez and Pérez Silva 2008). Under contract with Pemex, Ivancar's income jumped from 250,000 pesos in 2000 to 40 million pesos in 2005. Mouriño negotiated these contracts while he was a member of the Congreso Nacional, chairman of the energy commission in the lower house, and later adviser to the Ministry of Energy (Castillo Garcia 2008). Despite the evidence stacked against him, Mouriño was not found guilty of any charges of impropriety.

As a Campechano and a Panista with powerful family business ties to the companies contracting with Pemex in the Campeche Sound, Mouriño was perfectly placed to link up Campeche's political and economic aspirations with the uppermost echelons of the Calderón administration. Through 2008 Carmen's PAN municipal officials and Campeche's PRI state governor's office were counting on the interior minister to convince Calderón to push Pemex and the Congreso Nacional toward what they saw as a huge development boost for the region: a new refinery. Mouriño, trying to boost his own political clout and credibility in his home state, expressed his desire to advocate for the refinery on the state's behalf (*Tribuna Campeche* 2008b). Many suspected he was preparing a run for the governorship of Campeche in the 2009 midterm elections. A refinery for Campeche would be a huge win for Mouriño and seal the deal on his political fortunes.

On a scale far outweighing the bits and pieces brought by the social development program, Mexico's first new refinery in thirty years was at least a $10 billion project. But Campeche would have to campaign hard against stiff competition. Nine states—Campeche, Tabasco, Oaxaca, Veracruz, Puebla, Tamaulipas, Tlaxcala, Hidalgo, and Michoacán—competed for the refinery on the grounds that the facility would serve as a source of employment and of local and regional growth and development. The construction phase alone could bring up to 20,000 direct jobs and tens of thousands more indirectly. Once the facility went online, the permanently operating facility could give 40,000 jobs to a region.

Campeche soon mounted its campaign with a proposal to host a refinery on 750 hectares of land in the coastal community of Seybaplaya, on the coast between Carmen and the capital city of Campeche. State officials expected the plant to serve as a solid platform for regional development. The voices calling for the economic benefits of a refinery drowned out those wary of the effects of a refinery on air, water, and soil for generations to come. Even though the proposal promised "a new-generation" refinery designed to take advantage of the latest technology and have the lowest environmental impact, environmentalists and residents have long histories with and ongoing concerns about large installations in their communities. The Gas de Atasta recompression plant as well as the Planta de Nitrógeno de Cantarell have been embroiled for years in litigation over damages from contamination emanating from them.

In 1997 Pemex contracted a private firm, Compañía de Nitrógeno de Cantarell, to construct a plant and subsequently produce and supply nitrogen gas to 210 offshore wells. The commitment was for fifteen years. The plant, built on thirty hectares on the Peninsula of Atasta within the boundaries of the Laguna de Términos Flora and Fauna Protection Area, became operational in 2000. The Instituto Nacional Ecologísta (INE) and what was then the Secretaría de Medio Ambiente y Recursos Naturales y Pesca (Semarnap, the Ministry of Environment, Natural Resources, and Fisheries) granted permission for its construction in the protected area. An environmental impact report produced by the holding company of the plant's investment consortium concluded that the facility, which would produce upward of a billion cubic feet of nitrogen daily, would not have an adverse impact on the environment. And yet,

Cows grazing beside the gas recompression plant on the peninsula of Atasta in the Laguna de Términos protected area. The sign reads: "Protect Green Space." Author's photo.

predictably, problems with the plant abound, many of them related to the hundreds of miles of pipes running beneath the Peninsula of Atasta, some carrying nitrogen gas, others carrying the millions of gallons of seawater needed to cool the turbines that power the plant (Flores and Pérez 2004).

Even though the current corporate attitude at the "new" Pemex is based on transparency and accountability, the ethos is not retrospective. Over the past few years studies have emerged from other sources showing the very real effects of the presence of the oil industry, notably within the protected area. Residents of San Antonio Cárdenas, living just six miles from the Gas de Atasta recompression plant, worry about the constant flaring of sulfurous gas at the plant. They noticed that the corrugated metal on the roofs of their houses was corroding. What did that mean for their health and the environment? In 2004 a year-long study of rainwater collected in San Antonio Cárdenas conducted by researchers from the Universidad del Carmen demonstrated excessive sulfate levels, seven times higher than the normal level observed in the region. They concluded that flaring at the gas recompression plant was the source of humanly produced acid rain in San Antonio Cárdenas (Cerón et al. 2008).

The justification for the refinery as a platform for development ignored this kind of background on existing facilities' impacts. Instead, Governor Hurtado and refinery proponents argued that Campeche deserved the refinery as a way of making up for the severity of the oil industry's impact on the zone. He emphasized that the fishing sector is most affected by the oil industry: "In this state there were 600 shrimp trawlers in the ports of Campeche and Ciudad del Carmen. In 1978 they achieved a capture of 27,000 tons of shrimp. Now, we only have 150 trawlers. Of the 400 that were in Ciudad del Carmen, only 11 are left" (in *Tribuna Campeche* 2009e). Hurtado showed confidence that Campeche would receive the refinery: "We are going to start receiving a direct benefit from oil . . . It is a matter of justice that this refinery be established in Campeche because this will be the way of compensating many years of injustice" (ibid.). For thirty years the Bay of Campeche has been a major producer of Mexico's domestic and exported energy. Higuera and Pavón reported in 2009 that 83 percent of Mexico's crude and 34 percent of its natural gas came from the bay. The addition of the refinery was part of the fulfillment of the state's "vocation" as a petroleum production center. The argument was that Campeche was owed the refinery, and Hurtado went so far as to call the awarding of the refinery an act of "social justice" (ibid.).

Governor Hurtado's reasons for supporting the refinery initiative precisely paralleled reasons for opposing the installation. Hurtado stressed the large percentage of Mexico's oil that came from Campeche, and voices in opposition to the bid expressed the disproportionate burden this oil production placed on the region. Hosting a refinery would burden an already stressed coastal ecosystem. While Hurtado framed the refinery as a key step in the path toward development, how could local residents expect a different development outcome from further entrenchment in the extractive industry? What is more, while the state saw a refinery as a reward for enduring decades of oil impact, environmentalists and local communities may in fact perceive it as punitive. That the installation could, as a result of pollution, actually perpetrate social harm or injustice was an irony that did not come into the state's calculations.

The Campeche state government projected confidence with its bid, no doubt due to the intimacy with Interior Secretary Mouriño. But the campaign to bring the refinery to Campeche came to a shocking climax. On November 4, 2008 (the evening of Barack Obama's election in the United States), Mouriño was killed when his Lear jet went down in a fiery crash onto the rush-hour streets of downtown Mexico City. The immediate speculation was that Mouriño and his seven fellow passengers—including well-known former federal prosecutor José Luis Santiago Vasconcelos, who had recently resigned after a lack of success in fighting Mexico's increasingly powerful drug cartels—were intentionally brought down by a bomb. That speculation turned out to be unfounded, but rumors and suspicions abounded.

Campeche officials held out hopes to receive the bid. One state representative urged, "The least President Calderón can do is bring the refinery to Campeche and name it after his friend, Juan Camilo Mouriño" (in Ynuretta 2009). But in the end, Mouriño's death spelled doom for Campeche's refinery bid. Even though he was constantly embroiled in scandal and skewered by the Left, Mouriño embodied more than anyone else the closing of the PAN-PRI gap that had clogged the flow of resources and stymied political negotiations. Campeche's PRD state congressional coordinator, Alberto Cutz Can, said Campeche's plans for a refinery died with Juan Camilo Mouriño. The refinery was eventually awarded to Tula in the state of Hidalgo. Campeche, Cutz Can mused, has always been Mexico's "ugly ducking," and now it would continue to be (Arredondo Ortiz 2008).

## The Hydrocarbon Extraction Fund

In the immediate glow of peak production at Cantarell, state and municipal officials were constantly looking for new ways to garner resources based on oil impact. Even if some efforts failed, such as the refinery bid, others were bound to be successful. With the federal fiscal reform of 2007 that passed both chambers of the Congreso Nacional with overwhelming majorities, Pemex's fiscal framework underwent modification. At the center of the reform was how to allocate diminishing oil proceeds of the post-peak era. The reform specified a timeline by which the federal government would keep less revenue and the states would receive more. Additionally, the reform created the Fondo de Extracción de Hidrocarburos (Fexhi), a compensatory fund intended to level the playing field for oil-producing and non-oil-producing states across the country. The creation of the Fexhi constituted an admission that oil production creates developmental inequalities. This part of the fiscal reform package was obviously partisan, born out of a proposal sponsored by the PRI. The original proposal called for a redistribution of 2 percent of petroleum income directly back to the states most affected by extraction, refining, and production. This compensation would stand as an acknowledgement of the heavy toll the oil industry takes on host regions, particularly in Tabasco, Tamaulipas, Veracruz, and Campeche.

In its final approved version, the Fexhi became one of two means established to distribute funds to federal entities based on the Derecho Ordinario sobre Hidrocarburos (ordinary hydrocarbons duty) paid by Pemex. Created alongside the Fexhi in the 2007 fiscal reform was the compensation fund for ten low-income states involved neither in mining nor in petroleum that were now to share 20 percent of the proceeds of a new gasoline tax for regional development projects. At the outset, the Fexhi was based on 0.46 percent of the amount (*importe*) obtained through the ordinary hydrocarbons duty paid by PEP to the federal government. As declines in Fexhi contributions set in, modifications could be made to the compensation fund to increase contributions to states. Reformers at the state and municipal levels in Campeche have continually sought a higher-percentage distribution (making proposals to the Congreso Nacional for as high as 3 percent in 2010) to make up for declines in production and income. The greatest success was an increase in 2009 to 0.6 percent awarded to the four highest-priority states.

Members of the PRD, usually happy to promote social welfare, were against the increase proposal. They read it as cronyism and a concession to strengthen southern PRI governors. Indeed, all four of the named oil-affected states were PRI-governed states. At the same time, the rationale for defining oil-affected states is valid—namely, that the presence of Pemex has had consequences for development and infrastructure: roads, environmental damage, contaminated water and soil, and so on. The oil industry also spurs fundamental changes in people's livelihoods, notably in the displacement of agricultural and fishing activities. There has been little oversight of the use of these funds on a local level. However, at the crux of the debate is how to define the degree of "affectedness," even if it meant showing the extent to which the areas were stunted or underdeveloped because of oil.

Campeche was ready to make a good case for getting its share. On the occasion of his state of the municipality speech in September 2008, Carmen's municipal president Seara Sierra called for oil-affected areas to receive a more than 20 percent increase in the amount granted at the local level as well as a move toward decentralization in the distribution of funds as they arrived in the state from the Fexhi. Describing Carmen as "truly impacted" and thus distinguishing his town from other entities in the state, mainly those in the interior, Seara Sierra tried to distinguish Carmen as unique within Campeche. He called for a greater emphasis on the "petro municipalities" over and above the rest of the oil-affected state (Campeche 2008).

From the point of view of a municipal leader, local governance and local handling of finances is of the greatest concern. This is especially true when municipal leaders do not share the party affiliation of the governor. The state capital is not an oil-affected area. While Carmen might be a political backwater, any legislation that favors genuinely affected municipalities would benefit Carmen over the PRI-dominated Campeche capital city. And Seara Sierra's call for a greater amount from the fund would also represent his political dissent as a PAN party representative against the PRI legislation and Campeche's PRI governor, Hurtado.

Municipal leader Seara Sierra thus proposed a new method of local support for the municipio petrolero. At the first national meeting of petroleum municipalities, hosted in the state capital of Campeche, Seara Sierra suggested that rather than distributing 20 percent of Fexhi income to municipalities, why not 50 percent? Additionally, he proposed instituting a 12.5 percent direct line of income from the Fexhi, bypassing the state, and moving funds straight to the "directly impacted" municipalities (*CarmenHoy* 2008). Seara Sierra, backed by a host of state and local politicos, pitched this plan to decentralize funding and to "localize" state and federal funds while simultaneously opening up the use of funds to private-sector investment opportunities. In ongoing debates that filled newspaper pages for weeks on end, the municipal leader and the governor traded views. Hurtado emphasized the statewide nature of public works projects supported by Fexhi funds. The governor was quick to advertise the scope and number of projects in the state, and he stressed that construction was in the hands of Campechanos themselves.

Before the Fexhi, the state simply could not mount the projects that were needed. Some of the Fexhi projects are megamillion-peso projects. Among these were two major undertakings: a four-lane Mérida-Campeche highway and a cross-peninsula aqueduct project. In other instances, the funds are used for investments at the local level that are deemed necessary for governance. For example, in the summer of 2008, Hurtado used the state-apportioned Fexhi funds to purchase pickup trucks for local officials across the state who otherwise lacked access to reliable transportation. Funds are also regularly spent on ambulances and vehicles for health-care workers. Garbage trucks and other public works vehicles, in very short supply around the region, are occasionally found on the Fexhi budget.

As the top oil-producing state, Campeche has the most at stake in garnering funds from the Fexhi, and equally it has the most to lose if conditions change. Both the creation of the fund and the percentages that states would garner had been negotiated in 2007–2008 when production rates and oil prices were still strong. The budget was flexible enough to be generous to the oil-affected states. In turn, the states, which had waited long enough to be recognized, perhaps became shortsighted and failed to hold out for the most advantageous long-term scenario. With the drop in production and volatility in the oil market, the beneficial intentions of the Fexhi had been lost in Campeche by the second half of 2009. As the amount Campeche was receiving from the Fexhi increased, the amount the state drew from the federal government's general fund (to which all states are entitled regardless of resource wealth) fell. Campeche's general fund allotment dropped by 18 percent due to the higher percentage of Fexhi distributions allowed by fiscal reforms (Núñez Jiménez 2009).

The projected Fexhi income budgeted for Campeche for 2009 was more than 1.4 billion pesos. As the state began to experience a loss of overall income approaching nearly 10 percent, PRI politicians sought another reform in fall 2009, to raise the distribution to 0.8 percent. As economic conditions have deteriorated along with the production from Cantarell, the legislative pursuit of funds has not succeeded in keeping up with developmental needs at the state or local levels. In terms of politics and the conditions of oil production in the Campeche Sound, the Fexhi is the most precarious of the major project funds in Campeche. As an extraordinary fund, the Fexhi could disappear should conditions get bad enough in Gulf production, spelling major funding problems for Campeche if Pemex reneged on its commitment to local resources, which was exactly the next shoe to drop.

## Pemex's Post-Peak Funding Failures

Mexico's midterm elections in July 2009 shuffled leadership in the municipality of Carmen and the governor's office in the state capital. The election of PRI candidates in both places followed a dramatic nationwide trend toward a resurgence of the historically dominant party and away from President Felipe Calderón's right-of-center, pro-business PAN. In the atmosphere of the campaign and subsequent elections, lame-duck administrations, and transitions, the funding agreement between Pemex, the state of Campeche, and the municipality of Carmen expired. Pemex refused to award Campeche or Carmen any 2009 resources. Was it political maneuvering on the part of an outgoing administration, a desperate financial move by Pemex as the parastatal in a tight spot, or what amounted to no more than a terrible clerical error?

Clearly, it was more than a simple glitch. Tension was high during the course of the funding embargo, marking a change in the very nature of Pemex's relationship with the state. Gone were platitudes, deferential posturing, and groveling that marked the previous administrations' attempts to win Campeche's favor with the president and the parastatal. The only option for the new governor of Campeche, Fernando Ortega Bernés, was to take a harder line in order to demonstrate to his constituents that he was willing to fight for the state's patrimony. After several months of undelivered aid, I watched the governor tell his constituents in a televised speech, "Campeche feels defrauded and cheated, and I am not going to permit this." Knowing that the 2009 funding stoppage was more than accidental and certain that Pemex's finances were a matter of political will on the part of the parastatal and the Ministry of Finance as much as the geophysics of the ocean floor, Campeche officials went back to the negotiating table with Pemex. State and municipal officials signed the Acuerdo Marco in February 2010 to ensure the relationship would last at least another decade.

Though securely under obligations once again, Pemex delayed in actually delivering the aid. Fishers awaited the first payments to the fideicomisos of the altura and ribereño sectors, some 20 million pesos, and it finally arrived in September 2010. But citizens were wary of Pemex's renewed commitment to fund Carmen, as delivery dates for promised benefits checks came and went. Work crews awaited asphalt to continue road-paving projects. The material never arrived. Municipal president Aracely Escalante Jasso tried to be positive: "Pemex has made us this promise, and we are expecting that these materials that they have given us in kind will arrive" (*Tribuna Campeche* 2010).

A year later, Governor Ortega Bernés was still irritated. "It's not fair," he said in a December 2011 speech, "this situation that Campeche is facing" (in *YucatanAll* 2011). The governor pointed to a paradox: 1.9 mbpd of the nation's total oil production of nearly 2.5 mbpd came from the Campeche Sound. "Yet there is no correspondence between these oil contributions and either fiscal contributions or federal resources" received in return, he said. "We are looking for projects to compensate Campeche and especially the municipality of Carmen . . . to serve not only Campeche but the region and the whole of southeastern Mexico."

Because Pemex has generated a culture of compensation and wholly defined the parameters of what triggers the distribution of benefits, the term "oil-affected" has a strictly economic connotation in the Laguna de Términos region. Yet so much of everyday life is affected by oil, and much of it falls outside of the realm of what can be compensated. For the fishers, their frustration that Pemex will not admit to ever committing environmental damage is constantly growing. Pemex continues to "compensate" yet will not agree that declines across multiple fisheries are at least in part due to the environmental impact wrought by oil and gas exploration and production, a shell game that for fishers is no longer simply absurd, but criminal. In big, public tragedies like the Usumacinta accident, Pemex did pay up—with little ceremony, no admission of guilt, and certainly no apologies for environmental culpability. The compensation was just under $450,000 awarded to Carmen's 4,208 Sagarpa-credentialed fishers, giving each one enough, according to a fishing-union leader in Ciudad del Carmen, to buy fifty-three gallons of gasoline—two trips for a ribereño shrimper (*Tribuna Campeche* 2008a).

In terms of regional development on behalf of the municipality, the types of aid Pemex gives are essentially self-serving, shaping development toward the needs of Pemex itself. Infrastructural public works in the form of roads, bridges, electrification, sanitation, and potable water do have a trickle-down effect of helping residents. But first and foremost, the goals are to facilitate the workaday activities of Pemex and its contracted service providers. The major effects of the benefits may only serve to exacerbate the problems that the municipality of Carmen has experienced since the arrival of the oil industry in the region: out-of-control growth in an ecologically delicate environment.

The outlying areas around the Laguna de Términos have had mixed experiences with the social development offered by Pemex benefits. Long suffering from chronic underdevelopment because of the continuous pattern of natural resource exploitation and state neglect, these communities found themselves in need of basic infrastructural services such as roads, potable water, and electricity. OBM funds are designed to provide these services throughout the municipality. Also important are schools, health services, and social support services such as programs for women. Under the donativos and donaciones social development program, Pemex is much better at giving asphalt and fuel than cash for other community projects. The latter types of projects are not flourishing.

On the whole, the municipality of Carmen has fared better than neighboring municipalities because of its ability to garner proceeds from oil wealth. Of the state's eleven municipalities, Carmen is second only to the capital of Campeche in a social marginalization index published by Mexico's National Population Council (Conapo 2005). In stark contrast to neighboring municipalities on the interior of Campeche and the smaller rural municipalities of the Laguna de Términos that received only occasional funds from Pemex programs, Carmen was the state's only municipality registering a level of "low" rather than "medium" or "high" marginalization, in a state that ranks nationally as a high-marginalization entity.[7] The index, a multidimensional portrait comprised of factors such as housing (type, quality, size, and occupancy level), education levels and opportunities, and income, found across the nation as well as within states and municipalities "a profound inequality of participation in the process of development and in the enjoyment of its benefits" (Conapo 2005).

If the municipality of Carmen and indeed all of the oil-affected regions continue to struggle with Pemex over funds in the future and if those funds dwindle as the Gulf's shallow fields run dry, the prospects for the region's robust economy look uncertain. Economic growth and social development are skewed toward the occasional and hard-won rewards of the lasting scars of Pemex.

## PART 3

# POST-PEAK POLITICS:
# ENERGY REFORM AND THE RACE
# TO CLAIM THE GULF OF MEXICO

July 2008. Walking the littered and pot-holed streets of Isla Aguada as the sun went down and residents stirred from late-afternoon torpor into early evening activity, I could hear the hum and occasional blare of televisions from the open windows and doors. Without fail, I would catch a snippet of a government-sponsored advertisement in support of the Calderón administration's energy reform. One ad portrayed a middle-class young man putting gas in his car and musing about the irony of importing refined oil from the United States. Another showed a thirty-something schoolteacher with books in his hands standing in front of a white board covered with complicated equations. The message was always the same. "Let's not fool ourselves," chided the schoolteacher. "No one wants to privatize Pemex, not the politicians or the president or the citizens. All we want is for our gas to be produced here." That was why this earnest (and numerate!) schoolteacher was supporting the PAN-sponsored energy-reform proposal, the ad's voice-over informed me. The tagline confirmed the take-home message: "With the reform of Pemex, everybody wins."

Another TV ad sponsored by the federal government regularly shown in the summer of 2008 on the major network Televisa likewise aimed at working- and middle-class Mexicans. A woman appeared in the foreground against a backdrop of simple, black and white, animated drawings that appeared in quick succession: a refinery, pipelines, and an oil rig. The pictures dissolved into a map of Mexico with a giant oil well in the middle spurting crude. The young woman warned, "If you reject the [energy] reform we will have less oil, we will continually have to import more cooking and heating gas and gasoline, and this fuel will be more expensive. So, we have to support the president's reforms." According to the voice-over's conclusion, "The majority of Mexicans *do* want the energy reform."[1] But do they, really?

Demonstrating evidence much to the contrary, when the proposal for energy reform was presented to lawmakers and the Mexican public in 2008, it was met with explosive opposition. An organized left-of-center alliance representing political parties, unions, and various entities of civil society including academia, fronted by left-wing, populist leader Andrés Manuel López Obrador (AMLO, as he is known), showed that the message offered in the federal government's television commercials was not the opinion of all Mexicans. Among the opposition, "energy reform" was widely understood as code for denationalization if not the dreaded outright privatization of the nation's most revered asset: hydrocarbons. And the charismatic leader AMLO was not about to sit idly by while another national political fraud swept the country.

López Obrador, 2006 presidential candidate for the PRD, was still smarting from the loss of Mexico's most contentious national election ever. The hotly contested election went to the courts, which determined Calderón's victory by 240,000 votes among 41 million cast. After months of turmoil and protests, it seemed that López Obrador's star would fade into a Calderón administration-as-usual. But AMLO, who hails from the oil-producing state of Tabasco and was a very popular mayor of Mexico City, gained a new foothold in national politics by leading a nationwide effort to derail the Calderón administration's energy-reform efforts. Calling himself the "legitimate president" and supported by a whole shadow cabinet, AMLO launched a broad-based opposition movement in early 2008 that at times drew hundreds of thousands of supporters to the streets of Mexico City and public squares across the nation as he tirelessly traveled. The energy-reform opposition movement countered the neoliberal drive of the Calderón administration with rallying cries "No to privatization," "El petróleo es nuestro," and "El patrimonio no se vende, se defiende." The oil is ours! Patrimony is not for sale!

On the frontlines in Isla Aguada, where the pro-energy-reform ads were a constant presence in a family evening of *telenovelas*, visiting with friends and neighbors, and even doing some ethnographic interviewing, discontent with neoliberal privatization programs indeed exists. But local residents do not take to the streets to demonstrate that "oil is not for sale." Discontent with privatization in Isla Aguada exists alongside a host of other attitudes, including ambivalence and uncertainty that oil will be around long enough to fulfill its promise to finally benefit rather than continually harm local communities. Antiprivatization sentiment here on the frontlines at the height of the 2008 debates over the Calderón energy reform did not resemble the public protests on the streets of Mexico City. And nationalist slogans in defense of oil sovereignty are not sufficient in capturing how residents grapple with the nation's patrimony in their midst.

However, here in the region where voters staunchly supported Calderón's party candidates to fill offices from local to state levels in the 2006 elections, no one was demonstrating in favor of the right wing's energy-reform proposal, either. The sticky question of public versus private ownership of oil is tied to the historic experience of natural resource exploitation in resource-rich areas of Mexico including the Laguna de Términos. Since the seventeenth century, private-sector interests have garnered control of the natural resources of the Laguna de Términos, extending into the Gulf of Mexico—from palo de tinte to chicle to shrimp. In each case, state interests did try, however unsuccessfully, to wrest control of the resource back from the private sector. The state (the Spanish crown in the early exploitation of palo de tinte) attempted to claim each resource as patrimony. But private, often foreign capital consistently won the upper hand in profiting before the peak of each resource.

Oil is different. Since the expropriation, Mexico has worked very hard to safeguard oil from private—especially foreign—interests and protect this symbolically and economically valuable resource under the constitution as part of the national patrimony. Pemex, as a national oil company, is far from unique in guarding hydrocarbon resources as national assets. Pemex was on the vanguard in 1938 with the first small wave of state-owned oil companies with Argentina's Yacimientos Petrolíferos Fiscales (YPF) and Colombia's Ecopetrol. It was not until the 1970s that a real tidal wave swept across resource-rich countries. A growing sense of nationalism combined with an increasing global demand for energy commodities made the creation of state companies a good bet. Modeled on state intervention and exclusion of the private sector, a consortium of national oil companies (NOCs) formed the Organization of Petroleum Exporting Countries (OPEC);[2] a host of other NOCs operated around the globe. But by the 1980s, some NOCs found themselves compromised in an atmosphere of falling oil prices and a surging neoliberal model calling for free-market economic reforms. Some countries completely privatized their NOCs, among them Britain and Argentina. Other NOCs opened up to private-sector participation, including those of Brazil, Norway, and Indonesia.

Rather than fading like artifacts of a bygone era, NOCs are currently experiencing a resurgence. Countries are bringing oil resources to the global marketplace through the establishment of NOCs, while historic NOCs are maintaining relevance under changing political and economic tides and even recapturing lost resource sovereignty. Not only are energy assets remaining in national coffers, but in some cases oil, gas, and utilities once lost are actually being brought back into the national fold in a surprising reversal of the neoliberal trend. Rather than folding and collapsing, NOCs are retrenching (Bolivia), being newly created (Chad and Mauritania), and under serious consideration for establishment (Uganda). New technologies and the drive to find fossil fuels in new places, primarily off shore, have made countries as varied as East Timor and Ghana oil producers with newly formed NOCs.

National oil companies now dominate the global oil and gas industry in terms of market and reserves. They represent the top ten reserve holders across the globe, with 77 percent of the world's reserves in their hands (Baker Institute 2007).[3] Of the top twenty oil and gas enterprises in the world, sixteen are NOCs. According to the World Bank (2008: 3), 90 percent of the world's oil reserves and 75 percent of oil and gas production are in the hands of national oil companies, or NOCs, representing a global tide turning away from the dominating power of private oil companies such as ExxonMobil, Shell, and BP to resource sovereignty of nation-states controlling their own oil and gas resources. Even though neoliberal trends of the past thirty years would seem to indicate that privatization is the contemporary and future wave of ownership of the most valuable commodities on the planet, the continuity and even new creation of national oil companies indicates a different trend in the energy sector.

This is not to say, however, that transnational corporations have stepped back from conducting much of the business of everyday life in our globalized economy. In the energy sector, private companies still play a key role in exploiting oil. Oil companies themselves and oil-services providers contracted by NOCs stand to make great profits under current conditions. What is more, NOCs do not necessarily play a strong role in "downstream" activities that include refining, one of the most profitable components of the energy industry. Even among the most protective national oil companies, Mexico ranks high in international reputation as independent, highly nationalistic, and closed to foreign investment. But Mexico is no exception to providing a favorable climate for the private sector, either. Pemex regularly negotiates contracts worth billions of dollars for services, from feeding and transporting workers on offshore platforms to conducting seismic surveys of potential new finds to drilling and pumping oil. In Mexico, refining is a strictly nationalized activity within the boundaries of the state's territory, but refining abroad and other downstream activities are contracted to the private sector.

Under the post-peak condition, NOCs and the private sector vie for the power to profit from the last days of the fossil fuel age. While NOCs may maintain access to the global oil supply, private-sector multinationals—whether big oil companies like the familiar "seven sisters" or the lesser-known but incredibly robust oil-services companies—are often their codependent counterparts. In Mexico the decline of Cantarell has simultaneously increased the participation of the private sector in the work of oil exploration and production. As the national political situation heated up surrounding the Calderón administration's energy-reform proposal in 2008 (chapter 5), attention increasingly was drawn toward the confluence of private-sector activities in Pemex. The post-peak condition produced a current of neoliberalism and a nationalist upswell.

One of the strategic areas for private-sector involvement in the NOC was the Gulf of Mexico (chapter 6). Long before anyone heard of the Deepwater Horizon, both Mexico and the United States had set their hopes for a prosperous energy future in the deep waters of the Gulf. In the United States the average citizen would not even know about America's race to exploit one of the petroleum age's final frontiers that would be carried out through very attractive leases offered with great incentives to major multinational oil companies such as Shell, Chevron, and, as we all now well know, BP. Across the border in Mexico, however, just about the whole nation—anyone who picked up a newspaper, watched TV, talked to a neighbor, or basically had any sentient consciousness for the past couple of years, that is—knew all about the role of deepwater oil for Pemex and for the nation. *Aguas profundas* (deep waters) played a central role in Mexico's energy-reform debate, and these resources became even further enmeshed in issues of privatization, resource sovereignty, and national security. Deep waters became a symbol for Mexico's struggle not only domestically but across its national maritime borders as well.

## CHAPTER 5

# "No to Privatization": A Battle for Energy Independence

The summer of 2008 was a watershed moment for the global political economy of energy. A spike in prices driven by market speculation sparked an unprecedented oil price bubble across the global marketplace. Oil prices climbed to $147 per barrel. Surely the world's sixth-largest oil producer stood to benefit from the price spike, perhaps by as much as $3 billion (Malkin 2008). Governors in the priority oil-affected states and in others awaited the windfall money for their states' benefits programs and most of all for large infrastructural projects funded through the Obras de Beneficio Mútuo. But the windfall never appeared. What was going on?

The Calderón administration had a series of responses, none of them good. With a lack of refining capacity, Mexico had for years been importing its own oil from the United States as gasoline. According to a March 2008 diagnostic report of Pemex prepared by the Calderón administration, Mexico was importing three of every five gallons of gas consumed in the country. The rise in crude prices caused a rise in Mexico's own costs in imported refined products. Mexico was growing increasingly dependent on the expensive imported products as domestic use increased. Meanwhile, during the price spike, Mexico's crude production was decreasing. Production decreased 12.4 percent between the first quarter of 2007 and the same time in 2008 (Malkin 2008). Faced with the onset of declines in production from supergiant Cantarell, Mexico was in a post-peak condition, and a price-spike windfall was not nearly enough to make up the difference in budget projections or public expectations.

The neoliberal Calderón administration found itself well positioned to strike with a perfectly timed energy-reform proposal, one that would call upon the private sector to help, as the administration saw it, rescue the nation's patrimony from its less than productive life locked up in the parastatal Pemex. The Calderón administration, building on its neoliberal predecessors' efforts, attempted to parlay the geophysical reality of peak oil into an opportunistic move that Naomi Klein has called "the shock doctrine": in moments of crisis or disaster "societies often give up things they would otherwise fiercely protect" (2007: 17). The moment of crisis, as Klein describes it, is ripe for "disaster capitalism." In Mexico, disaster capitalism allows the basic tenets of neoliberalism—deregulation, the cutting of social spending, and above all, privatization—a reinvigorated life. Through a carefully timed and managed promotion and portrayal of a crisis in Mexico's petroleum sector, the "Calderonato" (a term used by critics to invoke images of the Porfiriato) sought to dismantle the nation's territorial resource sovereignty. Would the shock of peak oil pave the way for private-sector intervention in one of Mexico's last remaining state-owned assets?

Privatization has been a political hot potato in Mexico for decades. But when it comes to oil, we can even say that foreign private involvement in the exploitation of Mexico's most valuable natural resource has been a no-go area for almost a century. This is more than just a touchy subject: political careers have been made and broken on the nationalistic fervor for protecting and preserving Mexico's national patrimony. Presidents from the PRI's Carlos Salinas (1988–1994) to the PAN's Vicente Fox (2000–2006) showed that privatization was the backbone of Mexican modernity and that the exemption of oil from contributing to that modernity was a nonpartisan privilege. Under the sway of neoliberalism from the 1980s onward, Mexico's state patrimony would fall away. Hundreds of state-owned assets and enterprises were sold off to the private sector. Now, toward the end of the first decade of the twenty-first century, so many state-owned industries were gone, and only a few of any real significance to the Mexican people remained. Primary among these stood Pemex.

Staunch nationalist, defender of the nation's patrimony, and self-designated populist leader Andrés Manuel López Obrador found it improbable that Pemex would remain under constitutional protection much longer. "For 25 years the government has been acting in a deliberate manner . . . to ruin Pemex because they have only one goal: to make Pemex into booty to be plundered, and to privatize the oil business," López Obrador told the *New York Times* in April 2008 as president and former energy secretary (under Fox) Felipe Calderón's energy-reform bill was brought before Mexican lawmakers. For months the left-of-center leader had been organizing huge demonstrations against the expected bill, and now he and his citizen-based Movimiento Nacional en Defensa del Petróleo (MNDP) were ready to defend the nation's patrimony in the face of the latest attack on the public ownership of hydrocarbons.

Calderón was not the first to suggest opening Mexico's oil industry to the private sector, but he certainly proved the least subtle. Perfectly aware of the untouchability of oil, Calderón sought to liberalize Pemex and the nation's patrimony with a scalpel of legislative precision and a media war of rhetoric rather than with a jackhammer of constitutional obliteration. Overall, the Calderón energy reform sought to liberalize Mexico's oil sector—not to give Pemex financial autonomy from the state but to open space for direct private investment, including foreign investment, in the state-owned company. Liberalization of state assets was nothing new. By further opening the energy sector, Calderón would continue along a path that Mexico forged beginning in the 1980s. But Calderón's new reforms for the oil sector were perhaps a bit bolder than those of his predecessors, even those of the market-oriented PAN reformer Vicente Fox.

Over the decades since the 1938 nationalization of the oilfields in Mexico's national territory, the nation has been remarkably steadfast in maintaining a de jure resource sovereignty over hydrocarbons. The crowning achievement was the maintenance of an intact Mexican energy regime through the negotiations of the North American Free Trade Agreement (NAFTA) of the early 1990s. From the outset of deliberations between President Salinas and George H.W. Bush, Mexico was determined not to give up control of its oil sector. It did not. However, the liberalization measures accompanying NAFTA did establish a safe environment for Pemex's creditworthiness and foreign investment and an atmosphere conducive to the entrance of foreign multinationals in Mexico's oilfields (Orme 1996: 142–144).[1] NAFTA thus served as a crucial hinge in the liberalization of the hydrocarbon sector.[2] The Mexican energy regime emerged post-NAFTA with a clear fissure between de jure constitutional resource sovereignty and de facto private-sector participation in the everyday activities of the oil industry.

However reviled by the Mexican Left for its neoliberal tenor, even NAFTA did not openly cede Mexico's resource sovereignty. Under the weight of this history and because of the particular nature of Mexico's resource nationalism, Calderón's 2008 energy proposal would have to tread the path of reform very carefully. The administration thus specifically sought a technical route: the revision of contracts with multinationals for exploration and development. While private firms were allowed only on a fixed-fee basis, the energy reform would stretch Article 27's constitutional protection of oil as national property to allow contractors incentive-based contracts. The proposal also was to make changes downstream allowing local and foreign private firms to take part in refining, transport, storage, and distribution of crude and its byproducts through a permit system. For the Mexican public, any reform that would allow the further entrance of private-sector participation in Pemex—no matter the subtleties, intricacies, or complexities of the proposed arrangements—receives a blanket label: privatization. The 2008 energy reform was, in public opinion, a privatization proposal.

Given the circumstances under which the Calderón reform proposal emerged in spring 2008, there was little need, it seemed, for the façade of subtlety. Earlier in the Calderón administration, dire warnings were sounded that the nation's oil was running dry. Official data emerged just after Calderón took office in the 2007 *Reporte anual de las reservas de hidrocarburos de México* putting reserves at 12.8 billion barrels, a 6 percent decline from the previous year and suggesting that with steady production rates Mexico's oil would run dry in less than a decade. Six months later the reserves dropped again. In July 2007 Pemex stated in a report to the U.S. Securities and Exchange Commission (SEC) that Mexico's proven reserves—oil from developed fields with wells, investment, and infrastructure—would last for less than seven years (Cruz Serrano 2007b).[3] Politicians from the Left were incensed at what they perceived as a politicized fudging of reserve numbers, a practice not unheard of across the globe. Pemex managed a sleight of hand to manipulate production numbers and create an image of Mexico on the verge of an oil emergency. The left-of-center opposition PRD party's senate committee on economic development produced a report showing how Pemex "manipulates at will the volume of national oil reserves by confusing exploratory data with reserve numbers" (Garduño 2008). The PRD charged that the manipulation was part of a strategy to sway public opinion in the debate over the future of the oil industry.

In the first few months of 2008, more evidence emerged depicting a purposefully accelerated decline of Cantarell. Former Pemex chief Jesús Reyes Heroles (ousted in fall 2009) admitted in a leaked document originally presented to the Consejo de Administración inside Pemex that the decline was only partially due to a real fall in available oil. Rather, the major issues were in fact due to problems inside the PEP subsidiary. According to the document, Pemex produced 200,000 bpd less because of a deliberate underutilization of infrastructure. Of the 200,000 missing barrels, only 30,000 were due to natural decline. The overwhelming amount was not produced due to technical failures in PEP, among them fires in fields. Furthermore, during this time Pemex was sending into the atmosphere more than a billion cubic feet of natural gas through flaring due to equipment failure on Gulf platforms; this represented some 774 million cubic feet more than planned. Pemex deliberately underutilized refineries as well and thus imported more gasoline (Pérez 2009b).

Politics and nature combined to create the perfect moment for Mexico's right wing to go for energy reform in 2008. In this chapter we will examine that energy reform in detail, the campaigns for its passage, and the public debates over its passage. We will also look at the long history of "privatization" of one of the last remaining state assets in Mexico that is not yet privatized. But why should we be speaking of the long history of energy privatization when subsoil resources supposedly remain constitutionally protected as national patrimony?

### Energy Reform to Rescue Mexico's "Treasure"

The Calderón energy-reform proposal is a study in avoiding the word "privatization" with reference to a treasured national asset. Over the course of many months the right-wing campaign led by the Partido Acción Nacional tried everything to change the terms of energy-reform debate away from privatization. In March and April 2008, Pemex dedicated more than $20 million to promoting to the Mexican people the advantages and benefits of the Calderón energy-reform proposal; that single campaign exceeded the year's entire reported publicity budget of $16.5 million. Of these resources 73 percent went to the television networks Televisa and Azteca for "Modernization of Pemex," a campaign initiated a month before the PAN proposal came to the floor of the Congreso Nacional. In all, 93,000 ads, an average of 1,640 per day, were transmitted between March 4 and April 30. Besides the ads, "product placement" messages about energy reform ("spontaneous" mentions by hosts and actors) were seen on morning and afternoon chat shows and even during telenovelas on the country's two major television channels (Tinoco 2008).

By March 2008, before the energy-reform bill actually was introduced in the legislature, Pemex had already spent nearly 70 percent of its public relations budget. In the run-up to the bill's public unveiling, the Chamber of Deputies (akin to the U.S. House of Representatives) appealed to the Ministry of Energy and the director-general of Pemex to stop the campaign on the basis that it would only confuse a public that instead deserved measured, scientific information on the status of the nation's oil reserves (Gomez and Merlos 2008). The energy ministry officials rebuffed these concerns. What's wrong with publicizing our message to the people? they asked. After all, every democracy does it (ibid.). Equally adamant were the representatives of the publicity firms and the media outlets. The head of Televisa explained that getting across a message about deepwater oil exploration through sitcoms, telenovelas, or "news" programs was no different than promoting any product, "like Doritos" (Aguilar and Cruz Serrano 2008).

Thus the state set out to promote private-sector participation in oil exploitation as if it were a delicious snack chip. One of the centerpieces of the state's campaign was "El tesoro bajo el mar" (Undersea Treasure), a media blitz specifically focused on raising public confidence about the need to exploit deepwater reserves in the Gulf of Mexico. The centerpiece was a five-minute video released in February 2008. Opening to a scene of children playing on the white sands of a Gulf coast beach and Disneyesque music we hear the opening salvo: "Oil is our treasure, an enormous wealth that belongs to all Mexicans. It represents the principal source of energy that has permitted the modernization of the country and progress of the world. Mexico has experience and success exploiting oil on land and close to shore." Here the story line takes an ominous turn: "However, the world is now facing a new reality: most reserves are found in deep water, at depths of 3,000 meters or more—at fifteen times the depth of the tallest building in Mexico." Accessing these reserves, the narrator explains, presents enormous challenges that other nations, including Latin American countries like Brazil, are already confronting. Meanwhile, Mexico is facing a race from neighbors closer to home to exploit deep waters of the Gulf of Mexico. Here is where Mexico has hidden its treasure.

The video locates "Mexico's treasure" (deepwater oil) on a map of the Gulf of Mexico divided according to the international maritime boundaries of the United States, Mexico, and Cuba. The video overtly suggests an impending threat to national oil resources on the U.S.-Mexican maritime border where private multinational firms are currently developing leases on the U.S. side, shown as yellow targets dangerously close to the glowing aura of Mexico's treasure. The ad lays out the following argument: given the advanced technology Pemex needs to take on the new challenge of deepwater exploitation, the parastatal will have to make "alliances" or "associations" with private-sector partners to gain access to technology and, in turn, the nation's undersea treasure. In doing so, the company can simultaneously be strengthened and modernized.

The energy-reform infomercial, a study in twenty-first-century jingoism, delivers an on-point rationale for the privatization of Pemex disguised as a pitch to preserve the country's greatest national treasure. The campaign's central symbols—maps and treasure—are perhaps more appropriate to an adolescent fantasy fiction than high-tech petroleum geology and higher-stakes oil geopolitics. In his analysis of the ideologies of cartography, Black suggests, "Lines on the map are a clear expression of value . . . and the map can be a device as well as an icon of struggle" (1998: 87). The treasure map expresses the value of the nation's oil in terms that harken back to the days of piracy on the Gulf's high seas. As a propaganda device, "Undersea Treasure" works well to distract us from the weightier matters of resource sovereignty, control of Mexico's territorial seas, and the status of the constitutional ban on private-sector participation in oil extraction. The video ends with a rousing "Let's go for it!" thus initiating a narrative about the potential of deepwater oil that the Calderón administration would use over the course of the next months and even years to justify furthering private-sector involvement in exploiting the nation's patrimony—and profiting handsomely from it.

## AMLO's Crusade

If the Calderón administration was indeed tapping into the public's imagination of the contested politics of Mexican oil, it was unleashing a fury, most of it hostile to energy reform. Some months before the energy-reform proposal even formally appeared before the Congreso, a torrent of vociferous nationalist opposition spilled out onto the streets and into the media. Andrés Manuel López Obrador, called by biographer George Grayson a "Mexican messiah" (2007), stepped forward to lead a national campaign against the privatization of oil. The opposition had been simmering since the debacle of the presidential election victory of PAN candidate Calderón over PRD candidate López Obrador, a messier and even more contested election than Bush versus Gore in 2000. Who better to lead the effort to save the nation's oil and defend the very sovereignty of the nation than the man who, a full year after NOT assuming the presidential office, continued to tour the country giving widely attended speeches under the banner "legitimate president of Mexico." Supporters (who dubbed Calderón "El Espurio," the "spurious usurper" of the presidency, among other names) found a natural affinity between AMLO and the cause of battling against neoliberal energy reform.

López Obrador began denouncing privatization of Pemex on the national scene as a politician from the oil-producing state of Tabasco as early as the mid-1990s when he led mass marches including the April 1995 Exodus for Dignity and National Sovereignty from oil-production center Villahermosa, Veracruz, to Mexico City. This very popular former mayor of Mexico City ran for president as a prominent member of the left-of-center PRD. After the failed bid and debacle, he formed the Movimiento Nacional en Defensa del Petróleo officially on January 10, 2008, in anticipation of Calderón's coming energy reform. The rallies, demonstrations, speeches, symposia, books, editorials, blogs, and other forms of civic engagement successfully turned "energy reform" into "oil privatization" and kept the legislation in the light of day and under public scrutiny from before its introduction until the moment of the vote.

Public sentiment for the 2008 anti-energy-reform movement coalesced when López Obrador led hundreds of thousands to demonstrate in the Zócalo public square of Mexico City in the unofficial seventieth anniversary celebration of the 1938 oil expropriation at a moment when the national atmosphere could not have been more fraught. By placing himself at the helm of a popular Expropriation Day celebration, López Obrador attached himself to a long, deep, and symbolically rich nationalist history. The holiday commemorates the act by President Cárdenas to nationalize the oilfields and equipment, long under the control of foreign companies. López Obrador's movement defended the principles of the 1938 expropriation, which carried forward the vision of resource sovereignty laid out in the postrevolutionary 1917 constitution.[4]

The 1938 nationalization underlined the nature of oil as public patrimony and provided that oil rents be used for the public good and as the backbone for national development. The state needed to mobilize the natural resource as a financial asset for an administration that had just experienced a series of financial setbacks and a contracting economy. Oil became the state's lifeline. As it would come to pass over the next decades, the economic weight of oil would fuse with its symbolic density in the public's imaginary of Mexican nationalism, rendering the resource all the more important. Although it was not particularly good for oil production itself, the expropriation was a political boon inside Mexico. A strong spirit of nationalism would arise from the shambles of the oil industry that the Mexican state had expropriated from foreign oil companies.

In the first year of nationalized production, Mexico faced an adversarial situation. The amount of oil sold abroad dropped by 50 percent, to the United States by 61 percent, and to Latin American neighbors by 75 percent (Koppes 1982: 69). Hopes from abroad that the expropriation would fail only stirred Mexicans to support President Cárdenas (1934-1940). Days after the expropriation declaration, a mass demonstration of 100,000 people took place in Mexico City. For the first time, the whole of Mexico—a nation chronically torn by strife, dictatorship, and foreign occupation—was on the same side of a cause. Famously, women, rich and poor, turned out in Mexico City to donate whatever possessions they could muster in order to support the cause and help pay the national debt. Still celebrated annually in cities and towns across Mexico as a national holiday, Expropriation Day marks one of the deepest symbolic manifestations of nationalism in modern Mexico.

Would this seventieth anniversary be the last to celebrate Mexico's national resource sovereignty? Would energy reform cede the nation's hold over its valuable possession? Although reform has occurred in fits and starts through the decades and the specter of oil privatization raises a threat at least once every presidential sexenio, nothing compared to the "oil crisis" brought about by the proposed energy reform of 2008. The first warnings that an energy-reform proposal would emerge from the Calderón administration occurred in late 2007. The proposal did not actually appear in congressional chambers until April 2008. A nonbinding plebiscite was held in August 2008 (sponsored by the reform's opposition) to determine public support for the bill, and a final vote occurred in October 2008. During these tumultuous months, Mexico faced the question of who would win and who would lose if oil was privatized or remained property of the nation.

On the occasion of the seventieth anniversary of Expropriation Day, March 18, 2008, AMLO and Calderón had a standoff. While AMLO reached hundreds of thousands gathered in the Zócalo of Mexico City with a rousing speech, Felipe Calderón went to the frontlines of production at the Dos Bocas oilfield in Tabasco. Calderón spoke to an audience of mostly Pemex workers:

> On this anniversary I reaffirm that today, like seven decades ago, the oil is and will continue to be for all Mexicans. That's what the people want, that's what the constitution requires, and that's what the government assumes [as its responsibility]. Pemex will not be privatized. (Mexico, Office of the President 2008b)

At that very same ceremony, though, Pemex director Reyes Heroles urged authorities to modify Mexico's legal framework so the firm could form partnerships with other companies. He clarified that this would not "affect the nation's ownership of its resources, energy sovereignty, or the government's supervisory capacity." With the various de facto meanings already swirling around the term "energy reform," the Calderón administration could not prevent the surge of nationalist sentiment and deep suspicion over the true intent behind its proposal.

Calderón's appearance at Dos Bocas was met by thousands of protestors led by elected officials from the PRD, the left-wing Convergencia party, and even the PRI. Senators, representatives, and municipal leaders were among those who took part in what was to be a peaceful march, chanting, "Oil belongs to Mexicans" and "Our patrimony is not for sale" and singing the Mexican national anthem and songs from the Mexican Revolution. But the march devolved into a shouting and water-bottle-throwing match with the army and federal police. The demonstrators wanted Calderón out of the port of Dos Bocas because, according to one local official, "here there will be an opposition that will defend what is ours. They should know that they are not welcome in Tabasco" (in López 2008).

AMLO's forté clearly is the massive public gathering, and the Defensa del Petróleo citizens movement also fought hard on the media front. Even though they did not have the widespread television coverage of the federal government, they did have some. They also had social media—YouTube, blogs, and grassroots digital networks. Critics and skeptics had a heyday with the Pemex video. Through the feature on YouTube that allows users to directly link their videos as responses to existing contributions, many posted both serious and humorous revisions of the official text.

Two brief examples show the range of responses. The first is a mashup of the federal government's "Tesoro bajo el mar" and archival footage of President Lázaro Cárdenas's 1938 Expropriation Day speech. The effect of replacing the narration of the state-produced "Tesoro" video with audio of the moving speech given by Cárdenas on the occasion of one of the most symbolically significant moments in modern Mexican history is incredibly powerful. What is more, the Pemex ad is interspersed with overlays of 1930s archival images of oil workers marching and demonstrating in the lead-up to the expropriation. The mash-up generated more than 10,000 views just in the few months surrounding the 2008 energy-reform debates. An entirely different but particularly creative response to the "Undersea Treasure" video is a parody of a film trailer for *Lord of the Rings: The Two Towers*. The creators of the new video titled theirs "Bush, The Lord of the Rings, Pemex Tower." In the trailer, Gollum has George Bush's face and says over and over in a very creepy voice, "My treasure, my precious treasure in the Gulf of Mexico. My precious treasure, Mexican oil. I want my oil, my treasure. Thank you, Calderón."

AMLO used all forms of media as well to organize and communicate with the members of the citizens movement. In an urgent and moving message to the nation (López Obrador 2008b), sponsored by the PRD, the party under whose banner he ran his presidential bid, López Obrador appears in authoritative yet engaging form in front of the Mexican government seal under the banner "Legitimate President of Mexico." Beneath all of the pomp, he speaks plainly and directly, laying out the case against a nascent PAN energy-reform initiative. "There is no justification," he warns,

> not technical, technological, administrative, nor financial, to reform the laws and hand the oil over to foreigners. Oil can be well managed. Without corruption, with rationality. . . . It can still be a platform for national development. With a well-managed oil industry we can move forward. We can transform Mexico into an energy powerhouse.
>
> As Lázaro Cárdenas told us, any government or individual who would hand over natural resources is a traitor to the *patria*. We cannot permit anyone to do this. Our children will never forgive this.
>
> Don't let us end up slaves on our own land.
>
> *La patria no se vende; la patria se defiende.* (Don't sell the homeland, defend it!)

This message was AMLO's invitation for citizens to participate in peaceful acts of civil resistance. The movement began in January 2008 on the local level with the formation of municipal and state committees. López Obrador traveled across the country speaking in cities large and small and building up support, much the same as he had done on his presidential campaign. An agenda of activism was planned for the coming weeks, even months. The movement to defend the nation's patrimony and sovereignty was under way. No matter what energy reform looked like in practice, the only principle that mattered was that "el petróleo es nuestro," the oil is ours.

AMLO's crusade represented a coalition of young and old, men and women, educated idealists and working union members. The veritable citizens army of organized brigades had a significant number of women *brigadistas* among the rank and file. Known as *adelitas*, a term harking back to the women who fought with Pancho Villa in the Mexican Revolution, thousands of women organized in groups such as March 18 (Expropriation Day) and Enaguas Profundas (Deep Petticoats), a play on *aguas profundas*, the Calderón proposal's rationale for involving the private sector in order to open exploration in deep waters (Ross 2008).

When Calderón's reform finally was delivered to the Mexican Senate on April 8, 2008, brigadistas in the streets along with politicians on the inside were prepared for a spectacular act of peaceful civil disobedience. On April 10, members of the Frente Amplio Progresista (FAP), a left-wing coalition of the PRD, the Partido de Trabajadores (PT, Workers Party), and Convergencia, staged a shutdown of the Congreso. The opposition party members did not want the PAN (most likely with the complicity of the PRI) to be able to work quickly through the business of passing the energy-reform proposal. An enormous banner was unfurled across the entire gallery floor that read in bold letters: *CLAUSU-RADO* (CLOSED).[5] In this spectacular demonstration, dozens of legislators and staff members stood across the dais, holding block letters spelling out "DEFENDER LA CONSTITUCION."

Outside, citizen demonstrators, notably women, rallied in support of blocking the Congreso for days. Brigades of adelitas faced a showdown with a newly trained force of female federal police officers as they held the streets in front of the senate building. The adelitas responded: No one is passing, and we are not afraid. One of the adelitas interviewed in the Mexico City daily *La Jornada* said, "Here we are, even if on TV they say 'ay, those dirty, seditious, terrorist women, guerrillas trained in Israel!!' Even so, this B.S. initiative will not be debated!" (Mendez and Muñoz 2008).

Normal business came to a halt in both houses of the Congreso Nacional for fifteen days. They were released for normal functioning only five days before the close of the first session of the year. The demonstration was, for the FAP, successful because it prevented any fast-track approval by right-wing senators and representatives. The podium was only turned back over after an agreement had been reached between the left-wing coalition and the PRI and PAN whereby seventy-one days of public fora would take place, culminating in a nationwide consulta, or non-binding plebiscite. The possibility of a vote was now months away.

Beginning on May 31 and continuing until July 22, twenty-one public fora were held to debate the energy-reform proposal. Politicians, academics, technical experts, policy and energy analysts, legal scholars, and many others participated. Debates were organized along such themes as:

- constitutional analysis of the energy-reform proposal
- importance of the energy sector in national and regional development
- transport, storage, and distribution of hydrocarbons and their derivatives
- negotiation, exploration, and exploitation of cross-border reservoirs
- Pemex acquisitions, contracts, and public works
- financial situation of Pemex
- organization and administration of Pemex
- transparency, accounting, and combating corruption inside Pemex

The fora were transcribed and published on the Mexican Senate's website. They encompassed some moments of careful consideration and other moments of sheer ideological stagecraft. The debates muddied the waters over issues of the constitutionality of further revisions to contracts and releasing refining processes to the private sector, the viability of Pemex's deepwater prospects, and indeed the legitimacy of Pemex itself. By the conclusion of the debate period, one thing was very clear: the PAN proposal certainly was not any stronger and was perhaps in danger of not passing at all.

The leftist coalition appeared confident emerging from the public fora and ending the summer with the consulta. The referendum was held in twenty-two states and the federal district—areas where the FAP was able to maintain sufficient infrastructure to carry out the voting—on three Sundays: July 27, August 10, and August 24. The consulta posed two questions, to be answered by marking a box Yes or No for each:

1. Right now, exploitation, transport, distribution, storage, and refining are exclusive activities of the government. Do you agree that private businesses should participate in these activities?
2. Do you agree with the approval of the initiatives of the energy reform that are being debated right now in the Congreso?

The consulta was heavily advertised by the defense movement and the PRD-Left coalition. One particularly racy ad featured an anonymous, topless *ciudadana* (woman citizen) with strategically placed ballots over her bare breasts showing the referenda questions and claiming, "I'm patriotic and that's why I'm voting NO in the oil *consulta*, July 27."

Turnout for the 45.5-million-peso consulta met expectations in Mexico City. The response from participating citizens was overwhelming. In most locations upward of 80 percent answered "No" to both questions. Across Mexico, the administration of the consulta and rates of participation varied dramatically. Left-leaning Chiapas had high participation. Participation was lower in PAN-governed states and other regions where the Left is historically weak such as the northern border states of Chihuahua and Baja California. Turnout was also lower in some oil-affected areas.

In Campeche, where the vote was held on the second Sunday of voting, only 11,360 votes were cast. Even though this turnout actually exceeded the FAP's expectation of 10,000, FAP leaders criticized Carmen's media outlets for purposefully failing to cover the event (*Tribuna Campeche* 2008d), in which 93 percent voted against privatization. Campeche's votes rejecting privatization were joined by votes from across seven states that held the referendum on the same day; in them, 95 percent of the participants (286,306) rejected the first question and 94 percent (281,782) voted their disagreement with the proposed energy reforms outlined in question 2. The overall results leaned heavily toward rejecting the privatization of Pemex. However, PAN officials felt justified in rejecting the voluntary referendum due to its seemingly arbitrary administration and nonbinding nature and a number of null votes. Low turnout was compounded by a problem with the distribution of materials on the day of the consulta.

In Campeche, the turnout of only 11,360 people to voice their opinions on an issue that so directly affected their everyday lives and livelihoods was not so important to the antireform movement. Because it was a major symbolic victory, the representativeness of the consulta was not, for the Left, a problem. AMLO and the defense movement instead drew on the power of the citizens' voices exercised through the plebiscite. On August 31, López Obrador appeared in a taped message to the nation congratulating his followers on the success of the consulta: "The initial attempt to privatize the oil industry has been stopped. Now they can't carry out this robbery." The Left was spinning the success, but the battle against the energy reform would go on until the final vote before the Congreso Nacional in October. Even though the stakes were high, these battles were part of a much longer war for control over Mexico's national patrimony.

## Resource Alienation

The immediacy of the debate over the privatization of Mexican oil belies a much longer, tumultuous battle in which generations of Mexican citizens, labor, multinationals, and the state have fought over the value, ownership, and resource distribution of Mexican crude. There was a time when Mexico's own national resources including the oil beneath its territory could not have been more alienated. As we saw in chapter 1, Porfirio Díaz enacted a series of laws to ensure that U.S. and British oil companies had legal access to Mexico's subsoil resources by declaring hydrocarbon deposits to be the property of surface owners.[6] In doing so, he intervened in a deep legacy of subsoil ownership that has profound economic and symbolic dimensions.

In her study *American Pentimento* (2001), historian Patricia Seed details the origin of the tradition of ownership of mineral wealth in the Americas. Mexico's state ownership of the subsoil has its direct origins in Spanish colonialism. But this juridical tradition also had a much older history of conquest and occupation, older than Mexico's own experience. This is Spain's experience of the Muslim presence on the Iberian Peninsula in the eighth century. Islamic jurisprudence left its mark on Spanish law through the concept of direct dominion over the subsoil. Rather than private ownership by a surface owner (according to Anglo-American concepts of property ownership in the tradition of English common law), particularly valuable subterranean resources were conceptualized as God-given gifts and thus meant to be shared among his people (59).

This notion gradually came to influence Spanish law—with the major adaptation that subterranean wealth would fall under the stewardship of the monarch. Through divine right, the monarch would not have proprietorship over the subsoil as an individual or private owner per se but instead would hold its resources in trust as the Spanish crown. The conquistadores brought this idea to the New World, where indigenous Mexica, Maya, Zapotec, and others living atop the resources would come to have no say in how the subsoil would be owned or exploited. The genealogical succession of subsoil dominion thus passed from God to the Spanish crown and finally was inherited through the legacy of colonialism by the Mexican state. The state would employ the same principle by acting as custodian of the patrimonial assets of the subsoil.

Díaz reinterpreted centuries of tradition in order to align Mexico with U.S. law on subsoil ownership based on principles in English common law, which came from Roman law and the principle of *cuius est solum eius est usque ad coelum et ad infernos* (for whoever owns the soil, it is theirs up to the sky and down to the depths). This principle grants a surface owner rights over the minerals in the ground under his land.[7] Though unusual among nation-states in granting subsoil rights to the surface owner, the United States chose to use this legal regime through the eighteenth and nineteenth centuries to incentivize mineral exploration and exploitation. British and American companies arriving in Porfirian Mexico to exploit hydrocarbons thus found a familiar rather than foreign property regime. Because Díaz had so radically altered the law, the foreign companies did not seek (as many sources would have it) *concessions* for oil exploitation; rather, their right to Mexican oil was free and clear by dint of their ownership of land. While oil concessions were given in Mexico in 1865 under Emperor Maximilian, this was while subsoil resources were still regarded as the property of the nation. Only a few dozen concessions were granted, primarily to Mexican nationals and French interests, before Díaz changed the law to further attract private interests—and especially foreign capital—to exploit Mexican oil (Brown 1993b: 10). The Mining Law of 1884 stressed private ownership by alienating the subsoil from the nation and making it available not only to the private sector but to the foreign private sector. Land that was drilled had to be purchased or leased from surface owners so that the oil companies could access a surface title—and, in turn, the subsoil.

## Resource Nationalism

During the Porfiriato the interests of foreign private capital were generally supported over and above those of local populations and ecologies. The Mexican Revolution was fought to remedy these perceived abuses and to wrest the patrimony back under the nation's control. There were two related outcomes. The first was the establishment of Article 27 of the 1917 constitution, which simply represented a return to the legislative domination that the state held before the Porfiriato. The other outcome was the 1938 expropriation of the oil companies and the nationalization of the industry, which mobilized that patrimonial dominion in an entirely new way by laying a foundation for resource nationalism. Rather than an act of renationalization, this moment lives on in collective memory as "nationalization" per se and serves as a touchstone for national identity.

Liberalizing trends of the 1990s reversed such nationalization, and resource-rich countries bowed to the pressures of the free-market policy reforms of international institutions like the International Monetary Fund (IMF). Nowhere were these reforms more keenly felt than in Latin America. Neoliberal policies sought to open valuable energy resources to the global marketplace through private-sector investment. A prime case in point is the experience of Ecuador. In the 1990s the state-owned oil industry opened to multinational companies. The government provided incentives for multinational oil companies to participate in intensive exploration and production activity, largely in the ecologically sensitive and delicate Ecuadorian Amazon (Sawyer 2004: 109). Neoliberal privatizations came as well to Argentina, Bolivia, Peru, and Brazil. The policies proceeded across the globe as full and partial privatization occurred in the national oil companies of Canada, Russia, Norway, Malaysia, and beyond.

While once the private majors dominated the global landscape of oil production, state-owned oil companies are now reasserting themselves. In the post-peak condition national oil companies across the world from Venezuela to Nigeria to Russia have increasingly gained control of the global energy supply. Across the post-peak energy landscape, where fewer resources are being developed in the hardest places to reach, the multinationals appear to be the losers in de jure control over hydrocarbons. After all, of the world's proven oil reserves, more than 1 trillion barrels, approximately 77 percent are under the control of national oil companies with absolutely no equity participation of foreign international oil companies (Mares and Altamirano 2007: 3). Why, then, toward the end of the first decade of the twenty-first century, were Mexican citizens still fighting over privatization? Even though the NOCs including Pemex control the global energy supply, they are not in control of their own futures. What is more, the post-peak condition sets the stage for a climate of uncertainty for how oil will contribute toward the future of frontline communities. For communities banking on benefiting from the national wealth, the post-peak condition has presented a risk. To the private sector, on the other hand, it presents an opportunity. Even if oil supplies are held under de jure resource sovereignty, the de facto pressures of the post-peak condition have threatened to throw open an opportunity for investment in hydrocarbons long awaited by the private sector.

Against the prevailing current of what is now more than three decades of neoliberalism in the political economy of the Global South, one profound contradiction remains in the face of persistent programs of deregulation, structural adjustment, and perhaps above all, privatization. It is the irony of subsoil resource sovereignty. Today, even after decades of pressure from neoliberal agendas, states tend to be the owners of most mineral resources. In fact, state ownership of subsoil resources is far more common that legal regimes that permit private ownership of mineral or hydrocarbon deposits. Private property rights in subsoil resources including oil and gas tend to be historical vestiges rather than newly granted privileges. The key role played by NOCs does not mean, however, that private companies do not play an important, not to mention profitable, role in the exploitation of these resources. Some of the "big six" oil companies—Shell, ExxonMobil, BP—ranked among the ten largest corporations in the world on *Fortune*'s 2011 Global 500 list. Even if the multinational majors do not own reserves themselves, they find, extract, process, distribute, and sell oil, often in concert with NOCs.

The private sector still looms as a threat on the near horizon for several reasons. Most significantly, despite asserting resource sovereignty on the one hand, NOCs cannot function without private-sector participation in their daily operations; on the other hand, even though the

NOCs control the oil, the private sector controls the profits. In other words, private companies continue to be more profitable than comparable NOCs (Mares and Altamirano 2007: 3). Some states with NOCs, like Mexico, often maintain privileged access to reserves. In some cases, states transfer their rights as original holders of these rights to commercial interests that pay royalties for the exploitation rights. Even states that maintain strict legal controls over resource sovereignty typically, however, contract the services of multinational private companies to aid in developing oil fields, drilling, refining, and so forth.

The kinds of contracting arrangements vary by NOC. The most conservative contracting arrangements, until very recently used by Mexico and traditionally employed by many Persian Gulf nations, are "technical service contracts" under which private companies carry out specific tasks for fixed fees under well-defined parameters. These differ from the "risk service contracts," which allow private companies their own opportunities to invest in projects. Because risk service contracts agree upon set rates of return at the outset of ventures, there is not really a chance for the private companies to profit excessively.[8] While other NOCs were exercising flexibility in how they work with private companies, Pemex has long prohibited anything but technical service contracts or bundled these as "multiple service contracts." As Pemex pursues new frontiers such as the deepwater Gulf of Mexico, where the parastatal claims it will confront a shortage of technology and a great expense, in the energy-reform proposal of 2008 the Calderón administration sought greater flexibility in developing contracts with oil-services companies.

NOCs exercise different forms and degrees of resource sovereignty. Some, unlike Pemex, welcome direct foreign investment in their operations at home. Some have done so since their founding. Angola, for example, allows private investment and partnership in its state-owned oil company, Sonangol. Others were founded as NOCs that have only gradually opened up to more private-sector participation through the types of contracts (risk- and production-sharing) they employ; an example is Norway's Statoil, which encouraged private-sector participation, an ethos that led to the company's partial privatization in 2001. On the international stage, NOCs even are operating like independent oil companies (IOCs) in pursuit of oil and gas exploration and production beyond their own national borders. Some NOCs that have less oil at home will pursue more aggressive expansion plans elsewhere, such as Thailand's PTTEP has done. In another case, an NOC may bid jointly with IOCs, as with the IOC-NOC consortiums for oil production in

Iraq. And some NOCs are forming partnerships with other NOCs, among them Cupet, Cuba's national oil company, and Brazil's Petrobras. The ability of Petrobras, formerly an NOC constitutionally closed off to partnership, to participate in such ventures was a partial privatization. Once echoing its own version of the Mexican nationalist sentiment, "O petróleo é nosso," with financial hardship and declining production it was not enough to justify maintaining the NOC's monopoly on production. Thus, in 1997, Petrobras was opened to foreign private-sector participation and competition. The state maintained a 51 percent share (McPherson 2010: 277).[9]

## Reforming, not Privatizing, Pemex

The pressure to privatize was keenly felt throughout Latin America as its economies were brought in line with the measures prescribed in the so-called Washington Consensus, a set of neoliberal reforms that began to be implemented in the 1980s, including trade liberalization, the reordering of public-expenditure priorities, tax reform, financial liberalization, liberalization of foreign direct investment and of interest rates, a competitive exchange rate, deregulation, and property rights (Williamson 2008: 16-17). It would be impossible for Mexico to successfully model all of these, but privatization would emerge among the most significant.

The sexenio of Miguel de la Madrid (1982–1988) ushered in the initial wave of privatization of state assets. The practice reached new heights with the administration of Carlos Salinas de Gortari (1988–1994) and continued through the term of Ernesto Zedillo (1994–2000). Like some of its Latin American neighbors, notably Chile and Argentina, Mexico privatized during times of economic crisis to generate revenues. Mexico sold profitable public-sector enterprises under generous terms for investors, as reported in the *Multinational Monitor*, "in sweetheart privatization deals and other benefits conferred on a select group of private investors with close ties to the PRI" (Summa 1994). The sales created an elite class of new billionaires and a state that did not fare equally well in the long term. Through short-term revenue gains Mexico was able to service internal and external debts. Yet the long-term effects of the asset sell-offs were consequential, engendering "reduced flows of revenue in the future, significant loss of employment opportunities, increases in poverty, the loss of economic autonomy and political sovereignty, and the further concentration of income and wealth in the hands of economically powerful and politically influential groups" (Ramírez 2003: 267).

Despite this prospect of long-term, widespread damage, leaders did not want to give up the chance to garner their own political capital while falling in line with the demands of the neoliberal model. Salinas, for example, claimed that the sales were going to fund social programs for education, health, and poverty reduction. In the sale of Telmex, however, most of the income generated went into a contingency fund to pay for the state's domestic debt rather than to enhance social welfare (Ramírez 2003: 279). Carlos Slim's purchase of Telmex in 1990 paved the way for the Mexican billionaire to become the richest man in the world. With the help of the state, Slim's investment group turned the national phone company into a private near-monopoly on land lines and later cellular communications and even Internet access. Slim has gone from simply charging Mexicans outrageous phone-service prices to building a global corporate empire with telecommunications but also financial and industrial interests from retail and restaurants to infrastructure and oil services.

Even though many state-owned industries in Mexico were completely sold off, privatization takes many partial forms that can eventually bring about total divestiture or denationalization. The most common methods include breaking up state-owned enterprises into smaller parts (subsidiaries), opening national companies to private investment, offering private shares (for example, to corporate investors) or public shares (such as on a stock exchange), introducing competitive features into state-owned enterprises (performance-related incentives), and demonopolizing certain activities of state companies. Another path toward privatization is through attrition, whereby the state gradually allows the private sector to take over its own investments because it fails to renew critical infrastructure. Yet another is contracting out, when the state substitutes private contractors (through appropriate government procedures) to provide services (Vuylsteke 1996: 454–455).

Salinas would go where no administration had gone before. Bold reforms of the Salinas administration include reprivatization of the banks, privatization of the ejido land-tenure system, and the successful pursuit of the North American Free Trade Agreement. But not even Carlos Salinas de Gortari would dare touch the nation's most sacred patrimony. In an Expropriation Day speech, Salinas, like other presidents under the pressures of neoliberalism after him, promised that Pemex would stay "uniquely and firmly under the control of the Mexican state . . . the exclusive patrimony of Mexicans" (in Jensen 1993: 82). The promise was kept, at least in rhetoric and in public. Even though the PRI governments were selling off the nation's assets seemingly willy-nilly, a boundary was drawn between the cut-and-dried expedience of economic reform and the untouchable quality of Mexico's generations-old political structures: the PRI and its supporters, including Pemex and the state-owned electricity company CFE (Comisión Federal de Electricidad) and their powerful labor unions. Thus, throughout the 1980s and 1990s, oil stayed in the nation's coffers.

Amid the sweeping sell-offs of the Salinas years, there is no way the citizenry would have stood for the privatization of oil. So instead, key changes began in a less scrutinized area of Pemex: the petrochemical division. A program of trade liberalization, deregulation, and elimination of subsidies began in the mid-1980s. In 1986 "private companies were authorized to import basic petrochemicals that PEMEX could not supply, 36 of the 72 basic petrochemicals were reclassified as secondary by decree, and a flexible pricing policy was enacted" (Martínez Laguna 2004: 2037). By 1992 the number of basic petrochemicals was reduced to only nine, effectively ending Pemex's monopoly. Leading up to that reduction, the labor structure of Pemex's petrochemical branch began an inevitable collapse. "In 1989, the government strengthened the privatization phase by restructuring labor, with a 50% reduction in salaries, massive lay-offs of almost 71,000 workers from 1987 to 1993, and the annulment of the union's participation in Pemex's activities" (ibid.).

Subsequent administrations chipped away at Pemex, carefully tiptoeing around oil itself. In 1995 the administration of Ernesto Zedillo successfully privatized "secondary petrochemicals" and natural gas distribution. In doing so, he appeased nationalist sentiment around oil, assuring the people that "the energy resources belong to the nation and ought to be utilized in accordance with the law for the progress of Mexico and the well-being of all Mexicans" (in de Palma 1996). Zedillo's reform was completed despite thunderous opposition from the Left and from the oil workers union, which read the move as a warning sign of a major rollback from state ownership. In Tabasco, protestors—many of them oil workers—seized dozens of Pemex installations because of the privatization plans. For local residents privatization signaled a further setback in achieving state recognition of the thousands of claims filed against Pemex for the severe environmental damage inflicted on land and water as well as health damage to those living near affected areas. Deeply involved in the movement was Andrés Manual López Obrador, who was present and injured by a billy club when protestors were violently dispersed by federal troops at an oil production facility (Wheat 1996).

The ability of PRI and PAN political leaders to delve into Article 27 of the constitution and interpret what precisely constitutes the strategic dimensions of a resource or its management was troubling indeed. The pieces that were chipped away were rather profitable aspects of the company, yet they did not require the lumbering, capital-intensive infrastructure that weighed down other parts of Pemex. The selling off of these particular parts of Pemex was more strategic (that is, profitable) for the private sector than for the nation.

### PAN: New Politics, Old Designs on Pemex

Privatization as one tactic in the strategy of neoliberalism is not a partisan issue in Los Pinos, Mexico's White House. While the Mexican citizenry expected a new course for Mexico when the PRI's seventy-year rule was ended with the election of PAN candidate Vicente Fox, it should have been clear that the former Coca-Cola executive would bring an even more intensive neoliberalist vision to Pemex. At the outset of his campaign, Fox called for the privatization of Pemex, but he reneged on this position after seeing the uproar it provoked (Purcell 2004: 153). By the end of his administration, Fox found himself standing on an oil platform in the Gulf of Mexico proclaiming: "It would be stupid to privatize Pemex or even think about it!" (Davalos 2005). The stage upon which Fox was speaking, the Safe Britannia, a semisubmersible accommodation rig contracted from Prosafe, a multinational oil-services provider, perhaps spoke even louder than Fox's nationalist rhetoric. Throughout the Fox administration, as privatization per se became an increasingly hot potato, the private sector was nonetheless encouraged to participate in the everyday activities of Mexico's oil industry.

Although his rhetoric changed, Fox's actions spoke loudly. He appointed former Dupont-Mexico CEO Raúl Muñoz Leos to the helm of Pemex.[10] During his tenure Muñoz Leos caused Pemex to move away from being a state-owned monopoly that feeds on public resources and opened up the sector to private domestic and foreign investments. Emphasizing the importance of creating strategic alliances, Pemex under Muñoz Leos would stress the need to allow direct private investment in gas and refining in order for the state-owned company to move ahead. To critics of Fox, all of this sounded like a call for privatization.

The Fox sexenio contributed tactically to the strategy of privatization by developing a new kind of contracting system specifically for natural gas exploitation and by taking advantage of a new financialization scheme that allowed Pemex to invite the private sector to contribute to infrastructural development in an unprecedented fashion. The financing scheme, Pidiregas ("deferred expenditure impact projects") was conceived around 1995 under the administration of Ernesto Zedillo as a mechanism for off-balance-sheet financing to support infrastructural development projects. Through Pidiregas, Pemex would be able to finance itself in the wake of Mexico's atmosphere of severe economic instability of the 1994–1995 peso crisis.

Part of the problem that led to the mid-1990s currency crisis was Carlos Salinas's decision to peg the peso to the U.S. dollar in 1988 within a currency-stabilization program. This was another tactic in the neoliberal playbook, along with reduced government spending, tax reform, deregulation, privatization, and trade liberalization. The rapid reductions of tariffs played a part in paving the way for Mexico's entry into the General Agreement on Tariffs and Trade (GATT) and into NAFTA and put it on the path to becoming a member of the OECD. While heralded as successful for a short time—curbing high inflation and stabilizing the economy enough to draw foreign investment—the pegging did not stick. Mexico could not maintain the foreign exchange rate of the peso within the 2 percent fluctuation rate allowed by the IMF. The result was that Mexico could not meet its balance of payments; the peso was not viable enough for Mexico's transactions abroad, and Mexico was becoming a deficit nation. Investors lost confidence not only because of an economically unstable Mexico but a politically unsteady country after the Zapatista rebellion and the assassination of PRI presidential candidate Luis Donaldo Colosio. With depleted foreign exchange reserves, the peso was floated so its value decreased quickly and dramatically and ended up being devalued by 40 percent (Kim and Kim 2006: 106).

With the currency devaluation and the closure of capital markets to the federal government and parastatal companies, a new financing scheme had to be devised to keep Pemex up and running and the oil pumping. Before Pidiregas, Pemex investments had been limited to their government allocations (Moroney and Dieck-Assad 2005: 26). In 1995 the Congreso Nacional approved a modification in federal financing law to allow companies to carry out "productive infrastructure projects for priority activities" on behalf of Pemex. The projects could be carried out by third parties and paid off over time. The expense of the projects was deferred, meaning that they would not immediately appear as debt.

Pemex did not use Pidiregas extensively during the Zedillo administration. But under the Fox administration, Pidiregas was used much more even though the context of the peso crisis had passed. Absent a financial crisis, there was a self-generated crisis in the oil sector. Director Muños Leos cried out early in the Fox administration that Pemex would collapse and the oil would run dry without the intervention of the private sector, a cry that would be etched into the PAN-Pemex playbook and whipped out again during the Calderón administration. Without privatizing Pemex, the private sector was nevertheless welcomed in. Between 1997 and 2003, private enterprise increased its investment participation in Pemex activities from 38 percent to nearly 67 percent (Shields 2003: 89). The more private enterprise participated, the deeper the debt grew. Furthermore, no one seemed to know how much the debt really was, but estimates put Pidiregas investments between 2000 and 2008 at $96 billion in long-term projects.

The Pidiregas scheme was a disaster in terms of the amount of accumulated debt amassed under the financing scheme. Moving into the Calderón administration, three-quarters of Pemex financing fell under Pidiregas until "Pidiregas not only drowned Pemex but also the country" (Morales Villegrán 2009: 75). In 2008 Pemex's Pidiregas commitments became part of Mexico's general public debt, and Pemex was restricted from undertaking further Pidiregas authorizations or projects. Pidiregas was another form of de facto privatization within Pemex, or what David Shields calls "privatización furtiva" (2005: 83), for which opposition groups in Mexico blamed the executive branch of government for lobbying for the private sector's participation.

The tool facilitating the "furtive" privatization was the Fox administration's introduction of the multiple service contract (MSC) in 2002. The MSC was a new contractual arrangement between Pemex and private oil-services providers—usually large and often foreign multinationals—that initially was used in the exploitation of an area of the hydrocarbon sector thought less ideologically volatile than oil itself: natural gas. The Fox administration eased into the introduction of new contracting arrangements with the private sector by focusing on downstream gas activities rather than on upstream crude. Privatization (or any degree of private-sector involvement) is a tougher sell for the actual exploration and production of crude (upstream) than for the refining of crude oil and the sales and distribution of natural gas and products derived from crude oil—or so have politicians long thought as they presented energy reforms to the Mexican public. What is more, natural gas already had been a privatization target. In 1995 the Zedillo administration argued for privatizing the transmission and distribution of natural gas.

The Fox administration used MSCs negotiated with private-sector companies on a fee-for-service basis to exploit gas in nonassociated fields. The contracts are for predetermined lengths of time and do not permit the companies to share in proceeds of the finds. Even though the MSCs in effect invited private-sector participation to an unprecedented degree, the Fox administration made assurances at the time of their introduction that in line with the constitution, hydrocarbons belong to the state and Fox would keep his campaign promise not to privatize public enterprises in the energy sector (Stojanovski 2008: 25).

Despite the strongly nationalistic rhetoric used by Fox throughout his administration regarding the protection of Pemex and oil as national patrimony, the involvement of the private sector grew. After approval of the multiple service contracts by the Congreso, by 2003 the first MSCs were offered for natural gas production in the Burgos Basin. Critics perceived the MSCs as unconstitutional because of the broad nature of the work performed by foreign companies under the contracts (such as seismic processing and interpretation, geological modeling, field engineering, production engineering, drilling, facility design and construction, facility and well maintenance, and natural gas transportation services). But Pemex defended the MSCs, saying the contractors only received cash payments based upon the fixed prices for the finished works and services rendered. MSCs in the Burgos Basin were awarded to the private companies Repsol-YPF (Spain/Argentina), Teikoku Oil (Japan), Tecpetrol (Argentina), Industrial Perforadora de Campeche (Mexico), Grupo Diavaz (Mexico), Lewis Energy (United States), and the Brazilian national oil company, Petrobras.

Reforming Pemex rather than tackling oil itself is always the better political tactic in Mexico. The gut instinct of the public is to protect oil, while Pemex is far from beloved. For years Pemex has been accused of cronyism, bloated bureaucracy, and inefficiency. Given that Notimex, the government's own news agency, dubbed Pemex "the Company with the Most Employees and Lowest Productivity in the World," certainly no one could accuse the state of being overtly nationalistic. Critics often cite the number of Pemex workers as a sign of the parastatal's inefficiency. At the time of its founding, three months after the expropriation in March 1938, Pemex counted 17,600 workers. This number grew 25 percent to 21,940 workers in just the first two years. Sometimes the labor increase does not correspond to production increases. In 1927, annual production was 64 million barrels with 12,500 workers. Two decades later, with 18,822 workers, in 1947 Pemex produced 11 percent less oil, 57 million barrels (Pazos 2008: 40). In 2004 Pemex employed 138,215 workers in its core and across its four subsidiaries (Exploration and Production, Refining, Gas and Basic Petrochemicals, and Petrochemicals). Meanwhile, the major multinationals, most of which operate simultaneously in dozens of countries, employed fewer workers: Exxon Mobil employed 88,000, BP 103,700, and Shell 119,000.

Another unfavorable public perception is of the powerful Pemex union, STPRM (Oil Workers Union of the Mexican Republic). Unionized Pemex workers benefit from an array of extensive social services provided by the company—a hospital system, home-financing plans, schools, day care, libraries—all envied by the broader Mexican public. The STPRM played a key role in the 2008 energy-reform debates, with union head Carlos Romero Deschamps actively criticizing the structure of Pemex and calling for its modernization through the reform. Romero Deschamps's "complicity" with the plan to privatize Pemex was not supported through all of STPRM's 90,000 members. On the occasion of Expropriation Day 2008, an article in Mexico's *Reforma* newspaper quoted Romero Deschamps as stating, "Today Pemex is a complex, diverse, vast company that could only simplistically be catalogued as inefficient." He also threw a barb at the PRD, AMLO, and the citizens' antiprivatization movement: "It goes without saying that we oil workers have no need to hark back to the past with misplaced patriotic sentiment or hog the limelight" (in Fuentes Berain and Rico 2009: 9).

Since the late 1980s unions have been the target of Mexico's sweeping tide of neoliberalization. Part of the divestiture of state enterprises entailed cutting ties between the state and labor unions (Teichman 1996: 160). Even though Pemex itself was not denationalized and oil was not privatized as a commodity, Salinas brought his spirit of reform to bear on the Pemex union. Social services were cut, and between 1989 and 1993 almost half of the unionized positions within Pemex, nearly 100,000 jobs, were eliminated. Since then the positions added have been nonunionized. Furthermore, fewer and fewer of those actually contributing to the oil industry are Pemex workers; rather, more often they are contract workers for private oil-services companies. Of the 20,000 workers on platforms in the Bay of Campeche in 2010, for example, fewer than a quarter worked for Pemex; the rest worked for private firms. In Mexico's parallel "private oil industry," workers run the risk of facing "restrictions on trade union freedoms, lack of insurance and health coverage, low wages, poor training and corrupt practices" as only some of the prevailing irregularities (Godoy 2010).

In the 1990s, Salinas's rebuke of the Pemex union by renegotiation of its collective bargaining agreement changed neither the public perception of the elite nature of the parastatal nor the tide of scandal and corruption. The average Mexican has good reason to look to both the union and the Pemex leadership for reasons to hold the parastatal in low esteem. There are abundant books and investigative reports showing that Pemex officials or union leaders used occasionally as allies by recent governments have obtained special funds that go toward things like building vacation homes or buying first-class airplane tickets.

"Pemexgate" remains one of the most notorious scandals involving the parastatal. It was connected to the historic election in 2000 of PAN candidate Vicente Fox that broke more than seventy years of PRI domination. Pemex former director-general Rogelio Montemayor was accused of diverting millions in Pemex funds to support the political campaign of Fox's opposition, PRI candidate Francisco Labastida, and laundering the money through the Pemex union. The flying accusations put the oil industry and the country on the brink of an emergency as Pemex workers threatened a crippling strike. Perhaps cowed by the prospect, courts declared that no money laundering took place. The parties involved, including the top official of the powerful Pemex labor union, were found not guilty. When the Congreso Nacional threatened union head Romero Deschamps's immunity protection, serious threats of a walkout emerged from the STPRM. The government sought to prosecute Montemayor, who fled to the United States. When he was finally extradited back to Mexico, charges were dropped. The first nationwide strike since Pemex was founded in 1938 was averted (Weiner 2002).

In the Pemexgate case, union leaders accused the Fox administration of trying to persecute and weaken the union in an attempt to pave the way for privatization as Fox claimed to be pushing for modernization and transparency. The Fox push for private-sector transparency could not penetrate the historic interworkings of the parastatal or its old-style networks of clientelism. Meanwhile, part of the Fox transparency was to bend the constitution as far as it could go regarding private-sector participation without having to amend Article 27 regarding national sovereignty over strategic subsoil resources. The Fox administration was taking a lot of liberties with energy policy without proposing major energy-policy reform.[11]

## Calderón's More Comprehensive Reform

Fox's approach was only testing the waters for the reform attempted by the Calderón administration, which from its earliest days worked toward an energy reform aimed directly at the heart of Pemex. Calderón was familiar with energy policy but also energy-reform efforts. He served as the secretary of energy in the Fox administration from September 2003 until June 2004; his resignation was connected with the administration's failure to carry out one of its top priorities, restructuring the energy sector. Under Fox, the mission was to privatize not oil but electricity. After Zedillo's failed privatization effort in 1999,[12] Fox wanted to change the constitution to regularize and expand the operations of the private and foreign companies generating and selling electricity in Mexican national territory.[13] As Fox's energy secretary, Felipe Calderón had the specific task to push deregulation and private-sector participation, particularly the state-run electricity agency, CFE.[14]

Felipe Calderón's election to the presidency was a chance not just to finally fulfill his party's vision of energy reform but to carry out the nonpartisan strategy of neoliberal privatization of Mexico's remaining state-owned assets. Even though the official energy-reform proposal did not appear before the Congreso Nacional until April 2008, energy reform was in the works from the moment he took office in January 2006. The proposal was really a collection of proposals, both new ideas and modifications to existing laws, some more and some less controversial. It contained a revision of overseeing structures intended to reduce the bloat of Pemex's bureaucracy and thus increase its autonomy and efficiency. Under the existing law, Pemex had to go to the finance ministry for every spending decision; the proposed reform would allow the parastatal to manage its budget independently. Most significantly, Pemex would be able to negotiate its own contracts, and these contracts could be performance-based. Another part of Pemex's proposed new financing would be citizen bonds and debt securities issued by Pemex that would grant their holders a return linked to the entity's performance. Pemex had in fact already been issuing bonds in foreign markets; in January 2009 Pemex sold $1 billion worth of 10-year bonds in the United States and offered another $2 billion in 10.5-year bonds in July of the same year. Both offers underperformed.

Administratively the proposed reform would change the composition of the board of directors, introducing four new "outside" members, professionals in related fields. The reform also proposed the creation of a hydrocarbons commission to work in conjunction with Sener, the Ministry of Energy, in the regulation and supervision of exploration and production activities. The creation of a transparency and auditing committee was also proposed to reinforce the promise of full disclosure of all information and to improve Pemex's record of public accountability. The goal of these changes was to introduce the structure of corporate governance within the parastatal that would, in turn, increase transparency and accountability.

In order for the energy reform to pass, the minority PAN legislators would have to work across party lines—namely, with PRI members of the Congreso. But the PRI, with the benefit of knowing public reaction to the PAN energy reform, rolled out its own energy-reform proposal on July 24, 2008, hoping to emerge between the embattled PAN and enraged PRD as the rational compromise. The PRI held the position that its effort modernized and strengthened Pemex without privatization, "neither open nor hidden," and without endangering the constitution (Becerril and Ballinas 2008). Just like the PAN proposal, the PRI envisaged Pemex negotiating and entering into performance-based contracts. In other words, their payment would be based on success in drilling and exploration of finds, especially in deep water. Andrés Manuel López Obrador, emboldened by the success of the citizens' movement against Calderón energy reform, now rallied against the PRI as well. He called the PRI energy proposal the "dirty work" of Felipe Calderón and accused the two parties of collaborating to produce a seemingly "alternative" proposal under the guise of the PRI. In a press conference, PRI leaders feigned surprise and stressed the differences of their party's energy-reform plan. Although both parties' proposals would open participation in contracting to the private sector, the PAN proposal was not clear on performance benefits in exploration contracts (whether contractors' pay would depend on the projects' success, for better or for worse).

To back the accusation of collusion, AMLO's people released a side-by-side comparison of the two documents showing many similarities between the two proposals. But another distinction between the two proposals regards one of the most contentious issues in the PAN energy-reform proposal: privatization of the downstream activities of oil refining, transport, and storage. Knowing that there was no way the PAN could get away with saying the refinery issue was not privatization, the PRI took the opportunity to present a modified approach and offered instead a tactical path to privatization by suggesting that downstream activities be turned over to decentralized Pemex "affiliates." These affiliates, essentially subsidiaries, would have their own budgetary and management autonomy, with the right to negotiate their own contracts for projects, acquisitions, services, and leases. The refineries in the PRI proposal would not be private undertakings because their capital was to be 100 percent national or self-generated (Becerril and Ballinas 2008).

### The Left's Answer

On August 25, the leftist FAP coalition finally produced the "Citizens Energy Reform Initiative." The eighty-page document makes certain unequivocal statements. In contrast to the PRI and PAN, the alternative proposal calls for "a Pemex with pipelines and refineries, all property of the nation, no risk or multiple service contracts, neither open nor disguised." The document urged strengthening rather than weakening the constitutional guarantee of the nation's dominion over hydrocarbons. Strengthening it would involve the state's putting more investment into developing national engineering, emphasizing research in scientific institutions rather than paying the private sector for technology, and supporting public education in institutions that Mexico already has but that are underfunded.

The proposal discussed how Pemex might contribute to national development. Pemex needed an adequate budget to modernize and grow, and so the proposal suggested giving Pemex the resources it needed to make the investments to strengthen its operation, maintenance, and development. At the center of the FAP's proposal was the issue of Pemex's proceeds. The proposal outlined several new funds, including a stabilization fund to guarantee a secure source of income for states through Pemex proceeds. The FAP initiative proposed a review of the terms of distribution of Pemex's proceeds, implementation of strict guidelines for distribution, and substantial increases in the distribution of the proceeds to municipalities with the highest levels of marginalization.

Agreeing with both the PAN and PRI reforms, the FAP proposal pushed for Pemex's budgetary autonomy. But diverging from both, the leftist coalition called for reintegrating the parastatal's subsidiaries, thus moving Pemex back to a vertically integrated company. As vertical integration gives more control, the proposal claimed this would increase efficiency, avoid unnecessary overlap of functions, and increase industrial security. As opposed to the PAN reform proposal that takes no notice of renewable energy or alternative energy sources, only hydrocarbons, the FAP initiative introduced a national energy savings plan and a national energy council. Subsequently, the PRI and the Partido Verde Ecologista de México (PVEM) put forward sustainable- and renewable-energy initiatives to fill the gaping hole left by the original PAN proposal. A PAN committee then had to scramble to add its own initiative just weeks before the final vote, clearly as an afterthought.

## The Vote

On October 23, 2008, a modified PAN energy-reform bill passed Mexico's Senate with overwhelming approval. Yet, the approval belies the truth of the surrounding atmosphere. López Obrador rallied the troops once again to demonstrate against the reform. As riot police met protesters around the building, politicians moved the energy-reform vote to another government facility some distance away. Regardless, López Obrador, who had been expressly fighting against privatization per se all along, claimed that the energy-reform bill was simply not strong enough in protecting oil as a national resource. He continually pushed the question of the contracts, even suggesting additional language to clarify that no exploration or production contracts would be awarded for "blocks" or "exclusive areas," as this was thought to be too close to concessions. The change regarding contracts proposed by López Obrador was rejected. Lawmakers conducted proceedings from a makeshift stand on the floor of the Congreso Nacional after opposition legislators allied with AMLO to seize the usual podium, waving Mexican flags and setting off air horns and sirens in a bid to derail the vote.

On October 28, 2008, Mexico's energy reform met its final hurdle in the lower house, the Chamber of Deputies, where the package of legislation went for a vote. At the eleventh hour, the PRI-PAN alliance in the chamber attempted to revert the bill to the original Calderón proposal's risk contracts and incentives. The FAP threatened to derail the negotiations entirely over the contract issues if the original PAN proposal went up for the vote, but to little avail. The Chamber of Deputies approved the package of reforms—the same package approved by the

Senate—with 326 votes in favor, 133 against, and 5 abstentions. That night, Calderón made a television appearance to celebrate the passage of the "most important oil reform since the 1938 nationalization." Most importantly, Calderón stressed, "Pemex was not privatized," and "Mexicans continue to be the only owners of the oil" (Mexico, Office of the President 2008a).

"Strengthening" and "modernizing" Pemex are consistent goals of energy reform and are agreed upon by Left and Right in Mexico. Many believe that the package of amendments to seven laws that was passed in 2008 does in a sense begin to fulfill these goals because they grant unprecedented autonomy to the parastatal. In the reform, Pemex was moved away from the direct oversight of the Congreso and granted greater autonomy. The reform also gave Pemex budgetary autonomy in place of the previous system whereby the state-owned company needed federal approval for every item in its budget. But for those who believed that strengthening Mexico's energy future could truly be accomplished with the muscle of the private sector alone, the reform package was only a collection of baby steps.

It initially appeared that the PAN suffered two major losses, first on the issue of contracts and second on the privatization of refining. Over time, the party made up a lot of ground on the contracts issue, however, by leaving ambiguous language in the approved reform as to what leeway the parastatal would have in dealing with the private sector, especially now that Pemex would be able to exercise more autonomy. With the help of a December 2010 Mexican Supreme Court decision that backed the measure's constitutionality, Pemex may enter into integrated service contracts for drilling and exploration that offer incentives for the contractors. However, the incentives are limited: under no circumstances do contractors have ownership rights over the reserves. To reduce the sense that the contracts are indeed performance-based, payments on contracts cannot be calculated by reference to a percentage of production, nor may production be calculated on the contractors' own balance sheets. However, to enhance the sense that contractors are rewarded for bringing technological advances, lower-cost equipment, or other increased efficiency to a project, contractors can receive cash (and only cash) bonuses.

Regarding the privatization of Mexico's refineries, though, Calderón remained at a stalemate. Campeche in particular paid the price for Calderón's anger about the failure of the privatization of refining inside Mexico's borders. The state, which had mounted a vigorous campaign to host a new refinery, had high hopes of using the facility as a platform for regional development. The hopes were endangered when Campeche's inside track to Los Pinos—Calderón's Interior Secretary Juan Camilo Mouriño—died when his Lear jet crashed in downtown Mexico City only a week after the energy reform passed. On a visit to Campeche for Mouriño's memorial service, Calderón stopped off at a highway-dedication ceremony. The president spoke about the refinery that Campeche was vying for in a stiff competition with several other states. Calderón would ultimately decide which state offered the best location for the new Pemex facility. In his off-the-cuff comments Calderón shocked PRI Governor Hurtado standing by his side on the dais. Had the PRI, PRD, and other parties backed his energy-reform proposal, Calderón said, the private sector could provide financing for building a new refinery. States would not be competing with each other for only one Pemex facility; instead, three or four refineries could be under construction at the same time. Campeche would surely have been the site of one of those refineries. But now, without the participation of the private sector, only one refinery would be built. Where would it go? The decision would not be political, Calderón assured his audience. These decisions, he stressed, are strictly technical, not political (Herrera Beltrán 2009).

## Privatization and the Post-Peak Condition

States under neoliberalism take multiple approaches to privatization. Although in Mexico in the 1980s some industries were brought straight to the auction block, privatization is not always a wholesale process. In the case of Pemex, there have been many financial and structural tactics over the past thirty years (breakdown of the parastatal into subsidiaries, the Pidiregas scheme, the introduction of MSCs, and the 2008 reform), all of which contribute to an overall neoliberal strategy of privatization. These have not yet culminated in a constitutional amendment to denationalize oil. Under the post-peak condition in Mexico, oil is maintained as de jure national patrimony while the state has encouraged de facto participation of the private sector to profit from oil. The ideal mise-en-scène for the reformist sleight of hand is off shore, a neoliberalized frontier land of opportunity and opportunism (Cameron and Palan 2004: 105).

Yet it is difficult to assess who won and who lost the battle of the

2008 energy reform. In a sense, nobody and everybody. Some say Calderón lost: the package passed in October 2008 was a watered-down facsimile of what the PAN originally wanted and the country needed in order to save Pemex and the dangerously dwindling oil supply. As passed, the reform fell short of permitting private companies to buy equity stakes in oilfields or receive compensation directly in the form of oil. On the other hand, some say López Obrador, the adelitas, and the Left as a whole lost the energy-reform battle. In the ensuing months leading up to the 2009 midterm elections it became clear that AMLO's antiprivatization crusade snuffed out this iteration of Mexico's left-leaning party politics. When the issue died, what was left of a fractured PRD and a loose coalition of left-of-center parties splintered; along with their cause their alliances and power faded. In summer 2010 López Obrador announced his candidacy for the 2012 presidential race.

Back on the frontlines, after the privatization came and went with all of its protests and passions, lives in Gulf coast communities continued on as before. The national movement led by López Obrador did not sweep the residents of Isla Aguada into its fervor for defending oil as the patrimony of the nation. While the citizen referendum held months earlier clearly indicated a strong rejection of the Calderón reform on a state level, in Isla Aguada some ignored and others disdained the slogan "El petróleo es nuestro." The nationalist claim alienated Aguadeños disenchanted by thirty years of being unable to claim the oil as theirs. For the frontline community marginalized by the oil industry, the phrase could have and thus should have had a tangible dimension. The management of the nation's most valuable patrimony should have enhanced and not damaged citizens' livelihoods.

While the debate over privatization raged at demonstrations in Mexico City, on the frontlines of the messy and polluting extractive industry it appears that the nation has sold out already. One needs only to look at the seas and skies in Campeche's Ciudad del Carmen to find the evidence. Neon-orange-clad Halliburton, Schlumberger, and Baker Hughes workers scurry on land and in helicopters performing the duties required and allowed under their state-sanctioned multiple service contracts. Some have called the hundreds of millions of dollars in contracts awarded each year by Pemex to these and other companies a de facto privatization. While many think first of the big oil companies like Shell, ExxonMobil, Chevron, BP, ConocoPhillips, and Total, it is in fact the oil-services providers that are today's key players, especially in countries with state-owned oil companies. Under the Calderón administration, the multinational Schlumberger, headquartered in Houston, became the principal contractor and oil-services provider in Mexico, rapidly growing its portfolio to 194 contracts worth more than $4.5 billion. Many recent contracts are for drilling in Chicontepec, where progress has been much criticized for several delays and a failure to produce substantial results (Cardoso 2010). The company has more contracts valued much higher than its competitor Halliburton. Such contracts are only going to proliferate under the improved terms of the energy reform.

However, there is some good news on the horizon for the frontlines. The 2008 energy reform promised preference to contract bids that employ Mexican human resources, goods, or services and to small and medium-size companies. To guarantee follow-through, the reform requires minimum percentages of national content in the procurement of certain goods and services. On the frontlines in Campeche Governor Fernando Ortega Bernés and municipal president Aracely Escalante Jasso signed an accord with Pemex to ensure that the reform was carried out in Carmen. They created a council with representatives from state and local governments, Pemex, and the Carmen business community intending to facilitate the bidding process for local businesses in Carmen to obtain Pemex contracts. However, given that Pemex claims that its sights are set on developing difficult areas for exploration and extraction, such as deep water, for which Mexico does not already have the technology, equipment, and know-how, this new turn is unlikely to render the anticipated boost to local businesses and workers.

Meanwhile, the people in the coastal communities of Campeche are living with the current problems of the management of natural resources on our planet: privatization is a problem, but as the case of Pemex shows, NOCs are a problem, too. In the interests of democracy, Mexico maintains the de jure nationalization of hydrocarbons. Time and time again, administration through administration, this has been shown. The model of state ownership of subsoil resources is criticized mercilessly by the neoliberal Right, but looking at energy resources across the globe, we can see that 90 percent of oil is now in the hands of NOCs. Even so, in the interests of justice, patrimony should belong to everyone.

CHAPTER 6

# Energy Security on the U.S.-Mexican Maritime Border: Transboundary Oil in the Deepwater Gulf

## A Tale of Two Borders

In May 2010 Mexican President Felipe Calderón paid an official state visit to Barack Obama at the White House. Calderón's visit occurred during the immediate fallout of an unpopular Arizona immigration bill, SB1070, a law intensifying the criminalization of undocumented migration in the U.S.-Mexican border region. In their opening public addresses, both Calderón (a critic of the legislation) and Obama (a proponent of a differently focused national, comprehensive, immigration-reform policy) emphasized the spirit of cooperation necessary to lead their nations and the region toward a prosperous future. While the media helped stir public discourse into its usual frenzy by focusing on immigration and border security, the topic at hand behind closed doors took a different turn. The two leaders were faced with a different, long-standing, high-stakes border issue—the U.S.-Mexican maritime border in the Gulf of Mexico. Since the 1970s, geologists, oil-company executives, and politicians have become increasingly preoccupied with the underwater hydrocarbon resources in the Gulf. Particularly in the maritime border region, these oil resources are thought to be deep, valuable, exceedingly abundant, and thus—if not handled with both the proper technology and the most careful diplomacy—the stuff of a potential political border battle.

Calderón's visit coincided with one of the biggest environmental crises of the Obama presidency, the Deepwater Horizon oil spill. Just as the Ixtoc I blowout in Gulf waters in 1979–1980 was far from an exclusively Mexican event, the Macondo well blowouts and the BP rig disaster were not a tragedy entirely bound within the confines of impermeable national U.S. borders. Felipe Calderón, like many in the Mexican public as a whole, was no doubt watching the Deepwater Horizon event unfold with great interest and deep concern. The Gulf was Mexico's backyard, too. But given the very different ways the neighboring countries structure the relationship of the ocean's hidden yet valuable resources to national sovereignty and patrimony, the two leaders had potentially quite different needs and expectations of how to manage Gulf hydrocarbons and especially how to manage these resources under crisis conditions—whether that crisis be political, economic, or environmental.

Since coming to office, Calderón had found himself in a permanent storm of a Gulf oil emergency. At the center of the storm, citizens looked to the state to protect, not cede, the resources found in their patrimonial seas. For the Calderón administration, Cantarell's peak status, the political struggle over energy reform, and the economic conditions in Mexico deeply affected by recession and an uncertain oil future gave very little legitimacy to a national Mexican energy policy. For Pemex, the shallow waters of the Gulf of Mexico are the problematic past, and the deep waters hold the solution for the future. Though failing to pass his fully envisioned energy reform based on a private-sector-driven acceleration of deepwater drilling, Calderón nevertheless was succeeding in a piecemeal expansion of private service contracts for multinationals operating in deep waters of the Gulf. Pemex has continued to dedicate more and more of its exploration budget in deepwater projects, up to $20 billion in the Gulf in 2011. Meanwhile, no deepwater wells significantly contribute to the dwindling national production.

On the U.S. side of the maritime border, the Gulf of Mexico represented endless possibility for U.S. energy policy still tied to fossil fuels with pretensions toward energy independence. In early 2010, just weeks before the Deepwater Horizon disaster, Obama was all systems go on new plans for offshore drilling by the private sector. Even though part of the western Gulf's outer continental shelf was already open to leasing and drilling and companies were busy off the coasts of Gulf states, Obama had just rescinded the decades-old moratorium on offshore drilling along areas previously closed to drilling. Along with much of the eastern coastline (Delaware to Florida) and northern Alaska, a drilling moratorium on the eastern Gulf of Mexico was lifted. Though actual production would be many years in the future, billions of dollars in cost, and highly uncertain in its yield, one thing was certain on both sides of the Gulf: who stood to benefit from the uptick in Gulf drilling. Despite all of the uncertainties and strong protests from environmental

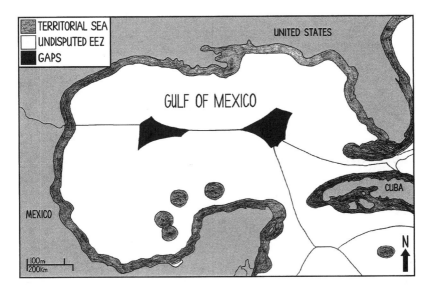

Gulf maritime boundaries. Map by Deanna Breglia.

groups and citizens especially in affected states, both leaders were eager to appease transnational companies that stood ready and eager to provide the infrastructure the new undertakings required.

As Obama and Calderón met under the shadow of the oil-spill tragedy, the sense of a shared horizon of interest was obvious. Yet the United States and Mexico as well as Cuba each holds its own vested interests in the Gulf's resources. While the countries have different histories of shallow-water oil exploitation, they perhaps share an interest in developing a future on their deepwater frontiers. However, these frontiers are now the subject of some considerable controversy and even dispute. Because of recent developments in international law, national maritime boundaries have been extended to a 200-nautical-mile exclusive economic zone for countries with coastlines. This gives those countries a considerable safety net for exploiting resources including the ever more valuable deepwater petroleum reservoirs. The new cartography of the Gulf of Mexico under this legal regime has also produced a curious dilemma of geology and geopolitics: drawing the EEZs produces areas of overlap and areas of gap. Thus the countries racing to leverage multiple and competing interests against peak oil in the Gulf of Mexico are also contending with a maritime border skirmish playing out at more than 5,000 feet below the water's surface and in congressional halls, board rooms of oil companies, and national protests over energy reform. I heard the echoes in communities along Mexico's Gulf coast where those who make their livelihoods in these waters understand that sovereignty over all of the Gulf's declining resources—whether oil, fisheries, or delicate ecological heritage—could be decided, perhaps symbolically and juridically as well, at the maritime border.

## Contested Politics of Maritime Boundaries

Over the past three decades the Gulf has become increasingly important to the energy security of the United States and Mexico. The Gulf is vital to the U.S. petroleum industry; drilling there accounts for 25 percent of U.S. domestic oil production and 15 percent of U.S. domestic gas output. Drilling off the coasts of Louisiana and Texas began in the 1930s. With shallow-water production now in significant decline, hopes are that deepwater areas of the Gulf will be able to make up for the loss. Exploratory drilling in 2008 produced estimates that deepwater reservoirs in the U.S. Gulf territory hold as much as 6.6 billion barrels of oil. Even though deepwater drilling is highly sophisticated and expensive, several new Gulf oilfields are already on the verge of contributing toward significant production. Four fields together—Thunder Horse, Shenzi, Tahiti, and Atlantis—were projected to supply about 14 percent of the daily production of the lower forty-eight states by 2010 (EIA 2009b).

One of the most serious symptoms of Mexico's oil addiction is the nation's heavy reliance on the Gulf to an even greater extent than in the United States. Since Pemex's initiation of offshore oil operations in the Campeche Sound in the 1970s, crude has flowed abundantly from the Gulf. Up to 80 percent of the nation's petroleum comes from the Gulf. With oil as a state-owned industry in Mexico and crude as a strategic national asset, oil rents fund approximately 40 percent of Mexico's federal budget. Revenues from Gulf of Mexico petroleum are especially important to the fiscal health of coastal states such as Campeche, Tabasco, and Veracruz. After the peak of the Gulf's supergiant Cantarell in 2004 and its subsequent annual decline of 14 percent, the country's overall output has decreased by nearly 20 percent. Hopes are that the Gulf's deepwater reservoirs hold the resources to rescue Pemex's declining production and, in turn, the federal budget.

Though the economic dimension of oil is key to the nation's security,

Gulf oil also involves a deeply symbolic dimension for Mexico, one in which nationalism—manifest as the desire to protect national resources from foreign plunder—plays a central role. The protection of Gulf oil resources is part of a longer and broader historical drive to spatially fix control over territory, thereby asserting dominion over resources. This drive is most apparent in the Gulf fisheries as Mexico exercised sovereignty over shrimp resources by manipulating maritime boundaries.

In his 1998 book *Maps and Politics*, Jeremy Black explains that "the impact of economic gains has been an intensification of frontier disputes. And these have had consequences in terms of contested cartographies. These disputes are not restricted to the land surface, but extend to the sea and also involve issues of underwater and underground rights" (87). Rather than a pro forma technical exercise, the execution of the U.S.-Mexican maritime border in the Gulf of Mexico is a fraught and contested process of political and economic negotiation. The history of maritime boundary delimitation in the Gulf is one of the calculated efforts to effect control over a widening scope of each nation's sovereign rights. Increasing a country's boundaries can help it to expand the scope of its resources and enhance national security vis-à-vis its resource security. The effort is only effective if these maritime borders are justly derived and the resources are developed or, equally importantly, conserved and protected. The strategic regulation of resources is one of the most compelling reasons for a nation to delimit its maritime borders. In the Gulf of Mexico the skyrocketing rise in the potential value of its undersea resources with the discovery of oil and gas prompted a corresponding intensification of attention to what piece of the Gulf belonged to which nation. The same contested politics of territory and sovereignty, mixed with ardent nationalism (at least from the Mexican side), is historically characteristic of border tensions between the United States and Mexico that were about to play out on a new frontier.

Beginning in the 1970s, attention not only from the public but also the private sector turned to stricter and more strategic mappings of maritime boundaries in the Gulf of Mexico. In line with the United Nations Convention on the Law of the Sea,[1] Mexico and the United States established maritime delimitations that stood in accordance with international law, regularizing sovereignty and territory in the Gulf. When Mexico attempted to secure its oil and gas resources in the Gulf of Mexico, an intricate legal framework of national and international law for establishing resource security in Gulf waters was already in place. Spurred by a decades-long battle (1940s–1970s) with U.S. fishermen over rights to exploit Gulf shrimp and Pacific tuna, Mexico extended its territorial sovereignty to 12 nautical miles and in 1976 established an EEZ of 200 nautical miles seaward (*Diario Oficial* 1976b,c). In those 12 miles of territorial sea Mexico has the same sovereignty as on land. In its EEZ, a nation has sovereign rights (but not sovereignty) over activities such as exploring, exploiting, conserving, and managing the natural resources on the surface and subsurface of the seabed. While boats and ships may travel freely through the waters of the EEZ (as the EEZ is coextensive with the "high seas"), nobody can, for example, set up an oil-drilling platform without permission. No nation may exercise rights over the mineral resources of other nations without consent. The EEZ is particularly important for hydrocarbon resources because it also gives coastal states the right to conduct other activities with a view to exploring and extracting economic benefits from the zone.

With the establishment of its EEZ in 1976, Mexico converted its maritime jurisdiction in the Gulf of Mexico into more than that of a "territorial sea" or an "exclusive economic zone." Because it contains resources vital to the nation's domestic security in terms of economics and sociocultural identity, the Gulf of Mexico is a patrimonial sea. The term "patrimonial sea" is specifically Latin American in origin and was first used as an antecedent to the concept of the EEZ. In a 1971 document presented to the Organization of American States (OAS), Edmundo Vargas coined the term to refer to a maritime territory beyond the limits of the territorial sea, up to a maximum limit of 200 miles, defined as

> that maritime zone in which the coastal state has exclusive rights for the exploration, conservation and exploitation of the natural resources of the waters adjacent to its coast, and of the sea-bed and the sub-soil thereof up to a limit determined by the said State in accordance with reasonable criteria and on the basis of its geographical, geological and biological characteristics. (In Yturriaga 1997: 26)

The patrimonial sea concept reached further than international law at the time by specifically functioning in the socioeconomic interest of coastal states. The concept reflected nations' exercise of sovereignty over their waters specifically to access fisheries; it was codified in the 1972 Declaration of Santo Domingo, one of the pillars of the UNCLOS in 1982.

In the Vargas definition of "patrimonial sea" and the later definition of the EEZ, maritime zones extending 200 nautical miles from a nation's coastlines are not territorial seas in which the nation has sovereignty. Rather than spaces of sovereign jurisdiction, they are spaces of economic access for exploitation only (Sepúlveda 1974: 68). Even though the term has been used to define the economic jurisdiction for the territory we simply now refer to as the EEZ, a revival and slight redefinition of "patrimonial sea" can help us to better describe Mexico's interests (and, in turn, the U.S. problem—or vice versa) in securing energy resources in the Gulf of Mexico. All of the Mexican Gulf is a patrimonial sea for Mexicans because the resources it contains, from fisheries to hydrocarbons, are symbolically tied to the nation-state's project of providing for the national welfare.

Taking the concept of the patrimonial sea as offered by the Declaration of Santo Domingo and broadening its scope to practical and symbolic dimensions, we can include the quotidian meaning of "patrimony" for Mexican citizens. This allows us to account for how Mexicans understand the Gulf's oil resources. As valuable as oil is, the symbolic value of petróleo as patrimonio to Mexican citizens is priceless. By this I mean that the maritime jurisdictional redefinitions have produced a deep symbolic effect by underlining the importance of oil as Mexican national cultural patrimony. A proper analysis of past maritime boundary negotiations as well as the success of upcoming agreements over this "other" U.S.-Mexican border will depend a great deal upon maintaining an awareness of how the Gulf of Mexico functions, in legal and popular public discourse, as a patrimonial sea. The concept of the patrimonial sea is critical to bring to our understanding of Mexico's claim of sovereignty over hydrocarbon resources in the negotiation of transboundary reservoirs in the western Gulf along the maritime border with the United States.

## Race to Deepwater Reserves

Mexico's dependence on conventional hydrocarbon resources of the Gulf has shaped its energy security for the past thirty years. Now Pemex is looking to maintain the nation's oil supply with the Gulf's nonconventional oil resource. Pemex estimates that within the 222,000 square miles of the deepwater Gulf are approximately 30 billion barrels of recoverable oil. PEP head Carlos Morales Gil announced during one of the summer 2008 energy-reform debates that of Pemex's 53.8 billion barrels of prospective reserves (neither proven nor probable or even on the horizon yet as possible), 55 percent would come from deep water (Comisiones Unidas 2008). In the post-peak condition deepwater resources are among the most viable of the remaining fossil fuels. For those who still see an energy future composed of fossil fuels, the problem is not only how to get them but how to get them before it is too late.

The hydrocarbon resources of the Gulf are vital to U.S. energy security. According to the U.S. Energy Information Agency (EIA 2010), the Gulf contributes 30 percent of total U.S. production and upward of 90 percent of the nation's offshore production. Gulf discoveries have revealed such a bonanza that one oil and gas journalist reported: "You can tune out all the scare talk about Peak Oil for a while—probably a long while" (Morrison 2006). The Minerals Management Service (MMS), the division of the U.S. Department of Interior charged with regulating oil and gas contracts and leases, in 2011 became the Bureau of Ocean Energy Management (BOEM).[2] According to the agency's figures, projections for 2007–2016 show that Gulf oil production has the potential to exceed 1.7 mbpd. Most of this will come from deep (more than 1,000 feet) and ultradeep (more than 5,000 feet) sources. Given the potential of undiscovered resources, this number could reach up to 2 mbpd (Karl et al. 2007: 11–12).

The United States and Mexico have high hopes for the promising potential for oil and gas reserves in the Gulf of Mexico. Like most other oil reserves in the twenty-first century, the fields on the Gulf's newest frontier are more expensive and difficult to reach than the cheap and easily extractable resources previously drawn from shallower Gulf fields. Rather, the new frontier lies in deep and ultradeep water, some more than five miles below the ocean's surface. Ultradeep oil is included in the suite of "unconventional fuels" (along with oil sands, shale oil, and biofuels) upon which the world will increasingly rely in the coming decades as production of cheap and easily refinable crude falls into steep decline (EIA 2009a).

Accessing such oil and gas is difficult not only practically but politically as well. Drilling at such depths is a multibillion-dollar investment requiring specialized technology, equipment, and labor. These deepwater reservoirs present another, increasingly common problem as the search for new reserves across the globe reaches uncharted territories. That is, underwater oil and gas deposits often lie in waters that have not been delimited; thus sovereign rights over exploration and resource exploitation are a matter of dispute or arbitration. The Gulf of Mexico's rich deepwater hydrocarbon deposits are contested spaces of national and transnational politics.

The race to secure offshore hydrocarbons is characteristic of what Klare has called "the era of xtreme energy," when the easily obtained conventional hydrocarbons like Cantarell crude are gone. Klare asserts that as we come to the end of the petroleum age we find ourselves entering a no-man's-land in which "we will remain for years to come . . . until an age that will see the great flowering of renewable energy" (2009a). Parsing resource rights in the Gulf of Mexico deepwater maritime borderlands demonstrates that the high seas are quite literally a no-man's-land where sovereignty and energy security hang in the balance.

## Legislating the Gulf of Mexico

Securing rights to access rich resources across the shared waters of the Gulf of Mexico has a history much longer than the race for oil reserves; it goes back as far as the battles the Spanish waged against English pirates and privateers for access to ports and coastal resources. Across the centuries, the principle of resource sovereignty—the control of access to resources within a set of territorial boundaries—remains an ideal for the Westphalian nation-state. While the tools and techniques for determining the technicalities of resource rights (mapping the high seas, for example) may be quite different, the modern negotiation between nations to claim sovereignty over resources is based on the same principle. Two treaties between the United States and Mexico (1978/1997 and 2000) establish maritime boundaries in the Gulf of Mexico and their effects on resource sovereignty.[3] The first (1978/1997), which took nineteen years to ratify, established a 200-nautical-mile zone for each country in which it may have sovereign rights to exploit resources. The second treaty (2000) deals with a problem created by the earlier treaty. It specifies what to do with the maritime territory in the gap beyond the reach of either country's 200-mile EEZ.

### Boundaries in Limbo in the 1978 Treaty

In 1976 the United States and Mexico set out provisional maritime boundaries for the eastern and western Gulf of Mexico as well as the Pacific. The instigating issue for the negotiation was the need for a bilateral fishing accord to resolve the jurisdiction of tuna-fishing rights in the Pacific Ocean, not hydrocarbon resource exploitation rights in the Gulf. The goal was to set the boundaries of each country's 200-nautical-mile EEZ. The delimitation was a clear-cut, technical measurement exercise (of equidistance between the farthest outlying land masses of the two countries, including islands). Using the principle of outlying islands, Mexico measured its zone from the Arrecife Alacranes, an exposed reef sixty-five nautical miles off the Yucatán Peninsula. The 1978 Treaty on Maritime Boundaries was signed in Mexico City by José López Portillo and Jimmy Carter to make the provisional maritime boundaries permanent. When the treaty was being negotiated, the U.S. State Department was primarily concerned about fishing rights and obtaining the best boundary possible in the Pacific, where rich fishing banks were at stake. Although the treaty also covered seabed resources, these were considered of secondary importance (Applegate 1997: 71).

The boundaries remained provisional for the next nineteen years as the treaty lingered unratified by the U.S. Congress. On the surface, the issue at the center of the debate was fishing rights. But one petroleum geologist, Hollis Hedberg, testified in 1980 before the U.S. Senate Foreign Relations Committee about what U.S., British, and other foreign interests in Mexico's onshore and offshore Gulf region had suspected for decades: the real issue was oil. Hedberg urged the Senate not to cede any of the Gulf's seafloor mineral exploitation rights to Mexico in exchange for Pacific tuna-fishing rights. Although deepwater exploration was in its infancy in the late 1970s and early 1980s and drilling in waters deeper than 2,000 feet was not even a reality, Hedberg's urgent testimony compelled a delay in ratification of the maritime boundary by convincing some senators that the Gulf seabed in the area of concern contained valuable petroleum resources.[4]

By 1980 Mexico was well under way with drilling in the Gulf, elated with the discovery of Cantarell, the world's second-largest oilfield, in the shallow waters of the Campeche Sound. Some of the drilling sites were only forty miles or so offshore, safely within the officially established EEZ. Cantarell, although it was Mexico's first offshore drilling venture, was manageable for Pemex, which had no previous offshore experience. Given its relative proximity to shore, its uncomplicated geomorphology, and the help of foreign contractors, production in Mexico's EEZ proceeded apace.

On the U.S. side, the 1978 treaty provoked little reaction from the major petroleum companies, which apparently shared the State Department's view that the agreement genuinely concerned fishing rights only. However, by the mid-1990s, oil interests began to get involved in pushing for ratification. Industry groups including the American Petroleum Institute and the Independent Petroleum Association of America lobbied for treaty ratification and mounted a letter-writing campaign to the then chairman of the Senate Foreign Relations Committee, Jesse Helms (R-NC), the Energy and Natural Resources Committee chairman Frank Murkowski (R-AK), and a consortium of Gulf Coast state senators led by majority leader Trent Lott (R-MS) and Senator Kay Bailey Hutchison (R-TX). On October 23, 1997, the treaty (known as the Clinton-Zedillo Treaty) was finally ratified, helped along by the efforts of the Departments of the Interior and State (U.S. Congress 1997).

## The Clinton-Zedillo Treaty

The unanimous approval of the 1978 treaty meant that Mexico could move ahead on negotiations with the United States regarding the Gulf maritime territory not covered by the treaty: two oddly shaped gaps, one western and one eastern, situated more than 200 nautical miles from either coast and beyond the extension of the EEZ of either country. These two gaps are colloquially known as "doughnut holes" (in Spanish, *hoyos de dona*). The western gap commands the most intense scrutiny and debate, as its seabed holds deepwater oil and gas reservoirs. It covers 5,092 square nautical miles ($nm^2$) that are the territory of neither the United States nor Mexico. The rights to exploit its seabed resources would be split between the two in proportions based on equidistant extensions of their respective EEZs. Estimates of the reserves in the western gap differ widely, anywhere from 2.4 billion to 22 billion barrels of oil and a minimum of 5 billion cubic feet (bcf) of natural gas to a maximum of 44 bcf (Estrada 2009).

Following ratification of the Clinton-Zedillo Treaty in 1997, the United States and Mexico quickly moved to agree on a division of the western gap. This was, after all, the intent made clear in a report to the U.S. Senate from its Foreign Relations Committee:

> Delimitation of the western gap has become increasingly important to U.S. interests as petroleum exploration has moved into deeper waters. The Department of Interior is now receiving bids for exploration in this area. Several new drilling vessels capable of operating in water depths of up to 10,000 feet are under construction . . . The Committee urges the

Executive Branch to commence negotiations on the western gap without delay, once this treaty enters into force. (U.S. Senate 1997)[5]

Although oil interests motivated the ratification of the Clinton-Zedillo Treaty, the voice of the oil lobby in the United States subsequently grew stronger and more insistent. By 2000 technology was quickly revealing the potential of oil and gas reservoirs in the maritime borderlands. Private-sector companies wanted the assurance of clear legislation to facilitate exploration and drilling in the region. The 2000 Continental Shelf Treaty reveals this intense interest in hydrocarbons. The treaty distinguishes the seabed (and its resources) from the water column (which remains high seas and subject to international law). The significance of this distinction is that it enables a nation to secure resource rights to undersea minerals without infringing upon international law (Charney and Smith 2002: 2626).

The continental shelf divides the western gap utilizing the same methodology employed for the 1978 treaty, meaning the boundary was drawn using a line (also known as a median line) equidistant from the two coasts. In this case, islands were given full consideration when calculating the EEZs. The equidistant lines were drawn from each national territory's farthest outlying islands. Using this principle of equidistance to measure each country's claim on the resources in the gaps, Mexico gained 62 percent of the territory (3,179 nm², or 17,000 km²) and the United States 38 percent (1,913 nm², or 10,500 km²) (US MMS 2000).

During the negotiation of the 2000 treaty, both parties suspected that hydrocarbon reservoirs existed in the deepwater gaps. The negotiators strategized to preempt the anxieties arising (more so on the part of the Mexican committee) over the strong likelihood that common petroleum deposits straddled the already set maritime boundaries. It was a problem of illegal migration across the U.S.-Mexican border in reverse. Because hydrocarbons migrate, a shared reservoir may be drained by whoever drills it first. The phenomenon is called "drainage" and is known colloquially as the "drinking straw" or in Spanish *popote* effect, meant to call to mind the sucking of oil from one side of the boundary to the other. Alarmists in Mexico popularized the popote effect as a U.S. border incursion on Mexico's resource sovereignty.

Thus, to avoid problems with the possible existence of transboundary reservoirs, the 2000 treaty established "the Area," a 1.4-nautical-mile buffer zone on each side of the maritime boundary, effectively creating a 2.8-mile strip.[6] The parties agreed to a ten-year moratorium on

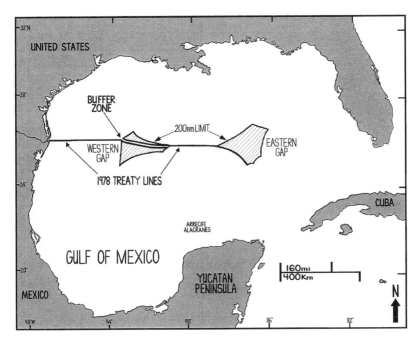

Gulf of Mexico gaps and buffer zone. Map by Deanna Breglia.

drilling in the buffer zone, set to expire in January 2011. In May 2010, at the height of the Deepwater Horizon disaster, Presidents Calderón and Obama negotiated an extension of the moratorium on drilling in the border region's buffer zone. The moratorium and its extension were beneficial for Pemex. Given its chronic lack of research and reinvestment, the parastatal was completely unprepared at the time the moratorium was originally established for launching a deepwater drilling program on the maritime border. In the years leading up to the 2000–2010 moratorium PEP made some efforts in exploring the "new oil geography" of the Gulf of Mexico with an investment of $1 million to find an initial drill site in the deepwater Gulf and to acquire seismic data (using sound waves to create images of the seabed) on more than 6,800 miles of Gulf waters at depths from 650 to 9,000 feet. PEP even prepared a proposal to drill an exploratory well close to the U.S. projects at the Baha and Trident fields. The latter project was never undertaken. As the end of the initial moratorium approached, energy analyst David Shields said Pemex still had "practically no relevant deepwater experience" (2008). Perhaps it was difficult for Pemex to be genuinely motivated to find new sources of crude, blinded by the success of its shallow-water production at the prolific Cantarell, which at the time was pumping 1.8 mbpd.

## Shifting Borders and Disappearing Islands

Not all was cut and dried between the United States and Mexico with the Gulf claims. In the quick maneuvering to divide the western gap's deepwater spoils under the private-sector-driven Clinton-Zedillo agreement, a sleight of hand occurred. The whole purpose of the 1978 treaty was the establishment of a 200-nautical-mile EEZ. The method employed to calculate the EEZ was to measure from the outermost land territory of each nation. In Mexico, an island off the coast of the Yucatán Peninsula was used to determine the Mexican maritime boundary in the Gulf and eventually the country's stake in the oil and gas reserves. When geologists saw the draft legislation of the 1978 treaty going before the U.S. Congress, they pointed out that by this reckoning the United States stood to lose claims on oil and gas deposits in the western Gulf. If Mexico measured from the mainland only, then the United States stood to gain some 25,000 square miles more of Gulf area. Thus, legislators were wary of employing the practice. However, the argument also goes the other way: if islands were not factored into the boundary determination, the United States would stand to lose ground off the Alaska, California, and Florida coasts (Schmitt 1982: 147). Hollis Hedberg argued the case on this point saying that Mexico should instead measure from the underwater slopes of the continental shelf, a method of maritime boundary delimitation unprecedented in international practice (R. Smith 1981: 404).

Alberto Székely, a former Mexican diplomat and an expert on maritime boundaries and resources, weighed in. The Hedberg proposal, Székely suggested (1982: 158), was not only misguided but illegal because it was standard practice in international maritime law to measure a median or equidistant line from each nation's farthest outlying coastal territory when determining a maritime boundary. If the Hedberg proposal for drawing the Mexican line only from the continental coastline was attempted and then the marine space between the outer limits of the two 200-mile zones was divided between the two countries, they would be appropriating for themselves, as for the waters, a part of the high seas. Regarding the soil and subsoil, they could be taking a part of the International Sea-Bed area that had been declared by the United Nations a Common Heritage of Mankind.

Hedberg was seemingly overridden: although the treaty was not ratified until nineteen years later, when the U.S. Senate finally voted for its approval the EEZ was indeed measured from Mexico's outermost island. Thus, the international practice of measuring from islands was preserved in the 1978 treaty and used by the United States and Mexico to determine their respective 200-mile EEZs.

Still, an old debate that consistently plagued the maritime boundary negotiations on the Mexican side would just not go away. A controversy repeatedly erupted among senators, in the media, and from the public regarding an island in Gulf waters that, should its existence be verified, would give Mexico a substantially larger extension. The historical and cartographic record charting Isla Bermeja, as the island is known, is thin but consistent across several centuries. Bermeja is referenced in numerous archival sources dating between 1539 and the end of the eighteenth century, and it appears on Mexico's national map.[7] In the maritime border negotiations with the United States, science, politics, international law, and popular culture mixed and clashed to produce a strange narrative concerning this Isla Bermeja, an island upon which a serious and valuable claim for Mexico's sovereignty over a large part of the western gap might rely.

Debate over the existence of Bermeja took place during the 2000 treaty negotiations and has arisen again more recently. At stake in the Bermeja controversy is that the definitive knowledge of the presence of the island at known coordinates would determine Mexico's new frontiers. The coordinates given are 22° 33′ north and 91° 22′ west, marking a location approximately 100 nautical miles off the coast of the Yucatán Peninsula. A 1997 reconnaissance mission carried out by the Mexican navy came up empty on the search for Bermeja, but not all parties were satisfied that the matter was settled. Among those opposed to passing the treaty so readily was the head of the Mexican Senate's foreign relations committee, Senator José Angel Conchello of the conservative PAN. He fought for the interests of Mexico's territorial sovereignty in the Gulf maritime border negotiations. In his capacity as committee head he accused President Zedillo and fellow senators of bowing to the pressures of the interests of both the United States and the transnational petroleum companies in acquiring Gulf resources. The mysterious disappearance of Isla Bermeja allowed the United States and private enterprise more access to the western gap (Egremy 2005). As an alternative, Conchello proposed laying claim to the whole western gap as an extension of the Mexican continental shelf. In the end, the island was not used in the calculations of the 2000 treaty. Although Bermeja was not a part of the mapping or negotiations in the 2000 treaty, it emerged later to haunt the proceedings. Mexican critics were furious with Zedillo for conspiring with Clinton and the private sector, failing to protect the nation's patrimony, and purposely not pursuing the mystery of the disappearance of the island.

The question of the island of Bermeja resurfaced in 2008 as the expiration of the moratorium on the western gap was approaching. Interest was increasing in potentially oil- and gas-rich areas of the northwestern Gulf such as the Perdido Foldbelt, and Mexicans were growing more anxious by the day about the nation's deepwater interests. The Zedillo administration's insistence on the nonexistence of Bermeja in 1997, followed by the death of Bermeja proponent Senator Conchello in a 1998 car accident (due to "mechanical failure"), riled conspiracy theorists. They pressed: Wasn't the mystery of Bermeja long overdue for a proper investigation? In November 2008 six PAN senators, led by Luis Coppola of the state of Baja California, were working on a special commission investigating the loss of national sovereignty from the Treaty of Guadalupe Hidalgo (1848) to the present; as part of their inquiry they requested a detailed report on the suspicious disappearance of Bermeja. The PAN senators were backed by colleagues from the PRI and Convergencia representing the energy, national defense, and marine committees. The Congreso Nacional ordered an investigation. In June 2009 a multidisciplinary team of researchers from the Universidad Autónoma de México (UNAM) delivered the results of its search for Isla Bermeja. Although the record seems compelling, present-day scientific findings showed that the island does not in fact exist at the coordinates given in historical documents. However, the researchers could not rule out the possible existence of the island at another location. Sensitive to the widespread rumors that Bermeja had been purposely destroyed, the researchers also concluded that no features were found that could be considered traces or ruins of an island.[8]

The Bermeja controversy added a strain to the already highly charged issue of sovereign rights in the Gulf of Mexico. Despite its earlier efforts to avoid a controversy by switching Mexico's point of measurement for the EEZ, the Zedillo administration managed only to reawaken conspiracy theories. Three decades after the 1978 treaty, the PAN attempted to wrest control of the Bermeja situation by spearheading a call for another thorough investigation. The Bermeja issue struck a nerve in Mexico's nationalist sentiment precisely because of the Gulf's status as a patrimonial sea. The very notion that Mexico, with its deep-seated culture of nationalism based in territorial sovereignty and sovereign rights to exploit the resources of national patrimony, would be complicit in ceding the same to the United States was an untenable proposition. In the context of the 2008 energy-reform debates, the Zedillo administration's disowning of Bermeja looked like antinationalist collaboration with U.S. oil interests. It also appeared to be part of a longer-term plan to pave the way for the foreign ownership of Mexican oilfields. But even if Isla Bermeja had miraculously appeared off Yucatán's coast in spring 2009, one of Mexico's problems with deepwater oil exploitation would still remain: transboundary reservoirs.

## The Popote Effect

When the western gap was created, it was thought too deep for oil exploration. But by the time the parcel of seabed was divided up in the Clinton-Zedillo Treaty, oil companies were more than ready to tackle deep and ultradeep offshore fields. Meanwhile, the issues of sharing transboundary reservoirs and overlapping territory such as the Perdido Foldbelt remain unresolved. What appeared to trouble Mexican negotiators was the wide difference in the two nations' legislative postures toward subsoil natural resources. Specifically, Mexican negotiators voiced concerns that private companies leasing blocks on the U.S. side or in overlapping territory would follow customary U.S. principles for the exploitation of oil and gas reservoirs. In U.S. law, surface property owners own subsoil minerals; under the historical customary principle known as the rule of capture, the person who brings oil up to the surface is the owner of the oil. This is quite unlike the law in Mexico, where minerals are the property of the nation regardless of the ownership of the surface.

The assertion of property rights through the rule of capture plays into the naturally migratory behavior of hydrocarbons. Oil and gas have the tendency to move around in an underground or undersea structure. In a transboundary reservoir, if one side is drilled, the other side will potentially lose pressure. Thus, access to the hydrocarbons in a shared reservoir is potentially lost to the second party that drills. In theory, the rule of capture stimulates oil production because it motivates one property owner to drill if a neighbor drills, so as not to lose oil to the neighbor. In America's early oil boom, the rule of capture produced a competitive atmosphere for production. According to Daniel Yergin,

> Owners of adjacent wells were in heated competition to produce as much as they could as swiftly as possible, to avoid having the pools drained by another. The impetus to rapid production contributed to

the instability of both production and prices. . . . The rule of capture led to considerable waste and damage, to the detriment of ultimate production from a given pool. (2008: 16)

If a rule of capture scenario were to play out with transboundary reservoirs in the western gap, Pemex would stand at a considerable disadvantage. This argument has been made in Mexico's Congreso Nacional since the late 1990s. If the private companies leasing shared oilfields develop transboundary reservoirs first, they will apply the rule of capture principle to encourage any shared oil to flow to the U.S. side. For Mexico, however, the oil will be difficult and costly to reach. Mexicans' fears are that U.S. drilling of a transboundary reservoir could siphon oil from Mexico's side of the maritime border, enacting the "popote effect," which requires no deliberate act on anyone's part. In fact, the United States even prohibits horizontal drilling in the border zone, thus avoiding a practice that would stimulate the popote effect. Yet the results of the popote effect would be disastrous for Pemex. In the event that Pemex is able to drill from the southern side of the maritime boundary side, the reservoirs might already be depleted.

One area of particular concern for Mexico is the Perdido Foldbelt, an area outside the western gap and thus not delimited by treaty with the United States. This remote, ultradeep region is thought to contain transboundary reservoirs at depths of 7,500 to 10,000 feet. But ascertaining whether the Perdido Foldbelt or western gap are indeed susceptible to the popote effect would require seismic studies that would allow petroleum geologists to model the area. Additionally, Pemex would have to drill exploratory wells. Some studies have been done, but there have been no exploratory wells. This poses a problem because of Pemex's restricted budget and limited technological capabilities (Melgar Palacios 2008). Members of Mexico's Congreso Nacional have looked on with growing anxiety while Mexico's own deepwater development lags far behind that of its northern neighbor.

Pemex has taken some tentative steps, however. Pemex's first well in waters deeper than 1,640 feet (500 meters) was Nab-1, completed in 2004. The well was installed ninety miles northeast of Ciudad del Carmen in waters 2,234 feet deep. The well was drilled to a depth of 13,287 feet. Estimates put its production at 1,200 bpd of heavy crude (Pemex 2004). As of July 2009 Pemex has drilled ten wells in waters deeper than 1,640 feet. In some of them, PEP found significant volumes of crude and natural gas. However, production from deepwater wells will not start until 2015 at the earliest. According to Pemex director Reyes Heroles, the only way forward into deep water is to have foreign oil companies extensively contribute to Mexico's deepwater drilling program (Friend 2009). The expansion of Pemex's exploration and drilling program into deepwater fields stood at the center of Felipe Calderón's rationale for pushing to rely more upon the equipment, technology, and personnel of the private sector in the parastatal's operations. For a critically vociferous though increasingly fractured Left, any Pemex development in the Gulf's deep waters is a boondoggle constructed by the right wing, and all the hype about moving production to the Gulf deep waters is merely a thinly veiled excuse for privatizing Pemex. An analysis by the U.S. Energy Information Administration, the *International Energy Outlook* (EIA 2009a), pessimistic about Mexico's deepwater capabilities and supportive of private-sector investment, would concur with the energy-reform policy of the Calderón administration in Mexico. The EIA found that "Pemex currently does not have the technical capability or financial means to develop potential deepwater resources in the Gulf of Mexico" and asserted that deepwater reserves can make up for worse than projected declines at Cantarell only if foreign investment is allowed.

Deepwater extraction is a major undertaking, and the Calderón administration would not be wrong to assert that Pemex needs major sources of additional revenue to take on ambitious projects the likes of which are in the works near the maritime border zone. Due to the extreme expense of deepwater drilling and the high level of capital investment, these projects heavily involve private-sector participation. In U.S. waters deepwater extraction is incredibly expensive, and the payoff is far from immediate: almost ten years from an initial lease to oil flow. Capital investment in a field can reach $1 billion. Yet most leases in the Gulf since the 1990s have been in deep water, and there are nearly 3,500 deepwater platforms on the U.S. side today. Why do companies want to get involved in deepwater exploitation? It is a question no one would have asked in July 2008 when oil was hitting $147 dollars per barrel. But six months later, with a barrel of oil losing two-thirds of its market price, perhaps the deepwater Gulf is not the gold mine it seemed before. However, given the "lead" (that is, the time and investment it takes before any production), companies are committed to their deep and ultradeep projects. Once a company makes a huge capital investment in a deepwater field, perhaps there is nowhere to go but onward.

While Mexico is struggling to maintain the façade of resource sovereignty on the maritime border, on the U.S. side private companies are beginning to profit from the deepwater frontier in the Western Gulf. As opposed to the way that Mexico operates, the U.S. government acts only as a landlord to the private sector. This is not to say, however, that the state does not benefit. Indeed it does, and those benefits are on the rise. According to MMS data (Nixon et al. 2009), the total federal revenue from offshore areas averaged about $5 billion to $7 billion in recent years. As shallow-water production in the Gulf (mostly for natural gas) is steadily declining, deepwater production (mostly for crude) is increasing. By the end of 2007, the MMS reported that 130 projects were already producing oil and gas in the deepwater Gulf of Mexico, double the number of five years earlier. Deepwater reservoirs are most attractive to the lessees on the U.S. side. In 2007 a record fifteen rigs were drilling for oil and gas in water depths of 5,000 feet or more.

Soon after its production began in 2008, the Thunder Horse field (operated by BP with a 25 percent share held by ExxonMobil) became the most prolific field in the deepwater Gulf. In mid-2009 the field was producing almost 300,000 bpd, three-quarters of BP's total production in the Gulf (Gonzalez 2009). Thunder Horse has since been plagued by a series of problems, leading to a partial shutdown in 2010 and a 50 percent reduction in its production capacity.

When deepwater leasing began in the mid-1990s, the U.S. Congress tried to make private companies as comfortable as possible.[9] As John Duff has explained (1998: 57), private-sector activity in the U.S. Gulf was motivated by the passage in 1995 of the Outer Continental Shelf Deep Water Royalty Relief Act (DWRRA), a royalty holiday for a proportion of new production. Numbers clearly confirm the commercial motivation that this royalty relief spurred. Only 17 percent of leases issued in 1994 were in deep water and 39 percent in 1995, but after the 1995 deepwater royalty relief went into effect, 59 percent of leases issued in 1996 and 70 percent issued in 1997 were in deep water (Kallaur 2001). Although this blanket act has since been suspended, royalty relief is still granted on a lease-by-lease basis. There is some controversy over the royalty relief programs, much of it because for the first years no provisions were made for price thresholds. In other words, if oil prices went sky high, companies stood to make huge profits, no matter the cost of their capital investments. Subsequent amendments to the royalty relief program set price thresholds. According to one analysis, "Although DWRRA spurred a surge of interest in deepwater oil and gas development, major production directly related to the act's incentives has yet to be realized. For leases containing price thresholds, relatively little royalty relief has been granted" (Humphries 2008: 5).

Motivated by incentives and regular leasing auctions, deepwater production in the U.S. Gulf expanded at a rapid pace. Of the 8,000 active leases in the Gulf, more than half are in deep water. U.S. offshore production in the Gulf was hit following the Deepwater Horizon disaster. The human toll (including eleven deaths) and prospect of irreparable environmental damage across the U.S. Gulf coast prompted the Obama administration to quickly issue a moratorium on new drilling in Gulf waters. The uncontrollable Macondo well blowout temporarily halted but did not stop U.S. deepwater production. The moratorium was lifted on October 12, 2010. Since then, production has picked up its heady pace.

Continued strong interest in leases in the western Gulf persists even after the Deepwater Horizon spill exposed the high risks of drilling in deep water. Some leased blocks in the western Gulf are right on the edge of the U.S.-Mexican maritime border. Dozens of multinationals and independents have drilling rights within ten miles of the maritime border. When Shell began drilling just eight miles north of the Mexican border at the 8,700-foot-deep Great White field in 2007, the company assured the public that "none of these reservoirs extend beyond the U.S.-Mexican international boundary; all are completely within U.S. waters. So, there is no chance for cross-border drainage of oil" (in Millard 2007).

On the southern side of the maritime border, the politics of transboundary oil development reached a fever pitch during the 2008 energy-reform debates. The Calderón administration used the fact of U.S. leasing on the northern side to present a geopolitical map of the Gulf under siege by rule of capture development. In the "Tesoro bajo el mar" ad campaign sponsored by the federal government, a map of the Gulf highlighted the western gap and showed clusters of deepwater leases (represented as flashing alarm lights) sitting just along the maritime border. The eastern gap, too, showed a worrisome acceleration of Cuban exploration projects very close to the Yucatán Peninsula. Foreign development was closing in on Mexico's oil. Surely the federal government knew how to ring patriotic alarm bells: set the stage for a border incursion, only this time in reverse. One only has to imagine U.S. rigs crossing 3,000 feet below the water into Mexico's territory using their deepwater technology to suck Mexico's reserves dry. For the Calderón energy-reform initiative, in order to protect Mexico's resource sovereignty, the only response was to loosen the nation's grip on oil and allow for greater participation of the private sector in deepwater exploitation. Unfortunately for Calderón, to many this presented too great a paradox.

But is the popote effect all smoke and mirrors? In autumn 2008 Mexico's Foreign Minister Patricia Espinosa confirmed the opposition's claim that there was no popote effect happening on the maritime border. Testifying before a Mexican congressional committee regarding negotiations she had undertaken with U.S. counterparts, Espinosa reported the nations' mutual intentions to establish, on the one hand, general principles for the exploration and exploitation of transboundary reservoirs (whether on maritime or land borders), and to produce, on the other hand, an efficient and equitable set of regulations for the two countries. Just weeks before Espinosa's testimony, Mexico's Chamber of Deputies and Senate voted on Calderón's ambitious energy-reform package, which was heavily promoted by TV ads that cited the popote effect and claimed that oil was already being extracted on the maritime border (Saldierna 2008). The foreign secretary thus distanced herself from her party's own message and propaganda.

Given the elasticity of the issue in the Mexican public sphere, it is difficult to tell whether the popote effect is a real danger to transboundary reservoirs or a political ploy. While some geologists and other experts have dismissed the power of the popote effect, Pemex representatives insist on the possibility of hydrocarbons from deposits on the Mexican side of the maritime border flowing to U.S. wells and pumps. Then director-general of Pemex Reyes Heroles defended the reality of the popote effect, claiming that private oil companies on the U.S. side of the border had an advantage in extracting Mexican oil. According to another Pemex official, Mexico could go as far as seeking compensation from production fields such as Trident and Hammerhead or in Perdido near Great White. These are fields that sit very close to the border (Trident only three miles away) and yet were leased by the U.S. government. Pemex threatened that Mexico would try to seek damages from the U.S. government (Millard 2008).

Even though some scientific opinion dismisses the popote effect, it is a captivating and politically powerful image for the public at large. Knowing this, spin doctors effectively used the popote effect to garner support for the PAN's energy-reform campaign. But López Obrador, the leftist leader of the Movimiento Nacional en Defensa del Petróleo, tried to pull the wool off the nation's eyes regarding the national drama instigated by the popote effect. He charged that the whole thing was a "practical joke" that Pemex and the Calderón administration were playing on the Mexican people. López Obrador, as nationalistic as they come, was quick to spot a faux-nationalist ruse. By pushing the popote effect, the federal government could garner support for its energy-reform package, which would expand the role for the private sector especially in exploiting the deep waters of the Gulf of Mexico. But given the long history of territorial disputes between the United States and Mexico, the nature of the perceived power inequity between the two nations, and the strong sense of resource sovereignty long enshrined in Mexico's constitution, the persuasion of the popote effect to grip a nation was strong.

Given the PAN's failure to pass legislation that would legitimately attract partners to share risk as well as the continued failure to actually produce deepwater crude, public support for the deepwater crusade waned. Mexicans swayed to support deepwater drilling efforts by the Calderón administration's "Undersea Treasure" campaign only had to see the images emanating from the cameras trained on the Macondo well spewing gallon upon gallon of crude into the sea to rethink the true cost of these riches. The post–Deepwater Horizon moment was a good time for Pemex to pull back the reins on racing to the farthest energy frontiers. Even with mounting reasons to doubt deepwater drilling, Pemex director Carlos Morales Gil announced that Mexico would forge ahead, doubling drilling capacity in deep water. As if to bring a wary public back on board by rallying the nationalist spirit, Morales Gil revealed that the ramped-up drilling program would include a well that might strike a transboundary reservoir, a promise that Mexico would be competitive in the race for cross-border oil (Carriles 2010).

### Conflict or Cooperation in Deepwater Development?

The U.S.-Mexican border is not the only place in the world where oil exploitation has run into complication, complexity, and dispute. Border fields are common around the globe, and transboundary reserves are forcing states into negotiation (and indeed, arbitration) over the exploitation of hydrocarbon deposits. There are different models for dealing with hydrocarbon flow between structures on different sides of the international boundary. One step Mexico could take is to apply to the United Nations to claim sole title over the reservoir based on the 1982 UNCLOS. Under Article 76 of the convention, Mexico may, as a party to the convention, submit a claim to resources outside of the 200-mile EEZ for a review by a special commission. In 2007 Mexico officially submitted its request for an extended continental shelf boundary claim to the Commission on the Limits of the Continental Shelf. It was approved in 2009.[10] The extension did not change the maritime boundaries agreed upon in the 2000 bilateral treaty with the United States. However, it does demonstrate another dimension of Mexico's legal entitlement over resources within the determined coordinates of the western gap, key in addressing Mexicans' anxiety over the exploitation of transboundary reservoirs.

Other solutions to the problem of cross-border resources vary, based on models offered by other countries negotiating transboundary gas and petroleum resources since the 1960s. Nearly all of these solutions suggest that Mexico should cooperate rather than compete with the United States and, looking to the future, with Cuba as well. Cooperation most often would involve two countries jointly developing an oilfield or sharing in the proceeds of production. In February 2012 the United States and Mexico took a major step in resolving the issue of cross-border resources in the western Gulf. At a meeting of the G20 leaders in Los Cabos, Mexico, U.S. Secretary of State Hilary Clinton and her counterpart Mexican Foreign Minister Patricia Espinosa signed the Transboundary Hydrocarbons Agreement. According to the agreement, each nation maintains its own rights over mineral resources. In the event of a transboundary reservoir or a dispute over the same, the agreement spells out who should extract the resources and how much. Upon entry into force, the moratorium on oil exploration and production in the western gap (otherwise due to stand until 2014) would end.

In the new agreement, transboundary fields will be subject to unitization, a common way of dealing with similar issues. Cross-border unitization agreements are used when a common reservoir underlies the delimited boundary between two nations. Unitization is the joint, coordinated operation of a petroleum reservoir by all of the owners of mineral rights in the territory (Bastida et al. 2007). Unitization requires that the two states agree on three points: the petroleum field is indeed a transboundary reservoir and it should be developed; the states will individually grant the authorizations for development according to their respective national laws; and in the event the transboundary reservoir is to be exploited as a single unit, the parties will establish joint procedures for its exploitation (Estrada 2009).

In her remarks at the signing, Clinton called the agreement "win-win" and said she was pleased to be "following through on the commitment that Presidents Calderón and Obama made in 2010 to improve energy security for both countries and to ensure a safe, efficient, responsible exploration of the oil and gas reservoirs in the Gulf of Mexico" (U.S. Department of State 2012). Though the agreement was pitched as a solution to the problems of sovereignty, territory, and resource rights in the western Gulf, critics in Mexico were infuriated by the agreement's unprecedented level of opening Mexico's resources to foreign exploitation. As Duncan Wood points out, "The Treaty allows for the tantalizing prospect of operators other than Pemex to drill for oil on the Mexican side of the Gulf. If and when this happens, it would mark an extraordinary step forward in breaking the taboos over foreign companies and Mexican oil" (2012: 4). Indeed, despite all of the reforms and the de facto leanings toward privatization, Article 27 of the Mexican constitution still protected subsoil resources as property of the nation. Licensing and concessioning remained prohibited. By far the most liberalized area of Pemex's operations was contracting, but even under the reformed contracting regime the sharing of production, revenues, and reserves was prohibited.

Signed just as Mexico's 2012 electoral campaign was moving into full gear, the left-of-center Citizens Movement senate block was ready to battle the PRI, PAN, and PVEM, whom they accused of supporting the "regressive and submissive" transboundary hydrocarbons agreement (Movimiento Ciudadano 2012). Given the impulses of the Calderón administration, the coalition viewed the agreement as yet another privatization tactic. Attempting to delay a ratification vote, a PRD senator made a motion to suspend the senate's consideration of the agreement. The motion was rejected, and the treaty was ratified with sixty-nine votes in favor, twenty-one against, and one abstention on April 12, 2012.

## Resource Sovereignty in the Maritime Borderlands

The drive toward intensifying the exploitation of transboundary resources in the deepwater Gulf, a primary characteristic of the post-peak condition, forges ahead despite hopes among frontline communities for alternative energy futures and environmental protection of the vulnerable marine environment. The deep waters of the Gulf have yet to produce substantial oil for Mexico, and suspicions are high that their promise is a Calderón-administration ploy for privatization, conflicting with the nationalist sense of the Gulf as a patrimonial sea. As the private sector gains a greater foothold in the Western Gulf, sovereign rights have to be reconciled with parastatal capabilities. The result of the deepwater surge is the alienation of the offshore from both the citizenry and the parastatal Pemex.

The intertwined issues of commercial exploitation, resource sovereignty, and nationalism in the Gulf of Mexico can only get more com-plicated in the immediate future. As the western gap and the Perdido Foldbelt heat up, the eastern gap silently looms off the coast of Flor-ida. This as yet undelimited territory has the further complication of in-volving Cuba, much to the consternation especially of the anti-Castro constituency that watches Gulf waters from the nearby Florida coast. Deepwater oil stands at the center of Cuba's energy future as well, since Cuba presently is heavily reliant on imports from Venezuela and is fac-ing a crisis of energy independence (Brookings Institution 2009). With-out the equipment or technology, Cupet, the state-owned oil company, has been drilling off Cuba's north coast, although its preferred method of exploiting offshore blocks is through production-sharing agreements that have been in place for several years with China's Sinopec and Cana-dian companies. Cupet has attracted several oil companies to explore for oil in Cuban deep waters, where the company is projecting a potential 4 billion to 6 billion barrels of oil. Exploratory drilling has commenced just sixty miles off the Florida Keys, and Cuba's operations in its EEZ are a truly multinational bonanza—Chinese-built rigs and leases of at least twenty of the fifty-nine blocks 6,500 to 13,000 feet deep to Vene-zuela's PDVSA, the Spanish company Repsol, and Norway's Statoil, among others.[11] Expectations are that the eastern gap, created during the Carter administration, will be delimited shortly and that each of the three countries sharing the Gulf of Mexico will get a portion.

For the past thirty years, states sharing the Gulf have been concerned with dividing and delimiting the Gulf into sovereign territories and zones of resource exploitation. All the while, the risks to sea life, shore-lines, and fisheries increase with the intensification of drilling efforts, especially those plunging deeper and deeper and running unknown and untold risks. Even in the wake of the Deepwater Horizon disaster, all signs point to an increase in deepwater exploration on the part of all three countries sharing the waters of the Gulf of Mexico. The three hydrocarbon exploitation regimes in different parts of the Gulf demon-strate that this single marine resource constitutes a very different kind of patrimony for the three nations. For the United States and Mexico, even though the border face-off appears on the surface to be one of Pemex versus the multinationals, only time will tell if it is actually the same few private companies that stand to benefit all across the Gulf wa-ters from the dangerous work of deepwater drilling.

# Post-Peak Futures

Cantarell was born out of apocalypse, its rich oil deposits left in the destructive aftermath of an asteroid hitting the Yucatán Peninsula 65 million years ago. The ancient impact event caused an "armageddon"—setting off wildfires and tsunamis, darkening skies with soot and ash, and causing storms of acid rain. It was enough to kill off the dinosaurs, explains Walter Alvarez in his book *T. Rex and the Crater of Doom* (1997). As early as the 1950s, oil prospectors surveying the peninsula's northwest coast began to detect the result: a 125-mile-wide impact crater known as Chicxulub. More recently, geologists have determined that the seismic shaking and tsunami waves produced by the impact caused the Yucatán platform to slump into the Gulf, leaving trapped underwater layers of carbon-rich material (Grajales-Nishimura et al. 2000). From booming inception to trickling demise, Cantarell's ancient history and modern fate are a heritage of apocalypse.

But Mexico's current oil crisis is far from the end of days imagined by Mad Max scenarios or peak-oil "doomers." The peak of Cantarell is not the end of oil for Mexico. The significant decline of one of the world's supergiants is a red flag that Mexico's energy sector now stands at a crossroads. On the one hand, the country can continue to maintain pre-peak production levels by opening Pemex to the private sector and engaging in riskier and more expensive drilling efforts. On the other hand, an alternative energy policy may be pursued, one that reduces the energy sector's overall reliance on fossil fuels and scales down the national budget's dependence on oil rents. Current efforts to maintain production demonstrate a drive to produce at any price—even if the price is compromised resource sovereignty and environmental protection. The pressure to maintain high levels of production without a concomitant replacement of reserves certainly means a shortened oil future for Mexico, the logic of which pro-privatization arguments for rationality and efficiency in the oil industry take no account. Geopolitics and the peculiarities of markets have, at least in the short term, mitigated the effects of the decline. The lower volume of oil has been offset by continued reliance on Mexican exports, which have brought higher prices. In the global cartography of oil supply, Mexico remains a safe and secure source. This "other Gulf" oil (much closer to home than the Persian Gulf in the Middle East) is preferable for the insatiable U.S. market. Meanwhile, net exporters have benefited from the recent historic highs in oil prices in the international oil market. As a result, Mexico's oil rents in the five years after the peak of Cantarell have increased while actual volumes have decreased (Morales 2011: 10).

Even if Mexico's energy crisis does not promise a sudden apocalypse, there remains some urgency to the nation's energy problems, exacerbated by its vulnerability to the combined pressures of declining production, unstable market prices, rising domestic consumption, and a chronically low refining capacity that increases the nation's dependence on imported consumer products. Given that Mexico's oil crisis stems from the energy sector's imbalance tipped toward nonrenewable hydrocarbons, new national policy is looking toward renewable alternatives in the energy mix. Currently, more than three-quarters of the nation's energy generation comes from fossil fuels. Mexico is the highest emitter of greenhouse gases in Latin America and the thirteenth highest in the world. Legislation including the 2008 renewable energy law passed concurrently with the Calderón energy reforms is designed to reduce domestic consumption of fossil fuels and move the nation toward 35 percent of all energy production deriving from renewable energy sources by 2024 (*Diario Oficial* 2008b). Renewable alternatives will help the country back its strong demonstrated interest in promoting the international agenda on climate change. Still, renewables are far from a panacea and not quite politically neutral. Debates over the promotion and provision of renewables call attention to the politics of resource sovereignty in energy realms beyond hydrocarbons, as critics saw renewables as another path for multinationals to enter Mexico's decreasingly protected energy sector.

As the domestic and global energy landscape grows and changes, what are the prospects for a post-peak future in Mexico? The answer begs the question of perspective. From inside the centers of decision making, whether in the offices of Pemex or the halls of state governance, the post-peak future is one with less cheap and easy-to-find crude, slimmer oil revenues for the state, and compromised resource sovereignty. From the perspectives of communities on the frontlines of oil production, which are so often the margins of politics, the post-peak future is mixed. Having for so long lived with oil, living without oil is not an apocalyptic nightmare. Instead, the post-peak future in Gulf coast communities is one that must overcome the crippling past cycles of boom and bust. In Isla Aguada, prospects of the post-peak future are buoyed by the hope that local entrepreneurship combined with a genuine commitment from the municipal and state governments will restore the struggling town into a picturesque fishing village with the security of livelihood that had, with the rise of the oil industry, been trickling steadily away.

Without fishing and now without a secure future in oil, the residents of Isla Aguada are turning to what resources remain within the surrounding natural environment to revive local industry. Campeche's Gulf coast fishers are counting on state-backed local entrepreneurialism to get them out of the vicious cycle of resource depletion and compensation dependence. Beginning several years ago on an ad hoc basis and more formally in 2008, fishers began to use their lanchas to take visitors on short excursions, known as *recorridos* or *paseos en lancha*, through the Laguna de Términos. Highlights of such a trip include a look at tropical bird nesting grounds and at dolphins.

The state of Campeche and municipality of Carmen recognize the need for new enterprise in coastal communities and are sinking millions of pesos into tourism development in the region. Isla Aguada is a major focus of improvements in infrastructure and promotion. The stars of the campaign are the lagoon's most beloved residents, a population of approximately 1,200 bottlenose dolphins that can regularly be observed off the shores of Isla Aguada. The fishers' boat tours allow visitors to closely observe the dolphins in their natural habitat.

The protected area is also the space of everyday life that local residents wish to recapture and convert into post-peak livelihoods. They, along with municipal and state officials, are right to look toward a future in tourism. Historically on the Yucatán Peninsula, tourism generates greater economic growth than the oil industry. In a study comparing the peninsula's three states—Campeche, Yucatán, and Quintana Roo—researchers found that tourism gave Quintana Roo, home to "Maya Riviera" resort towns like Cancún and Playa del Carmen as well as nearby archaeological treasures, stronger economic performance than

Campeche. Investments in tourism infrastructure and services helped the economy of Quintana Roo grow while that of Campeche stagnated, notably in the 1980s and 1990s (Peña Chapa, Martín Castillo, and Gonzalez Avila 2000). What is more, tourism linked Quintana Roo to the international marketplace, while Campeche's oil did not achieve the effect of bringing outside investment or foreign currency into the state in a significant way. During the 1970s through 1990s, Pemex had only a marginally beneficial effect on Campeche's economy because it brought employees from other states and bought goods and services from companies located outside the state (112).

During the development of megatourism on Yucatán's Caribbean coast, the Mexican state made an all-out investment and promotion effort to build an international tourist destination. The Gulf coast of Campeche was left out of the equation. Where the state failed Campeche in previous decades, it is now seeking to make up lost ground in the post-peak era. So close yet a world away from the famous Maya Riviera, the Gulf coast of Campeche waits in development limbo: Will or won't the Mexican state sponsor the same sort of megadevelopment that spawned Cancún in the 1970s? Perhaps the days of public financing are over. Will the post-peak condition motivate the state to give the private sector incentives to step in and capitalize the future of the Laguna de Términos instead? Either way, expectations run high that now is the time to chart a new course for the future: tourism.

Despite thirty years of intensive oil exploitation, the Laguna de Términos remains attractive and almost beautiful, its aesthetic health contingent only upon the proximity of Pemex infrastructure to shore and the incidence of oil spills. Some of its resources are exceptionally rich, and although fishers have lost their commercial livelihoods, the lagoon hosts a semi-intact wildlife refuge that promises to draw visitors. Dolphins and a variety of nesting birds top the list of appealing assets, not to mention the lagoon's attractive beaches.

Organized into cooperatives, fishers vie for the business of increasing numbers of visitors, predominantly fellow Mexicans who are attracted by state-financed publicity campaigns promoting Isla Aguada in national media. The town's nineteenth-century lighthouse has been restored as a small museum of underwater heritage and public library. The ever-smiling "Flipper" bottlenose dolphin serves as the community's mascot on billboards, postcards, and television commercials. In the flurry of the post-peak turn to tourism, Aguadeños are upbeat. Fishers are excited about receiving small development grants and taking night courses to aid them in turning their lanchas into festive, canopied tour boats and reinventing themselves as cosmopolitan, multilingual tour guides. Fishers without even a secondary-school education now have Facebook pages where they "friend" clients from nearby states of Tabasco and Veracruz and as far away as Sweden. In Isla Aguada, fishers have formed several cooperatives offering nature-based tourism services to visitors. The local fishers have converted their lanchas to passenger boats outfitted with deck chairs and safety gear. They offer two- and three-hour scenic rides through the lagoon.

In the contemporary post-peak condition, Isla Aguada is constructing its sunny future in tourism under the dark shadow of intensified oil production not only in the Campeche Sound but possibly the Laguna de Términos itself. Pursuing entrepreneurial opportunities in nature-based tourism may be more than simply an economic advantage for fishing communities facing collapse. It may also represent a politically savvy maneuver against further encroachment of Pemex operations in the immediate vicinity. As the state demonstrates a broader and more intensive commitment to tourism development in Isla Aguada, it stands to reason that the buffer that failed to protect fishing will finally be erected. "Strengthening tourism," Anna Zalik notes (2006: 39), "would build socioeconomic interest against ecological deterioration and against the visible presence of installations." (The same can be said of strengthening other weak sectors in the region such as agriculture.) Nature-based tourism can indeed raise ecological awareness of the rich resources of the region that have, for many centuries, been exploited without reserve.

Standing in the face of the oil industry's decline, the natural environment of the Laguna de Términos cannot be sustained without a major effort on the part of all stakeholders. This includes every level of government and Pemex, too. The question remains as to whether, in the post-peak period, Pemex will be able to work against its own interests in order to preserve the Laguna de Términos and on the other hand help develop nature-based tourism in the region after the environment has been exploited by one of the most dangerous extractive industries on the planet. As a remaining option for making a sustainable livelihood from resources on Mexico's Gulf coast, nature-based tourism appears a rather precarious endeavor.

# Notes

## Introduction

1. Mexico produces other grades for export—Isthmus and Olmeca, for which there is generally much lower production and demand. Other receiving countries for these exports include Spain (the second greatest amount after the United States at just over 7 percent of exports in 2007), Dutch Antilles, India, and various Central American and Caribbean nations, dividing just over 2 percent among them (Sener 2008: 42).

2. The Maya area of northern Campeche has received anthropological attention (Faust 1998; Gates 1993, 1998). Nora Haenn's long-term ethnographic scholarship (1999a,b, 2000, 2002, 2005) has emerged as the most prominent work in an array of multidisciplinary studies of the interior forests of the state (centered in the region of the Calakmul Biosphere Reserve). Other studies also have mostly been concerned with political ecology, development, and conservation (Acopa and Boege 1998; Alayón Gamboa and Gurri-García 2008; Chowdhury 2006; Ericson 2006; Keys 2005; Murphy 2007; Porter-Bolland, Ellis, and Gholz 2007). Coastal Campeche and the Laguna de Términos are, to date, nearly absent from the ethnographic record, especially in English-language publications. Scholarly attention to the region has instead heavily focused on historical investigations (Bolívar Aguilar 2001, Justo Sierra 1998, Sosa Solís 1984), often on the impact of the shrimping industry in Carmen (Leriche Guzmán 1995, Melville 1984). We also have a predominance of scientific investigations of the watershed ecosystem (Bach et al. 2005). Notable exceptions are works by Rodríguez C. (1984) and Currie-Alder (2001, 2004) that take a more nuanced perspective of the ground-level socioeconomic relations of coastal communities in the 1980s and 1990s, respectively.

3. For technical discussions of the Ixtoc I blowout see Pearson 1980, Torrey 1980. For its effects on coastlines and fisheries see National Research Council 1985, Seoánez Calvo 2000.

4. My interests here follow from the theoretical traditions of Henri Lefebvre (1991) and Michel de Certeau (1984) as well as from attention to spatial politics in the work of David Harvey (2001), Neil Smith (1984), and others.

**Part One**

1. Energy companies often measure their outputs in potential energy such as "crude-oil equivalent." A barrel of oil equivalent is a standardized unit equal to the amount of energy contained in a barrel of crude oil, approximately 5.8 million British thermal units (Btu), or 1,700 kilowatt-hours (kWh). A barrel is a liquid measure equal to forty-two gallons.

**Chapter One**

1. The "foreignness" of Mexican oil seemed, at times, to escape President Bush. Among his well-known malapropisms is this line uttered at an October 3, 2000, presidential debate: "I've been talking to Vicente Fox, the new president of Mexico . . . I know him . . . to have gas and oil sent to U.S. . . . so we'll not depend on foreign oil."

2. According to 2011 statistics from the U.S. Energy Information Administration (EIA 2012), Mexico's contributions have dropped, but the strength of exporters in the Western Hemisphere remains. U.S. imports by country were: Canada (64%), Saudi Arabia (14%), Nigeria (11%), Venezuela (9%), Mexico (7%). By region they were: Western Hemisphere (49%), Africa (23%), Persian Gulf (18%), other (10%).

3. In the 1970s the United States was dependent on OPEC for more than 70 percent of its imports. Since 1992, more petroleum has come into the United States from non-OPEC countries than from OPEC countries (EIA 2012).

4. Private contractors participated heavily in the development of Cantarell, with companies like Brown and Root entering work in the Campeche Sound during Pemex's "crisis of self-sufficiency"; Pratt, Priest, and Castañeda 1997: 180. Contractors carried out substantial engineering and construction tasks for Cantarell from 1977 through 1982 with their operations base in Ciudad del Carmen; ibid., 185.

5. I will not pretend to cover the history of the Mexican oil industry here. For excellent work by others on this topic see Brown 1993b, Meyer 1977, and Rippy 1972. For specific coverage of the 1938 expropriation see Brown and Knight 1992, Gordon 1976, and Jayne 2000.

6. The foreign companies complained about excessive taxation even though, as Gordon points out (1976), the taxes were not excessive compared to U.S. taxes; in fact, they were lower than taxes paid at the same time on oil production in Oklahoma and Texas. The political problem was that oil companies, in the light of the 1917 constitution, interpreted the situation as a de facto nationalization of oil conducted by way of "confiscatory" taxation; 55.

7. The actual implementation of a taxation scheme posed a shock to the oil companies. Even though taxes had technically been introduced during the last term of Porfirio Díaz, for years no real system of taxation was enforced. President Venustiano Carranza was the first to make a real attempt to garner a tax that would support Mexico's national budget (Gordon 1976: 59).

8. Article 27 also, significantly, addresses surface landholdings important in

land-tenure issues affecting hundreds of thousands of indigenous and peasant agriculturalists across the country. One provision of the article limits the situations in which corporations might acquire, hold, and administer rural properties. Article 27 originally contained a provision that prevented foreigners from owning land within fifty kilometers of any coastline. In 1992 Article 27 was amended to allow for the privatization of communal (*ejido*) landholdings.

9. The problem was exacerbated by import-liberalization policies the International Monetary Fund (IMF) imposed in 1976 following the institution's bailout loan to Mexico after a currency crisis. Moreno-Brid and Ros 2009: 130.

10. The financial assistance oil deal was the second of two in two years negotiated between the United States and Mexico for oil to stock the U.S. reserve. In August 1981 Mexico and the U.S. Department of Energy made the first government-to-government oil negotiation between Pemex and the United States. In the initial contract the United States agreed to buy 110 million barrels of oil to be delivered over a five-year period. The contract would extend through July 1986. Prices were to be negotiated quarterly. U.S. officials at the time said they were satisfied with the long-term security of Mexico as an oil supplier (Beaubouef 2007: 128).

11. Aleklett and Campbell 2003; Deffeyes 2005; Hirsch, Bezdek, and Wedling 2005; Robelius 2007.

12. The suggestion raised the hackles of Mexicans. Foreign Secretary Patricia Espinosa responded to the 2009 Pentagon report that cited Mexico along with Pakistan as a "weak and failing state" with a denial of the assessment. Mexico often cites the state's fight against cartels by using its military, an obvious symbol of the state, as evidence that the state is neither weak nor failing.

13. Webber and Kirshenbaum in an editorial in the *Boston Globe* (2010) suggest that the effects of climate change (mostly on agricultural production) will increase immigration to the United States. They add, however, that declining oil production is another significant factor in increasing outward migration from Mexico. They suggest finding energy policy solutions like large-scale renewable-energy partnerships that are not impeded by Mexico's constitutional prohibitions on private ownership or investment in the subsoil as means to prevent some migration from Mexico.

14. Many contend that Pemex's greatest problem is the high taxing scheme. Until 2006 the rate held steady at 62 percent. A relief reform was introduced in 2006 in which the treasury got 60.8 percent of monthly gross revenue (and then any remaining surplus after Pemex paid expenditures, taxes, and interest). The legislature divided the upstream and downstream activities for taxation purposes, introducing a variable tax rate for oil production (the scale varied from 78.68 to 87.81 percent), a windfall tax for oil prices over $22 per barrel, and an extraordinary tax on oil exports. Refining and distribution activities would pay a regular corporate tax. The tax break should have provided relief for reinvestment in exploration. As a result of these changes, Pemex paid taxes and duties equivalent to 55 percent of its gross revenue in 2006, compared with 62.5 percent in 2005. The tax rate Pemex is paying now is still around 60 percent. Quiroz 2009.

15. "En este momento no existe ningún tipo de tecnología que nos permita sacar del subsuelo los hidrocarburos."

16. Mexico's reserves are annually reported by PEP. In 2002 Mexico revised the total number of proven reserves based on the standards of the U.S. Securities and Exchange Commission (SEC). Since 2004 PEP has certified reserves accordingly. Sener 2008: 68.

## Chapter Two

1. "Términos" was abbreviated "TRS" on Spanish colonial maps (Ancona 1881). Carmen Island was and is known also as Isla de Tris, taken from the abbreviation TRS (del Castillo 1866: 151). "Tris" was misinterpreted by some as "triste," which in Spanish means "sad" or "melancholy." Isla Aguada was the victim of maritime misconstruals as well. Isla Aguada got its European name early in the Conquest from Europeans who took shelter in the cove formed by the calm waters of Puerto Real, the inlet across the lagoon from Isla Aguada. Here they found a spring of fresh water, an *aguada*, a much-needed and scarce resource for sailors on the open ocean. They believed the place to be an island rather than a peninsula, though there is some debate over whether Isla Aguada was indeed at the time an island rather than the sandy peninsula it is today, connected to land on its eastern side.

2. Not all loggers in the Laguna de Términos were pirates. Jarvis (2010), for example, describes Bermudians who sailed their own small sloops to the shores of Campeche to cut logwood in the 1680s and 1690s. The small ships were light and easy to navigate directly to shore to load the wood (223).

3. Producing colorfast dyed cloth, especially black, was surprisingly difficult through the Industrial Revolution and even into the twentieth century. This is why palo de tinte was an especially valuable commodity. As McJunkin points out (1991), perhaps the easiest way to get colorfast black was simply to shear a black sheep! Beyond this, the advantage for high-quality black dye went to palo de tinte (13).

4. In his text Dampier uses the term "carrion crows" to refer to vultures (in Spanish, *zopilotes*). He clearly identifies the turkey vulture, very common in the region today, and the king vulture as present around the Laguna de Términos. Because of the critical role these carrion eaters play in quickly dispatching decaying bodies, the Spaniards banned their killing. The English in Jamaica adopted the same position. According to Dampier, the English loggers, though far outside of so many laws, took this one to heart and did not harm vultures. Dampier 1699: 67–68.

5. Beef Island was a colonial land grant pertaining to an absentee owner resident in the capital city of Campeche and was occasionally occupied by fugitive indigenous inhabitants escaped from Spanish hands. Dampier 1699: 93–98; Johnstone 1832: 224.

6. The several-month effort by the Spanish to expel the pirates lasted from December 1716 until July 16, 1717, the feast day of Nuestra Señora del Carmen, made patron saint of Ciudad del Carmen. Daniel Defoe, author of many works of fiction and nonfiction dealing with pirates, seafaring, and adventure

such as the famous Robinson Crusoe, gives an account: "Five Spanish Frigates, whereof two carried 44 Guns each, came into the Bay, took or burnt 12 English Ships belonging to New England, New York, and the Colonies thereabouts, and burnt all the Logwood they could find already cut, pursuing the Fellows that had cut it as far as they could into the Woods, where many of them were kill'd; and the rest had as well have been kill'd, for being left without Tools to work, or Ships to carry them off, they must certainly have perish'd, or been oblig'd to surrender to the <u>Spaniards</u>, which they always think worse than Death"; 1728: 301–302, emphasis in original. The logwood cutters that were caught by the Spaniards were typically sold into slavery, either in Mexico City or Campeche. Others returned to seafaring life, and those who continued as loggers moved farther south to the Bay of Honduras in present-day Belize.

7. Colonial agrarian projects in the Spanish-settled areas of Yucatán only required mild labor-recruitment efforts. The common "corn and cattle" haciendas needed little in the form of intensive human labor. Into the 1800s most of the countryside was dominated by free villages where peasants lived subsistence lifestyles. Not until the nineteenth century well after Mexico achieved independence in 1821 did a full-fledged industrial agricultural plantation system develop on the backs of exploited labor of indigenous Maya, other Mexicans, and imported indentured servants from the Far East. First, the haciendas transformed into more labor-intensive sugar plantations. Then henequen production dominated the peninsula, altering labor relations dramatically.

8. In 1936 fifty concessions were granted for harvesting chicle from the Campeche forests. These lands were subsequently converted into sixty-nine ejidos, or communally held government land grants. The Campeche forests were then settled by colonists from across Mexico with the newly acquired right to access land. Acopa and Boege 1998: 84.

9. In 1984 and 1985 almost 20,000 Guatemalan refugees crossed the border into the southern state of Chiapas, Mexico, to flee the violence of their home communities. Between 1996 and 2001, approximately 5,000 refugees who chose to stay in Mexico participated in a naturalization process to obtain their Mexican citizenship.

10. This slowed, according to the 2010 census: the overall population of the municipality of Carmen (221,094) demonstrated a 1.7 percent growth rate in 2005–2010. INEGI 2011a.

11. As of 2010 Mexico established 171 areas under the auspices of the Sistema Nacional de Áreas Protegidas (Sinap) in the following categories: biosphere reserve, national park, natural monument, national marine park, natural resource protection area, urban park, flora and fauna protection area (wildlife and marine), and zones subject to ecological conservation. Terrestrial protected areas (ANPs) cover nearly 10 percent of Mexico's national territory.

## Chapter Three

1. Although some of the product did go to market dried, the boats still brought the delicate shellfish to cleaning and peeling factories as a fresh catch.

The industry required building from the ground up—boats, docks, factories—and much of the capital outlay came from foreign investment.

2. Mexico did allow U.S. boats access to the Mexican EEZ but not the Campeche bank. The United States and Mexico also signed a fisheries agreement in November 1976 allowing U.S. fishers access to the Mexican EEZ for snapper, grouper, and shrimp. Meanwhile, Mexico had an ongoing problem with Cuban fishing vessels and likewise negotiated a fishing agreement with Cuba. Mexico, Ministry of Foreign Affairs 1976.

3. The establishment of laws and regulatory agencies to enforce them have been attempts to keep Gulf fisheries sustainable. Since 2000, fisheries institutions have been placed within the federal Ministry of Agriculture, Livestock, Rural Development, Fisheries, and Food (Sagarpa). Sagarpa has state and local offices around the country, among them a station in Isla Aguada that was never actually staffed on any of the occasions I went there. The agency responsible for fisheries management, monitoring, and enforcement is the National Commission of Fishing and Aquaculture (Conapesca). As fishery resources and legislation are federally controlled, local governments have little room for flexibility in management. The legal framework is detailed in the Ley de Pesca, which undergoes periodic modification and updating.

4. *Caracol*, or conch, is one of the top ten marine resources in Campeche. The state of Campeche produces the highest conch capture in the nation by volume. In 2008 a closed season was initiated by official decree (*Diario Oficial* 2008a). At that time, eighty-nine licensees and a fleet of 266 boats took in a capture of just over 7,000 tons, down from 8,300 five years before. To keep the resource at a sustainable level, a seasonal veda was imposed by fishing authorities. The open season for caracol is mid-March to mid-July. While a substantial majority of the caracol fishers come from the town of Champotón, some of the capture comes out of the Laguna de Términos, with one of the principal areas of capture being the shallow waters around Isla Aguada. Caracol harvesting in the lagoon has long occurred, according to one study on conch sustainability as an "informal fishery" (Wakida Kusunoki, Amador del Angel, and Santos Valencia 2007). The characteristics of this include very minimal regulation on caracol harvesting in the lagoon (only a minimum size standard for capture of two species found in lagoon waters), unlicensed fishing, and unreported and thus unrecorded capture. The effects of placing a veda on an informal ribereño fishery are multifold. Aid cannot be given in proportion to loss if the loss is not properly known. Further, aid cannot be received for loss of capture if the fisher is not licensed or credentialed.

5. A regionwide closed season on shrimp that included Gulf waters did not begin until 1994.

6. The other coincidence that occurred with the Ixtoc blowout was the coming of a devastating lethal yellowing disease (*amarillamiento letal del cocotero*) that struck coconut palms in the late 1970s. It wiped out 90 percent of the region's palm trees, a cash crop for dried copra. Many locals blamed the air fouled by the Ixtoc spill.

7. Evidence takes the form of either eyewitness accounts of crude or tar on the beach or unusual deaths of marine life, whether fish or mammals. Fish-

ers in this region are not the only ones to struggle with "proving" the effects of oil contamination. For example, despite the obvious effects of contamination in the Niger Delta, Fentiman (1996) points out that overfishing and overpopulation are often considered co-culprits for that region's devastating fishing decline.

8. Villaseñor et al. (2003) produced the first comprehensive environmental impact study of exploration and production activities to asses air quality. The study was funded by Pemex. In all, 174 platforms, the gas recompression station at Atasta, the Dos Bocas marine terminal, tankers, and helicopters were studied. The researchers measured the total pollutants at 660,000 tons per year (3727). The 2003 report stated that specifically at the Atasta gas plant, levels of nitrogen and sulfur oxides were not found in levels that violated Mexican air quality standards. In addition to measuring air quality, the researchers used modeling to understand how polluting emissions moved from installations around the region. According to the study, "Mass fluxes of SO2 issuing into atmospheric air from the re-compressing station of Atasta and the Dos Bocas crude-oil facility treatment plant do not seem to have a large radius of influence, hence their impact on neighboring communities is not as pronounced as one might have guessed" (3726). The report acknowledges that the data were preliminary and that more work needed to be done to examine the range of environmental impacts from exploration and production activities in the area such as water discharges and spills on soil (3728).

9. The boundaries are formed by the parallels 18°50′00″ north and 20°00′00″ north and meridians 92°50′00″ west and 91°40′00″ west. The zone around the Dos Bocas terminal includes a circular surface of 450 square nautical miles with a radius of 12 nautical miles whose center lies at latitude 20°12′00″ north, longitude 091°57′30″ west. Martinez Tiburcio 2005: 3.

10. Ribereños and commercial aquaculture producers receive gasoline for their lanchas at tax-free and subsidized prices through Sagarpa's Programa de Apoyo al Diesel y Gasolina para el Sector Agropecuario y Pesquero (Diesel and Gasoline Aid Program for the Fish and Agricultural Sector). The beneficiaries are not only fishers but also agricultural producers who use fuel for tractors and other equipment. Those who receive aid depend upon Sagarpa to make the funds available through the use of "smart cards" that can be used at Pemex stations. In Isla Aguada the management of fuel subsidies is another way bodegueros wield power over the cooperative members. As it turns out, the fishers do not actually see their fuel subsidy cards because the bodega owners maintain control over the cards and distribute fuel to the fishers. This is a cause of great consternation for the fishers, especially since the "cost of fuel" is then leveraged against the price the fishers receive for their catches.

## Chapter Four

1. The fund aims to give each claimant just under $115. The actual amount received will go up or down based on how many claimants are on the rolls. According to my accounting, in 2007 recipients in Isla Aguada received about

$86, compared across the municipality to $83 in Sabancuy, not quite $80 in Carmen, and about $76 in Atasta. In 2009 the baja captura program paid nearly 5,000 fishers in the municipality of Carmen. In Atasta, each claimant received slightly less than $77, and in Sabancuy, each received a little over $90.

2. The matter was not settled for Isla Aguada. When Javier Aguillón Osorio, the leader of the local fishers association, went to the Scotiabank Inverlat in Ciudad del Carmen with the check from the state of Campeche, the bank refused to cash it. The bank, where the Federaciones y Cooperativas Pesqueras Ribereñas themselves held its own account and where for four years all of the fideicomiso checks had been cashed, claimed that a problem verifying the check would delay its clearance by ten days. Aguillón commented, frustrated, "It's another attempt to hold back the resources, especially from the fishers of Isla Aguada."

3. As Haenn documents (1999b, 2005), residents balked at the imposition of the state's establishment of the Calakmul Biosphere Reserve and its attendant restrictions. In contrast, the management plan for the APFFLT contains few if any restrictions for residents inside the protected area. The only restrictions fought for in the public consultation process during the development of the site management plan were on Pemex's oil-drilling activities.

4. The general funding categories for donativos and donaciones are: productive projects and job training; rural and urban infrastructure and supplies; the environment; financial security; and civil protection and public safety. Also supported is the conservation of archaeological heritage affected by the oil industry.

5. The rules and regulations for distributing the donativos and donaciones are spelled out in the guidelines for awarding them to third parties by Pemex and its subsidiaries as well as in Pemex's criteria for designating them; Pemex 2007b. The legal framework guiding the rules on cash disbursements (donativos) is found in the Ley Federal de Presupuesto y Responsabilidad Hacendaría and the Reglamento (Articles 10, 80, and 184). The legislation informing the in-kind donaciones is the Ley General de Bienes Nacionales; this category of donations includes *bienes muebles* (chattel, Article 133) and *bienes inmuebles* (real estate, Article 84).

6. The Office of Social Development list is posted at http://www.pemex .com/index.cfm?action=content&sectionID=113&catID=14162.

7. Taken from 2005 data, this compared to four municipalities registering "medium" (Calkiní, Hecelcekán, Champotón, and Escárcega) and five "high" (Tenabo, Hopelchén, Calakmul, which upgraded from "very high" in 2000, and in the Laguna de Términos region Palizada and Candelaría).

## Part Three

1. An ad produced and paid for by Calderón's PAN indeed supports this last statement. A twenty-second ad showing the bold headline "La mayoría la quiere" (The majority wants it) only flashes for the briefest moment actual data from three surveys. The results show that among those surveyed by the firm

Varela and Associates in July 2008, 49 percent answered in favor, 35 percent opposed, and 15 percent "Don't know." Those questioned in the same period by ARCOP answered 56 percent in favor, 36 percent opposed, and 12 percent "Don't know." In the survey conducted July 19–21, 2008, by GEA-ISA, 55 percent answered in favor, 36 percent opposed, and 9 percent "Don't know." The firm BGC-Ulises Beltrán and Associates found that 48 percent answered in favor, 46 percent opposed, and 6 percent "Don't know" (PAN 2008).

2. OPEC has twelve member countries. The oil consortium was founded in September 1960 by Iran, Iraq, Kuwait, Saudi Arabia, and Venezuela. Later, Qatar (1961), Indonesia (1962), Libya (1962), the United Arab Emirates (1967), Algeria (1969), Nigeria (1971), Ecuador (1973), Gabon (1975), and Angola (2007) joined. Ecuador suspended its membership from 1992 to 2007. Gabon left in 1995 and Indonesia in 2009, neither to return.

3. Using 2008 data, *Petroleum Intelligence Weekly* (*PIW*) published a list of the top fifty oil companies. Among the top twenty oil producers worldwide, fourteen were NOCs or newly privatized NOCs, and the international majors were relegated to second-tier status in terms of controlling the world's oil production. *PIW* ranked these among the world's most important gas- and oil-producing companies: Saudi Aramco; Russia's Gazprom, Rosneft, and Lukoil; Iran's NIOC; Pemex of Mexico; Algeria's Sonatrach; Iraq's INOC; PetroChina; Kuwait Petroleum Corporation; Brazil's Petrobras; Malaysia's Petronas; ADNOC of Abu Dhabi; PDVSA of Venezuela; and Nigerian National Petroleum Corporation (NNPC).

### Chapter Five

1. In the NAFTA negotiations, Mexico famously laid out the "Five no's" by which it stood fast: 1) no reduction of state control over ownership, development, or exploration of hydrocarbons or basic petrochemicals; 2) no ceding of control over storage or distribution; 3) no foreign ownership of gas stations; 4) no commitments on energy supplies to foreign countries; and 5) no contracts paid in reserves. NAFTA permanently exempts Mexico from any U.S. oil import fees, a win for Mexico. Yet Mexico conceded the right to set quota caps and punitive tariffs on exports. Orme 1996: 145; Ortiz Mena 2003.

2. Morales 2011 (22) emphasizes that as the "most important energy reform of the past 20 years in Mexico," NAFTA enacted liberalization across the entire sector, affecting gas and electricity as well. NAFTA opened the construction of pipelines and storage facilities to private investment and recognized a new class of private power suppliers, all without making any changes to the constitutional laws.

3. The proven reserves number was verified by certifying companies contracted by Pemex.

4. According to the constitution's self-imposed limitations (made explicit in Article 14), the provisions securing the subsoil as the property of the nation (in Article 27) were not retroactive. Yet within a year after its passage, certain new measures regarding the property regime of subsoil resources were effected

by the administration of President Venustiano Carranza. In effect, Carranza moved the foreign oil companies from an ownership regime to a concession system. His decree of February 19, 1918, required that oil companies had to register their lands and receive permits to continue drilling. They would now have to pay rental for their lands and royalties on production, regardless of when lands had been acquired; Haber, Maurer, and Razo 2003: 6. Some of the companies complied with the registration, but none agreed to payment of royalties. Nevertheless, the Carranza administration pressed on with an interpretation of Article 27. He issued subsequent decrees that called for the forfeiture of unregistered lands and distributed unregistered lands to Mexican citizens and even mobilized the military to occupy oil fields and cap newly drilled wells. Clark 1928: 604; Haber, Maurer, and Razo 2003: 7; Meyer 1977: 43–45. Carranza, however, did not triumph in fighting the oil companies, which turned toward the U.S. government to intervene on their behalf. The Mexican president backed down after diplomatic intercession.

5. The chamber was taken at the exact moment that representatives on the floor of the legislature were voting to authorize Calderón's travel to the United States, Canada, Mexico Security and Prosperity Partnership summit in New Orleans on April 21–22. Much more than symbolic, this coincidence shows the deeply interconnected relationship between the push for the privatization of Mexico's oil and the hemispheric strategy of the U.S. energy-security plan.

6. To allow and encourage foreign oil companies to enter Mexico, Díaz enacted the Mining Law of 1884, the first post-independence code dealing with subsoil resources. Article 10 established that the owner of the surface of a piece of land is also a subsoil owner. Thus, the law granted subsoil exploitation rights to surface owners. He subsequently enacted a series of other measures to specify, reiterate, and shore up the rights for private owners to exploit subsoil resources. In the second significant piece of legislation, the Mining Code of 1892, the law was refined regarding petroleum exploitation, stating that surface owners could freely exploit subsoil wealth without special permission from the government as long as they paid property taxes. An attempt to nationalize oil in 1905 would declare the oil finds to be of public utility and therefore requiring permission from the Ministry of Development (Fomento). The proposal was considered failed at the starting block because the "previous legislation had created perfect private property"; Meyer 1977: 24; see also Brown 1993b: 93. The 1905 depression produced something of a nationalist reaction against foreign investors. U.S. oilman Edward Doheny's leases and sales were investigated, but the Mexican laws that had adopted the Anglo-American concepts of private property were upheld; Brown 1993b: 39. In an extension of the liberalization of the national territory to subsoil exploitation, in 1901 Díaz opened federal lands (a substantial part of the national territory) to concessions for oil drilling and even granted tax exemptions to firms willing to invest in oil exploration; Haber, Maurer, and Razo 2003: 4. Just to make sure there were no misunderstandings about his intent, a third law, the Petroleum Code of 1909, returned to the language of the 1884 mining law in which Díaz declared hydrocarbon deposits to be the exclusive property of the surface owners; Clark 1928: 601–602. Halleck 1859 provides an English text of the mining laws themselves, and

Rippy 1972, Meyer 1977, and Brown 1993b offer comprehensive analyses of the legal status of hydrocarbon deposits during the Porfiriato.

7. This principle of absolute ownership may get reined in by the courts, for example, in cases of "wandering" or "fugitive" minerals like petroleum, which by its liquid nature may escape the property of the landowner and flow under the property of a neighbor.

8. When an NOC is more fully inviting privatization, risk-sharing contracts are used. For example, in Ecuador's partial privatization in the 1990s, the state institutionalized neoliberalism in its energy-exploitation policies through the mechanism of the contracts, made explicit in the 1993 hydrocarbon law. Sawyer 2004: 109.

9. Petrobras was subjected to the same fiscal regime as private companies, and Petrobras would no longer receive subsidies to conduct noncommercial activities. In addition to taxes, the oil company was to pay a 25 percent dividend to its owners, public and private. The Agência Nacional de Petróleo (ANP), an independent oversight agency, was created to regulate Petrobras.

10. The term of Muñoz Leos as Pemex director-general during the Fox administration was short and rocked by scandal. He negotiated directly with the union a nearly 8 billion-peso increase in benefits. Muñoz also used $12,500 in Pemex funds to pay for two liposuction surgeries for his wife. In July 2007 Muñoz avoided jail time and instead was fined heavily and banned from holding public office for ten years for the misuse of funds and the illegal transfer of more than $170 million to the oil workers union.

11. The Fox administration set out with perhaps more hope for privatization reforms in the electricity sector, picking up on a proposal initially presented in 1999 by the Zedillo administration.

12. The successful blockage of Zedillo's proposal was due to the mobilization spurred by the CFE workers' power union, SME (Sindicato Mexicano de Electricistas). According to Bacon 2003, "The union formed the National Front of Resistance to the Privatization of the Electrical Industry, collected 2.3 million signatures on petitions in three weeks, and brought a million angry *capitalinos* into the streets. Zedillo was defeated."

13. Salinas in 1992 permitted private companies including foreign ones to build and operate power plants in Mexico as long as they consumed or exported all the energy they produced or sold it to CFE.

14. Later, as president, Calderón would order a police raid to seize the headquarters of Luz y Fuerza del Centro, the financially troubled state-owned power company in Mexico City backed by a strong labor union. As a result, 44,000 workers were laid off. The move was widely understood as paving a path for privatization.

## Chapter Six

1. UNCLOS entered into force November 16, 1994. The United States is a signatory and recognizes the principles of the convention as customary international law yet has not ratified UNCLOS.

2. Within the Department of the Interior, the agency responsible for regulating oil and gas contracts and leases was, until June 2010, the Minerals Management Service (MMS). Revelations of inefficiency and irregularity in the MMS in the wake of the Deepwater Horizon spill prompted a restructuring and renaming of the federal agency, resulting in the establishment of the Bureau of Ocean Energy Management, Regulation, and Enforcement (BOEMRE). In 2011 the regulatory function of BOEMRE was siphoned off into the newly established Bureau of Safety and Environmental Enforcement (BSEE), which would function as a entity distinct from the Bureau of Ocean Energy Management (BOEM).

3. Maritime borders between Mexico and Cuba (which I will not discuss extensively here) were negotiated through an exchange of diplomatic notes specifically regarding fishing rights. Mexico, Ministry of Foreign Affairs 1976.

4. Hedberg argued in 1980 that the continental shelf, rather than any island, should be used to measure the 200-mile EEZ. The measurement from the continental shelf instead of from the shore of an island would greatly favor the United States in accessing deepwater hydrocarbon deposits in the Gulf of Mexico. Hedberg's arguments were not taken very seriously, and the Foreign Relations Committee approved the treaty, sending it to the Senate floor for a final vote. When the treaty went up for a final vote, Hedberg's alarm bells finally impressed some senators, and the U.S. Geological Survey was enlisted to undertake a two-year study of the issue. By the time this was accomplished, ratification of the treaty was dropped from the congressional agenda. Applegate 1997.

5. MMS first began offering western gap leases at the annual western Gulf sale in 1983 but suspended offering the blocks in 1997 following complaints from Mexico, which claimed that the leases were premature before signing a treaty to formally divide the gap. According to Ralph Ainger, chief of leasing division for MMS who participated in negotiating the 2000 treaty, "We've always asserted that the northern portion of the gap would have been U.S. territory in the end anyway, but it seemed productive to defer offering in those blocks until we agreed on a line"; in *Oil and Gas Journal* 2000. The MMS claimed to have acted in good faith and not to have even opened the bids received prior to the 1997 treaty ratification; US MMS 2000.

6. A spokesperson for the MMS called the buffer zone, which covers about 10 percent of the U.S. part of the gap, an "unusual" arrangement made to allay the Mexicans' anxiety regarding the probability of companies working on the U.S. side much sooner than on the Mexican side and as a tool to help the treaty pass more quickly through the Mexican Senate. *Oil and Gas Journal* 2000: 30.

7. Bermeja appeared on maps as part of the claim of the viceroyalty of New Spain. Historical texts locate the island 100 miles off the coast of the Yucatán Peninsula's port of Sisal, close to Cayo Arenas. Bermeja is included in Antonio García Cubas's *Carta general de la República Mexicana* (1863) and Manuel Orozco y Berra's *Carta etnográfica de México* (1864). Documentation of Bermeja continues to appear as recently as 1946, with its entry in *Las islas mexicanas* by Manuel Muñoz Lumbier, an edition produced under the auspices of Mexico's Ministry of Education.

8. This meant that Mexico would have to maintain the 200-mile EEZ as established in 1978/1997 treaty, using as a reference point Arrecife (or Isla) Alacranes eighty miles off the Yucatán Peninsula's port of Progreso at latitude 22°22′5″ north and longitude 89°40′57″ west.

9. This only refers to areas of the Gulf that were not under a drilling moratorium at the time. In 2006 George W. Bush signed the Gulf of Mexico Energy Security Act (GOMESA), freeing for lease 8.3 million acres in the eastern Gulf that included 5.8 million acres previously held under congressional moratoria. Oil and gas leasing remained banned within 125 miles of the Florida coastline in the eastern planning area, and both areas remain banned until 2022. GOMESA also allows companies to exchange certain existing leases in moratorium areas for bonus and royalty credits to be used on other Gulf leases.

10. Using the formula allowable by the boundary commission, Mexico calculated its maximum potential extent of entitlement to implement Article 76. In determining the claim to the western polygon, the boundary commission allowed Mexico to calculate that the submerged continental shelf is a natural prolongation of Mexico's land territory. To determine how far into the sea this extends, geophysical surveys are used to measure sediment thickness.

11. In September 2011, in a bipartisan effort, thirty-four members of the U.S. House of Representatives sent a letter to Repsol, the largest Spanish oil company (in which Pemex has a large share and long history) "urging Repsol to reassess risks inherent in partnering with the Castro dictatorship, including the risk of its commercial interests in the United States." The letter asks that Repsol "abandon any of its proposed oil drilling activities in Cuban waters." Ros-Lehtinen et al. 2011.

# References

Acopa, Deocundo, and Eckart Boege. 1998. The Maya forest in Campeche, Mexico. In *Timber, tourists, and temples: Conservation and development in the Maya forest of Belize, Guatemala, and Mexico,* ed. Richard Primack, David Bray, Hugo A. Galletti, and Ismael Ponciano. Washington, DC: Island Press.

Agamben, Sergio. 2005. *State of exception.* Trans. Kevin Attell. Chicago: University of Chicago Press.

Agencia Comunicación del Mayab. 2008. Complace a gobernador campechano voluntad política para la reforma energética. *Reporteros Hoy,* October 25. http://www.reporteroshoy.net/Notas/NotaCompleta2.aspx?ClaveNota =3071.

Aguilar, Davis, and José Grande-Vidal. 2008. Shrimp fishing in Mexico. In *Global study of shrimp fisheries,* technical paper 475, ed. J. Gillet. Rome: UN Food and Agriculture Organization. ftp://ftp.fao.org/docrep/fao/011 /i0300e/i0300e02b.pdf.

Aguilar, Davis, and Noé Serrano Cruz. 2008. Pemex detrás de la campaña en TV. *El Universal,* March 13. http://www.eluniversal.com.mx/finanzas /63188.html.

Aguilar Ibarra, Alonso, Chris Reid, and Andy Thorpe. 2000. The political economy of marine fisheries development in Peru, Chile, and Mexico. *Journal of Latin American Studies* 32, no. 2:503–527.

Alayón Gamboa, José A., and Francisco D. Gurri García. 2008. Home garden production and energetic sustainability in Calakmul, Campeche, Mexico. *Human Ecology* 36, no. 3:395–407.

Alba, Francisco. 2010. Mexico: A crucial crossroads. (Migration Policy Institute) *Migration Information Source,* February. http://www.migration information.org/feature/display.cfm?ID=772.

Alberro, José Luis. 2007. Mexico's oil: Who needs it? In *Oil as a strategic resource in Mexico?* by Luis de la Calle, José Luis Alberro, and Pamela Starr. Washington, DC: Woodrow Wilson International Center for Scholars. http:// www.economia.unam.mx/cegademex/DOCS/Oil.pdf.

Alcántara Vega, Raúl. 2011. Pemex construirá el nuevo Puente de la Unidad. *Campeche Economía.* http://campeche-economia.webnode.es/news/pemex -construira-el-nuevo-puente-de-la-unidad-ciudad-del-carmen-isla-aguada/.

Aleklett, Kjell, and Colin J. Campbell. 2003. The peak and decline of world oil and gas production. *Minerals and Energy* 18, no. 1:5–20.

Alvarez, Walter. 1997. *T. Rex and the crater of doom.* Princeton, NJ: Princeton University Press.

Álvarez Aguilar, Luis F., and Juan José Bolívar Aguilar. 2003. *El presidio de Nuestra Señora del Carmen (1717-1821).* Colección Documentos e Investigación. Cuidad del Carmen: Universidad Autónoma del Carmen.

Álvarez-Legorreta, Teresa, Gerardo Gold-Bouchot, and Omar Zapata-Pérez. 1994. Hydrocarbon concentrations in sediments and clams (*Rangia cuneata*) in Laguna de Pom, Mexico. *Bulletin of Environmental Contamination and Toxicology* 52:39–45.

Ancona, Eligio. 1881. *Compendio de la historia de la península de Yucatán.* Mérida: El Eco de Comercio.

Anderson, Adam. 1787. An historical and chronological deduction of the origin of commerce: From the earliest accounts. Vol. 3. London: J. Walter.

Applegate, David. 1997. Doughnut holes in the western Gulf of Mexico. *IBRU Boundary and Security Bulletin,* Autumn, 71–73. http://www.dur.ac.uk /resources/ibru/publications/full/bsb5-3_applegate.pdf.

Arias Rodríguez, José Manuel, and Hugo Ireta Guzmán. *Pesca y petróleo en el Golfo de Mexico.* 2009. Villahermosa, Tabasco: Asociación Ecológico Santo Tomás. http://aestomas.org/wp-content/uploads/2008/07/pescay petroleo-public.pdf.

Arredondo Ortiz, María Alejandra. 2008. Con Mouriño "murió" la refinería para Campeche: ACC. Agencia SIEN, November 25.

Athearn, Frederic J. 1998. Contributions of the oil and gas industry to cultural heritage management in public lands. *Southwestern Lore* 64, no. 2:21–34.

Auty, Richard M. 1993. *Sustaining development in mineral economies: The resource curse thesis.* New York: Routledge.

———. 1998. *Resource abundance and economic development.* Helsinki: UN World Institute for Development Economics Research.

———. 2001. The political economy of resource-driven growth. *European Economic Review* 45:839–946.

Bach, Leslie, Rafael Calderón, María Fernanda Cepeda, Autumn Oczkowski, Stephen Olsen, and Don Robadue. 2005. *Managing freshwater inflows to estuaries, level one site profile: Laguna de Términos and its watershed, Mexico.* Narragansett, RI: Coastal Resources Center, University of Rhode Island.

Bacon, David. 2003. A charged atmosphere. *American Prospect,* January 21. http://prospect.org/article/charged-atmosphere.

Baker Institute. 2007. The changing role of national oil companies. *Baker Institute Policy Report,* no. 35 (April). http://www.policyarchive.org/handle /10207/bitstreams/6756.pdf.

Ballard, Chris, and Glenn Banks. 2003. Resource wars: The anthropology of mining. *Annual Review of Anthropology* 32:287–313.

Ballve, Marcelo. 2003. Mexico rejects oil for migrants proposal. El norte digest, *New America Media*. http://news.newamericamedia.org/news/view _article.html?article_id=bb9ccb840dade5fd263ea7d7f3e7628b.

Baptiste, A. Karen, and Brenda J. Nordenstam. 2009. Impact of oil and gas drilling in Trinidad: Factors influencing environmental attitudes and behaviors within three rural wetland communities. *Environmental Conservation* 36, no. 1:14-21.

Barry, Andrew. 2006. Technological zones. *European Journal of Social Theory* 9, no. 2:239-253.

Basedau, Mattias, and Wolfram Lacher. 2006. A paradox of plenty? Rent distribution and political stability in oil states. (German Institute of Global and Area Studies) GIGA working paper 21 (April). http://www.giga-hamburg .de/dl/download.php?d=/content/publikationen/pdf/wp21_basedau -lacher.pdf.

Bastida, Ana, Adaeze Ifesi-Okoye, Salim Mahmud, James Ross, and Thomas Walde. 2007. Cross-border unitization and joint development agreements: An international law perspective. *Houston Journal of International Law* 29, no. 2 (Winter): 355–422.

Beaubouef, Bruce. 2007. *The strategic petroleum reserve: U.S. energy security and oil politics.* College Station: Texas A&M University Press.

Becerril, Andrea, and Victor Ballinas. 2008. Propone el PRI incluir a la IP en tareas de exploración petrolera. *La Jornada*, July 24.

Bermúdez, Antonio J. 1963. *The Mexican national petroleum industry.* Palo Alto, CA: Stanford University Press.

Black, Jeremy. 1998. Maps and Politics. Chicago: University of Chicago Press.

Bolívar Aguilar, Juan José. 2001. *Monografía del estado de Campeche.* Ciudad del Carmen: Universidad Autónoma del Carmen.

Booth, William. 2009. State dept. cites 'large firefights' in travel alert on Mexico. *Washington Post*, February 21.

BP. 2008. Statistical review of world energy. June. http://www.bp.com /liveassets/bp_internet/globalbp/globalbp_uk_english/reports_and_pub lications/statistical_energy_review_2008/STAGING/local_assets/down loads/pdf/statistical_review_of_world_energy_full_review_2008.pdf.

Breglia, Lisa. 2006. *Monumental ambivalence: The politics of heritage.* Austin: University of Texas Press.

Brookings Institution. 2009. Cuba: A new policy of critical and constructive engagement. Proceedings, April 22, Brookings Institution, Washington, DC. http://www.brookings.edu/~/media/Files/events/2009/0422 _cuba/20090422_cuba.pdf.

Brown, Jonathan C. 1987. Domestic politics and foreign investment: British development of Mexican petroleum, 1889–1911. *Business History Review* 61, no. 3 (Autumn): 387–416.

———. 1993a. Foreign and native-born workers in Porfirian Mexico. *American Historical Review* 98, no. 3:786–818.

———. 1993b. *Oil and revolution in Mexico.* Berkeley: University of California Press.

Brown, Jonathan C., and Alan Knight, eds. 1992. *The Mexican petroleum industry in the twentieth century.* Austin: University of Texas Press.

Butler, Edward C. 1903. Americans in Mexico. *Los Angeles Times,* June 9, A4. ProQuest Historical Newspapers, *Los Angeles Times* 1881–1986.

Cameron, Angus, and Ronen Palan. 2004. *The imagined economies of globalization.* Thousand Oaks, CA: Sage.

Campbell, Colin J. 2005. *Oil crisis.* Essex, England: Multi-Science.

Campbell, Colin J., and Jean Laherrere. 1998. The end of cheap oil. *Scientific American,* March.

Campeche, State of. 2004. Propuestas del estado de Campeche a la Ley de Coordinación Fiscal. May. http://www.indetec.gob.mx/cnh/propuestas/376.pdf.

———. 2008. Segundo informe de gobierno José Ignacio Seara Sierra. Cuidad del Carmen, Campeche. September 28.

Cardoso, Victor. 2006. Para 2006 se reducirá 17% restitución de reservas de crudo, calcula Pemex. *La Jornada,* March 30.

———. 2008. No se recuperará la producción petrolera de 3.1 millones de barriles al día: Sener. *La Jornada,* December 11.

———. 2010. En seis años Schulmberger se posicionó como el principal proveedor de Pemex. *La Jornada,* February 24.

*CarmenHoy.* 2008. Propuesta para una mejor distribución de recursos en municipios petroleros. August 16. http://www.carmenhoy.com/Noticias/Noticias/Locales/mtids,34/mtcat,82/Noticia,1032/Propuesta-para-una-mejor-distribucion-de-recursos-en-municipios-petroleros.html.

Carriles, Luis. 2010. Pemex perforará su primer pozo transfronterizo. *El Milenio,* April 16.

Castillo Garcia, Gustavo. 2008. Mouriño rendirá declaración escrito sobre contratos de Ivancar con Pemex. *La Jornada,* April 12.

Centro de Estudios de las Finanzas Públicas (CEFP). 2009. Análisis de los informes sobre la situación económica, las finanzas públicas, y la deuda pública: cuarto trimestre de 2008. CEFP/013/2009. February. http://www.cefp.gob.mx/intr/edocumentos/pdf/cefp/2009/cefp0132009.pdf.

Cerón, Rosa María, Julia Griselda Cerón, Manuel Muriel-García, and Beatriz Cárdenas. 2008. Identification of ion sources in rainwater of a coastal site impacted by the gas and oil industry in the southeast of Mexico. *Global Nest Journal* 10, no. 1:92–100.

Charney, Jonathan, and Robert Smith, eds. 2002. *International Maritime Boundaries.* Vol. 4. The Hague: Martinus Nijhoff.

*Chicago Daily Tribune.* 1915. Tribune investors' guide. July 30, p. 15. ProQuest Historical Newspapers, *Chicago Tribune* 1849–1986, *Chicago Daily Tribune* 1872–1963.

Chim, Lorenzo. 2010. Acusa Marea Azul a la Semarnat de violar norma en Campeche. *La Jornada,* May 22.

Chim, Lorenzo, Luis Boffil, and Angelica Enciso. 2007. Reconoce la Semarnat contaminación por crudo en Tabasco y Campeche. *La Jornada,* October 31.

Chowdhury, Rinku Roy. 2006. Landscape change in the Calakmul Biosphere

Reserve, Mexico: Modeling the driving forces of smallholder deforestation in land parcels. *Applied Geography* 26, no. 2:129–152.

Clark, J. Reuben. 1928. The oil settlement with Mexico. *Foreign Affairs* 6, no. 4:600–614.

Clemente, Jude. 2008. Cantarell is not Mexico's only oil production problem. *Pipeline and Gas Journal*, August, 51–54.

Colby, Frank, ed. 1921. *The new international yearbook.* New York: Dodd, Mead.

Comisión Nacional de Población (Conapo). 2005. Campeche: Grado de marginación municipal. Map. http://www.conapo.gob.mx/publicaciones/mar gina2005/anexoB/mapas/b_0400.pdf.

Comisiones Unidas de Energía y Estudios Legislativos. 2008. Séptimo foro de debate con el tema "Exploración, explotación y restitución de reservas petroleras." Mexico City, June 3. Transcript. http://www.teledicion.com .mx/artman2/uploads/2/VERSI_N_ESTENOGR_FICA_COMPLETA _DEL_S_PTIMO_FORO.pdf.

Connor, Steve. 2009. Warning: Oil supplies are running out fast. *The Independent*, August 3. http://www.independent.co.uk/news/science/warning-oil -supplies-are-running-out-fast-1766585.html.

Coronil, Fernando. 1997. *The magical state: Nature, money, and modernity in Venezuela.* Chicago: University of Chicago Press.

Corredor, Jamie. 1983. The significance of Mexican petroleum. In *U.S.-Mexico relations: Economic and social aspects*, ed. Clark Reynolds and Carlos Tello. Palo Alto, CA: Stanford University Press.

Cortesi, Arnaldo. 1940. Mexico voids title of 3 U.S. concerns to 1,500,000 acres. *New York Times*, March 27, p. 1. ProQuest Historical Newspapers, *New York Times* 1851–2005.

Cruz, Nancy. 2009. Mexico: An oil nation in crisis. Council on Hemispheric Affairs. October 22. http://www.coha.org/mexico-an-oil-nation-in-crisis/.

Cruz Idiáquez, Jeanette. 2008. Entrega Pemex recursos a pescadores ribereños. *Diario 40*, March 25.

Currie-Alder, Bruce. 2001. Collaborative management of the Mexican coast: Public participation and the oil industry in the Terminos Lagoon Protected Area. Master's thesis, resource management, Simon Fraser University.

———. 2004. Sharing environmental responsibility in southeast Mexico: Participatory processes for natural resource management. International Development Research Center, working paper 16. http://web.idrc.ca/uploads /user-S/1117113685116CurrieAlder.pdf.

Currie-Alder, Bruce, and John C. Day. 2003. Public participation in Mexican protected areas: Términos Lagoon Campeche. In *Protected Areas and the Regional Planning Imperative in North America*, ed. James G. Nelson, John C. Day, and Lucy Sportza. Calgary, Canada: University of Calgary Press.

Dampier, William. 1699. *A new voyage round the world.* Vol. 2. London: James Knapton.

Davalos, Renato. 2005. "Sería tonto privatizar Pemex o pensar en hacerlo": Vicente Fox. *La Jornada*, August 6.

Davidson, Charles. 2008. Plumbing the Gulf's depths for oil and gas. (Federal

Reserve Bank of Atlanta) *EconSouth* 10, no. 3 (third quarter). http://www
.frbatlanta.org/invoke.cfm?objectid=94FF86BC-5056-9F12-122F97FCB6
F6C556&method=display_body.

Day, John W., Alejandro Yáñez-Arancibia, William J. Mitsch, A. L. Lara-
Dominguez, Jason N. Day, Jae-Yung Ko, Robert Lane, Joel Lindsey, and
David Zárate Lomelí. 2003. Using ecotechnology to address water quality and wetland habitat loss problems in the Mississippi basin (and Gri-
jalva/Usumacinta basin): A hierarchical approach. *Biotechnology Advances*
22:135–159.

de Certeau, Michel. 1984. *The practice of everyday life*. Berkeley: University of
California Press.

Deffeyes, Kenneth. 2005. *Beyond oil: The view from Hubbert's Peak*. New York:
Farrar, Strauss, and Giroux.

Defoe, Daniel. 1728. An historical and geographical description of the coasts
and rivers, colonies and ports of America [. . .] in six parts. June 3.

de Landa, Diego. 1978. *Yucatán before and after the conquest*. Trans. William
Gates. Mineola, NY: Dover.

Délano, Alexandra. 2011. Mexico and its diaspora in the United States: Policies of emigration since 1848. Cambridge, England: Cambridge University Press.

del Castillo, Jerónimo. 1866. *Diccionario histórico, biográfico y monumental de
Yucatán*. Vol. 1. Mérida: Castillo y Compañía.

de Palma, Anthony. 1996. Mexico renews its intention to sell off parts of oil
monopoly. *New York Times*, February 13.

*Diario Oficial de la Federación*. 1974a. Acuerdo que determina como zona de
reserva de cultivo para el camarón, la Laguna de Términos del Estado de
Campeche. April 18.

———.1974b. Acuerdo que determina las artes de pesca que pueden ser utili-
zadas en la pesca comercial de la de especies de escama en la Laguna de Términos del estado de Campeche. April 19.

———. 1976a. Bilateral fisheries agreement with the United States.

———. 1976b. Decreta por el que se adiciona el Artículo 27 de la Constitución
política de los Estados Unidos Mexicanos para establecer una zona económica exclusiva situada fuera del mar territorial. February 6.

———. 1976c. Decreta que fija el límite exterior de la zona económica exclusiva de México. June 7.

———. 1998. Reglas por las que se establece el sistema de organización del trá-
fico marítimo en el Golfo de Campeche y en la terminal marítima petrolera
en Cayo Arcas, Campeche. July 22.

———. 2001. Acuerdo por el que se dan a conocer los formatos de permiso ex-
cepcional de pesca para embarcaciones cubanas en la zona económica exclusiva de México. November 9.

———. 2008a. Acuerdo por el cual se establece veda para la captura de todas
las especies de caracol en aguas de jurisdicción federal correspondientes al litoral del estado de Campeche. May 6.

———. 2008b. Ley para el aprovechamiento de energías renovables y el finan-
ciamiento de la transición energética.

———. 2009. Acuerdo por el que se da a conocer el establecimiento de épocas y zonas de veda para la captura de todas las especies de camarón en aguas marinas y de los sistemas lagunarios estuarinos de jurisdicción federal del Golfo de México y Mar Caribe. April 30.

———. 2010. Acuerdo por el que se da a conocer el establecimiento de épocas y zonas de veda para la captura de todas las especies de camarón en aguas marinas y de los sistemas lagunarios estuarinos de jurisdicción federal del Golfo de México y Mar Caribe. April 30. http://www.dof.gob.mx/nota _detalle.php?codigo=5141328&fecha=30/04/2010.

Díaz del Castillo, Bernal. 1844. *The memoirs of the conquistador Bernal Díaz del Castillo.* Vol. 1. Trans. John Ingram Lockhart. London: J. Hatchard and Son.

Díaz de León, Antonio, José Ignacio Fernández, Porfirio Álvarez-Torres, Oscar Ramírez-Flores, and Luis Gerardo López-Lemus. 2004. *The sustainability of the Gulf of Mexico's fishing grounds.* Corpus Christi, TX: Harte Research Institute.

Duff, John. 1998. Royalty relief act spurs oil and gas exploration in deep waters of Gulf of Mexico: United States ratifies maritime boundary treaty with Mexico. *In Proceedings of the 16th International Conference of the Coastal Society, Minding the coast: It's everybody's business,* ed. Maurice P. Lynch, 56–62. William and Mary College, July 12–15. Reprinted by Mississippi-Alabama Sea Grant Program, http://www.masgc.org/pdf/masgp/98-016 .pdf.

Energy Information Administration (EIA). 2007. Mexico energy data, statistics, and analysis. http://www.eia.gov.

———. 2009a. *International energy outlook.* May 27. ftp://ftp.eia.doe.gov /forecasting/0484(2009).pdf.

———. 2009b. *Short-term energy outlook.* July 7. http://www.eia.gov.

———. 2009c. *World energy outlook 2010.* Executive summary. http://www .eia.doe.gov/oiaf/aeo/pdf/execsummary.pdf.

———. 2010. Gulf of Mexico fact sheet. http://www.eia.gov/oog/special /gulf/gulf_fact_sheet.html.

———. 2011a. Country analysis briefs: Mexico. July. http://www.eia.gov /cabs/Mexico/pdf.pdf.

———. 2011b. Oil crude and petroleum products explained. Imports and exports. June. http://www.eia.gov/energyexplained/index.cfm?page=oil _imports.

———. 2012. How much petroleum does the United States import and from where? http://205.254.135.7/tools/faqs/faq.cfm?id=36&t=6.

———. N.d. U.S. imports by country of origin. http://www.eia.gov/dnav /pet/pet_move_impcus_a2_nus_ep00_im0_mbblpd_a.htm.

Egremy, Nydia. 2005. Una isla que México perdió ante EU. *Contralínea,* July.

Eifert, Benn, Alan Gelb, and Nils Tallroth. 2003. Managing oil wealth. *Finance and Development* 40, no. 1 (March).

Ericson, Jenny. 2006. A participatory approach to conservation in the Calakmul Biosphere Reserve, Campeche. Mexico. *Landscape and Urban Planning* 74, no. 3–4:242–266.

Escobar, Arturo. 1996. Constructing nature: Elements for a poststructuralist political ecology. *Futures* 28, no. 4:325–344.

Espinoza, Martin. 2000. Cheney's oil investments and the future of Mexico's democracy. *CorpWatch*, August 8. http://www.corpwatch.org/article.php ?id=464.

Estrada, J., K. Tangen, and H. O. Bergensen. 1997. *Environmental challenges confronting the oil industry*. Toronto: John Wiley and Sons.

Estrada, Javier H. 2009. Reservoirs that cross country lines need special agreements. *Offshore*, July 1. http://www.offshore-mag.com/articles/print /volume-69/issue-7/latin-america/reservoirs-that-cross.html.

Farriss, Nancy. 1984. *Maya society under colonial rule*. Princeton: Princeton University Press.

Faust, Betty Bernice. 1998. *Mexican rural development and the plumed serpent*. Westport, CT: Greenwood.

Fentiman, Alicia. 1996. The anthropology of oil: The impact of the oil industry on a fishing community in the Niger Delta. *Social Justice*, no. 23:87–100.

Ferry, Elizabeth Emma. 2003. Envisioning power in Mexico: Legitimacy, crisis, and the practice of patrimony. *Journal of Historical Sociology* 16, no. 1: 22–53.

———. 2005. *Not ours alone: Patrimony, value, and collectivity in contemporary Mexico*. New York: Columbia University Press.

Fiedler, S., C. Siebe, A. Herre, B. Roth, S. Cram, and A. Stahr. 2008. Contribution of oil industry activities to environmental loads of heavy minerals in the Tabasco lowlands, Mexico. *Water, Air, and Soil Pollution: An International Journal of Environmental Pollution* 197, nos. 1–4:35–47.

Fitzgerald, David. 2006. Inside the sending state: The politics of Mexican emigration control. *International Migration Review* 40 (Summer): 259–293.

Fitzsimmons, Kevin. 2000. Tilapia aquaculture in Mexico. *Tilapia aquaculture in the Americas*, ed. B. A. Costa-Pierce and J. E. Rakocy. Vol. 2. Baton Rouge, LA: World Aquaculture Society.

Flores, Nancy, and Ana Lilia Pérez. 2004. Cantarell daños irreversibles. *Contralínea*, March. http://www.contralinea.com.mx/archivo/2004/marzo /capitales/index.html.

Friend, Phaedra. 2009. In deepwater: Pemex looks for help from foreign oil companies. *Rigzone*, February 13. http://www.rigzone.com/news/article .asp?a_id=72949.

Fuentes Berain, Rossana, and Daniel Rico. 2009. *Oil in Mexico: Pozo de pasiones. The energy reform debate in Mexico*. Washington, DC: Woodrow Wilson Center for Scholars, Mexico Institute. http://www.wilsoncenter.org/sites /default/files/Oil%20in%20Mexico.%20Pozo%20de%20Pasiones1.pdf.

Fundar. 2007. La contribución de PEMEX para el desarrollo local de las comunidades petroleras: un caso de contraloría social. http://www.fundar.org .mx/ingresospetroleros/pdf/la_contraloria.pdf.

García Méndez, Lorena. 2010. Más de $48 millones esperan para temporada de camarón. *El Sur*, June 29.

Garduño, Roberto. 2008. Manipula el gobierno federal las cifras sobre reserves. *La Jornada*, February 17.

Gates, Marilyn. 1993. *In default: Peasants, the debt crisis, and the agricultural challenge in Mexico.* Boulder, CO: Westview Press.

————. 1998. Eco-imperialism? Environmental policy versus everyday practice. In *The third wave of modernization in Latin America*, ed. Lynne Phillips. Wilmington, DE: Scholarly Resources.

Gentile, Carmen. 2009. Mexican oil production hits 14-year low. UPI, January 28. http://www.upi.com/Energy_Resources/2009/01/28/Mexicos-oil-production-hits-14-year-low/UPI-89551233179740/.

Gentleman, J. 1984. *Mexican oil and dependent development.* New York: Peter Lang.

Gillet, R. 2008. Global study of shrimp fisheries. FAO fisheries technical paper 475. Rome: UN Food and Agriculture Organization. ftp://ftp.fao.org/docrep/fao/011/i0300e/i0300e.pdf.

Godoy, Emilio. 2010. Oil workers at sea without a safety net. Inter Press Service, August 13. http://ipsnews.net/news.asp?idnews=52481.

Gold-Bouchot, Gerardo. 2004. Hydrocarbons in the southern Gulf of Mexico. In *Environmental analysis of the Gulf of Mexico*, ed. Kim Withers and Marion Nipper. Corpus Christi, TX: Harte Research Institute.

Gold-Bouchot, Gerardo, E. Noreña-Barroso, and O. Zapata-Pérez. 1995. Hydrocarbon concentrations in the American oyster (*Crassostrea virginica*) in Laguna de Términos, Campeche, Mexico. *Bulletin of Environmental Contamination and Toxicology* 53:222–227.

Gomez, Ricardo, and Andrea Merlos. 2008. Piden a Sener y a Pemex cancelar campaña en tv. *El Universal*, Finanzas, March 14. http://www.eluniversal.com.mx/finanzas/63221.html.

Gonzalez, Angel. 2009. BP becomes largest GOM producer from Thunder Horse output. *Rigzone*, April 15. http://www.rigzone.com/news/article.asp?a_id=75095.

Gonzalez, Susana. 2008. Líder del STPRM, clave en propósitos de vender Pemex. *La Jornada*, August 17.

Gordon, Wendell Chaffee. 1976 [1941]. *The expropriation of foreign property in Mexico.* New York: Arno Press.

Grajales-Nishimura, José M., Esteban Cedillo-Pardo, Carmen Rosales-Domínguez, Dante J. Morán-Zenteno, Walter Alvarez, Philippe Claeys, José Ruíz-Morales, Jesús García-Hernández, Patricia Padilla-Avila, and Antonieta Sánchez-Ríos. 2000. Chicxulub impact: The origins of reservoir and seal facies in the southeastern Mexican oil fields. *Geology* 28, no. 4:307–310.

Grayson, George W. 1980. *The politics of Mexican oil.* Pittsburgh: University of Pittsburgh Press.

————. 1988. *Oil and Mexican foreign policy.* Pittsburgh: University of Pittsburgh Press.

————. 2007. *Mexican messiah: Andrés Manuel López Obrador.* University Park: Pennsylvania State University Press.

Griffin, Wade. L., and Bruce R. Beattie. 1977. *Mexico's 200-mile offshore fishing zone: Its economic impact on the U.S. Gulf of Mexico shrimp fishery.* TAMU-SG-77-210. College Station: Center for Marine Resources, Texas A&M University.

Grove, Noel. 1974. Oil, the dwindling treasure. *National Geographic*, June, 792–825.

Haber, Stephen, Noel Maurer, and Armando Razo. 2003. When the law does not matter: The rise and decline of the Mexican oil industry. *Journal of Economic History* 63:1–32.

Haenn, Nora. 1999a. Community formation in frontier Mexico: Accepting and rejecting new migrants. *Human Organization* 58 no. 1:36–43.

———. 1999b. The power of environmental knowledge. *Human Ecology* 27, no. 3:477–491.

———. 2000. "Biodiversity is diversity in use": Community-based conservation in the Calakmul Biosphere Reserve. America Verde working paper 7. Arlington, VA: Nature Conservancy. http://evols.library.manoa.hawaii.edu/bitstream/10524/1526/1/diversity_in_use.pdf.

———. 2002. Nature regimes in southern Mexico: A history of power and environment. *Ethnology* 41, no. 1:1–26.

———. 2005. *Fields of power, forests of discontent: Culture, conservation, and the state in Mexico.* Tucson: University of Arizona Press.

Halleck, H. W. 1859. *A collection of mining laws of Spain and Mexico.* San Francisco: O'Meara and Painter.

Hart, John Mason. 1987. *Revolutionary Mexico.* Berkeley: University of California Press.

———. 2002. *Empire and revolution: The Americans in Mexico since the Civil War.* Berkeley: University of California Press.

Hartley-Alcocer, Adrian. 2007. Tilapia as a global commodity: A potential role for Mexico? PhD thesis, University of Stirling, Scotland.

Harvey, David. 2001. *Spaces of capital: Toward a critical geography.* New York: Routledge.

Headlam, Cecil, ed. 1930. America and West Indies, September 1717, 17–30. *Calendar of state papers colonial, America and West Indies.* Vol. 30, *1717–1718*, 30–50. British History Online. http://www.british-history.ac.uk/report.aspx?compid=74027.

Headlam, Cecil, and Arthur Percival Newton, eds. 1939. America and West Indies: January 1733, 16–31. *Calendar of state papers colonial, America and West Indies.* Vol. 40, *1733* (1939), 15–29. http://www.british-history.ac.uk/report.aspx?compid=79263.

Henderson, Peter. 2000. *In the absence of Don Porfirio.* Wilmington, DE: Scholarly Resources.

Hernandéz, Álvaro, and Willet Kempton. 2003. "Changes in fisheries management in Mexico: Effects of increasing scientific input and public participation." *Ocean and Coastal Management* 46:507–526.

Hernandez, Daniel. 2010. Drug group may have set off oil blast that killed 28 in central Mexico. *Los Angeles Times*, December 20.

Hernández Montejo, Carmen. 2007. *El petróleo en Campeche: del espejismo económico a la realidad social.* Campeche: Instituto de Cultura de Campeche, Gobierno del Estado de Campeche.

Herrera Beltrán, Claudia. 2009. Reprocha Calderón a opositores su rechazo a construir refinerías privadas. *La Jornada*, February 4.

Higuera, Cecilia, and Olivier Pavón. 2009. Claman refinería como "justicia social." *La Crónica de Hoy*, March 26.

Hirsch, Robert, Roger Bezdek, and Robert Wedling. 2005. Peaking oil production: Sooner rather than later? *Issues in Science and Technology Online*, Spring. http://www.issues.org/21.3/hirsch.html.

Holden, Robert. 1994. *Mexico and the survey of public lands: The management of modernization 1876-1911*. DeKalb: Northern Illinois University Press.

Höök, Mikael. 2009. The evolution of giant oil field production behavior. *Natural Resources Research* 18, no. 1:39–56.

Höök, Mikael, Robert Hirsch, and Kjell Alekett. 2009. Giant oil field decline rates and their influence on world oil production. *Energy Policy* 37, no. 6:2262–2272.

Hubbert, M. King. 1956. Nuclear energy and the fossil fuels. Presented at the spring meeting of the Southern District Division of Production, American Petroleum Institute, San Antonio, TX, March 7–9. http://www.hubbert peak.com/hubbert/1956/1956.pdf.

Humphries, Marc. 2008. Royalty relief for US deepwater oil and gas leases. Congressional Research Service (CRS), Library of Congress report for Congress. September 18. http://assets.opencrs.com/rpts/RS22567_20080918 .pdf.

Iliff, Laurence. 2010. Pemex vows to stick with Chicontepec project. *Rigzone*, April 16. http://www.rigzone.com/news/article.asp?a_id=91168.

*Informador.com.mx*. 2008. Tendrán pesca y acuicultura 10 por ciento más presupuesto: Sagarpa. http://www.informador.com.mx/mexico/2008/54469 /6/tendran-pesca-y-acuicultura-10-por-ciento-mas-presupuesto-sagarpa .htm.

Instituto Nacional Estadística Geográfica (Inegi). 2002. Cuadernos estadísticos del Municipal de Carmen, Campeche.

———. 2004. Sistema de cuentas nacionales de México, producto interno bruto por entidad federative, 1997–2002. Año base 1997.

———. 2006a. II Conteo de población y vivienda 2005, México y sus municipios.

———. 2006b. Producto interno bruto por entidad federativa, 2001–2006.

———. 2010. Sistema de cuentas nacionales de México, producto interno bruto por entidad federativa 2003–2008. Año base 2003.

———. 2011a. Censo de población y vivienda 2010.

———. 2011b. Perspectiva estadística de Campeche. December. http://www .inegi.gob.mx/est/contenidos/espanol/sistemas/perspectivas/perspectiva -cam.pdf.

Inter-American Development Bank (IDB). 2009. IDB estimates of 2008 remittance flows to Latin America and the Caribbean. http://idbdocs.iadb.org /wsdocs/getdocument.aspx?docnum=1662094.

International Energy Agency (IEA). 2008. *World energy outlook 2008*. Paris: IEA/Organization of Economic Cooperation and Development (OECD).

———. 2010. *World energy outlook 2010*. Paris: IEA/Organization of Economic Cooperation and Development (OECD).

Jaime, Edna. 2004. Fox's economic agenda: An incomplete transition. In *Mex-

*ico under Fox*, ed. Luis Rubio and Susan Kaufman Purcell. Boulder, CO: Lynne Rienner.

Jarvis, Michael J. 2010. *In the eye of all trade*. Chapel Hill: University of North Carolina Press.

Jayne, Catherine. 2000. *Oil, war, and Anglo-American relations*. Westport, CT: Greenwood.

Jensen, Kenneth. 1993. Chapote: Interdependence and the liberalization of the oil industry in Mexico. *California Western International Law Journal* 24:81–116.

Jiménez Valdez, Gloria Martha. 1989. Poblaciones costeras de Tabasco y Campeche. *Anales de Antropología* 26, no. 1:99–105.

Johnstone, Christian. 1832. *Lives and voyages of Drake, Cavendish, and Dampier*. New York: J. and J. Harper.

*La Jornada*. 2007. Las nuevas Siete Hermanas. *Petróleo: presente y futuro*, March 27. Economist Intelligence Unit.

Joseph, Gilbert. 1982. *Revolution from without: Yucatan, Mexico, and the United States: 1880–1924*. Cambridge, MA: Cambridge University Press.

Joseph, Gilbert M., and Timothy J. Henderson, eds. 2002. *The Mexico reader: History, culture, politics*. Durham, NC: Duke University Press.

Justo Sierra, Carlos. 1998. *Breve historia de Campeche*. Fideicomiso Historia de las Américas. Serie Breves Historias de los Estados de la República Mexicana. Mexico City: Colegio de México, Fondo de Cultura Económica.

Kallaur, Carolita. 2001. The deepwater Gulf of Mexico: Lessons learned. In *Proceedings, Institute of Petroleum International conference on deepwater exploration and production in association with OGP*. February 22, London. http://www.gomr.boemre.gov/homepg/offshore/deepwatr/lessons_learned.html.

Karl, Kevin, Richie D. Baud, Angela G. Boice, Roy Bongiovanni, Thierry M. DeCort, Richard P. Desselles, and Eric G. Kazanis. 2007. Gulf of Mexico oil and gas production forecast: 2007–2016. OCS report, MMS 2007-020. May. New Orleans: U.S. Department of the Interior, Minerals Management Service, Gulf of Mexico OCS Region. http://www.gomr.mms.gov/PDFs/2007/2007-020.pdf.

Karl, Terry Lynn. 1997. *The paradox of plenty: Oil booms and petro-states*. Berkeley: University of California Press.

Keys, Eric. 2005. Exploring market-based development market intermediaries and farmers in Calakmul, Mexico. *Geographical Review* 95, no. 1:24–46.

Kim, Suk H., and Seung Hee Kim. 2006. *Global corporate finance: Texts and cases*. Malden, MA: Blackwell.

Klare, Michael. 2008. *Rising powers, shrinking planet*. New York: Metropolitan Books.

———. 2009a. The era of extreme energy: Life after the age of oil. *Toms Dispatch.com*, September 22. http://www.tomdispatch.com/blog/175127/tomgram:_michael_klare,_energy_xtremism/.

———. 2009b. It's official—the era of cheap oil is over: Energy department changes tune on peak oil. *TomDispatch.com*, June 12. http://www.tom dispatch.com/post/175082.

———. 2010. BP-style extreme energy nightmares to come. (Post Carbon Institute) *Energy Bulletin*, June 22. http://www.energybulletin.net/node/53212.

Klein, Naomi. 2007. *The shock doctrine: The rise of disaster capitalism*. New York: Metropolitan Books.

Knight, Alan. 1990. *The Mexican Revolution*. Vol. 1. Lincoln: University of Nebraska Press.

———. 1992. The politics of the expropriation. In *The Mexican petroleum industry in the twentieth century*, ed. Jonathan Brown and Alan Knight. Austin: University of Texas Press.

Koppes, Clayton. 1982. The Good Neighbor Policy and the nationalization of Mexican oil: A reinterpretation. *Journal of American History* 69, no. 1:62–81.

Krikorian, Mark. 2003. Oil for illegals? Mexico, and the Democrats, have a fit over House vote. *National Review Online*, May 14. http://www.national review.com/comment/comment-krikorian051403.asp.

Kunstler, James Howard. 2005. *The long emergency*. New York: Grove.

Kuo, J. C., Doug Elliot, Javier Luna-Melo, and José B. de León Pérez. 2001. World's largest N2-generation plant. *Oil and Gas Journal*, March 12.

Lane, Kris E. *Pillaging the empire: Piracy in the Americas: 1500–1750*. Armonk, NY: M. E. Sharpe.

Larson, Alan. Geopolitics of oil and natural gas. *Economic Perspectives: Journal of the US Department of State* 9, no. 2:10–12.

*Latin American Economy and Business*. 2006. "Mexico, boom to bust." February 21.

Ledward, K. H., ed. 1930. *Journals of the Board of Trade and Plantations*. Vol. 7, *January 1735–December 1741*, 51–61. Institute of Historical Research, *British History Online*. http://www.british-history.ac.uk/report .aspx?compid=81651&strquery=Campeachy.

Lefebvre, Henri. 1991. *The production of space*. Trans. Donald Nicholason-Smith. Oxford, England: Blackwell.

Leis, Brian, Richard Chidester, Stephanie Flamberg, John Olson, Susan Rose, Julio Aysa, Mauricio Moreno, José Chapela, and Thomas Thomas. 2008. Análisis de causa raíz de incidente entre la PAE Usumacinta y el KAB-101 23 de octubre 2007. Report prepared by Battelle's Energy Systems for Pemex's Dirección Corporativa de Operaciones. http://www.pemex.com /files/content/usumacinta/informe_battelle.pdf.

Leriche Guzmán, Luis Fernando. 1995. *Isla del Carmen: La historia indecisa de un puerto exportador: El caso de la industría camaronera (1947–1982)*. Mexico City: ENDESU.

López, Luis Ruben. 2008. "¡Fuera el pelele de Calderón de Tabasco!" *Por Esto*, March 19.

López Obrador, Andres Manuel. 2008a. Mensaje a la nación. August 31. http://www.youtube.com/watch?v=aLcBrgNPd_M.

————. 2008b. Mensaje de Andrés Manuel López Obrador in defensa de petróleo. February 6. http://www.youtube.com/watch?v=vJB8kk7sf-A.

Lustig, Nora. 1998. *Mexico: The remaking of an economy*. Harrisonberg, VA: R. R. Donnelly and Sons.

Malkin, Elizabeth. 2008. Mexico, an oil producer, hasn't benefited from soaring prices. *New York Times*, Business, June 7.

*Manatt*. 2007. Mexico takes legal steps aimed at oil exploration in central Gulf of Mexico. December 18. ManattJones Global Strategies.

Mares, David, and Nelson Altamirano. 2007. Venezuela's PDVSA and world energy markets: Corporate strategies and political factors determining its behavior and influence. Working paper. March. Houston: James A. Baker III Institute for Public Policy and Japan Petroleum Energy Center, Rice University. http://www.rice.edu/energy/publications/docs/NOCs/Papers/NOC_PDVSA_Mares-Altamirano.pdf.

Martin, Jeremy. 2009. Chicontepec debate could redefine energy sector. *Mexbiznews.com*, November 25. http://www.mexbiznews.com/chicontepec-debate-could-redefine-energy-sector.

Martin, Jeremy, and Sylvia Longmire. 2011. The perilous intersection of Mexico's drug war and Pemex. *IAGS Journal of Energy Security*. March 15.

Martínez Laguna, Norma. 2004. Oil policies and privatization strategies in Mexico. *Energy Policy* 32, no. 18 (December): 2035–2047.

Martínez Tiburcio, Félix. 2005. Maritime protection of critical infrastructure assets in the Campeche Sound. Master's thesis, Naval Postgraduate School, Monterey, CA.

Mathews, Jennifer. 2009. *Chicle: The chewing gum of the Americas*. Tucson: University of Arizona Press.

Mayer, Brantz, and Frederick Albion Ober. 1906. Mexico, Central America, and the West Indies. In *The history of nations*, ed. Henry Cabot Lodge. Vol. 22. Philadelphia: John D. Morris.

McJunkin, David. 1991. Logwood: An inquiry into the historical biogeography of Haematoxylum Campechianum L. and related dyewoods of the neotropics. PhD diss., Department of Geography. University of California, Los Angeles.

McPherson, Charles. 2010. State participation in natural resource sectors. In *The taxation of petroleum and minerals: Principles, problems and practice*, ed. Philip Daniel, Michael Keen, and Charles McPherson. New York: Routledge.

Melgar Palacios, Lourdes. 2008. Yacimientos transfronterizos: negociación, exploración, explotación. Presentation before the senate of the nation, June 5. http://www.15diario.com/15diario/documentos/debatepemexsenado/05junio2008_3melgar.pdf.

Melville, Roberto. 1984. Condiciones laborales de los pescadores camaroneros en Ciudad del Carmen. In *Los pescadores de la Laguna de Términos*, ed. Roberto Rodríguez C. Mexico City: CIESAS.

Méndez, Enrique, and Alma E. Muñoz. 2008. El proyecto privatizador "¡no pasará!," advierten *adelitas* en resistencia civil. *La Jornada*, April 11.

Méndez, Enrique, and Ciro Pérez Silva. 2008. Mouriño firmó contratos por más de $26 millones. *La Jornada*, February 29.

Méndez Romellón, Leydi. 2006. Visitan pescadores de altura la sala interactive de Pemex. *El Sur*, July 27.

———. 2009. Promueve Sagarpa programa de concientización de respeto de veda. *El Sur*, September 29.

Mendoza Novelo, Adely. 2009. Responsibilidad, pide Hurtado a miembros de sector pesquero. *El Sur*, June 7.

Metz, W. D. 1978. Mexico: The premier oil discovery in the Western Hemisphere. *Science*, December 22, pp. 1261–1265.

Mexico. 2005. Campeche. *Enciclopedia de los municipios de México.* Instituto Nacional para el Federalismo y Desarrollo Municipal, Gobierno del Estado de Campeche. http://www.e-local.gob.mx/work/templates/enciclo/campeche/Mpios/04003a.htm.

Mexico, Cámara de Diputados. 2009. Comunicación social, June 23. Boletín 4316.

Mexico, Ministry of Foreign Affairs. 1976. Acuerdo de pesca entre los Estados Unidos Mexicanos y la República de Cuba. Exchange of notes constituting an agreement on the delimitation of the exclusive economic zone of Mexico in the sector adjacent to Cuban maritime areas. July 26.

Mexico, Office of the President. 2007. Confianza en las instituciones públicas. *Plan nacional de desarollo.* http://pnd.calderon.presidencia.gob.mx/pdf/PrimerInformeEjecucion/1_5.pdf.

———. 2008a. Mensaje a la nación de President Felipe Calderón. October 28. http://www.presidencia.gob.mx/2008/10/mensaje-a-la-nacion-del-presidente-felipe-calderon/.

———. 2008b. Presidente Calderón en la ceremonia conmemorativa en el 70 aniversario de la expropriación petrolera. http://www.presidencia.gob.mx/2008/03/el-presidente-calderon-en-la-ceremonia-conmemorativa-del-70-aniversario-de-la-expropriacion-petrolera/.

Mexico, Secretaría de Economía. 1956. Estadísticas sociales del Porfiriato 1877–1910. Mexico City: Talleres Gráficos de la Nación.

Mexico, Secretaría de Energía (Sener). 1956. Estadísticas sociales del Porfiriato 1877–1910. Mexico City: Talleres Gráficos de la Nación.

———. 2008. Prospectiva del mercado de petróleo crudo, 2008–2017. http://www.sener.gob.mx/webSener/res/PE_y_DT/pub/Prospectiva%20PC%202008-2017.pdf.

———. 2009. Reservas de hidrocarburos. http://www.sener.gob.mx/portal/las_reservas_de_hidrocarburos_de_mexico.html.

Mexico, Secretaría de Hacienda y Crédito Público. 1912. *Mexican yearbook.* London: McCorquodale.

Secretaría de Medio Ambiente, Recursos Naturales, y Pesca (Semarnap)/Instituto Nacional de Ecología. 1997. Programa de manejo de la Zona de Protección de Flora y Fauna Laguna de Términos. http://www.conanp.gob.mx/que_hacemos/pdf/programas_manejo/lagunaterminos.pdf.

Meyer, Lorenzo. 1977. *Mexico and the United States in the oil controversy 1917–1942.* Austin: University of Texas Press.

Millard, Peter. 2007. As deepwater drilling booms, Mexico's oil could leak to U.S. Dow Jones Newswires, September 7.
———. 2008. Mexico concerns run deep as US accelerates border oil push. Dow Jones Newswires, July 7.
———. 2009a. Halliburton, 4 Mexican firms to get Chicontepec contracts. Dow Jones Newswires, July 22.
———. 2009b. Mexico state oil co. optimistic on two largest fields. Dow Jones Newswires, June 12.
Millman, Joel. 2009. Remittances to Mexico fall more than forecast. *Wall Street Journal*, January 28. http://online.wsj.com/article/SB12331069511 0822547.html.
Millor, Manuel. 1982. *Mexico's oil: Catalyst for a new relationship with the US?* Boulder, CO: Westview.
Mitchell, Timothy. 2007. Carbon democracy. Paper presented at the Oil and Politics Conference Goldsmith's College, London.
Morales, Isidro. 2011. Energy trade and security issues at the U.S.-Mexico border. *The future of oil in Mexico*. James A. Baker III Institute for Public Policy and Oxford University. April 29. http://bakerinstitute.org/publications /EF-pub-MoralesTrade-04292011.pdf.
Morales Villagrán, Vicente. 2009. *El túnel oscuro . . . del petróleo mexicano: la reforma energética del 2008*. Published by Vicente Morales Villagrán.
Moreno, Saúl. 2007. *Dilemas petroleras: cultura, poder y trabajo en el Golfo de Mexico*. Mexico City: Casa Chata, CIESAS.
Moreno-Brid, Juan Carlos, and Jaime Ros. 2009. *Development and growth in the Mexican economy: A historical perspective*. New York: Oxford University Press.
Moreno Gullón, Amparo. 2004. La matrícula de Mar de Campeche (1777–1811). *Espacio, tiempo y forma*. Series 4, *Historia Moderna* 1, no. 17:273–291. http://e-spacio.uned.es/fez/eserv.php?pid=bibliuned:ETFSerie4-EA2 F7080-C23A-3B10-ED07-54BC46D2CD8F&dsID=Documento.pdf.
Moroney, John, and Flory Dieck-Assad. 2005. *Energy and sustainable development in Mexico*. College Station: Texas A&M University Press.
Morrison, Mark. 2006. Plenty of oil, just drill deeper. *Business Week*, September 7.
Movimiento Ciudadano. 2012. El acuerdo sobre yacimientos transfronterizos de hidrocarburos con EU, "regresivo y entreguista." Press release. April 12. http://www.movimientociudadano.org.mx/index.php?option=com_con tent&view=article&id=630:el-acuerdo-sobre-yacimientos-transfronterizos -de-hidrocarburos-con-eu-regresivo-y-entreguista&catid=32:boletines -&Itemid=49.
Muñoz Lumbier, Manuel. *Las islas mexicanas*. Mexico City: Secretaría de Educación Pública.
Murphy, Julia. 2007. Anthropological perspectives on environmental concerns in rural Mexico ethnography in the Calakmul Model Forest, Campeche. In *Across borders: Diverse perspectives on Mexico*, ed. Karen Campbell and Jessica Perkins. Toronto: ISC Mexico.
Nadel, Jane Hurwitz. 1988. Changing waters: A cross-cultural survey of petro-

leum development impacts on artisanal fishing communities. In *Idenitidad y transformación de las Américas*. Bogotá: Ediciones Unidades.

National Research Council, Steering Committee for the Petroleum in the Marine Environment Update. 1985. *Oil in the water: Inputs, fates, and effects*. Washington, DC: National Academy Press.

Nations, James. 2006. *Maya tropical forest: People, parks, and ancient cities*. Austin: University of Texas Press.

Negrete Salas, María Eugenia. 1984. Petróleo y desarrollo regional: el caso de Tabasco. *Demografía y Economía* 18, no. 1:86–109.

Ness, Jeannie. 2009. Mexican minister: Swine flu could cut GDP by 1%. Associated Press Worldstream Newswire, May 11.

*New York Times*. 1914. Americans in distress. May 22, p. 2. ProQuest Historical Newspapers, *New York Times* 1851–2005.

Nill, Andrea. 2010. DeMint compares influx of undocumented immigrants to an oil leak. *ThinkProgress Security*, May 28. http://wonkroom.think progress.org/2010/05/28/demint-border-oil/.

Nixon, Lesley, Nancy K. Shepard, Christy M. Bohannon, Tara M. Montgomery, Eric G. Kazanis, and Mike P. Gravois. 2009. Deepwater Gulf of Mexico 2009: Interim report of 2008 highlights. OCS report, MMS 2009-016, May. New Orleans: U.S. Department of the Interior, Minerals Management Service, Gulf of Mexico OCS Region. http://www.gomr.mms.gov /PDFs/2009/2009-016.pdf.

Núñez Jiménez, Arturo. 2009. Iniciativa con proyecto de decreto por el que se reforma el primer párrafo del artículo 4o.-B de la Ley de Coordinación Fiscal. *Gaceta Parlamentaria*, no. 2878-1, October 30.

Offen, Karl. 2000. British logwood extraction from the Mosquita: The origin of a myth. *Hispanic American Historical Review* 80, no. 1:113–135.

*OffshoreTechnology.com*. N.d. Cantarell oilfield, Gulf of Mexico, Mexico. http://www.offshore-technology.com/projects/cantarell/.

*Oil and Gas Journal*. 2000. Gulf of Mexico western gap division agreed. July 10, p. 30.

Ong, David M. 1999. Joint development of common offshore oil and gas deposits: "Mere" state practice or customary international law? *American Journal of International Law* 93, no. 4:771–804.

Organization of Economic Cooperation and Development (OECD). 2009. Economic surveys: Mexico. OECD.

———. 2011. Recent changes in migration movements and policies (country notes): Mexico. *International Migration Outlook*. http://www.oecd.org /dataoecd/44/28/48356260.pdf.

Orme, William. 1996. *Understanding NAFTA: Mexico, free trade, and the new North America*. Austin: University of Texas Press.

Ortiz, Alicia, Anayantzin Romero, and Catalina Díaz. 2010. 1979: Cantarell, el salvador de un país. *CNNExpansión*, September 1. http://www.cnnexpansion .com/bicentenario/2010/08/27/bicentenario-historia-petroleo-mexico.

Ortiz, Edgar. 1994. NAFTA and foreign investment in Mexico. In *Foreign investment and NAFTA*, ed. Alan Rugman. Columbia: University of South Carolina Press.

Ortiz Mena, Antonio. 2003. Getting to "no": Defending against demands in NAFTA. Paper for Developing Countries and Trade Negotiation Process. Geneva International Academic Network (GIAN). http://www.ruig-gian .org/research/outputs/output.php?ID=120.

Palan, Ronen. 2003. *The offshore world.* Ithaca, NY: Cornell University Press.

Pan American Union, 1911. *Mexico: A general sketch.* 1911. Washington, DC: Byron S. Adams.

Parks Watch. 2003. Park profile: Mexico, Laguna de Terminos Flora and Fauna Protection Area. http://www.parkswatch.org/parkprofiles/pdf/ltpa _eng.pdf.

Parra, Francisco. 2004. *Oil politics: A modern history of petroleum.* New York: Palgrave Macmillan.

Partido Acción Nacional (PAN). 2008. *La mayoría de los mexicanos quiere la reforma de Pemex.* Video.

Payne, Martin. 2008. Mexican oil exports: Start saying adios! *Peak Opportunities,* March 19. http://peakopps.blogspot.com/2008/03/mexican-oil -exports-start-saying-adios.html.

Pazos, Luis. 2008. Los dueños de Pemex: del saqueo a la reforma. Mexico City: Editorial Diana.

Pearson, John F. 1980. Fighting the world's worst oil spill. *Popular Mechanics,* May.

Pemex (Petróleos Mexicanos). 1990. *Statistical yearbook 1990.* http://www.ri .pemex.com/files/content/anuario1990(ingles).pdf.

———. 2001. *Anuario estadístico 2001.* http://www.ri.pemex.com/files /content/AnuarioEstadistico2001.pdf.

———. 2004. Pemex confirma la presencia de petróleo pesado en aguas profundas. Press release, November 24. Boletín 285. http://www.pemex.com /index.cfm?action=news&sectionID=8&catid=40&contentID=2640.

———. 2007a. Drenaje pluvial y red de agua potable en las colonial Francisco I. Madero y Pedro Saenz Baranda.

———. 2007b. Lineamientos en materia de donativos y donaciones de Petróleos Mexicanos y organismos subsidiarios. http://www.pemex.com/files /content/Lineamientos%20en%20materia%20de%20donativos%20y%20 donaciones.pdf.

———. 2007c. Petróleos Mexicanos aportó más de 54 millones de pesos en el period 1995–2006, para el desarrollo de diversos proyectos en el sector pesquero en el estado de Campeche. Press release. Boletín regional 002, Ciudad del Carmen. January 5. http://www.pemex.com/index.cfm ?action=news&sectionID=118&catID=11381&contentID=16252.

———. 2008a. Cantarell: pasado, presente y futuro. July 18. http://www .pemex.com/index.cfm?action=content&sectionid=137&catid=12222.

———. 2008b. Donativos y donaciones autorizados por el Consejo de Administración de Petróleos Mexicanos. Table. http://www.pemex.com/files /content/Cuadro32008.pdf.

———. 2008c. Gerencia corporativa de desarollo social. http://www.pemex .com/files/content/PresentacionGCDS.pdf.

———. 2008d. Responsibilidad social 2008 (versión completa). *Informe 2008, desarollo sustentable.* August 6. http://desarrollosustentable.pemex.com /portal/index.cfm?action=content&sectionID=2&catID=921.

———. 2009a. *Anuario estadístico 2009.* http://www.ri.pemex.com/files /content/7s4_aee_pep.pdf.

———. 2009b. Aportó Pemex dos mil 667 millones de pesos al desarrollo social del país en 2008. Press release, February 3. Boletín 023. http://www .pemex.com/index.cfm?action=news&sectionID=8&catID=40&content ID=19597.

———. 2009c. 2008 informe de responsibilidad social. http://desarrollo sustentable.pemex.com/files/content/inf08/pemex_rs.pdf.

———. 2009d. 30 aniversario de la Sonda de Campeche. Video. Pemex.tv. http://tv.pemex.com/index.cfm?mode=entry&entry=0FB99EE8-CE2F -47A1-E0CA6698C3A9E683.

———. 2010a. 2009 informe de responsibilidad social. http://desarrollo sustentable.pemex.com/files/content/inf09/inf_ds09.pdf.

———. 2010b. *10 anuario estadístico.* http://www.ri.pemex.com/files/con tent/7sae10.pdf.

———. 2011. Desarollo social. *Información estadística.* http://www.pemex .com/index.cfm?action=content&sectionID=113&catID=14163.

———. N.d.a. Cifras que debemos conocer. http://www.pemex.com/index .cfm?action=content&sectionid=135&catid=11820.

———. N.d.b. Reservas de hidrocarburos. http://www.pemex.com/index .cfm?action=content&sectionid=112&catid=12660.

Pemex Exploration and Production (PEP). 2009. Aspectos relevantes de la ex-ploración y producción de hidrocarburos. President Carlos Morales Gil. http://www.pep.pemex.com/Paginas/default.aspx.

Pemex/Sener (Petróleos Mexicanos/Secretaría de Energía). 2008. Diagnós-tico: situación de Pemex. March.

Peña, Moises T. de la. 1942. *Campeche económico.* 2 vols. Mexico City: Go-bierno Constitucional del Estado de Campeche.

Peña Castillo, Agustín. *Campeche histórico: guía breve.* Mérida: Maldonado Editores, 1986.

Peña Chapa, Juan Luis, Manuel Martín Castillo, and Juan Carlos Gonza-lez Avila. 2000. The performance of the economy of the Yucatán Penin-sula 1970–1993. In *Population, development, and environment on the Yu-catán Peninsula: From ancient Maya to 2030,* ed. Wolfgang Lutz, Leonel Prieto, and Warren Sanderson. July. Laxenburg, Austria: International In-stitute for Applied Systems Analysis. http://www.iiasa.ac.at/Admin/PUB /Documents/RR-00-014.pdf.

Pérez, Ana Lilia. 2007. Los azules copan Pemex. *Contralínea,* February 15. http://contralinea.info/archivo-revista/index.php/2009/02/15/los -azules-copan-pemex/.

———. 2009a. Donativos de Pemex benefician a gobiernos del PAN. *Contra-línea,* February 15. http://contralinea.info/archivo-revista/index.php/ 2009/02/15/donativos-de-pemex-benefician-a-gobiernos-del-pan/.

———. 2009b. El informe secreto de Reyes Heroles. *Contralínea,* July 19. http://contralinea.info/archivo/2009/julio/140/.

*Petroleum Intelligence Weekly.* 1984. February 27, p. 5.

Philip, George. 1992. The expropriation in comparative perspective. In *The Mexican petroleum industry in the twentieth century,* ed. Jonathan Brown and Alan Knight. Austin: University of Texas Press.

Philip, George, and Alan Knight. 1982. *Oil and politics in Latin America: Nationalist movements and state governments.* New York: Cambridge University Press.

Piña Chan, Román, ed. 2002. Enciclopedia histórica de Campeche. 7 vols. Mexico City: Gobierno del Estado de Campeche.

Pinet Plascencia, Adela. 1998. La península de Yucatán en el Archivo General de la Nación. San Cristóbal de las Casas: UNAM, CHIMIECH, Estado de Chiapas.

Pirker, Kristina, José Manuel Arias Rodríguez, and Hugo Ireta Guzmán. 2007. *El aceso de la información para la controlaría social.* Mexico City: Fundar.

Ponce Jiménez, Martha Patricia. 1990. *La montaña chiclera: vida cotidiana y trabajo (1900–1950).* Mexico City: CIESAS.

Ponce Vélez, Guadalupe, and Alfonso Vásquez Botello. 2005. Niveles de hidrocarburos en el Golfo de México. In *El Golfo de México,* ed. Alfonso Vásquez Botello, Jaime Rendón von Osten, Gerardo Gold-Bouchot, and Claudia Agraz-Hernández. 2nd edition. Universidad Autónoma de Campeche, Universidad Autónoma de México, and Instituto Nacional de Ecología.

*Por Esto.* 2010. Endeudados y con poco esperanza. Campeche, July 31. http://www.poresto.net/ver_nota.php?zona=qroo&idSeccion=31&idTitulo=34389.

Porter-Bolland, Luciana, Edward A. Ellis, and Henry L. Gholz. 2007. Land use dynamics and landscape history in La Montaña, Campeche, Mexico. *Landscape and Urban Planning* 82, no. 4 (October 17): 198–207.

Purcell, Susan Kaufman. 2004. The changing bilateral relationship: A U.S. view. In *Mexico under Fox,* ed. Luis Rubio and Susan Kaufman Purcell. Boulder, CO: Lynne Rienner.

Pratt, Joseph, Tyler Priest, and Christopher James Castañeda. 1997. *Offshore pioneers: Brown & Root and the history of offshore oil and gas.* Houston: Gulf.

Quiroz, Juan Carlos. 2009. Modernizing Pemex: New reforms focus on regulation. Revenue Watch Institute. http://www.revenuewatch.org/news/news-article/mexico/modernizing-pemex-new-reforms-focus-regulation.

Rabalais, Steven C., and R. Warren Flint. 1983. Ixtoc-1 effects on intertidal and subtidal infauna of South Texas Gulf beaches. *Contributions in Marine Science* 26:23–35.

Ramírez, Miguel D. 2003. Privatization in Chile and Mexico. In *International handbook on privatization,* ed. David Parker and David Saal. Northampton, MA: Edward Elgar.

Ramos-Miranda, Julia, Domingo Flores-Hernández, and Thang Do Chi. 2009. *Assessment of the white shrimp fishery (Litopenaeus setiferus) on the Campeche Bank.* Campeche: Centro Epomex, Universidad Autónoma de Campeche.

*Reforma.* 2006. Pemex postpones investments in crude oil. *Reforma,* March 15.

Respuesta Spot Pemex. 2008. *Extreme machines: Oil rig.* Discovery Channel video clip mash-up with comments. http://www.youtube.com/watch ?v=meaMr0v2scs&NR=1.

Restall, Matthew. 2009. *The black middle: Africans, Mayas, and Spaniards in colonial Yucatan.* Palo Alto, CA: Stanford University Press.

Restall, Matthew, and Christopher Lutz. 2005. Wolves and sheep? Black-Maya relations in colonial Guatemala and Yucatán. In *Beyond black and red: African native relations in colonial Latin America,* ed. Matthew Restall. Albuquerque: University of New Mexico Press.

Reyes Heroles, Jesús. 2009. Palabras de Dr. Jesús Reyes Heroles G.G. en la ceremonia conmemorativa del 30 aniversario de la producción de hidrocarburos en la Sonda de Campeche. Transcript, July 10, Ciudad del Carmen, Campeche, Mexico.

Richardson, G. Ed, Lesley D. Nixon, Christy M. Bohannon, Eric G. Kazanis, Tara M. Montgomery, and Mike P. Gravois. 2008. *Deepwater Gulf of Mexico 2008: America's offshore energy future.* OCS report, MMS 2008-13. New Orleans: U.S. Department of the Interior, Minerals Management Service, Gulf of Mexico OCS Region. http://www.gomr.mms.gov /PDFs/2008/2008-013.pdf.

Rico F., Carlos. 1992. Migration and U.S-Mexican relations, 1966–1986. In *Western Hemisphere Immigration and United States foreign policy,* ed. Christopher Mitchell. University Park: Pennsylvania State University Press.

Rippy, Merril. 1972. *Oil and the Mexican Revolution.* Leiden, Netherlands: Brill.

Robadue, Don, Rafael Calderón, Autumn Oczkowski, Leslie Bach, and Mafer Cepeda. 2004. Characterization of the region of the Términos Lagoon: Campeche, Mexico. Draft for discussion. Narragansett: Coastal Resources Center, University of Rhode Island. http://www.crc.uri.edu/download /23s_L1Profile_Draft_Terminos_2004.pdf.

Robbins, Lynn Arnold, and Steven McNabb. 1987. Oil developments and community responses in Norton Sound, Alaska. *Human Organization* 46, no. 1:10–17.

Robelius, Fredrik. 2007. Giant oil fields, the highway to oil: Giant oil fields and their importance for future oil production. PhD diss., Department of Nuclear and Particle Physics, Uppsala University, Sweden. http://publications .uu.se/abstract.xsql?dbid=7625.

Roberts, Paul. 2004. *The end of oil: On the edge of a perilous new world.* New York: Houghton-Mifflin.

Robinson, Karen. Mayan Goldmine? *Sunday Times* (London), July 2, Home section.

Rodríguez, Israel. 2010a. Cae producción de Cantarell 23% en lo que va del año: CNH. *La Jornada,* August 13.

———. 2010b. Despacho externo debe auditar y evaluar el desempeño de Chicontepec: Fluvio Ruiz. *La Jornada,* October 11.

———. 2010c. La producción de Ku Maloob Zaap caerá a partir de 2014. *La Jornada,* October 4.

———. 2012. Produjo Chicontepec 63 mil 313 barriles diarios de crudo en enero, según Pemex. *La Jornada,* January 31.

Rodríguez, Israel, and Claudia Herrera Beltrán. 2007. Anuncia Felipe Calderón alianza estratégica de Pemex con Petrobras. *La Jornada*, economía, March 2.

Rodríguez C., Roberto. 1984. *Los pescadores de la Laguna de Términos.* Mexico City: CIESAS.

Rodríguez Marin, Julian. 2006. Expert: Mexico's oil reserves estimates near delirious. EFE World News Service, March 17.

Roig-Franzia, Manuel. 2007. Mexico launches 8th offensive in its drive against drug cartels. *Washington Post*, December 1.

Ronfeldt, David. 1980. *Mexico's oil and U.S. policy: Implications for the 1980s.* Santa Monica, CA: Rand.

Ros-Lehtinen, Ileana, Albio Sires, Mario Diaz-Balart, et al. 2011. Letter to Antonio Brufau Niubó, chairman of Repsol, from members of U.S. Congress. September 27. http://www.hcfa.house.gov/IRLettertoChairman RepsoldeepwaterdrillinginCuba.pdf.

Ross, John. 2006. First Iraq, then the world! Halliburton wrecks Mexico. *Counterpunch*, November 18–19. http://www.counterpunch.org/ross1118 2006.html.

———. 2008. AMLO's "adelitas" shut down Mexico's congress. *UE International, Mexican Labor News and Analysis* 13, no. 4 (April 22). http://www.ueinternational.org/MLNA/mlna_articles.php?id=131#ttoc.

Ross, Michael. 1999. The political economy of the resource curse. *World Politics* 51:297–322.

———. 2001. Does oil hinder democracy? *World Politics* 53:325–361.

Rosser, Andrew. 2006. The political economy of the resource curse: A literature survey. Paper. Brighton, England: Institute of Development Studies, University of Sussex.

Rudolf, John Collins. 2010. Is peak oil behind us? *New York Times*, November 14. http://green.blogs.nytimes.com/2010/11/14/is-peak-oil-behind-us/.

Sachs, Jeffrey D., and Andrew M. Warner. 1997. Natural resources and economic growth. Discussion paper, revised version. Cambridge: Harvard Institute for International Development.

———. 2001. The curse of natural resources. *European Economic Review* 45:827–838.

Saldierna, Georgina. 2008. Negocian México y EU pacto sobre yacimiento transfronterizos: SRE. *La Jornada*, September 18.

Sales Heredia, Francisco Javier. 2007. Participación de PEMEX en el gasto social de algunos de los estados de la república. Centro de Estudios Sociales y de Opinión Pública. Documento de trabajo no. 27, December. http://www3.diputados.gob.mx/camara/content/download/164086/404788/file/Documento_27_Donativos_Pemex.pdf.

Sánchez, Daniel. 2007. Ningún riesgo en ductos de Pemex. *Por Esto*, September 10.

Sánchez-Gil, Patricia, Alejandro Yáñez-Arancibia, José Ramirez-Gordillo, John Day, and Paul Templet. 2004. Some socio-economic indicators in the Mexican states of the Gulf of Mexico. *Ocean and Coastal Management* 47:581–596.

Sangkoyo, Hendro. 2003. Indonesia: The coming decline of a ludicrous carbocracy. Paper presented at the Berkeley Centers for African Studies and

Southeast Asia Studies Workshop on Human Rights and Oil in Southeast Asia and Africa, University of California, Berkeley, January 31.

Santiago, Myrna. 2006. *The ecology of oil: Environment, labor, and the Mexican Revolution, 1900–1938.* New York: Cambridge University Press.

Savage, Melissa. 1993. Ecological disturbances and nature tourism. *Geographical Review* 83, no. 3:290–300.

Sawyer, Suzana. 2001. Fictions of sovereignty: Of prosthetic petro-capitalism, neoliberal states, and phantom-like citizens in Ecuador. *Journal of Latin American Anthropology* 6, no. 1:156–197.

———. 2004. *Crude chronicles: Indigenous politics, multinational oil, and neoliberalism in Ecuador.* Durham, NC: Duke University Press.

Schell, William. 1990. American investment in tropical Mexico: Rubber plantations, fraud, and dollar diplomacy, 1897-1913. *Business History Review* 64, no. 2:217-254.

Schmitt, Karl M. 1982. The problem of maritime boundaries in US/Mexican relations. *Natural Resources Journal* 22:139–154.

Seed, Patricia. 2001. *American pentimento: The invention of Indians and the pursuit of riches.* Minneapolis: University of Minnesota Press.

Seelke, Clare Ribando. 2010. U.S./Mexico relations: Issues for Congress. Washington, DC: Congressional Research Service.

Sener. See Mexico, Secretaría de Energía (Sener).

Seoánez Calvo, Mariano. 2000. *Manual de contaminación marina y restauración del litoral.* Madrid: Ediciones Mundi Prensa.

Sepúlveda, Bernardo. 1974. Mexico and the law of the sea. In *The changing law of the sea: Western Hemisphere perspectives,* ed. Ralph Zacklin. Leiden, Netherlands: Sijthoff.

Serrano Cruz, Noé. 2007a. Descenso acelerado de reserves petroleras. *El Universal,* July 26. http://www.eluniversal.com.mx/finanzas/59098.html.

———. 2007b. Reporta Pemex caida de reservas. *El Universal,* July 26. http://www.eluniversal.com.mx/notas/439161.html.

———. 2009a. Cantarell, en estado de emergencia. *El Universal,* September 11. http://www.eluniversal.com.mx/finanzas/73534.html.

———. 2009b. México halla reserva histórica de petróleo. *El Universal,* February 17. http://www.eluniversal.com.mx/notas/577412.html.

Shields, David. 2003. *Pemex. Un futuro incierto.* Mexico City: Editorial Planeta.

———. 2004. Pemex ready to drill in deepwater Perdido area. *Offshore,* June, p. 38.

———. 2005. *Pemex. La reforma petrolera.* Mexico City: Editorial Planeta.

———. 2007. *Problemática de las reservas y producción de petroleo en México.* Fundad. http://www.fundad.org/word/petroleo/t2Shields.doc.

———. 2008. Faced with sharp declines, Mexico eyes deepwater. *Offshore,* January, pp. 45–59.

Silva Herzog, Jesús. 1963. *Una vida en la vida de México.* Mexico City: Siglo Veinteuno.

Simmons, Matthew R. 2001. The world's giant oilfields. http://energyconversation.org/sites/default/files/062006GiantOilFields.pdf.

———. 2005. *Twilight in the desert.* Hoboken, NJ: Wiley.

Smith, Geri. 2009. The oil crisis slamming Mexico. *Bloomberg Businessweek*, September 17. http://www.businessweek.com/magazine/content/09_39 /b4148036488158.htm.

Smith, Neil. 1984. *Uneven development: Nature, capital, and the production of space*. Oxford, England: Blackwell.

Smith, Robert W. 1981. The maritime boundaries of the United States. *Geographical Review* 71, no. 4:395-410.

Soberanes Fernández, José Luis. 1994. Historia contemporanea de la legislación pesquera en México. In *El régimen jurídico de la pesca en México*, ed. Manuel González Oropeza and Miguel Ángel Garita Alonso. Mexico City: Universidad Nacional Autónoma de México.

Sorrell, Steve, Jamie Speirs, Roger Bentley, Adam Brandt, and Richard Miller. 2009. *An assessment of the evidence for a near-term peak in global oil production*. Report. London: Technology and Policy Assessment, UK Energy Research Centre.

Sosa Solís, Federico. 1984. *Datos para la historia del Carmen*. Ciudad de Carmen: Ayuntamiento del Carmen.

SourceMex. 2009. Negative impact on Mexican tourism continues from April outbreak of swine flu. SourceMex Economic News and Analysis on Mexico. Published by AllBusiness.com, April 5. http://www.allbusiness.com/travel -hospitality-tourism/lodging-lodging-industry/12616969-1.html.

Stojanovski, Ognen. 2008. The void of governance: An assessment of Pemex's performance and strategy. Program on Energy and Sustainable Development at Stanford University, working paper 73. http://iis-db.stanford.edu /pubs/22156/WP_73,_Stojanovski,_Pemex,_12_Apr_08.pdf.

Suárez, S., and I. Palacios. 2001. PEMEX y el desarrollo económico mexicano: aspectos básicos. Mexico City: Instituto de Investigaciones Económicas, UNAM.

Summa, John. 1994. Mexico's new super-billionaires. *Multinational Monitor*, November. http://www.multinationalmonitor.org/hyper/issues/1994/11 /mm1194_09.html.

*El Sur*. 2009a. Infraestructura y terreno a refinería. March 26.

Székely, Alberto. 1982. A comment with the Mexican view on the problem of maritime boundaries in US-Mexican relations. *Natural Resources Journal* 22:155–159.

Székely, Gabriel. 1983. *La economía política del petróleo en México, 1976–1982*. Mexico City: El Colegio de México.

———. 1989. Dilemmas of export diversification in a developing economy: Mexican oil in the 1980s. *World Development* 17, no. 11:1777–1797.

Teichman, Judith. 1996. Economic restructuring, state-labor relations, and the transformation of Mexican corporatism. In *Neoliberalism revisited*, ed. Gerardo Otero. Boulder, CO: Westview.

Thorpe, Andy, Alonso Aguilar Ibarra, and Chris Reid. 2000. The new economic model and marine fisheries in Latin America. *World Development* 28, no. 9:1689–1702.

Tinoco, Yenise. 2008. Derrocha Pemex 220 mdp en publicidad de "aguas profundas." *Contralínea*, July 1. http://www.contralinea.com.mx/archivo

/2008/julio/html/derrocha-pemex-220-mdp-publicidad-aguas-profundas
.htm.

Torrey, Lee. 1980. Black tide from the Bay of Campeche. *New Scientist*, January 24.

*Tribuna Campeche*. 2008a. Pemex no cubre daños que ha hecho a pesca ribereña. March 28.

———. 2008b. Por instalación de refinaría: Mouriño. August 9.

———. 2008c. Pulpo rentable: pulpo deja más de 154 mdp; beneficia a 5 mil pescadores. December 9.

———. 2008d. Votaron mas de 11 mil. August 12.

———. 2009a. Acuacultura, única opción de pescadores. July 21.

———. 2009b. Aún no dan a ribereños 15 mdp que dona Pemex. August 11.

———. 2009c. Carmen, centro logístico de Pemex. August 16.

———. 2009d. En un mes cayó 15% la pesca. August 19.

———. 2009e. Esposas de pescadores exigen que las apoyes. July 16.

———. 2009f. Infraestructura y terreno a refinería. March 26.

———. 2009g. Impacto negativo de Pemex en la pesca de altura. August 19.

———. 2009h. Operan en IA 257 embarcaciones. March 17.

———. 2010. Pemex aún no entrega apoyos ofrecidos. September 14.

Turriza Muñoz, Patricia. 2007. Carmen, Campeche y Palizada. Municipios petroleros. *El Sur*, July 10.

United Nations. 1982. Convention on the Law of the Sea. December 10. http://www.un.org/depts/los/convention_agreements/texts/unclos
/unclos_e.pdf.

*El Universal*. 2008. México tiene finanza públicas petrolizadas: Carstens. April 4.

———. 2009. Depradación baja captura de en Campeche. December 19.

U.S. Congress. 1997. *Hearings on Maritime Boundaries Treaty with Mexico before the Senate Committee on Foreign Relations*. 105th Congress, 1st Session. Washington, DC: Congressional Information Service.

U.S. Department of State. 1978. Treaty on maritime boundaries between the United Mexican States and the United States of America. Senate Treaty Document EX. F, 96-1.

———. 2000. Treaty between the government of the United Mexican States and the government of the United States of America on the delimitation of the Continental Shelf in the western Gulf of Mexico beyond 200 nautical miles. UNTS, vol. 2143, I-37400.

———. 2012. Remarks at the signing of the U.S.-Mexico Transboundary Agreement. Hillary Rodham Clinton, Secretary of State, Los Cabos, Mexico, February 20. http://www.state.gov/secretary/rm/2012/02/184236
.htm.

U.S. Joint Forces Command (US JFCOM). 2008. The JOE. Joint operating environment 2008. Challenges and implications for the future joint force. November 25. Suffolk, VA: U.S. Joint Forces Command, Center for Joint Futures. http://www.jfcom.mil/newslink/storyarchive/2008/JOE
2008.pdf.

U.S. Mineral Management Service (US MMS). 2000. MMS lauds U.S. and

Mexico continental shelf boundary treaty agreement. Press release, June 13. http://www.mms.gov/ooc/press/2000/061300.htm.

U.S. Senate. 1997. Executive report, 105-4, 105th Congress, 1st session, October 22.

Vadillo López, Claudio. 2001. *Los chicleros en la region de la Laguna de Términos, Campeche, 1890–1947.* Ciudad del Carmen: Universidad Autónoma de Carmen.

Vásquez Botello, Alfonso, Guadalupe Ponce Vélez, and Stephen Macko. 1996. Niveles de concentración de hidrocarburos en el Golfo de México. In *El Golfo de Mexico: contaminación e impacto ambiental,* Epomex serie científica 5, ed. Alfonso Vásquez Botello, Jorge Rendon-von Ostén, Gerardo Gold-Bouchot, and Claudia Agraz-Hernández. Campeche: Universidad Autónoma de Campeche.

Vásquez Botello, Alfonso, Guadalupe Ponce Vélez, Alejandro Toledo, Gilberto Díaz-González, and Susana Villanueva. 1992. Ecología, recursos costeros, y contaminación en el Golfo de México. *Ciencia y Desarrollo* 18, no. 102: 28–48.

Vásquez Botello, Alfonso, Jaime Rendón von Osten, Gerardo Gold Bouchot, and Claudia Agraz-Hernández, eds. 2005. *El Golfo de México: contaminación e impacto ambiental.* 2nd edition. Universidad Autónoma de Campeche, Universidad Autónoma de México, and Instituto Nacional de Ecología.

Vásquez León, Marcela, and Thomas R. McGuire. 1993. La iniciativa privada in the Mexican shrimp industry: Politics of efficiency. *MAST* 6, nos. 1–2:59-73.

Vazquez Castillo, Maria Teresa. 2004. *Land privatization in Mexico.* New York: Routledge.

Villaseñor, R., M. Magdaleno, A. Quintanar, J. C. Gallardo, M. T. López, R. Jurado, A. Miranda, M. Aguilar, L. A. Melgarejo, E. Palmerín, C. J. Vallejo, and W. R. Barchet. 2003. An air quality emission inventory of offshore operations for the exploration and production of petroleum by the Mexican oil industry. *Atmospheric Environment* 37:3713–3729.

Villegas Sierra, Javier, and Ramón Martínez Beberaje. 2009. La organización social, modernización y utopías entre los pescadores ribereños de la Península de Atasta e Isla Aguada en Campeche. International Development Research Centre. http://web.idrc.ca/en/ev-137411-201-1-DO_TOPIC.html.

Vuylsteke, Charles. 1996. Techniques of privatization of state-owned enterprises. In *Privatization: Critical perspectives on the world economy,* ed. George Yarrow and Piotr Jasinski. London: Routledge.

Wakida Kusunoki, Armando T., Luis Enrique Amador del Angel, and Josefina Santos Valencia. N.d. *La pesquería de caracol en el ANPFF Laguna de Términos, Campeche, Mexico.* Foro Regional de Caracol del Golfo de México y Mar Caribe. http://www.inapesca.gob.mx/portal/documentos/publicacio nes/MEMORIAS%20DE%20FORO%201/2.pdf.

*Wall Street Journal.* 1906. International lumber and development. *Wall Street Journal,* August 23, p. 6. ProQuest Historical Newspapers, *Wall Street Journal* 1889–current.

*Washington Post.* 1913. Her estate is seized. August 9, p. 2. ProQuest Historical Newspapers, *Washington Post* 1877–1992.

Watts, Michael. 2005. Righteous oil? Human rights, the oil complex, and corporate social responsibility. *Annual Review of Environment and Resources* 30:373-407.

———. 2008. Imperial oil: The anatomy of an oil insurgency. *Erkunde* 62, no. 1:27–39.

———. 2009. Crude politics: Life and death on the Nigerian oil fields. Niger Delta Economies of Violence working papers 25. http://oldweb.geog .berkeley.edu/ProjectsResources/ND%20Website/NigerDelta/WP/Watts _25.pdf.

Weaver, Jacqueline Lang, and David F. Asmus. 2006. Unitizing oil and gas fields around the world. *Houston Journal of International Law* 28, no. 3: 61-105.

Webber, Michael E., and Sheril R. Kirshenbaum. 2010. Energy and immigration: Global warming and declining oil production will drive more Mexicans to the United States. *Boston Globe*, op-ed, November 26. http://www .boston.com/bostonglobe/editorial_opinion/oped/articles/2010/11/26 /energy_and_immigration/.

Weddle, Robert S. 1995. *Changing tides*. College Station: Texas A&M University Press.

Weiner, Tim. 2002. President Fox trying to avert oil strike throughout Mexico. *New York Times*, September 28.

———. 2003. Corruption and waste bleed Mexico's oil lifeline. *New York Times*, January 21.

Wells, Allen, and Gilbert Joseph. 1996. *Summer of discontent*. Stanford, CA: Stanford University Press.

Wheat, Andrew. 1996. Oil country blowout. *Multinational Monitor*, October. http://www.multinationalmonitor.org/hyper/mm1096.04.html.

Wilkinson, Tracy. 2010. Mexico under siege: Mexican drug cartels cripple Pemex operations in basin. *Los Angeles Times*, September 6. http://articles .latimes.com/2010/sep/06/world/la-fg-mexico-pemex-20100906.

Williamson, John. 2008. A short history of the Washington Consensus. In *The Washington Consensus reconsidered: Towards a new global governance*, ed. Narcís Serra and Joseph Stigliz. New York: Oxford University Press.

Wood, Duncan. 2012. US-Mexico cross border energy cooperation: A new era in the Gulf of Mexico. *Woodrow Wilson Center Mexico Institute Monthly Report on Pemex and U.S.-Mexico Energy Cooperation*. March. http://www .wilsoncenter.org/sites/default/files/March_2012_Transboundary_Oil _Agreement_0.pdf.

World Bank. 2008. *A citizen's guide to national oil companies*. Part A: Technical report. October. Washington, DC: International Bank for Reconstruction and Development/World Bank and Center for Energy Economics/University of Texas. http://siteresources.worldbank.org/INTOGMC /Resources/NOC_Guide_A_Technical_Report.pdf.

Yáñez-Arancibia, Alejandro, José J. Ramírez-Gordillo, John W. Day, and David Yoskowitz. 2009. Environmental sustainability of economic trends in the Gulf of Mexico: What is the limit for Mexican coastal development? In *Gulf of Mexico origin, waters, and biota*, ed. J. Tunnell, D. Felder, and S. Earle. College Station: Texas A&M University Press.

Yergin, Daniel. 2008 (1991). *The prize.* New York: Simon and Schuster.

Ynuretta, Francisco. 2009. Edil pide que refinería lleve nombre de Juan Camilo Mouriño. *El Universal,* March 19. http://www.eluniversal.com.mx/notas /584998.html.

Yturriaga, Jose Antonio. 1997. *International regime of fisheries.* The Hague: Martinus Nijhoff.

*YucatanAll.* 2011. "La situación que enfrenta Campeche es injusta": Ortega Bernés. December 6. http://www.yucatanall.com/turismo/turismo-cam peche/interior-del-estado/6383.

Zalik, Anna. 2006. Re-regulating the Mexican Gulf. Paper no. 15. Berkeley: Center for Latin American Studies, University of California at Berkeley. http://www.clas.berkeley.edu/7001/Publications/workingpapers/index .html.

———. 2009. Zones of exclusion: Offshore extraction, the contestation of space and physical displacement in the Nigerian Delta and the Mexican Gulf. *Antipode* 41, no. 3:558–582.

Zárate Lomelí D., T. Saavedra, J. L. Rojas Galaviz, A. Yáñez-Arancibia, and E. Rivera. 1999. Terms of reference towards an integrated management policy in the coastal zone of the Gulf of Mexico and the Caribbean. *Ocean and Coastal Management* 42, nos. 2–4:345–68.

Zárate Lomelí, D., and A. Yáñez-Arancibia. 2003. Conclusiones. Segundo panel Necesidades para la Gestión y el Manejo Integrado de la Zona Costera del Golfo de México y Mar Caribe. Panel MIZC-Golfo/Caribe, INECOL, Semarnat. Xalapa, Mexico.

Zedillo, Ernesto. 1996. Acciones para el desarrollo del estado de Campeche. Transcript of Expropriation Day speech, Ciudad del Carmen, Campeche, March 18. http://zedillo.presidencia.gob.mx/pages/disc/mar96/18mar96 .html.

# Index

*adelitas*, 208, 231
Agamben, Sergio, 13
Aguillón Osorio, Javier, 134
Alvarez, Walter, 259
American Petroleum Institute, 243
Angus, Cameron, 13, 230
aquaculture, 100, 142–144, 156, 159, 169, 270n.3, 271n.10
Argentina, 213
Arias Rodríguez, José Manuel, 136, 143, 144, 174
Arrecife Alacranes 242
Auty, Richard, 146, 147

Belize, 71, 83, 132, 269n.6
Bermeja Island, 247–249
Bermúdez, Antonio, 55
Black, Jeremy, 203, 237
Bolívar Aguilar, Juan José, 34, 265n.2
Bolivia, 194, 213
BP (British Petroleum), 194, 195, 214, 223, 231, 233, 252
Brazil, 45, 54, 193, 202, 213, 216
Britain, 37, 211; colonial territorial claims 72–75, 77
British Petroleum. *See* BP
Brown, Jonathan, 87, 212, 266n.5, 274–275n.6
Brown & Root, 25, 45, 266n.4
Burgan oil field, 44
Burgos Basin, 51, 52, 222

Bush, George H. W., 199
Bush, George W., 29, 31, 32, 43, 207

Calakmul, 90, 96–97, 165–166
Calderón, Felipe, 45, 48, 51, 61, 62, 178, 187, 191, 195, 197, 201, 203, 215, 221, 228, 229, 230, 233, 234, 245, 251, 253, 256
Cameron, Angus, 13, 230
Campeche, 2–8, 14, 16, 17; demography, 88–90; development, 4, 20, 24, 26, 65, 77, 78, 149, 160–161, 165, 166, 173 (*see also* Pemex Social Development); foreign investment, 78–88; labor, 75–76, 84, 120; natural resources, 4, 5, 24, 27, 65–66, 68, 76, 78, 90; oil impact, 20, 23, 93, 96, 181–182, 184; oil incomes, 90, 148, 160–161; as an oil state, 163–164. *See also* Laguna de Términos
Campeche, City of, 68, 90, 92, 185
Canada, 19, 29, 31, 213, 266n.2, 274n.5
Canainpesca (Cámara Nacional de Indústria Pesquera y Acuícola), 134, 143
Cantarell, 1–4, 13, 23; discovery and development, 6, 24–25, 33–34, 91, 112, 242; peak and decline, 1, 6, 16, 17, 20, 24, 27, 32, 42–

Cantarell (*continued*)
46, 47, 49, 52, 64, 183, 197, 234, 236, 241; production, 1, 6, 23–26, 31, 38, 42, 52–53, 56, 63, 147, 148
Cantarell Jiménez, Rudesindo, 33–34, 37
Cárdenas, Lázaro, 31, 38, 86, 87, 112, 115, 204, 205, 207
Carmen Island. *See* Ciudad del Carmen
Carranza, Venustiano, 266n.7, 274n.4
Carstens, Agustín, 32, 47, 162
Carter, Jimmy, 242, 258
CFE (Comisión Federal de Electricidad), 218, 225, 275nn.12,13
Chevron, 195, 231
Chiapas, 6, 84, 90, 92, 163, 168, 171, 172, 177, 210, 269n.9
chicle, 4, 19, 66, 79–87, 110, 115, 117, 193
Chicontepec, 57–60, 63, 232
Chicxulub, 259
Ciudad del Carmen, 8, 13, 23, 26, 33, 34, 57, 67, 84, 88, 90, 92, 100, 103–104, 107, 111, 115, 117, 141, 157, 158, 160, 168; founding of, 67, 72; impact of oil industry, 3–4, 9, 93–94, 99, 185, 231
Clemente, Jude, 50
Clinton, Hillary, 256
Clinton-Zedillo Treaty, 243–244, 246–249
Colosio, Luis Donaldo, 220
Comisión Federal de Electricidad (CFE), 218, 225, 275nn.12,13
Conapesca (Comisión Nacional de Acuacultura y Pesca), 126, 134, 158
Congreso Nacional, 222, 224, 225, 228, 229, 248, 250
conquest, 66, 71, 76, 95, 109, 110
Convergencia Party, 206, 248
Coppola, Luis, 248
Coronil, Fernando, 66
Cortés, Hernán, 67

Cuba, 60, 67, 114, 202, 235, 253, 256, 258
Cupet, 216, 258
Currie-Alder, Bruce, 165, 265n.2

Dampier, William, 69–71, 109
De Alminos, Antón, 67
debt crisis, 41–42, 64, 119
debt peonage, 78, 79, 83
Declaration of Santo Domingo, 238, 239
Deepwater Horizon, 12, 51, 121, 195, 233, 234, 245, 253, 258
deepwater oil, 20, 60, 63, 195, 202–203, 209, 215, 226, 232, 235–236, 239–241
Deepwater Royalty Relief Act, 252
De Grijalva, Juan, 67
De la Madrid, Miguel, 216
De Landa, Diego, 67, 68, 95, 109
DeMint, Jim, 51
Díaz, Porfirio, 37, 77, 80, 81, 83, 84, 211, 212
Doheny, Edward, 37, 274n.6
Dos Bocas, 91, 136, 206, 271n.8
drainage, 244. See also *popote* effect
drug cartels, 29, 31, 45, 46–47, 49, 50, 127, 137, 183; oil theft, 51–52
Dutch disease, 40

Echeverria, Luis, 50
Ecopetrol, 193
Ecuador, 213, 273n.2
Energy Information Agency (EIA), 63, 240, 251, 266nn.1,3
Energy reform, under Calderón, 20, 45, 48, 61, 62, 149, 191–193, 197–211, 225, 234, 253, 260; under Fox, 219–222, 225
energy security, 1, 10, 26, 29, 31, 36, 63, 136, 236, 256
Escalante Jasso, Aracely, 187, 232
Escobar, Arturo, 165
Espinosa, Patricia, 47, 254, 256
Exclusive Economic Zone (EEZ), 114, 235, 239, 241–248, 255, 258

ExxonMobil, 194, 214, 223, 231, 252

FAP (Frente Amplio Progresista), 208, 209, 227
FEXHI (Fondo de Extracción de Hidrocarburos), 183–186
Fideicomiso pesquero, 150, 154–156
Fifopesca (Reconversión Pesquera del Golfo de Mexico), 142, 143, 144
fisheries, 66–67, 91, 98; aid programs, 149–151, 154–160; artisanal, 13, 111, 121–127, 140, 145, 150, 151, 156, 164, 168, 173, 188; as cultural heritage, 19, 103–106, 109, 110, 144; decline, 103–104, 123, 125, 127, 128, 130, 137, 145, 154, 182; illegal capture, 125, 126, 127, 133, 140; industrial, 19, 67, 87, 110, 112, 115–121; seasonal closures, 117, 121, 128, 130–135, 141, 150; women, 150, 158–159. *See also* shrimp industry
fishing cooperatives, 87, 112, 115, 116, 118, 119, 120, 126, 133, 137–141, 156
fishing licensing and permits, 140–141
Fox, Vicente, 51, 54, 59, 148, 178, 198, 199, 219, 220, 222, 224
frontlines, 1–10, 14–20, 24, 27, 51, 93–95, 145–149, 192–193, 205, 214, 231–232, 257, 261
Fundar, 174, 175

Gas de Atasta, 180, 181
Gentleman, Judith, 41
Ghawar oil field, 44, 57
Gold-Bouchot, Gerardo, 129
Grayson, George, 203
Guatemala, 66, 80, 83, 85, 87, 89, 97, 269n.9
Gulf of Mexico, 1, 8, 13, 26, 43, 45, 51, 56, 60, 83, 90, 95, 105, 121, 122, 124, 127; as a commons, 112, 119, 120; marine environment, 126, 127–128; pat-rimonial sea, 14, 18, 21, 111, 113, 145, 234, 238–239, 257; resources, 3, 10, 20, 26, 33, 36, 57, 63, 107, 115, 193, 233; territorial disputes, 113–114, 135–137; U.S. drilling, 12, 195, 203, 234. *See also* Cantarell; deepwater oil; Exclusive Economic Zone; maritime boundaries

Haenn, Nora, 90, 97, 165
Halliburton, 45, 52, 59, 106, 231, 232
Hart, John Mason, 81, 83, 84, 86, 87
Hedberg, Hollis, 242, 246
henequen, 79, 82, 83
Hernández de Córdoba, Francisco, 67
Hernandez Montejo, Carmen, 76, 85, 93, 98, 119
Hirsch, Robert, 44, 64, 267n.11
Huasteca 37, 86
Hubbert, M. King, 15, 43–44
Hubbert's Peak, 15, 16, 17, 43, 46. *See also* peak oil
Hurtado Valdéz, Jorge, 23–24, 27, 151, 182, 185, 230

independent oil companies (IOCs), 215
Inter-American Development Bank, 46
International Energy Agency (IEA), 44
International Energy Outlook, 63
International Monetary Fund (IMF), 42, 213, 220, 267n.9
Ireta Guzmán, Hugo, 136, 143, 144, 174
Isla Aguada, 8, 9, 11, 14, 17; aid, 134, 149–151, 154–160 (*see also* Fideicomiso Pesquero); fishing, 110, 111, 125, 127, 130, 134, 135, 137, 144; population, 90, 94; social relations, 137–140, 152–153; tourism development, 21, 261–263

Ixtoc I oil spill, 11–12, 118, 128–129, 233

Jarvis, Michael, 71, 74, 268n.2
Justo Sierra, Carlos, 71, 78, 117

Kab-101, 12, 154
Karl, Terry Lynn, 146
Kessel, Georgina, 60
Klare, Michael, 45, 241
Klein, Naomi, 198
Knight, Alan, 80, 81, 266n.5
Ku Maloob Zap (KMZ), 57–58, 63

Labastida, Francisco, 224
Laguna Corporation, 83, 85, 86
Laguna de Términos, 2, 8, 33, 67, 78, 83; environmental impact, 3, 11–12, 26, 129–130, 180; natural resource exploitation, 3, 4–5, 10, 11, 18, 23, 27, 65, 66, 68, 74–75, 78, 96, 188, 193; protected area, 9, 56, 95–101, 164, 165, 166. *See also* chicle; fisheries; palo de tinte
Leriche Guzmán, Luis Fernando, 76, 83, 112, 114, 116, 117, 118, 265n.2
Ley de Colonización y Terrenos Baldíos, 80–81
Ley General de Bienes Nacionales, 114
Ley General de Pesca y Acuacultura Sustenables, 130
López Obrador, Andrés Manuel, 192, 198, 203–208, 219, 223, 226, 228, 230, 254
López Portillo, José, 39, 40, 118, 119, 162, 242
Los Zetas, 51–52. *See also* drug cartels

Marea Azul, 11, 98, 101
maritime boundaries, 60, 112, 233, 235, 237, 241; and fishing, 113–114, 237–238; and oil, 195, 202–203, 239–247, 250, 251, 255. *See also* Exclusive Economic Zone;

Transboundary Hydrocarbons Agreement; Treaty on Maritime Boundaries
Mathews, Jennifer, 80
Maya crude, 3, 6, 34, 48
Maya people, 8, 33, 67, 70, 75, 79, 80, 89, 110, 212, 265n.2, 269n.7
Melville, Roberto, 117, 118, 265n.2
Mérida, 68, 94, 185
Mexican Constitution, 86, 193, 198, 199, 203, 204, 206, 209, 222, 227, 229, 230; Article 27, 5, 39, 87, 113, 119, 200, 213, 219, 225, 257
Mexican Eagle (El Aguila), 37, 86
Mexican Oil Industry: concessions, 212, 228; exports, 6, 39, 40; expropriation, 31, 32, 38, 94, 193, 204–205, 207, 213; foreign ownership, 31, 37, 211; production, 37, 38, 42, 63, 200; reserves, 61–63, 200, 202, 239; revenues, 32, 40, 148, 161; role in national development, 39, 40, 42, 54, 148, 161, 204, 207, 227. *See also* Pemex
Mexican Petroleum Company, 86
Mexican Revolution, 83, 84, 88, 206, 208, 213
Middle East, 1, 29, 31, 36, 38, 39, 260
migration, 41, 50, 89–90, 233, 244, 267n.13
Minerals Management Service (MMS), 240, 252
Mining Law of 1884, 212
Mitchell, Timothy, 15
Montemayor, Rogelio, 224
Morales Gil, Carlos, 59, 60, 239, 255
Mouriño, Juan Camilo, 178–180, 182–183, 230
Movimiento Nacional en Defensa del Petróleo, 199, 204, 206, 254, 257
multinational oil companies, 7, 213, 219, 224, 233
multiple service contracts (MSCs), 215, 220–221, 229, 230, 231

Municipality of Carmen, 4, 10, 11, 20, 24, 83, 90, 94, 95, 98, 115, 116, 123, 134, 151, 155, 156, 158, 160, 168, 171, 173, 187, 188, 261, 272n.1; as oil-affected, 26–27, 91, 93, 94, 97, 148, 149, 161, 163–167, 183–184, 188–189
Muñoz Leos, Raúl, 176, 219

NAFTA, 199, 217, 220
National Hydrocarbons Commission (CNH), 60
national oil companies (NOCs), 193–195, 213–216, 232
neoliberalism, 18, 20, 193, 198, 213, 214, 216; in Mexico, 5, 8, 10, 13, 15, 42, 49, 120, 192–194, 197, 199, 204, 217, 219, 220, 223, 225, 230, 232
Nigeria, 32, 147, 213; Niger Delta, 10, 14, 15
nitrogen, 12, 56–57; Planta de Nitrógeno de Cantarell, 180–181
nonconventional fuels, 17, 48, 239, 240

Obama, Barack, 182, 233, 234, 235, 245, 253, 256
offshore drilling moratorium, 234, 253
offshore oil production, 11–15, 241; environmental effects, 155; and fisheries, 104–105, 111, 112, 118, 120, 128–129, 135, 136; in Mexico, 23–27, 32–34, 37, 50, 63, 91, 93, 94, 170, 180, 195, 236, 242, 257; in U.S., 234, 240, 252–253
oil-affected areas, 6, 149, 160, 163, 170, 186, 189; priority states, 163, 166, 169, 171, 172, 175, 177, 184, 197
oil nationalism, 5, 15, 21, 50, 62, 94, 115, 179, 193–195, 198, 199, 203–206, 213, 216, 218, 219, 222, 231, 237, 248, 254, 255, 257–258
OPEC, 1, 31, 36, 39, 193

Organization of American States (OAS), 238
Ortega Bernés, Fernando, 187, 232

Palan, Ronen, 13, 230
palo de tinte, 4, 19, 66, 68–69, 71–76, 78, 103, 110, 112, 117; labor, 69, 74-75, 78
paradox of plenty, 146
Partido Acción Nacional (PAN), 62, 148, 157, 159–160, 176, 178, 183, 185, 188, 198, 201, 204, 207, 209, 210, 219, 221, 226, 227, 228, 229, 230, 248, 257
Partido de Trabajadores (PT), 208
Partido Revolucionario Democratico (PRD), 98, 184, 200, 204, 206, 207, 208, 210, 223, 230, 257
Partido Revolucionario Institucional (PRI), 148, 159, 178, 183, 185, 186, 198, 206, 208, 209, 216, 218, 219, 220, 226, 227, 230, 248, 257
Partido Verde Ecologista de Mexico (PVEM), 228, 257
Payne, Martin, 43
peak oil, 7, 15–17, 43–44, 235, 240; global, 44; in Mexico, 42, 49, 56, 61, 62, 198; in U.S., 36, 38–39
peak oil migrant, 50–51
Pearson, Weetman (Lord Cowdray), 37
Pemex, 1, 42; accidents and spills, 12–13, 118, 134, 149, 154 (see also Ixtoc I oil spill, Kab-101); compensation, 149, 161, 164, 165, 166, 168, 188; contracts, 59, 60, 200, 215, 220, 223, 225, 226, 229, 232, 234; distribution of oil revenues, 161–163, 227; effect on fisheries, 104, 105, 107, 121, 128, 135–137, 154; environmental effects, 3, 6, 11–12, 98, 101, 128–130, 154, 164, 170, 218; exports, 5, 6, 25, 39, 40, 42, 47–48, 53, 54, 56, 260, 265n.1, 267n.14; financing, 162, 187, 199, 220–221;

Pemex (*continued*)
labor, 55, 93, 173, 218, 223; natural gas, 10, 201, 218, 220; petrochemicals, 3, 39, 40, 98, 170, 218; production, 25, 31, 47, 57, 58, 197; refining, 10, 48, 179–180, 182, 194–195, 197, 200, 201, 209, 220, 223, 227, 229, 230; transparency and accountability, 224–225
Pemexgate, 224
Pemex Exploration and Production (PEP), 53, 56, 58, 59, 60, 63, 154, 167, 168, 170, 177, 201, 239, 245, 250
Pemex Social Development, 14, 53, 90, 93, 95, 97, 98, 123, 134, 139, 142, 148–152, 154, 156, 166–178; corruption, 175–176; transparency, 177–178
Peninsula of Atasta, 56, 70, 88, 92, 96, 98, 115, 125, 143, 154, 155, 158, 164, 165
Perdido Foldbelt, 248, 249, 250, 258
Pérez, Ana Lilia, 174, 176, 178
peso crisis, 220–221
Petrobras, 45, 54, 216, 222
Pidiregas (deferred expenditure impact projects), 220–221
piracy, 66, 68, 69, 71, 72, 76, 203, 241
*popote* effect, 244, 249–250, 254
Porfiriato, 66, 77, 78, 79, 80, 213
post-peak condition, 7, 17, 20, 21, 145, 149, 156, 162, 195, 197, 213–214, 230, 240, 260–263
privatization, 216–217; land, 77, 78, 79, 81, 83, 87, 217; oil, 20, 46, 49, 55, 149, 191–193, 197–211, 216–219, 251, 257
*pulpo* (octopus) fishing, 125–127

Ramsar Convention, 96
remittances, 46
renewable energy, 241, 260
Repsol, 258
resource curse, 146–147, 149, 166

resource security, 76, 237
resource sovereignty, 5, 6, 10, 14, 18, 32, 40, 64, 69, 72, 76, 105, 113, 148, 194, 198, 199, 203–205, 241, 248, 251, 255, 257, 260
Reyes Heroles, Jesús, 23, 200, 206, 250–251, 254
Rodríguez, Roberto, 93–94, 105, 124, 133, 265n.2
Romero Deschamps, Carlos, 223, 224
Rosser, Andrew, 146
rule of capture, 249–250
Russia, 87, 213

Sabancuy, 154, 155, 158
Sagarpa, 126, 131, 134, 140, 141, 142, 151, 158
Salinas de Gortari, Carlos, 112, 198, 199, 216, 217, 220, 223
Sawyer, Suzana, 213, 275n.8
Schlumberger, 52, 59, 231, 232
Seara Sierra, José Ignacio, 154, 184–185
Securities and Exchange Commission (SEC), 200, 268n.16
Seed, Patricia, 211
Semarnat (Secretaría de Medio Ambiente y Recursos Naturales), 100
Sener (Ministry of Energy), 48, 52, 63, 202, 226, 265n.1, 268n.16
Sepesca (Secretaría de Pesca y Acuacultura), 143, 149, 154, 158
Seybaplaya, 125, 180
Shell, 194, 195, 214, 223, 253
Shields, David, 221, 245
shrimp industry, 3, 40, 116–121, 193; state aid, 135, 137
Silva Herzog, Jesus, 41
Slavery, 68, 70, 72, 75–76
Slim, Carlos, 59, 217
Spain, 66, 67, 69, 71, 74, 241
Spanish colonialism, 69, 72, 76, 103, 112, 193
STPRM (Sindicato de Trabajadores Petroleros de la República Mexicana), 223, 224

subsoil resource rights, 211–213
swine flu, 46
Székely, Alberto, 246
Székely, Gabriel, 39, 40

Tabasco, 91, 92, 93, 96, 98, 109; environment, 6, 12; fishing, 132; oil, 118, 132, 163, 168, 184, 192, 206, 218, 236
Tamaulipas, 52, 98; fishing, 118, 131, 132; oil, 6, 163, 171–172, 177, 180, 184
Televisa, 191, 201, 202
Telmex, 217
tilapia, 143, 144
tourism, 46–47, 91, 261–263
Transboundary Hydrocarbons Agreement, 256
transboundary reservoirs, 249, 256, 257
Treaty of Guadalupe Hidalgo, 113, 248
Treaty of Madrid, 73
Treaty of Utrecht, 71, 75
Treaty on Maritime Boundaries, 242–243

UNCLOS (UN Convention Law of the Sea), 113, 237, 238, 255
UNESCO (United Nations Educational, Scientific and Cultural Organization), 96, 97, 130
Unión de Pescadores de Ckiquixo-coq, 134, 151, 155, 157
Unión de Sociedades de Pescadores Ribereños, 144
United Nations Food and Agriculture Organization (FAO), 127, 142
United States, 10, 12, 19, 25, 39, 44, 46, 49, 75, 80, 85, 86, 114–117, 130; offshore drilling, 60, 234, 236, 240, 251–252; oil imports, 6, 29, 30, 31, 39, 42; strategic petroleum reserve, 42; U.S.-

Mexican border, 16, 31, 39, 41, 50, 179, 202–203, 233, 234, 239, 244, 255
unitization agreements, 256
U.S.-Mexican energy relations, 1, 25, 29, 36–38, 39, 45, 50, 63, 64, 136, 234–235
Usumacinta, 12, 154, 188

Valladares, Yolanda, 154, 178
Vargas, Edmundo, 238
Venezuela, 32, 38, 69, 146, 147, 213, 258
Veracruz, 34, 68, 84, 93, 236, 263; environment, 6, 12; fishing, 132; oil, 31, 57, 59, 86, 92, 98, 118, 163, 168, 170, 171–172, 175, 177, 180, 184, 204
Villa, Francisco "Pancho," 84, 208
Virgen del Carmen, 103–106

Washington Consensus, 216
Watts, Michael, 15, 63, 148
Weatherford, 52, 59
Western Gap, 243–257
wind energy, 45
Wood, Duncan, 257
World Bank, 40, 206
World Energy Outlook, 44
Wrigley and Company, 80, 83

Xicalango, 70, 109, 110

Yacimientos Petrolíferos (YPF), 193, 222
Yergin, Daniel, 249
Yucatán Peninsula, 2, 3, 7, 8, 47, 67, 126, 131, 137, 185, 242, 246, 247, 253, 259, 261; resources, 68, 73, 74, 75, 78, 79, 85, 109, 125, 131

Zalick, Anna, 14, 263
Zedillo, Ernesto, 160–161, 216, 218, 220, 225, 248